THE

SOCIALIST REGISTER 1979

THE
SOCIALIST REGISTER
1979

EDITED BY

RALPH MILIBAND

and

JOHN SAVILLE

THE MERLIN PRESS
LONDON

First published in 1979
by the Merlin Press Ltd.
3 Manchester Road,
London, E.14.

Printed by The Garden City Press Ltd.,
Letchworth, Herts

SBN 0 85036 2520 cloth edition
0 85036 2539 paperback edition

TABLE OF CONTENTS

ACKNOWLEDGEMENTS

This is the sixteenth volume of *The Socialist Register,* and we wish once again to express our thanks for their help to our contributors; to Martin Eve and David Musson of Merlin Press; and to Mike Gonzalez and David Fernbach for their translations. As usual, we must point out that the views expressed by any one contributor are not necessarily shared by any other or by the Editors.

Andrew Gamble is in the Department of Political Theory and Institutions at Sheffield University. Ian Birchall teaches French at the Middlesex Polytechnic and Leo Panitch is in the Department of Political Science at Carleton University, Ottawa. Duncan Campbell now works for the *New Statesman.* Alun Howkins teaches History at Sussex University. Elmar Altvater and Otto Kallscheuer teach Political Sociology at the Free University, Berlin and George Ross is in the Sociology Department, Brandeis University. Julio Aramberri is a member of the Faculty of Political Science and Sociology of Madrid University and Jane Jenson is in the Department of Political Science, Carleton University. Jerome Karabel is at the Huron Institute, Cambridge, Mass. Domenico Mario Nuti teaches Economics in the Faculty of Economics, Cambridge University, and is a Fellow of King's College, Cambridge. Kevin Robins and Frank Webster are in the Department of Social Studies, Oxford Polytechnic. Hilary Rose is in the Department of Social Studies at Bradford University and Steven Rose is in the Department of Biology at the Open University.

July 1979

R.M.
J.S.

THE FREE ECONOMY AND THE STRONG STATE: THE RISE OF THE SOCIAL MARKET ECONOMY.

Andrew Gamble

I

During the last ten years the long post-war period of expansion and stability has come to an end. We are living through a crisis that should never have happened, the crisis that Keynesian techniques and social democratic policies and institutions were supposed to have banished for ever, because they had overcome the tendency of the capitalist economy towards deficient demand and underconsumption. No slump on anything approaching the scale of the 1930s has occurred, and the pattern of economic performance has been varied, but the overall slowdown in rates of economic growth has still been marked. There has been a deepseated crisis of profitability reflected both in declining short run rates of return and a fall in long-term opportunities for investment. Barriers to further rapid accumulation have multiplied and determined the ground on which major conflicts have erupted—struggles over pay, new technology and employment; struggles over the size and composition of public expenditure; and struggles over trade and financial imbalances between surplus and deficit states.

The most striking feature of the new recession which divides it so sharply from the last great crisis in the world economy is the behaviour of the price level. Unemployment has been rising steadily, but it has been inflation that has repeatedly threatened to get out of control, and in the face of which economic policy makers have appeared most powerless. Inflation is in turn a contributor to the instabilities in the financial markets, the imbalances in trade, and to the fiscal crisis of the state and has also done much to undermine the political cohesion of the major states. With the spread of uncertainty and instability it is hardly surprising that the reputation of governments for successful economic management has rapidly waned and that politicians, having benefited during the long years of boom from the identification of economic prosperity with

1

government economic policies, now suffer from the identification of those same policies with the dismal succession of crises and failures over which they have to preside. In Britain where the problem of relative economic decline has been aggravated by the impact of the recession, no government has won re-election after serving a full term since 1959, and there has been a significant decline in support for both major parties (most notably in 1974 but still marked in 1979).

The slow-down in the pace of accumulation has provided the opportunity for a widespread rejection of Keynesian political economy and an onslaught on the policies, values and organizations of social democracy. There has always been an element among British intellectuals which has never required much inducement to join a collective stampede to the right. We are constantly being told that 'intellectuals' are finally losing faith in socialism (this follows their previous final rejection of it in the early 1950s). They have been converted, even at this late hour, to the need to resist totalitarianism and the British Labour Party, and to reject the beliefs in collectivism and equality that were enshrined in the policies and institutions established in the 1940s.[1] Aside from these 'men who have changed their minds', swayed by the populist clamour of the new right, there has also been in recent years a real intellectual change, a remarkable revival of liberal political economy through the elaboration of the doctrine of the social market economy, a doctrine which, under different labels, has made increasing headway within the Conservative party in the last ten years. The Conservative Government elected in 1979 had a group of ministers in the crucial economic ministries (Treasury, Industry, Trade, Energy), who were all adherents of the doctrine and prepared to govern in accordance with its prescriptions.[2]

The term social market economy originated in Germany from the neo-liberal ideas that were current there after 1945.[3] In Britain and America similar ideas have been put forward by a number of theorists including F. A. Hayek and Milton Friedman, and popularized in Britain by organizations like the Institute for Economic Affairs and the Centre for Policy Studies,[4] by leader writers in the *Times* and *Daily Telegraph:* by economic commentators such as Peter Jay, Samuel Brittan, and Patrick Hutber,[5] and by Conservative politicians (Enoch Powell at first; more recently, Keith Joseph).

Although many of the intellectuals prominent in this broad

tendency, (often labelled, rather inaccurately, monetarist), like to imagine themselves as romantic outsiders breaking lances against the formidable walls of the Keynesian economic and political Establishment, the ease with which they have penetrated the citadel and the speed with which the Keynesian defences have crumbled in the past few years, suggests otherwise. At any other time the jousting between monetarists and Keynesians would probably have remained a technical debate about the best instruments for economic management. But the monetarists have not been content to carve a place for themselves within Keynesianism, but have launched a broad assault on the political forces that underpin Keynesianism, the forces and organizations of social democracy. So monetarism and economic liberalism have become linked with other ideas and movements, the most significant of which is the populist right in the Conservative Party, most vigorously represented by groups such as the Monday Club and the National Association for Freedom, which are strongly critical of trends in British society since the war and are closely identified with the beliefs and attitudes of the present Conservative Leader. The populist assault on social democracy has concentrated upon the burden of taxation, the abuse of welfare, the inefficiences of public provision and public enterprise, and the threat to public order and well-being posed by immigrants, unions, students, and other minority groups.[6] A big attempt has been made to appeal to that section of the working-class electorate for whom the policies and organizations of social democracy have become increasingly unpopular.

The self image entertained by the new ideologues of the right and the band of vociferous converts and roving spokesmen for management that consort with them, is that Britain, having just passed through its 'watershed' election, is about to experience a renaissance of liberty and the liberal society, the creation of a new national consensus by means of which the chains of collectivism will be thrown off, the trends of the past thirty years reversed, and Britain's national and economic fortunes revived. On the left two main views of Thatcherism and the new liberal political economy are evident. On the one hand there is the strongly held belief that the underlying trend in modern capitalism is towards some form of 'corporatism' with the state constantly tending to increase its powers of direction over the economy. Hence Thatcherism is regarded simply as an ideology, a veil drawn over the real development of capitalism, and a poor guide as to how goverments are obliged to behave. Liberal political economy is seen as appropriate to the era of competitive capitalism but no longer relevant to the problems of monopoly or corporate capitalism. If any attempt were made to apply its principles chaos would result; the experience of the Heath Government in its first two years is often cited. Many on the left go on to argue that so poorly adapted is the ideology of the right to the problems of managing modern capitalist economies that often the social democratic parties like the Labour Party are better suited for it, and secretly preferred by capitalists themselves to the explicitly capitalist parties.

A second response to Thatcherism and the revival of liberal political economy is to see them not simply as ideology but as a means for reorganizing the state sector in a period of recession, increasing spending on maintaining order and reducing it on certain kinds of welfare. The rolling back of the state in some areas is seen to involve rolling it forward in others. The crisis has to be policed as well as managed, and this implies a more active role for some state agencies (as well as more ample remuneration from a grateful people). Whilst there is much more to be said for this point of view than for the first it can lead to a neglect of the scope of the right-wing revival and the sources of its strength, because it focuses on the state sector and the mobilization of populist attitudes towards welfare, immigrants and strikes. But Thatcherism and liberal political economy should not be treated as one, however important is the fact of their present linking in practice. Liberal political economy has far deeper roots and permanence within capitalist social formations and contributes ideas and programmes to the conservative 'left' as well as the 'right'. Even many of the intellectuals who currently advocate a 'social market economy' do not by any means share the populist positions of Thatcherism and are extremely unhappy that monetarism and the social market economy should appear as 'right-wing' doctrines.

2

One of the main reasons why the social market economy has acquired right-wing asociations is because it is often regarded as a euphemism for laissez-faire economy, and because so many political issues are now defined as left or right depending on whether they involve the extension or the retreat of central government powers and responsibilities. The problem with the term laissez-faire is that it suggests a quiescent or inattentive state. Capitalist states have never been that. The crucial question is the dividing line between those areas where the state feels obliged to intervene and those where it does not. There have always been issues like the protection of property and the enforceability of contracts on which the state has never followed a laissez-faire policy. Where the dividing line comes has often been determined by political and social struggles. The importance of the social market doctrine is not that it is against all state intervention but that it wants the state to intervene less in some areas and more in others. 'Free economy—strong state' is no idle slogan, and marks the continuity of the doctrine with the tradition of liberal political economy, not a departure from it. Nobody in this tradition has seriously suggested that capitalism could do without a strong and active state,[8] although this has sometimes been obscured by laissez-faire ideologies of self-help and business enterprise. The key problem for economic liberals has always been how limits to the sphere and tasks of government should be fixed, i.e., where the strength of the state should be concentrated. This means that there is nothing in social market doctrine that rules out collective provision of welfare or public enterprise, provided that these are justified in terms economic liberals can accept.

During the boom the theoretical differences between the social welfare or 'mixed' economy in Britain, supported by the Labour Party, and the social market economy in Germany supported by the SPD was not very obvious (although the contrast in economic performance was sharp enough). There has always been a debate between liberal and collectivist social democrats about whether certain agreed ends can best be achieved through the market or through planning. The real significance of the social market doctrine has only appeared during the recession. In the vacuum caused by the discrediting of Keynesianism and the evident disarray of social democracy, the social market doctrine has provided the intellectual bedrock for the rallying of the right around a programme aimed at breaking theoretically with the universe of social democratic thought in order to establish the principles that will enable governments to break from social democracy in practice also. For the first time since the war the right has acquired a set of distinctive principles on which to base the conduct of economic policy and attempt to reverse some of the political advance made by organized labour. Social democrats, whatever their party affiliation,[9] accurately perceive the fundamental hostility of social market doctrine to their beliefs and policies, but have found themselves on the defensive because of the translation of the theoretical principles and distinctions of social market doctrine into the language and demands of the authoritarian populism of Margaret Thatcher.

At its most elementary level the break that social market doctrine seeks is with the basic standpoint of Keynesianism and social democracy. The standpoint of the Keynesian school in approaching problems of managing capitalism is that of the national economy. Social democrats have come increasingly to share that standpoint, particularly when they are in government, although they operate as well with an older frame of reference, usually when they are in opposition—the interests of the working class. Taking the national economy as the starting point for the development of a political economy, a set of principles for guiding economic policy, means adopting the standpoint of the nation-state and its agencies. This does not preclude reliance on free market methods, but it means they are evaluated in terms of their contribution to the success and progress of the national economy.

The true mark of a social market theorist is the rejection of this intellectual construction and the return to the concerns of liberal political economy—the standpoint of the market, the sphere of commodity relations regulated by law. This sphere is composed of a multitude of different markets, some of which reach well beyond national political structures, and their proper functioning is considered to be an important end in itself, as well as the best means to the achievement of certain national ends. This does not entail that adherents of social market doctrine are all internationalists and cosmopolitans, although some are. Others are passionate nationalists and British race patriots. But all accord an importance to markets and the voluntary relationships of exchange they establish, which they regard as setting definite limits to what national economic policy can and ought to accomplish.

The principles of liberal political economy on which the concept of the social market economy rests have been restated most fully and most influentially in Britain and America by Hayek, whose writings repay careful study.[10] There is very little written by the popularizers of social market doctrine that is not already contained (somewhere) in Hayek. His thought revolves around three crucial distinctions—those between liberty and democracy, law and bureaucracy, and the market and planning. From these oppositions flow most of the practical conclusions of the social market theorists. Hayek makes it very clear that whilst he is by no means hostile to democracy, it is liberty that is more important. A democratic state may protect liberty, if it is properly organized, but it is not the only kind of state that can do so. Liberty is defined as 'that condition of men in which coercion of some by others is reduced as much as possible in society'.[11] Coercion by individuals can be greatly reduced if one social agency, the state, is able to punish individuals who infringe laws governing individual exchange. The problem then becomes how to reduce coercion by the state itself; the answer is the construction of a private sphere free from public interference. Such a private sphere can only come into existence if there are certain activities and rights which are protected and cannot be infringed by the government. This requires that the state as well as individuals be bound by laws (the idea of a *Rechtstaat,* or constitutional state), and that decisions of government agents be subject to legal appeal and reversal in the courts. Such a notion of liberty naturally clashes with the notion of popular sovereignty because it implies that there are many laws which should be beyond the power of a government to alter, whereas the doctrine of popular sovereignty suggests that a government elected by the people has the right to overturn and refashion all laws.

It is not surprising therefore that in the era of mass democracy and popular sovereignty, liberal political economy should frequently inspire dreams of an apolitical state—a state whose agencies are so constituted that they supply the least possible scope for interference by the temporary democratic majorities that inhabit legislatures. Montagu Norman's [12] search for a system of central bank co-operation which would take the important questions of monetary policy out of the hands of politicians has found a recent echo in the advocacy of a Currency Commission which would remove control of the money supply from the Treasury and the Cabinet. The thinking behind such proposals is simple. A sound currency is one of the conditions for markets to function, hence for liberty to exist. 'Politicians and bureaucrats' are prone to interfere with the money supply in pursuit of other objectives, so its regulation should cease to be a matter of discretion and become a constraint within which all governments are obliged to operate.

What gives such notions credibility is that the modern state is organized in precisely this manner with many agencies, for example the judiciary, but also the military, and parts of the bureaucracy, enjoying varying degrees of autonomy from the government and constituting an orchestra which governments cannot command but must persuade to play. The great bulk of state agencies are not subject to democratic election and control and the liberal proposal is to strip away a few more functions of government and hand them to agencies who can be more readily trusted with the public interest than can politicians swayed by short-term political pressures.

An alternative approach to removing certain areas of state activity from political scrutiny and democratic pressure is the attempt to limit government activity by identifying individual rights which are presumed so fundamental that no government can infringe them and still be called free. This approach leads to Bills of Rights and written constitutions, which have enjoyed a considerable revival in recent years.[13] Robert Moss, a former director of the National Association for Freedom and speech writer to Margaret Thatcher, puts forward a list of measures which he argues should be beyond the powers of any elected government: the abolition of democracy, the banning of religious beliefs, the destruction of the family, the withdrawal of the right to own or bequeath property, and the prevention of the exercise of individual choice in health and education.[14]

The idea behind both approaches is that the preservation of liberty requires that there be very precise limits to legislation, however democratically constituted the legislative authority may be. Democracy is seen as the least harmful form of government, but still suffers from major flaws—there is for instance no 'budget constraint' to limit what the voter can vote for in the same way that there is limiting what the consumer can buy. Since voters are not obliged to consider costs, competitive bidding between the parties develops, and democratic governments come to offer more than they can deliver with serious consequences for their handling of economic policy. As Milton Friedman has put it:[15]

> The fundamental defect of the political mechanism (is that) it is a system of highly weighted voting under which the special interests have great incentive to promote their own interests at the expense of the general public. The benefits are concentrated; the costs are diffused; and you have therefore a bias in the market place which leads to ever greater expansion in the scope of government and ultimately to control over the individual … In the economic market … each person gets what he pays for. There is a dollar-for-dollar relationship. Therefore, you have an incentive proportionate to the cost to examine what you are getting.

Democracy therefore encourages ever greater bureaucratic interference with the privileged private sphere—the sphere of market relationships between individuals. As bureaucracy rises, so the law declines—the second of Hayek's basic distinctions. He does not suggest that bureaucracy can be dispensed with (his thought is never utopian in that sense), but he does argue that for liberty to flourish the realm of law must dominate the realm of bureaucracy. General laws, i.e., known rules that are applicable to all, must regulate social behaviour over as wide an area as possible and discretionary administrative decisions be minimized as much as possible. The essence of collectivism (what makes it, for Hayek, the prelude to totalitarianism and allows him to range welfare state and New Deal policies in the same continuum as socialism, fascism, and communism) is the disregarding of the distinction between law and administration, so that law becomes not a means for checking the growth of administration but a means of facilitating it, by providing new unspecified discretionary powers for government agencies. From this flows the opposition between planning and the market. The market is potentially the sphere of free, voluntary individual behaviour regulated by law, and protected from the coercion practised either by other individuals or by the state. Planning signifies the intrusion of the unregulated discretionary power of politicians and bureaucrats,[16] supposedly acting in the national interest, in accordance with the wishes of the electorate, but in practice interfering with and reducing the only kind of liberty that is possible.

The message that bubbles from the fermenting pot of social market writings is that democracy is dangerous and can threaten liberty, so needs to be rigorously controlled and limited. The attachment of these thinkers to democracy is precarious, because during times of economic difficulty the workings of democracy are one more burden that the liberal society must carry. It becomes very hard to pursue the right economic policies because the immediate consequences in terms of unemployment and living standards, and the active opposition of many parties, organizations, and groups, soon lead to the collapse of both electoral support and the political confidence and determination of the government.

How much easier the restoration of the liberal society would be, muse these theorists, if the need to secure a renewed popular mandate and to maintain civil liberties were removed or at least suspended for a time. Great play is made in this literature of the distinction between authoritarianism and totalitarianism. Authoritarian regimes, like Chile, are regarded as far preferable to totalitarian regimes like Russia and Nazi Germany, because whilst they interfere with political freedoms, they do not interfere with economic freedom; trade unions are of course disbanded or repressed, but foreign investment is not interfered with and citizens are still free to own and bequeath property, and to buy and sell their products and their labour power. The intellectual dishonesty of this position is glaring because Nazi Germany is regarded as totalitarian rather than authoritarian, despite the overwhelming evidence that, like Franco's Spain and Pinochet's Chile and Papadopoulos's Greece the regime did not interfere with the economic freedom of private capital, but considerably increased it, by suppressing trade unions and providing stable financial and commercial conditions and a climate of expansion. The destruction of political freedom is always regrettable, according to Friedman, but clearly it is not to be compared to the far more serious loss of economic freedom for capital.

3

Defining freedom as they do, and distrusting democracy and bureaucracy as a result, certain definite consequences follow for economic policy—a set of principles which rooted in the notion of the individual are extremely durable, capable of wide application, and form the backbone of the current intellectual revival on the right. The state has to be both strong and active—maintaining the conditions which guarantee 'individual liberty'. Three main ones are identified—the security of property and contract; free competition; and stable money. Or as Keith Joseph has put it more discursively:[17]

> Governments can help hold the ring, provide infrastructure, maintain a stable currency, a framework of laws, implementation of law and order, provision of a safety net, defence of property rights and all other rights involved in the economic process.

The contrast with Keynesian political economy is very marked. Post-war Keynesian thinking proposed four targets for economic policy—full employment, economic growth, stable prices, and a surplus on the balance of payments—and conceived managing the economy as a matter of fine tuning, of steering, of adjusting the economic aggregates through a constant process of intervention to keep the national economy in balance. The social market doctrine would still set targets, but only for those things like money supply and public expenditure that were specifically under government control. On all other detailed questions of economic policy—particularly employment, the rate of economic growth, and the exchange rate for the currency—the government would adopt a 'neutral policy stance', so disclaiming responsibility for economic outcomes.[18] Responsibility for employment would be passed to the trade unions, and responsibility for growth to the individual preferences of savers, investors, consumers, as well as external circumstances and divine providence. This means that no one need be unemployed so long as they are prepared to accept a wage low enough (negative if necessary), to make someone want to employ them, and so long as trade unions do not try to 'prevent' people taking or being forced into employment at such wages.

The centrepiece of this strategy is money, so it is no accident that monetarism has received such wide attention as the spearhead of the economic liberal assault on Keynesianism. Monetarism, however, as its advocates point out, is not a new doctrine and for most of the past two hundred years has been the orthodox approach of economists to monetary questions.[19] The ideals of sound money and a balanced budget and exchange rates fixed in terms of an incorruptible standard, gold, dominated the early development and spread of industrial capitalism. The idea of inflation as a 'monetary phenomenon' that can be traced to an over-expansion of the money supply by governments, has long been a central tenet of liberal political economy and conservative statesmanship. The significance of the restatement of this doctrine now, lies not in its efficiency as a technical device but in its implications for policy in other fields, particularly the management of demand and the public sector. As a technical device monetarism is merely one further instrument that can and has been added to the armoury of governments seeking to keep the confidence of the financial markets and external creditors. As the most recent Labour Government showed, monetarism, in the sense of firm monetary guidelines and control of public expenditure through cash limits, is quite compatible with incomes policies, price controls, industrial strategies, and all the other interventionist paraphernalia. The conversion of all governments to monetarist ideas is a concession that was forced on them in order to maintain the confidence of the international financial markets. The price of continuing to fund the public sector borrowing requirement and maintain external confidence in the currency was that governments had to reduce the domestic rate of inflation by restricting the money supply, announcing monetary targets and holding back the growth implications as to how governments should attempt to manage the economy.

For economic liberals, however, monetarism is not simply a means for easing the management problems of interventionist governments, but the only central obligation laid upon government in economic policy. The link between an expanding public sector and inflation is constantly stressed—inflation being regarded as a tax that is constantly redistributing income to the advantage of the state, and therefore one of the chief sources of finance for the government, whilst at the same time it destroys savings, enterprise and investment (although it greatly boosts speculation). At the root of this position is the notion that only in exceptional and highly temporary circumstances (some economic liberals think the 1930s was one) can unemployment be reduced by an expansion of demand that is initiated by central government and does not make the prospects for unemployment worse in the long run. If governments cannot reduce unemployment by tolerating a slightly higher rate of inflation, then commitment to expansionary demand policies undermines prosperity both by distorting the pattern of demand (stopping firms going bankrupt that otherwise would), and facilitating a constant transfer of resources and employment into the public sector.

Keynes's benevolent tolerance of inflation as a lesser evil than unemployment is what economic liberals so bitterly attack now, because they regard any acceptance of inflationary policies as undermining the basis of the market order. When Keynes argues that 'Inflation is unjust and Deflation is expedient. Of the two perhaps Deflation is the worse; because it is worse in an impoverished world to provoke unemployment rather than to disappoint the rentier', or again that 'the right remedy for the trade cycle is not to be found in abolishing booms and thus keeping us permanently in a semi-slump; but in abolishing slumps and thus keeping us permanently in a quasi boom',[20] he was making practical suggestions as to how governments could mitigate the impact of the Depression by using their control of the already vast state sector to manipulate the level of demand in the economy. Governments in many capitalist economies had long been interventionist, particularly in industrial and trade policy. Keynes, however, provided one of the first persuasive theoretical justifications for suspending the principles of orthodox finance, and so unwittingly provided a set of principles that underwrote the great inflationary boom of the 1950s and 1960s, which was certainly assisted, though not caused, by the relaxation of controls on private credit and the remarkable expansion of public sectors everywhere.

If the government's monetary policies are sound, then one major check to the encroachment of the public sector onto the private and to the undermining of thrift, industry and enterprise has been established. It relieves government of its responsibility for expansion and prosperity, but it does not relieve it of its obligation to make markets function as they should, nor does it rule out specific government expenditures or interventions in the private sector. The whole tradition of liberal political economy has insisted that governments have a duty to undertake the provision of 'public goods', defence being the case that is always cited. Aside from these, the presumption is that the market will normally supply goods at much lower cost than the state, and should be preferred. This argument turns on the notion of competition and the contrast between the 'imperfect' market and the 'imperfect' state—the imperfections of the state being so much greater because it has monopoly powers. John Jewkes expresses this standard liberal idea:[21]

> the efforts ... of governments to manipulate or 'restructure' a system as subtle and complex as competitive private industry are as likely to fail as would the efforts of a group of curious and playful children to repair a modern chronometer.

The industrial policy that would accompany sound money would therefore require drastic restrictions on all state economic activities, whether investment and regional subsidies, or help for mergers. It is typical of this approach that most economic liberals would think it more important to introduce competition into the nationalized industries by decentralizing them and ending their legal monopoly and accountability to ministers, than by handing them back to private owners. [22] It also follows that the government's chief role in preserving competition is to ensure freedom of entry into all industries and this necessarily involves a basic commitment to free trade, particularly in view of the growth of world trade and the increased interpenetration of capital and national economies over the last thirty years.

An emphasis on free competition and freedom from state interference is often regarded as a cardinal belief of shopkeepers and small manufacturers, and generates demands for the control and dispersal of private monopolies. Social market literature, however, at least in Britain and America, sees no need to present its proposals as the demands of an oppressed petit bourgeoisie or even of consumers. Corporate capital is explicitly vindicated. ICI is as respectable an economic individual as the next man and entitled to the same consideration, freedom, and rights. As Hayek says with his usual clarity:[23]

> The most conspicuous gap in the following survey is probably the omission of any systematic discussion of enterprise monopoly. The subject was excluded after careful consideration mainly because it seemed not to possess the importance commonly attached to it. For liberals anti-monopoly policy has usually been the main object of their reformatory zeal. I believe I have myself in the past used the tactical argument that we cannot hope to curb the coercive powers of labour unions unless we at the same time attack enterprise monopoly. I have, however, become convinced that it would be disingenuous to represent the existing monopolies in the field of labour and those in the field of enterprise as being of the same kind ... I have become increasingly sceptical ... about the beneficial character of any discretionary action of government against particular monopolies, and I am seriously alarmed at the arbitrary nature of all policy aimed at limiting the size of individual enterprises.

After inflation and anarchy the main threat to the foundations of the market order is seen as the privileges and organizations of trade unions. The legitimacy which is accorded to corporate capital is not extended to the unions. This might seem odd since most theories that justify corporate capitalism also regard trade unions as a necessary adjunct for the efficient planning and integration of the labour force. British and American social market theorists do not take this view because they regard monopoly powers of unions in the labour markets as the principal reason for growing government regulation of the economy and lax monetary policy. This is because trade unions 'distort' relative prices in the labour market, making many activities unprofitable that would otherwise be profitable, so creating unemployment; and they impede the introduction of new technology, so reducing mobility and freezing the pattern of employment whilst the pattern of demand is shifting. The economy performs less well than it should, and governments under pressure to retain and win votes intervene in private industry to try to make it more efficient, and expand demand to reduce unemployment. This creates inflation which keeps the economy prosperous for a while but at the expense of making the final crash and the scale of reorganization more extensive.[24] What is particularly irksome for economic liberals about the existence of trade unions is that they cannot discover any economic role for them at all. They are one of those unfortunate natural events like the Sahara Desert. Hayek grants that unions have social functions and assist in simplifying the bargaining process in large organizations, and thinks they perform a most valuable service as friendly societies, when they insure their members against illness and unemployment. But the idea that the unions have had anything to do with the permanent raising of absolute wages is vigorously resisted. They can only introduce artificial rigidities into the setting of relative wages, so pricing some non-unionists out of work and preventing the most rapid adjustment of the economy to new technology.

The basis of union power is seen as private coercion, the interference with the individual liberty of workers and employers. Enoch Powell argued in 1968[25] that union power rested on three legal privileges; the freedom to intimidate (i.e., picketing); the freedom to impose costs with impunity; and the immunity of trade unions from actions of tort. Withdrawal of these three privileges would certainly revolutionize the workings of the labour market; it would certainly keep the courts busy and, if successful, it would change decisively the balance of forces between the classes in production itself. In Marxist terms it would restore the full operation of the industrial reserve army of labour. The perennial problem of labour supply in capitalist social formations—the right labour, in the right quantity, at the right price, would be alleviated.

In its attitude towards trade unions the political character of social market doctrine becomes clear. This is corporate liberalism, but a corporate liberalism which in a period of recession chafes under the extra burdens which trade unions and interventionist bureaucracies impose on their operations. Social democracy could be afforded in times of expansion; in a period of recession it suddenly becomes costly. If the economy is to remain free the state has to become strong; and nowhere stronger than in its dealings with organized labour. The unions are excused direct responsibility for inflation (since wage rises can only cause inflation if the government allows the money supply to increase to finance higher prices). But they are made directly responsible for all other ills of the market economy—unemployment, stagnation, and disruption; and so the strongest measures can be justified against them as being in the 'public interest'. Social market doctrine offers intellectual reasons to fortify the political onslaught on social democracy and its main organizational support, the trade unions.

4

The doctrine of the social market economy as it has been presented here can be seen to be a restatement and revival of some of the key themes of liberal political economy, which have tended to be buried with the ascendancy of Keynesianism and the increasing specialization of economics as a branch of mathematics. What the social market economy is not, is any simple reversion to the ideal of a competitive laissez-faire economy which acts as an ideological veil for the present problems of capital accumulation. The continuing strength and new relevance of liberal political economy has to be sought in the basic structure of capitalist social formations. It is not just a question of ideological beliefs but of the social practices on which they arise.[26]

From this standpoint liberal political economy is the theory which treats capitalism primarily as a system of simple commodity production, what Marx termed the sphere of circulation or commodity exchange, 'a very Eden of the innate rights of man'. The problem of maintaining capitalism and improving its functioning is viewed almost entirely from the standpoint of how markets work. The market is viewed as the most efficient way of finding solutions to the problem of satisfying material needs because it searches out those methods of social co-operation that ensure maximum individual choice and minimum (measurable) costs. The key concerns of the social market doctrine are therefore with the basic conditions that make markets work—sound money, security of property, competition—and such is the commitment to the idea of individual exchange as a supreme value that all the problems of capitalism are ascribed to rigidities and inflexibilities in institutions and practices which prevent the market economy from working. One of the most notorious examples was the doctrine of the 1920s and 1930s that unemployment only existed because wage rates would not fall far enough. It is an idea that has been reborn today with Milton Friedman's doctrine of the natural rate of unemployment[27]—a rate which is determined primarily by the degree of 'imperfection' in the labour market, which includes such incidentals as trade union organization, subsidized council housing, and social security benefits. Two liberal economists were able recently to conclude that the real wage necessary for full employment was now some way below the social security minimum.

The social market doctrine seeks to dispose of unemployment as a matter for political concern or government intervention, by putting the blame for unemployment on the failure of individuals and institutions to adapt themselves to the requirements of the market, whatever the cost in low wages and poverty, demoralization and uprooted communities, lost skills and lost purposes. As Keith Joseph recently told workers on Clydeside faced with redundancy—100,000 workers change jobs in Britain every week, and you may have to do the same. With more than 15 million unemployed in the major capitalist states this doctrine serves to reconcile governments and electorates to permanent high levels of unemployment.

The power of the social market economy, therefore, is not that it revives an ancient ideology, but that it restores a way of looking at capitalism and its problems which has been pushed aside by other conceptions and by the political intervention of the working-class movement, but which has revived because of the continuing importance of the sphere of commodity exchange in the actual workings of capitalist economies. Indeed this sphere has not shrunk but expanded since the heyday of the so-called laissez-faire economy, as more and more areas of social life have been commercialized, i.e., brought within the sphere of exchange and made alienable. In a fully developed exchange economy, a catallaxy as Hayek prefers to call it,[28] everything has its price, and everyone is forced to become a merchant and live by buying and selling. A nation of self-acting commodities experience the truths of liberal political economy daily.

The grave defect, however, of liberal political economy lies in its handling of capital, in its failure to perceive how radically the structure of the market economy is transformed by first the emergence, and then the development of capital within it. To the logic of individual exchange is added the logic of capital accumulation. If simple commodity production were undisturbed and all men were merchants and independent producers the theory of the social market economy would accurately describe the economy that existed. But it is because it is possible for some of those independent producers and merchants to become capitalists, buying labour power, organizing production, and selling commodities to realize a surplus value, that imparts a quite different dynamic to the development of the market economy. Accumulation has to work through exchange, but it gives rise to a different order of problems and a different direction social development.

The first of these problems is class conflict between the two classes of agents that, having bought and sold labour power in the market, now confront one another in production. This conflict of interest brings the creation of defensive organizations which break with individual choice and exchange in favour of the benefits from collective action and solidarity. In acting thus they seriously impair the free working of labour markets. Such organizations have at times been suppressed but more often allowed to become legal institutions as trade unions and political parties. Since for social market theorists labour power is a commodity just like any other ('the worker has only his productivity to sell' is a favourite aphorism) they need to recommend either repression of trade unions in order to recreate an atomized labour market or a programme of measures which will strip away the harmful effects of the concessions that have been made to working-class organizations in order to reduce and control class conflict. The problem is that the benefits of collective action and defence normally outweigh the benefits from greater individual market freedom and choice. As many of its warmest admirers have noted regretfully, the legitimacy of market institutions is difficult to secure, because the market is essentially amoral, directionless, and to some extent arbitrary in the way in which it distributes income and wealth, rewarding luck and status as much as skill and effort. The older thorough-going petit-bourgeois moral justification for capitalism, which Thatcher regularly trumpets forth, is that reward is related to effort and skill. But such a crude notion has long been discarded by Hayek and the other advanced thinkers of liberal political economy.[29] They argue that it is fruitless to seek either merit or fairness in the pattern of market outcomes. Attempts to establish either lead to grave distortions of the market order. The way in which society develops means that unfair and unmerited opportunities and rewards are constantly being created. The sophisticated message of these theorists is that the amoral outcomes of the market should be accepted by everyone as legitimate because of the general benefits everyone receives from a maximizing of opportunities for individual exchange and choice. This notion has not proved a great popular success as yet, and has certainly either been misunderstood or ignored by those who write speeches for the Conservative Leader.

It points to a permanent weakness in the populist ideology of self-help, because only a minority can ever help themselves to the abundance the ideology promises. If the best hopes of Hayek were realized, and the legitimacy of capitalism were to be founded no longer on the traditional authority of Church and State or on populist ideologies of Race, Religion, or Empire, but squarely on the market order, then at the very least a capitalism of some abundance would be required, so that the vast majority of the population without property, without inheritance, and without luck, would at least derive some tangible benefit, and give thanks to the great international capitalist catallaxy which rules their lives. Such abundance is hard to guarantee due to the second set of problems which capital accumulation poses for the market order—the profitability of its enterprises. Since the driving purpose of production is no longer consumption but accumulation, profits assume great importance and at the same time appear highly precarious, a quality which increases as the scale of capitalist production expands. As a result capitalist development has been punctuated by severe crises, instabilities and depressions. The relentless search for new sources of profit has brought constant reorganization of its productive base, leading to increasing concentration and centralization of capital, rapid technological innovation, the gradual expulsion of living labour from the production process, and the establishment of a world division of labour.

So massive has been this development of social production and so radical its transformation of social institutions that it required the growth of public responsibilities and new state agencies in many fields. The social market theorists are mostly blind to this rather obvious fact. Milton Friedman ascribes the steady growth of public spending from 1906 onwards to a misplaced charitable intent.[30] Politicians and intellectuals wanted to do good to improve society, but they chose a method which was ultimately destructive of their intentions. According to Friedman the eleventh commandment should read 'everyone shall be free to do good at his own expense'. This would solve the problem of the growth of the state. Such extreme political naivety arises from a theoretical system in which the problems of capital accumulation for the organization of industrial societies do not appear, so the material basis for state intervention is generally not glimpsed. It is ascribed simply to political 'will' and mistaken ideas. This imposes severe limitation on the theory, because it means it contains no means for thinking through some of the most important problems confronting capitalist societies and their governments.[31]

One implication of the analysis in this essay is that the real test of the seriousness of a social market strategy in Britain does not lie in policies it prescribes for money supply, taxation and public expenditure, which only amount to an orthodox deflationary policy, but in the readiness to tackle the main obstacle to the realization of a social market economy—the organized working class.[32] Without measures to radically reduce trade union 'monopoly' powers, the success of a monetarist policy might be seriously hampered through the creation of a level of unemployment and rate of growth that would be hard to tolerate politically or electorally. One of the structural features of the political market which social market theorists often overlook, is that the great majority of electors are not capitalists and savers but workers and consumers. The achievement of prosperity has become something that is expected from government policies, not something that is the responsibility of each individual. Deflation if pursued for long enough may make money sound again and halt the encroachments of the state, but it will not bring prosperity unless the free functioning of the labour market is restored. The only alternative (the one U-turn this present Conservative Government might contemplate, despite doctrinal scruples and EEC opposition) would be to introduce the kind of import controls urged by the Cambridge Economic Policy Group, the one technical policy for managing the British economy which seems to have any chance of rescuing it from heavy and continuing deflation and stagnation to protect the balance of payments and keep control of the money supply for as long as the current recession lasts.

Social market doctrine encourages passivity and resignation by policy makers faced by stagnation and recession. Talk is already being heard of the 'libertarian' advantages of cuts in taxes and public expenditure, regardless of whether they succeed in stimulating expansion. Whether such policies can be maintained depends on whether the populist scapegoating of trade unionists, immigrants and welfare claimants, can retain sufficient political and electoral support, and further intimidate and demoralize the labour movement, so weakening its political opposition.

5

The argument presented here is that the social market economy must be distinguished from the populist presentation of some of its key themes in order to understand the driving force it has imparted to the intellectual revival on the right. It is its material basis as the theory of the sphere of commodity exchange that gives it its range and allows it to dominate so much of the intellectual assessment of the modern state and to prescribe policies for the recession that are rapidly becoming orthodoxy.

On the left the same clarity and fundamental rethinking has not occurred. The alliance between the state and the labour movement during the war created the political basis for the social democratic Keynesian consensus and the belief in the efficiency, desirability, and justice of state action. This consensus maintained a remarkable social peace through the long boom, but now that the problems of managing capitalism loom so large it is visibly failing. The revival of the perspective of liberal political economy is one response, and is proving extremely powerful, reinforced as it is by its easy translation into the themes of populism where all economic ills are seen both as the result of an overbearing and inefficient state, *and* as the work of ill-intentioned, subversive minorities who disturb order and threaten security.

The major response to this within the British labour movement has been the alternative economic strategy, a reaffirmation of the old collectivist faith of social democracy—the preference for solutions that involve greater centralization, more public ownership and more public expenditure, all of which entail the strengthening of parts of the existing state. The fight is for a socialist incomes policy, a socialist National Enterprise Board, and socialist import controls. The extension and strengthening of the state that was achieved by social democracy and Keynesianism is regarded as part of the conquests of the labour movement, to be defended against attack and to be used as the base from which to make the next advance.

Another response starts from the ideological and political weakness of the left and seeks to recreate the oppositional and independent role of socialists and the labour movement within capitalist society. It asks why the best efforts of socialists should go towards strengthening the existing agencies of the state or to extending their powers. This response is often criticized because it appears to accept much of the case for the social market economy, at least where the attitude to collectivism and state interference is concerned. It covers both the defensive celebration of the pluralism of the free market, on the grounds that free collective bargaining best preserves the ability of working-class organizations to defend working-class interests, and the currently strong revival of interest in guild socialism, industrial democracy, and co-operatives in housing, industry and education —attempts to create new socialist communities and experiments, using the freedoms a market order provides.

These two principal responses on the left to the current recession and the political challenge from the right both attempt to mark out an independent socialist line based on a class standpoint, one in terms of policies, the other in terms of institutions, but they are often too easily contained within the universe of thought and practice they seek to challenge. One reason why the social market doctrine is proving such a successful catalyst for populist ideologies on the right is that it goes back to fundamentals. Since exchange and the market do provide a basis upon which all social relations in capitalist society can be grasped and evaluated, social market doctrine has a universal reach, constantly suggesting ways of approaching and solving practical problems. If the right currently enjoys the advantage in arguments about how to cope with the recession, it is partly because of the skilful populist translation of its key themes into grievances about taxes, strikes, and bureaucracies, but it also because the social market doctrine goes deeper than the instrumental and managerial approach of Keynesianism, and restates the case for capitalism in its most fundamental and strongest form—as a market order which maximizes individual freedom and choice.

It is the case which Marx set out and analysed at length in the *Grundrisse* and in *Capital*, because he believed it was necessary to base socialist politics and socialist strategy upon a critique of it. He wanted to go beyond either a 'socialist political economy' or a 'socialist market economy' by providing instead a socialist critique of the assumptions on which liberal political economy was based, in order to assist the practical efforts of the working-class movement in transforming the social relations of a class society. It is this critique which needs reviving again today, now that fundamentals are once again at stake. It emphasizes the sphere of production relations and the labour process as the starting point for criticizing the bourgeois ideal of the market—the individual calculation and pursuit of self-interest, and the accommodation and adjustment of interests through competition—as the model of all social relations.

Fundamentalism, in the sense of a dogmatic adherence to the writings and precepts of past thinkers, is always sterile, but fundamentalism, in the sense of a rediscovery and rethinking of the essential positions of a political movement, is a necessity if its independence and vigour are to continue. In the present period technical and managerial doctrines will not by themselves provide the basis upon which socialists can win back the initiative in arguments and struggles, and develop a coherent strategy for socialist transformation. To do this it is not sufficient to know which institutions and policies have to be defended, but also which features of capitalist social relations have to be changed for a socialist society to come into existence. How, for example, does socialist theory cope with the three oppositions which lie at the heart of the social market doctrine: democracy/liberty; bureaucracy/law; planning/freedom? Can any set of social relations other than the market limit bureaucracy and state power? Must the basic forms of exchange relations, such as money, law, and the commodity be eventually superseded if a stage of social development is to be realized which does not reproduce the social relations and individual experience of a market order? Social market doctrine urges the furthest possible extension of alienated relations of commodity exchange and, through them, the rule of capital. Socialists can regain their intellectual conviction and confidence if they confront the arguments for the social market economy by restating and rethinking the basic premises on which the intellectual and practical case for socialism has been and must continue to be based.[33]

NOTES

1. Typical products of the right-wing upsurge are recent collections such as P. Cormack (ed.), *Right Turn*, London, 1978; and *The Coming Confrontation*, (IEA) London, 1978. The contributors range from Paul Johnson to Julius Gould, Reg Prentice, and the Duke of Edinburgh. They mostly see themselves as engaged on a crusade against evil doctrines and vested interests.
2. I have examined in greater detail the changing Conservative Party in two recent essays: 'The Conservative Party', in H.M. Drucker (ed.) *Multi-Party Britain*, London, 1979; and 'Conservative Economic Policy' in Z. Layton-Henry (ed.) *Conservative Party Politics*, London, 1979.
3. They are surveyed by C. J. Friedrich, 'The Political Ideas of Neo-Liberalism', *American Political Science Review*, 49 (1955), pp. 509-25.
4. The IEA was founded in 1957 and has produced a constant stream of pamphlets (over 250 publications). It recruits its writers mainly from academic economists. The Centre for Policy Studies was founded by Keith Joseph and Margaret Thatcher, in 1974 and has produced a number of pamphlets, including the keynote, *Why Britain Needs a Social Market Economy*, London, 1975. It has also published collections of the speeches of its two founders as well as a range of pamphlets the intellectual level of which has been variable.
5. Apart from their journalism they have all written more extended studies, especially Brittan, who has written pamphlets for both the IEA and the CPS. See also his recent and important book, *The Economic Consequences of Democracy*, London, 1977.
6. Cf. Stuart Hall *et al.*, *Policing the Crisis*, London, 1978.
7. See, for instance, S. Brittan, *Government and the Market Economy*, IEA, London, 1971 and *Participation Without Politics*, IEA, London, 1975.

8. Rustow, one of the German neo-liberals set forth his ideas under the engaging slogan 'Freie Wirtschaft—Starker Staat' (free economy, strong state). See Friedrich, *op. cit.*

9. See the onslaught contained for example in T. Russel, *The Tory Party*, Harmondsworth, 1978. Russel, a former Labour Party member is an active member of the Tory Reform Group.

10. *The Road to Serfdom* (London, 1944) is rather a slight work, although the best known of all Hayek's writings. Much more important are his later writings, particularly *The Constitution of Liberty*, London, 1960; *Law, Legislation, and Liberty* (3 volumes), London, 1973; and *Studies in Philosophy, Politics, and Economics*, London, 1967.

11. Hayek, *The Constitution of Liberty*, p. 11. This notion of coercion is absolutely vital to liberal theory and it leads to the notion of the state enjoying a monopoly of legitimate force, a notion that is often incorporated uncritically into Marxist theories of the state. The error of this conception is brilliantly demonstrated by Q. Rudland in *The Capitalist State as History and Logic*, mimeo, Sheffield, 1979.

12. Moreau's assessment of Norman was as follows: 'In his view politicians and political institutions are in no fit state to direct with the necessary competence and continuity this task of organisation (economic and financial organisation of the world) which he would like to see undertaken by central banks, independent at once of governments and of private finance', quoted by A. Boyle, *Montagu Norman*, London, 1967, p. 205

13. They make loyalty tests and the *Berufsverbot* much easier to impose.

14. R. Moss, *The Collapse of Democracy*, London, 1975.

15. M. Friedman, 'The Line We Dare Not Cross', *Encounter*, November 1976. See also G. Tullock, *The Vote Motive*, IEA, London, 1976.

16. A brief perusal of the social market literature will reveal how profound is the distrust of these writers of the state. The IEA has taken to translating the term 'state' as politicians and bureaucrats, to strip away from it the aura of omniscience and omnipotence and reveal the fallible agents that the term conceals. They have not yet shown the same readiness to translate their own idol 'the market' as entrepreneurs and lawyers. That would be consistent, for these are the agents that liberal political economy regards as essential for upholding the market order.

17. Keith Joseph, *Conditions for Fuller Employment*, CPS, 1978, p. 20.

18. See, for example, A. Walters, *Economists and the British Economy*, IEA, London, 1978. The bitterness of liberal economists against Keynesian economists is extraordinary. Cf. W. R. Hutt, *Politically Impossible?*, London, 1971.

19. See, for example, T. Congdon, *Monetarism*, CPS, 1978, and W. Rees-Mogg, *Democracy and the Value of Money*, IEA, 1977.

20. J. M. Keynes, *The General Theory of Interest, Employment, and Money*, London, 1973, p. 322.

21. J. Jewkes, *Delusions of Dominance*, IEA, 1977. See also the Centre for Policy Studies series on government intervention, 'The Way the Money Goes'.

22. Cf. S. Brittan, *Government and the Market Economy*.

23. Hayek, *The Constitution of Liberty*, p. 264. This represents a considerable shift from the position he adopted in *The Road to Serfdom*.

24. Hayek's views on inflation and the consequences of Keynesianism are usuefully collected in *A Tiger by the Tail*, IEA, 1972. See also his Nobel Lecture, *Full Employment at any Price?*, IEA, 1975.

25. J. E. Powell, *Freedom and Reality*, London, 1969, ch. 10. When Powell first emerged as an exponent of economic liberalism he was dismissed as a crank and widely derided. But he pioneered the analysis which has now become orthodox.

26. This is not the same, however, as arguing that the idea of the social market economy must be attributed to this or that fraction of capital. I regard the evidence for this as slim and the underlying argument unsound.

27. For an exposition of it see Friedman's Nobel lecture, *Inflation and Employment*, IEA, 1977; and S. Brittan, *Second Thoughts on Full Employment Policy*, CPS, 1975.

28. See Hayek, *The Confusion of Language in Political Thought*, IEA, 1968.

29. See, in particular, Hayek, *Law, Legislation, and Liberty*, vol. 2 and S. Brittan & P. Lilley, *The Delusions of Incomes Policy*, London, 1976.

30. Friedman, 'The Line We Dare Not Cross', *op. cit.*

31. A very different way of looking at capitalism comes from those who analyse capitalism as a system of production rather than as a system of markets. W. W. Rostow's *The World Economy*, London, 1978, is an example of the former approach which assigns a very small role to monetary factors. Rostow, whose own allegiance to capitalism is hardly in question, argues that the present recession will only be overcome and capitalism placed on a stable basis again if there is a further massive extension of state powers and investment, particularly in the energy field.

32. This is of course recognized and the necessary measures fully discussed. See, for example, K. Joseph, *Solving the Union Problem is the Key to Britain's Recovery*, CPS, 1979; and S. Brittan, *The Economic Consequences of Democracy*, ch. 19. One of the most drastic suggestions is for the creation of a professional specialized strike-breaking force, a kind of permanenet OMS which would be available to man essential installations in the event of strikes, and would presumably allow lockouts to be threatened and implemented more easily in some sectors.

33. One recent major attempt to rethink socialist strategy, although from a different position from the one proposed here, is A. Cutler *et al*, *Marx's Capital and Capitalism Today*, London, 1977.

THE PREMATURE BURIAL:
A REPLY TO MARTIN SHAW

Ian H. Birchall

Martin Shaw's 'unofficial' history of the International Socialists[1] makes an important contribution to the debate that has been taking place, over the last few years, in the pages of *The Socialist Register* about the sort of organization that the British left needs. Shaw has written, firmly if not without melancholy, an obituary for the political tendency represented by the International Socialists and (since 1977) the Socialist Workers Party. By 1976, Shaw tells us, the organization was 'radically deformed'; its politics had become 'opportunistic, unrealistic and sectarian'; its 'degeneration' represented a 'squandering of the potential for a new socialist movement'; it had undergone 'catastrophic changes'.[2]

These are serious charges and require a cool and objective response. Every failure has its lessons and every defeat is a stepping-stone to final victory. For example, the IS/SWP represents the most serious and consistent attempt in recent years to build a revolutionary socialist organization outside of and independent from the Labour Party. An acceptance of Shaw's case would be a strong argument on the side of those who believe that Marxists must continue to work within the Labour Party.

Moreover, any SWP member who reads Shaw's article will be willing to concede that some of Shaw's specific criticisms are at least partially correct. All the more pity that Shaw frames them in the context of an article which uses the weaknesses as the proof of irredeemable corruption rather than asking how they may best be corrected.

Shaw makes a wide range of criticisms, but behind them lie two fundamental points: firstly, that the IS/SWP has failed to develop an adequate form of internal democracy; secondly, that the IS/SWP is guilty of a political deviation described as 'workerism'. Rather than commenting on detailed historical points (though a few may be worth footnotes) I think the most fruitful way of replying to Shaw is to examine these two charges, and then to examine how they were—or were not—manifested in some of the main areas of IS/SWP activity.

I. *The Internal Regime*

Shaw chronicles in some detail—though not always accurately[3] —the constitutional changes in IS from 1968 to 1976 and the accompanying changes in leading personnel. But while the details of the account can be questioned, what is much more important is the method that lies behind the account. For Shaw, the changes in IS often seem to proceed in a vacuum, with only the thinnest references to what was going on in the world outside. (For example, Shaw's account makes no reference to the events in Portugal of 1974-5; yet not only did these events have an influence on the perspectives of Marxists throughout Europe, but also IS was deeply involved both in solidarity work and support for Portuguese revolutionaries, and in organizing delegations of workers to Portugal.) The form of an organization must be related to the situation the organization finds itself in and the tasks it sets itself. But Shaw seems more interested, say, in the decision-making process which led to the creation of the Right to Work Campaign, than in what the Campaign actually did, in the workplaces, in the labour movement, or on the streets.

In any revolutionary organization that is more than a sterile and immovable sect there will be a continuing dialectical relation between the forms of organization and the tasks posed by external reality. Habits of organization and of mind which serve well in one phase of development may be a conservative and inhibiting factor in the next.[4] Thus Shaw, writing of the IS unity proposals of 1968, describes them as 'not ... a well thought out "first step" on the road to a revolutionary party, but something of a panic response'.[5] The alternative categories proposed are revealing. Revolutionary organizations rarely have the time or the predictive powers to take well thought out steps; this does not mean that the need to respond rapidly and flexibly to new circumstances should be labelled as panic. In which category, one wonders, would Shaw put Lenin's *April Theses?*

Shaw's main contention is that there was a decline in the level of internal democracy between 1968 and 1976. There was less debate and discussion, more tight control from the top. Such a judgement in itself would be impressionistic, but fortunately Shaw gives us a clear criterion. The tight Central Committee control, its imposition of policies and expulsion of political opponents 'took IS further away from a serious and realistic appraisal of the situation in the working class'.[6] In this Shaw agrees with what has always been the dominant view in IS/SWP: internal democracy is not an end in itself, but a means whereby the party is able to effectively evaluate situations and critically assess its own intervention. It will be on the basis of this criterion that we shall be able to judge whether Shaw's analysis is correct with regard to the IS/SWP work with relation to trade unions, racism, unemployment, sexual politics and other topics.[7]

Unfortunately, Shaw does not always apply his own criterion. He gives a full account[8] of the various internal disputes in IS in 1975. Yet the account is lacking in any real presentation of what the debate was all about. As Shaw himself points out, the election of the Labour Government, and the shift in pace of the class struggle posed very real problems. In retrospect it is easy enough to see that we all got it wrong—Wilson, Callaghan and their allies in the trade union bureaucracy succeeded in dampening down class struggle for much longer than anyone had believed possible. The debate inside IS was a real, but necessarily confused, attempt to come to terms with the problems. Initially the Opposition's time-scale was scarcely less cataclysmic than the majority's:

> Jim Higgins argued that the honeymoon period might be longer rather than shorter—six or seven months rather than three or four.[9]

By early 1975 the majority had come to a reassessment of their position:

> The political perspectives put to the last IS Conference in September had telescoped events, Chris Harman told the IS National Committee on Saturday, opening the discussion on political perspectives for the next annual conference. Our *economic* analysis had been by and large correct, although unemployment had risen slightly more slowly than we had predicted, he said. Our real mistake had been *political*—in thinking that political consciousness among workers would rise completely in time with the economic crisis.[10]

From this basic question of perspectives flowed a number of other arguments. One concerned the possibilities of growth. Were the potential recruits to revolutionary politics to be found among those workers who had already some experience of the existing political organizations (Labour Party, Communist Party), or would they come from among young workers with few traditions and little experience of work in the labour movement? It was this question that lay behind the long debate on *Socialist Worker*—its content, level and presentation—which certainly involved every member of the organization over the 1974-5 period.

A second debate related to the question of work in the trade unions. Labour's accession to power had meant a general drift to the right in the movement, typified by the way in which Jack Jones, previously a pillar of the left, supported the Social Contract. The Communist Party and its allies in the Broad Left did not escape the drift; they were both unwilling to make a clean break with former allies such as Jones, and increasingly unable to mobilize, even on the electoral level. IS was faced with the problem of how to respond to this situation; how far should comrades continue to co-operate with the Broad Left, and in what ways could an independent alternative be built? (It is in this context that the dispute about AUEW elections must be placed. Shaw, however, distorts the issues by seeing it as conflict between Birmingham IS members and 'the leadership'; he leaves out of account IS engineers in many other localities who were strongly opposed to the policies of the Birmingham comrades.)

In short, Shaw's account of the alleged decline of democracy in IS/SWP gives us form without content. Debates, decisions and splits are catalogued without any account of the real issues that lay behind them. It is therefore necessary to turn to Shaw's second major accusation, that of 'workerism'.

2. *The Question of Workerism*

The problem of what Shaw describes as 'workerism' has implications which go beyond the history of the vicissitudes of one small revolutionary organization. It raises the whole issue of the analysis of the present epoch and the sort of intervention which revolutionaries can make.

It will therefore be useful to begin with Shaw's own definitions. 'Workerism', he tells us, is used in his article 'to describe the leadership's almost exclusive preoccupation with the economic struggles of male manual workers in industry, and its tendency to interpret all other issues in terms of them'. Behind this lay a 'question of general politics, of understanding that socialism is about more than economics, together with the way in which economic, cultural, ideological and political factors are inter-related in the current crisis'.[12]

On one level it is hard to disagree with Shaw here. The last ten years have given us a rich experience to be assimilated: student struggles, the rise of the women's movement, the extension of trade union militancy to a wide range of new sectors; and, on the other hand, a ruling class on the defensive thrusting cultural and ideological factors into the centre of the arena. Yet just because what he says is so obviously correct it is less than adequate, for it does not point towards action. It is one thing to grasp the social complex as a totality; it is quite another—especially for a small organization—to develop a strategic intervention.

There is also a more fundamental problem. When Shaw challenges IS/SWP's preoccupation with manual workers in industry, it is not clear whether he is simply making a point about the balance of activity, or whether he is calling into question the whole Marxist thesis that the industrial proletariat is the primary agent of socialist transformation. Of course Shaw has every right to do the latter; things are not true just because Marx said so. Indeed, if he were to develop the argument the point would be considerably more significant than the minutiae of constitutional change in the IS/SWP. The problem is that the question is left unresolved, with the result that it is hard to determine the status of Shaw's critique of IS/SWP 'fundamentalism'.

To take one aspect of the question, Shaw suggests that the IS/SWP leadership has played down the importance of work among white collar trade unionists. The whole experience of the last ten years refutes this charge. The teachers' journal *Rank and File*, founded in 1968 on the joint initiative of IS and Communist Party members, represented IS's first excursion into the realm of rank and file organization, and in many ways provided a model for similar work in other areas. The first Rank and File Conference in 1974 would scarcely have been possible without the sponsorship of such rank and file white collar papers as *NALGO Action*, *Redder Tape*, *Case Con*, *Rank and File Teacher* and *Tech Teacher*. It is unlikely that the right wing in the NUT, CPSA, NALGO or NATFHE would endorse the charge that IS/SWP had neglected work in these areas.[13]

Yet the category of 'white collar' worker is far from homogeneous. The term includes a very wide range of occupations, some of which are, in comparison to other groups of workers, relatively privileged in terms of security, working conditions, etc. Moreover, many white collar unions contain a whole hierarchy of grades (head teachers, managers, etc.) within their ranks.[14] For example, in the last couple of years we have seen both the heroic struggle by APEX members at

Grunwicks and the threat of withdrawal of labour by the Association of University Teachers. Both were examples of the extension of militancy to new sectors, and both deserved support. But scarcely anyone on the left can have had any doubts as to which was the more significant.

For specific historical reasons (radicalized students entering white collar professions, the relative weakness of the traditional left) revolutionaries have found it easier to make some impact on white collar unions than on the more traditional manual unions. This has great advantages, but also certain dangers; there is a constant risk of accommodation, of an economism which is especially pernicious because it adapts to a relatively privileged group. Revolutionary socialists have to constantly combat the dangers of craftism (and its white collar manifestation, professionalism) in the name of the most oppressed sectors of the working class—which include women, blacks and the unemployed. As Tony Cliff has put it:

> Some revolutionaries do suffer from elitist notions. They think of the barricades as follows: In the front row there is an Imperial Father of the Chapel representing craft workers in all their glory. He is wearing his gold chain of office to pay homage ...
> And then there are some representatives of section one of the Engineering Union.
> Only then if there is enough room in the street they would in their generosity allow some blacks, a few women and some youth—if they know their place, that is.
> Revolution has nothing at all to do with this hierarchical concept.
> Anyone who is in any doubt about it has no need to look further than the boys and girls of Soweto.[15]

The struggle against elitism and sectionalism in the labour movement has been central to IS/SWP politics. The Right to Work Campaign, seeking solidarity from employed workers with the (disproportionately black, female and young) unemployed, has been an important weapon in this struggle.

Moreover, Shaw fails to deal with the most important problem of all, that of priorities. Throughout the period in question IS/SWP has been a tiny organization; it has grown, unevenly, from around one thousand in 1968 to around four thousand at present. The failure of both the Labour left and the Communist Party to take necessary initiatives has become ever more marked; the revolutionary left inherited a range of tasks far in excess of its capacities. For a small group even to attempt to intervene in all the different struggles —political, economic, cultural, ideological, etc.—would require either a debilitating round of non-stop activism or a division of labour organized with military precision. Neither of these suited the model of an organization open to workers which IS/SWP has aimed at. The only other alternative was an insistence on priorities, a continuing emphasis by the leadership on intervention in the industrial working class. The limited but real success of ISA/SWP in developing a membership of industrial workers and a real presence in certain workplaces and unions has not been paralleled by any other revolutionary organization in Britain since the Communist Party in the 1920s. The achievement must be judged for what it is worth, and by the price at which it was bought. This price, indubitably, was a failure to intervene in a number of other important areas. Moreover, we can concede that opportunities were missed unnecessarily, that gross mistakes were made, and that some comrades interpreted the priorities of the organization in an insensitive and exaggerated manner. To this extent there is substance in some of Shaw's particular criticisms. But what Shaw fails to show is that an alternative set of priorities could in fact have been successful. This point can best be pursued by examining in more detail some particular areas of activity.

3. *The Rank and File Movement*

The project of a rank and file movement has for a long time been central to the political current represented by IS/SWP. The continuing class-collaboration of the trade union leaders makes it necessary to develop a current within the trade union movement which, while rejecting any attempt to by-pass the existing organizations or wander off into the dead end of breakaway unionism, none the less aims to organize the militants in the workplaces in order, when and if necessary, to act independently of the machine. The tradition of such a movement has deep roots in the British labour movement, going back to the shop stewards' movement during and after the First World War, and the subsequent emergence of the Minority Movement. For revolutionary socialists, such a movement is not only an important tool of the class struggle; it is also a bridge which links the revolutionaries to the most militant sections of the working class.

Until the early seventies IS was in no position to do more than propagandize for a rank and file movement. By the last year of the Heath government, however, things had begun to change. The role of the trade. union bureaucracy in collaborating with the state was becoming more obvious. Moreover, the body which up to this time had seemed that it might in some ways provide the basis for a rank and file movement—the Liaison Committee for the Defence of Trade Unions (largely under the political influence of the Communist Party)—was becoming increasingly ineffective. Its conferences were so arranged as to make it impossible to take any decision other than endorsement of the platform; there was no attempt to set up local liaison committees; and there was little in the way of co-ordination of struggle and solidarity action. Finally, IS members, in co-operation with other militants of various organizations and of none, had established rank and file papers and caucuses in a number of unions and industries.

It was in this situation that the first National Rank and File Movement Conference was held in March 1974, attended by 500 delegates from 270 trade union bodies. Up to this point Shaw does not disagree substantially—though perhaps he makes the success of the Conference seem too easy. It did not fall from the sky, but was the result of several months intense work by IS members and others; the size of the Conference was in fact a great surprise to all those involved in organizing it.

It is also possible to agree with Shaw that the Rank and File Movement did not continue to grow in line with the expectations its early success had raised. But while Shaw does not deny the objective circumstances—the Social Contract and the general drift to the right in the movement—he puts the main blame on what he sees as the manipulative politics of IS: 'An exaggerated emphasis on the rank and file movement's independence of IS, and encouragement of others to take their responsibility for it, was needed.'[16]

Here Shaw grossly simplifies the extremely complex problem of the relationship between the political organization and the rank and file movement. The IS position in the problem had in fact been clearly set out in an article by the industrial organizer written before the first Rank and File Conference:

In the initial stages of building a movement, there can be real problems. Because it is revolutionaries who usually take the initiative in calling for the movement, there is the grave danger that they set it up on a basis that makes it difficult for non-revolutionaries to participate. It is necessary to take concrete steps to prevent this happening: it is no good arguing about the need for the members of the rank and file movement to move towards revolutionary politics if there are no non-revolutionaries involved. Such arguments only make sense when the movement has already begun to gather some muscle and some base. In the early stages the greatest care has to be taken to involve broad support, even if it means revolutionaries keeping relatively quiet about their distinctive ideas.

Once the movement is really off the ground, the opposite danger can arise. IS members could be so involved in the mechanics of keeping the movement going as not to see the need to put their more general political ideas across. But precisely at such a point we have to insist that more is needed than a rank and file movement for fighting the immediate defensive economic struggles of the class. A revolutionary party is also needed, to fight the ruling class on every issue, to raise the level of consciousness of the advanced sections of the class, and to provide a combative leadership in the struggle for power. These are tasks which a rank and file movement, organised on a minimal programme aimed at involving rank and file CP and Labour Party members, can never do.[17]

Such an approach, recognizing pitfalls on either side, requires sensitivity and tactical skill. Doubtless IS comrades made mistakes, cut corners or misjudged the pace of events. But Shaw simply offers the panacea of 'the rank and file movement's independence of IS'.

What would such 'independence' have meant in the 1974-8 period? The drift to the right that afflicted the labour movement was not confined to the upper echelons; it permeated right down to the 'rank and file' (in the broad sense of the term). A lack of confidence in the power to win combined with a sense of loyalty to the reformist leaders, inhibited many workers from struggle. The problem in the labour movement was not the excessive influence of IS/SWP ideas, but the continuing grip of labourist and reformist ideas. IS/SWP members had no alternative but to fight for their ideas and policies; if they could find others to fight alongside them, so much the better, but if they could not, then they had to fight alone. If this meant that most of the burden, both of taking initiatives and of simply maintaining the apparatus (such as it was), fell on IS members, then this was a sign of weakness, but there was no available alternative. The 'independence' Shaw speaks of would have been nothing other than political abstention.

The drift to the right in the labour movement since 1974 has affected the whole of the left in Britain (and indeed throughout

Europe[18]). Many socialists saw no other choice than to swim with the stream, to adapt to the rightward-moving milieu, in many cases going back into the womb of the Labour Party. The IS strategy was quite consciously to 'steer left'; to put up a clear opposition to the rightward drift even at the price of temporary isolation. Part of the cost that had to be paid was that the possibility of rank and file initiative was limited. The signs are now that, after the election, the possibilities for the growth of a more meaningful rank and file movement are emerging. The rank and file organization that has been preserved will then be put to a real test.

4. *The Right to Work Campaign*

One initiative stemming from the national Rank and File Movement did achieve some considerable success—the Right to Work Campaign. Shaw, unfortunately, is not prepared to acknowledge this success, but actually sees the Right to Work as a key element in the sad decline of IS.

Partly this is because of Shaw's tendency to pay more attention to the forms of democracy than to the content of the decisions made. The Right to Work Campaign is seen as just another manipulation by the ubiquitous 'leadership';. in fact, it was comrades from the South-West London district of IS who urged that the organization should take an initiative on this matter. Shaw also complains that the Right to Work Campaign had not been mooted at 1975 Conference, held in late spring. [19] If this were a matter of IS 'leadership' and 'opposition' slogging it out in a vacuum this might seem outrageous. But Shaw omits to mention what was happening in the real world. Between the Conference and the autumn Callaghan and the TUC had cobbled up the six-pound wage policy. For the time being a systematic struggle around wages was ruled out; but the new situation made a campaign around the issue of rapidly mounting unemployment a viable possibility. To argue that any initiative on the question should have waited till the next annual conference is to reject, not only 'machine Leninism',[20] but all that is positive in democratic centralism.

Indeed, an uninformed reader would be hard put to it to learn from Shaw's account what the Right to Work Campaign was and why it happened. Unemployment had officially topped the million mark in the autumn of 1975 (in fact the figure was probably half a million higher, including a large number of unregistered women). Women and blacks were especially hard hit—and so were school-leavers unable to get jobs. (The latter category represent a particular problem for those who argue that everything should be done through the 'official channels'. What exactly are the 'official channels' for a youth who has never had a job and therefore never been able to join a union?) Unemployed youth, moreover, represent a potentially fertile recruiting ground for fascist and racist groups. Unemployment, moreover, was not an isolated issue; it was intimately linked to the whole struggle against the Social Contract. The Labour leaders had argued that wage restraint must be accepted to save jobs; yet unemployment was rising to levels higher than anything since the thirties. Moreover, the Broad Left was failing to take any effective initiatives. The London Co-op and the No. 8 London Confed District Committee did call an Assembly on Unemployment (after the Right to Work march had been announced) which attracted 3,000 delegates; but this impressive conference merely called an ill-supported day of action on 26 May and disappeared without further trace.

In this situation the Right to Work Campaign was able to fill an otherwise unoccupied political space. Basically the Campaign had three aims:

a) to confront employed workers and the organized labour movement with the seriousness of the unemployment problem as a step towards achieving unity of employed and unemployed workers;
b) to offer a focus to unemployed workers, especially youth, who had no other organizational channels to work through.
c) to initiate direct action, of a propagandist or agitational nature, on a limited scale in a period when a generalized response seemed impossible.

To a less jaundiced observer than Shaw it might well seem that the Campaign had modest success on all three counts.[21] Shaw comments that 'Had it been launched on a wider basis, with a stronger orientation to organised workers, it could have been more successful ... The effect on IS was to turn it away from serious ongoing work in the trade unions—and the women's and student movements—and from wider political campaigning against the policies of the Labour Government.'[22]

Of course the campaign could have been wider. It would have been better if it had been a mass movement, but unfortunately there are no recipes for launching mass movements in periods of downturn. The Campaign did get sponsorship from some 480 trade union bodies, despite the coolness of much of the Broad Left; there was active participation by members of the Labour Party—and of the Communist Party, despite the CP's official hostility to the Campaign. The second march, in September 1976, attracted 568 unemployed, mainly youth, when only 350 had been expected. Shaw's preoccupation with 'organised workers' is a little strange from one who has denounced 'workerism' so sharply, as is his remark about 'serious ongoing work in the trade unions'. Surely in 1976 'serious ongoing work' precisely required raising the question of unemployment—particularly among sectors of workers who had relatively secure jobs. To fail to do so would have been economistic routinism. Likewise it is hard to see how the Campaign turned IS away from the women's movement. As has been pointed out, women suffered particularly severely from unemployment, and many of them did not even receive benefit. The Right to Work Campaign was precisely drawing attention to an aspect of women's oppression which more middle-class sections of the women's movement had neglected. Finally the 'wider political campaigning' against the Labour Government that Shaw refers to is dangerously vague. In fact unemployment and the closely intertwined issue of public expenditure cuts were central to a critique of the Labour Government which showed that not only was Labour not achieving socialism (which few would have expected it to) but that it was not even able to preserve the minimal level of welfare measures that had been the principal achievement of the 1945 Labour Government.

If the first Right to Work march was not successful enough to satisfy Shaw, it at least provoked enemies elsewhere. On 19 March the march was attacked by police at Staples Corner. Forty-three marchers were arrested. Shaw unaccountably fails to mention this, or the subsequent successful campaign against the trial of John Deason, which won wide trade union support. This allowed the whole political question of the state and police action against trade unionists to be raised.

But perhaps the most important aspect of the Right to Work Campaign was the stress on direct action. The Right to Work marches were not simply propaganda exercises; they constantly attempted to intervene in local struggles. To quote one example among many:

> [On 5 March] the March Council read in a local paper that Spear and Jackson, a small garden tool factory at Dronfield, south of Sheffield, was sacking 43 of its 123 workers.
> Two hours later, eluding the persistent police escort, marchers invaded the factory.

Before gate security knew what was happening, the marchers were in among the machinery, urging the workers to stand up and fight the sackings.

They called a meeting of 30 workers outside the factory, and held a second in the canteen with another 30.

The sacked workers were delighted. They told the marchers that the redundancies had been hand-picked, that they left not a single shop steward in the factory, and that the GMWU official had known about them a week before, but had told no one.

Enraged, the marchers, with some of the sacked workers, stormed into the manager's office. London engineering worker and marcher Mick Brightman bellowed at him: 'Will you sleep at night with these 43 and their families on the dole?' The manager replied nervously: 'No comment.'

That afternoon, another delegation of marchers visited the AUEW office in Chesterfield. District secretary Bill Mitchell told them he had not heard of the sackings. But he promised he would go to the factory and fight for the sacked workers that afternoon.[23]

Examples could be multiplied many times over, both from the marches and from the activities of local Right to Work committees. Yet Shaw can write that 'major decisions, such as the launching of the Right to Work Campaign ... were received by the membership as *faits accomplis*'.[24] The picture of a passive membership, mechanically obeying orders from an omnipotent centre, does not fit the facts. The Right to Work Campaign gave scope to the imagination and initiative of hundreds of comrades, inside IS and outside. That has far more to do with real revolutionary democracy than Shaw's obsession with constitutional niceties.

5. *Sexual Politics*

Undoubtedly the strongest part of Shaw's case is that relating to sexual politics and the women's movement. His case that IS/SWP for too long neglected important developments is now generally accepted in the SWP. As a *Socialist Worker* editorial put it:[25]

Just like those male socialists 60 years ago, we on Socialist Worker have tended to turn our back on that movement: to denounce it as 'middle class', to protest that we were fighting for the rights of all workers and to ignore the discrimination against women.

The women in the Socialist Workers Party refused to accept this bias. They *acted,* as part of the women's movement, to change the party.

They organised themselves in Women's Voice groups, and changed the face and tone of their paper Women's Voice.
They tapped a great well of anger and enthusiasm which men-only socialism had never come near.

But to agree that Shaw makes some valid points about IS/SWP practice is not to endorse his analysis. For Shaw, IS/SWP's lapses and omissions on the women's and gay movements are not errors, however serious; they are a part of his case, indeed a central one, against the workerism and the undemocratic regime which characterize IS/SWP. A defence of the record may therefore be in order.

Socialist feminism was one of the offshoots of the great ferment of 1968. There was an earlier tradition, in the Second International and the first years of the Comintern, but the rise of Stalinism killed it, and it lay hidden for more than a generation. As a result there was no experience and very little theoretical analysis to draw on.[26] Hence comrades who were, after all, very busy and endeavouring to implement a set of priorities, took some time to recognize the significance of the new movement that was developing.

Secondly, the women's movement emerges in Shaw's account in a rather purer form that it had in reality. The women's movement itself suffered from the long break in the tradition; it threw up a diversity of ideas—some valuable, some less so; organizationally it was unstructured and hence effectively undemocratic. In composition it was predominantly middle class. None of this is stated to justify abstention or to play down the significance of the movement. It is to suggest that the relations between Marxists and feminists were necessarily complex, and that there were errors and abandoned responsibilities on both sides, rather than everything being attributable to the 'original sin' of IS/SWP. (A dangerous notion, since it suggests the possibility of a party without original sin, one that had everything right from the start without needing to learn from experience.)

Thus Shaw alleges that 'IS's support for the National Abortion Campaign was grudging and highly conditional, bringing it into immediate conflict with the majority of the activists, and accompanied by a constant tendency to call demonstrations in opposition to NAC whenever a disagreement on tactics arose'.[27] The problem in reality was more complex. NAC did not have an effective structure with an elected and responsible committee; its 'open committee' form meant that it was constantly liable to reverse its own decisions, and laid it wide open to packing by a variety of tendencies. This made NAC, after the highly successful demonstration in the summer of 1975, unable to take the necessary initiatives. At times in the 1976-7 period *Women's Voice* supporters found that there was no way of getting a proposal for action considered by NAC except to take the initiative and announce that it was going to take place.

A similar point can be made with regard to the gay question. Here there was an almost total absence of tradition and experience. Shaw draws heavily on Bob Cant's article 'A Grim Tale'[28], which presents a severe but generally honest[29] account of IS's attitude in the 1972-5 period. But Shaw's account is a one-sided one. Bob Cant's original article contains an element of self-criticism; he recognizes that the gay comrades had a responsibility to explain the problem to other IS members who could not be expected to have all the answers already given. He accepts that mistakes of strategy and presentation were made. In Shaw's account all this disappears; everything is laid at the door of the 'leadership'.

Nor can everything be blamed on workerism. While it is true that IS/SWP did for a time neglect women who were not workers, there can be no dispute as to the importance of industrial struggles involving women—Trico, Grunwick, etc.—for which IS/SWP played an important role in mobilizing solidarity.

Likewise, Shaw asserts that 'On the gay question, there could be no ... compromise with the workerist, economistic line of IS.'[30] On the contrary, there have been a number of cases of gay workers who have faced discrimination at work; John Warburton, a gay teacher was sacked by ILEA, while Wapping social workers struck in defence of a gay workmate who was victimized. Alan Burnside, a gay miner, has attempted to raise the issue in the NUM.[31] It is precisely cases like these (together with the crucial issue of the National Front's hostility to gays) that enable the question to be taken up concretely and operationally, rather than simply as a question of abstract propaganda.

Finally, on Shaw's thesis, change was impossible. 'After 1975 the leadership was, as one long-standing member described it, "unassailable". It was simply not conceivable that the membership could change it in any way, and any alterations would have to come from the top.'[32] Yet changes did happen. The 1976 Conference reversed the earlier line on the gay question; *Socialist Worker* now carried the statement 'We are for an end to all forms of discrimination against homosexuals', and a new IS Gay Group was established. All this in *1976*, the year in which according to Shaw IS touched rock-bottom.

And by 1978 not only had a Women's Voice organization been

launched, but Tony Cliff himself (the workerist villain of Shaw's history) was contributing to a *Socialist Worker* centre spread on the gay question:

> A lot of socialists still have difficulty believing that gays will be taking part in the revolution at all.
> On the contrary we should look forward now to the first leader of the London workers' council being a 19-year-old black gay woman![33]

Contrary to Shaw's picture, there has been intense discussion of sexual politics at every level of IS/SWP over the last few years. Only a sect has an unchanging programme; the changes in IS/SWP precisely show that it has been able to reappraise reality.

6. *Theory and Intellectuals*

Shaw's comments on theory and intellectuals may be dealt with more briefly. He accuses IS/SWP of 'theoretical stagnation' and alleges that there has been a 'flight' of intellectuals out of IS.[34]

This judgement is at best impressionistic. We can only begin to answer it by asking exactly what is meant by 'theory'. It is certainly true that IS/SWP has made little or no contribution to the flood of 'Marxist' literature published since 1968, mainly written in an incomprehensibly convoluted style, and concerning itself with the methodological status of Marxism, or with the marriage of Marxism to psychoanalysis, semiology, etc. Yet it is theory of this sort that is radiated by the 'Communist University' which Shaw unaccountably commends. The Communist Party has attracted intellectuals over recent years precisely because its anodyne brand of Marxism is able to coexist peacefully with the academic establishment.

What are the real theoretical issues facing Marxists in Britain today? The changing nature of the trade union bureaucracy; the lessons of the defeats in Chile and Portugal; the nature and potential of contemporary fascism. One would search in vain through the last twenty issues of *New Left Review* for any work on these topics. *International Socialism* (series one and two) will stand comparison with any other theoretical journals on these questions. Of course we have been weak on some topics—the nature of the economic crisis, sexual politics—but here too some significant work is being done.

As for the flight of the intellectuals,[35] it is hard to identify whether such a phenomenon has indeed taken place, for 'intellectuals' do not form a neatly defined category in IS/SWP. Indeed, eleven years on from 1968, higher education widely open to mature students, graduate unemployment and the spread of white collar trade unionism all tend to make Shaw's categories somewhat anachronistic.

7. *The Fight Against Racism*

But the most serious omission from Shaw's account is his almost total failure to refer to IS/SWP's work in the struggle against racism. Thus Shaw tacks on to the end of his account of the Right to Work Campaign:

> As the furore over immigration increased in the summer, IS leafleted on a massive scale with the slogan 'They're welcome here.' The issue was a godsend, since the media (and the membership) were tiring of repeated long-distance marches for the Right to Work.[36]

Shaw's language is almost unbelievably flippant. Following the press attack on Malawi Asians, a further outburst from Enoch Powell and an upsurge of National Front activity, three black youths (Dinesh Choudhri, Riphi Alhadidi and Gurdip Singh Chagger) had been killed; scores of other blacks had suffered physical attacks.[37] To call this a 'furore' is an understatement; to suggest that IS regarded it as a 'godsend' is a piece of unworthy cynicism.

Britain is an old imperialist country which since the Second World War has had a large influx of black immigrants. The question of racism must be central to any understanding of class struggle and class consciousness in Britain today. It is surprising that Shaw, who puts so much stress on the importance of ideology, has so little to say about what is certainly the key ideological issue in Britain at the present time. If Shaw can, with some justice, accuse us of neglecting sexual politics, we can equally accuse him of underestimating the racist threat. (To make things quite clear: it is not being suggested that the National Front or any other racist group is—at present—a serious contender for political power. What is being argued is that the activities of the racists in harassing, weakening and dividing the working class are a very serious challenge to the left.)

IS/SWP has a record of giving crucial importance to racism going back well before 1968. Shaw mentions the IS response to the surge of racism following the first Powell speech in 1968; though he strangely refers to the leaflet headed 'The Urgent Challenge of Fascism' as 'exaggerated' and 'inflammatory'.[38] Such a charge might be justified had the leaflet suggested that a fascist bid for power was imminent; in fact it spoke of 'long-term fascist development'. But Shaw's suggestion that we exaggerated the significance of a traditionally militant group of workers, the London dockers, striking and marching for an openly racist cause, is surely to underestimate the power of the racist poison in Britain.

When dealing with the more recent period Shaw simply refers to 'militant anti-racism' without giving any detail of the actions and initiatives taken by IS/SWP. From 1974 onwards IS took to the streets to confront the National Front, often almost the only organization to do so. In the summer of 1976 direct action by IS and various black organizations prevented the National Front staging a major demonstration in support of Robert Relf's right to advertise his home 'For sale to an English family'. Relf's sign was removed and publicly burnt, and the NF demonstration collapsed. In August 1977, when for Shaw IS/SWP had already degenerated and squandered its potential, the SWP was at the centre of a national witchhunt for its role in confronting the NF at Lewisham.

Many other initiatives of a similar sort could be listed. Could it be that Shaw gives them so little attention because there was virtually no internal dissension on the question of anti-racist work? Every member took up the struggle with enthusiasm.[39]

It is also striking that Shaw, who attributes, rightly, so much importance to 'cultural' struggle, finds no place to mention the initiative, in late 1976, by IS members and others, in launching Rock Against Racism in response to openly pro-racist statements by Eric Clapton and pro-fascist remarks by David Bowie.[40] RAR has undoubtedly been one of the most successful aspects of the anti-fascist mobilization over the last couple of years.

Nor does Shaw make any mention of the IS role in helping to launch the Anti-Nazi League.[41] Once again the key question was that of initiative. As the editorial in *Socialist Challenge*[42] put it:

> The carnival did not fall out of the sky. It was organised. The Anti-Nazi League and Rock Against Racism were the sparks that ignited the anti-fascist fire. The fusion of politics and culture was vital in offering an alternative to the tens of thousands of youth who carried ANL banners and placards on Sunday.
> But a further point also needs to be stressed. The Anti-Nazi

League did not fall out of the sky either. It was an initiative undertaken and launched by the comrades of the Socialist Workers Party. They threw the resources and political weight of their organisation to build the League: and ensure the organisation necessary to build the carnival.

True, they were not the only force, but without them this event would not have taken place. It would be crass sectarianism to try and underplay this fact.

Conclusion

For Shaw the conclusion is that it was a mistake to found the Socialist Workers Party. There are differences between us as to the facts of the case and the interpretation to be put on them. But the real argument is about the nature and role of a revolutionary socialist party in Britain today.

It has not been my intention in this article to make more than the most modest claims for the actual achievements of the IS/SWP. The adoption of the name 'Party' was simply a recognition of the tasks which faced us and which we had *begun* to take upon ourselves, not any claim to be already leading the class or even a small section of it. The struggle for political leadership in the British working-class movement will be fought out in the factories and on the streets not in the pages of the *Socialist Register*.

Since 1974 there has been a significant shift to the right in British politics, a shift which the recent Tory election victory does no more than confirm.[43] No tendency in the socialist movement has been able to escape the pressures of this period; we have all faced difficulties and problems. What we can do is to try to establish the best way to respond to this rightward movement.

Shaw, who writes of the 'long, gradual decline' of the Labour Party[44] does not disagree that it is necessary to build a political alternative outside the Labour Party. The question is the form of such an alternative, and, above all, what sort of activity it should engage in.

A substantial majority of the British working class still gives electoral support to the Labour Party.[45] But it is important to establish the nature of that support. There can be very few workers indeed who still believe that Labour will initiate sweeping social changes. The support that Labour does get is essentially pragmatic; Labour is seen as being the best of a bad bunch, and no viable alternative is perceived. Hence the strategies of 'exposing' Labour or of 'committing it to socialist policies' can be seen as equally misguided; they both start from an assumption of expectations that do not actually exist in workers' minds.

More generally, it can be said that at the present time in the British working-class movement, the crisis is not one of class consciousness, but of class confidence. It is not the case that workers have any positive commitment to a reformist view of the world. What inhibits struggle is rather a sense of powerlessness, a feeling that things cannot be changed. The most vital task for a party that claims to be revolutionary is to break down this lack of confidence. And this cannot be done primarily by means of propaganda (though this is in no way to suggest that political argument has no role to play). But the sense of powerlessness will collapse only through the experience of struggle.

Now if we look at the groupings that have inhabited the political space to the left of the Communist Party since the Second World War we can observe in their political style an inordinate preoccupation with the question of programme. Partly this derives from an attachment to Trotsky's *Transitional Programme* of 1938; but much more it is a response to decades of isolation. Getting the slogans right, raising the 'correct demands', even if there was no one to hear them, all too easily became a substitute for actual involvement in struggle.

Against this the IS/SWP has believed that the most important task is to take initiatives that show, albeit on a small scale, that things can be changed. Sackings can be prevented; hospital closures can be stopped; the fascists can be driven off the streets. A policy of giving priority to such initiatives has earned us criticism that we were 'economistic' and 'pragmatists' from many opponents prior to Shaw.

The point is relevant to another of Shaw's preoccupations —unity of the left. He welcomes the moves towards revolutionary unity made by the IMG through the vehicle of Socialist Unity.[46] Now no serious socialist can feel anything other than depression at the array of splinters and fragments that characterizes the revolutionary left. But this fragmentation has deep historical roots and it will take much effort to overcome it.

What is not so clear is whether the Socialist Unity strategy is the best way to overcome the divisions of the left. Thus far Socialist Unity has been essentially an electoral alliance. But the evidence thus far does not suggest that it is in elections that the revolutionary left is best able to make itself heard.[47] There has been far more impressive unity in the struggle around specific struggles—solidarity with Grunwicks, opposition to cuts, and, above all, against racism[48]—than in electoral alliances. This is scarcely surprising, for at the present time a revolutionary electoral intervention must be on the level of propaganda, and it is far more difficult to achieve unity in propaganda than in action.

More generally, too much discussion on revolutionary unity proceeds on the basis of what may be called the 'brush-and-pan' theory—i.e., the revolutionary movement is a beautiful vase which has been shattered into tiny pieces; the way to mend it is by collecting all the fragments into one receptacle.

The real task for revolutionaries today is not to regroup those who are already revolutionaries, but to fight for socialist ideas among the thousands of people who are becoming open to them. The title of Paul Foot's pamphlet *Why You Should Be A Socialist*[59] suggests the emphasis needed; we have to break with the introverted atmosphere of extreme left politics and fight for the most elementary ideas of socialist transformation.

At the time of writing it is impossible to predict the scale and rhythm of the Tory attack on working people, still less those of the resistance. But it is clear that the next two or three years will pose even more sharply the need for a revolutionary alternative to the existing organizations of the left.

To face this challenge all of us, whether in organizations or outside, will have to learn to adapt ourselves to new needs. To do so we need to learn from our mistakes, but not bury ourselves in an introspective search for their historical sources; we need to criticize our own practice, not blame everything on some villainous 'leadership'. Open and constructive debate is needed, and, to the extent that it encourages this, Shaw's critique is to be welcomed.

NOTES

1. Martin Shaw, 'The Making of a Party', *The Socialist Register 1978*. In this article Shaw refers frequently, and critically, to my own 'History of the International Socialists', *International Socialism*, Nos. 76 and 77. Shaw accuses my history of 'distortion', and sees my omissions as not only 'strange' but 'characteristic' and 'symptomatic'. (For the record, my article was in no way an 'official' history, but an individual, though unambiguously partisan, account.)
2. Shaw, *op.cit.*, pp. 127, 130, 138, 139.
3. Thus Shaw (*op.cit.*, pp. 124-5) devotes considerable attention to what he calls the '*coup*' of August 1973. But his account is misleading on

several points. Cliff and Harman were not the only members of the old EC to remain on the new body—Roger Protz also stayed, as did Andreas Nagliatti, the industrial organizer and a key figure up to the Rank and File Conference of March 1974. Jim Nichol was not an 'addition'—he had served on the EC for two and a half years previously. Among what Shaw classes as 'provincial organisers' and comrades not of 'national political standing' were Roger Rosewell, who had served on the EC for some years before moving to Liverpool; John Charlton, a member of over ten years' experience on leading bodies; and Granville Williams, who was to be a central figure in the IS Opposition. The only real newcomer was Roger Kline (who was subsequently to be one of the main opponents of the Right to Work Campaign). Rosewell and Nagliatti both left the organization by 1975. John Deason and Steve Jefferys, who became members of the first Central Committee in 1975, were not only not involved in the *coup*, but critical of aspects of it.

The exits and entrances of such largely unknown individuals may seem a matter of indifference to most readers of *The Socialist Register.* But perhaps they may show that the process of change was more complex and tortuous than Shaw's simplistic version of loss of 'balance' would indicate. The quest for a *rupture* in the history of IS may prove as problematic as that for the break between the young and old Marx.

4. One of the most interesting attempts to study this process is to be found in T. Cliff, *Lenin* (four volumes), Pluto Press, 1975-9.
5. Shaw, *op.cit.*, p. 108.
6. *ibid.*, p. 13.
7. Shaw gives a detailed account of the transition from a National Committee (a large body with non-full-time membership meeting infrequently) to a small, full-time Central Committee. Yet his evaluation of the effects is impressionistic. He cites John Phillips ('Laying the National Committee Ghost', *Internal Bulletin*, April 1976) to prove that the leadership was now 'unassailable'. Phillips, who advocated return to the National Committee structure, was a long-standing member whose views deserved respect. But for the sake of balance, Shaw might have quoted the case for the other side; for example (from a comrade with five years' National Committee experience): 'It is suggested that the old NC was able to control the EC. In my experience this was rarely if ever the case. The whole attention of the EC was devoted to how to sell things to the NC, and it generally succeeded.' Ian Birchall, 'The Myths of the Golden Past', *Internal Bulletin*, May 1976.)
8. Shaw, *op.cit.*, pp. 135-7.
9. National Committee report in *Socialist Worker*, 16 March 1974.
10. *Socialist Worker*, 22 February 1975.
11. Shaw, *op.cit.*, p. 135.
12. *ibid.*, pp. 130, 132.
13. Just as it is unlikely that Dr. G. Brosan, Director of North East London Polytechnic, would suggest that IS/SWP has neglected

student work, since he found it necessary to have SWP student Andy Strouthous jailed by the High Court. (*Socialist Worker,* 21 May 1977.)

14. For two attempts to evaluate the changing and contradictory situations of white collar workers, see Duncan Hallas, 'White Collar Workers', *International Socialism* 72, and Colin Sparks, 'Fascism and the Working Class, Part Two', *International Socialism,* series 2, No. 3.

15. *Socialist Worker,* 8 January 1977.

16. Shaw, *op.cit.,* p. 128.

17. A. Nagliatti, 'Towards a Rank and File Movement', *International Socialism* 66 (February 1974).

18. Cf. Chris Harman, 'Crisis of the European Revolutionary Left', *International Socialism,* series 2, No. 4.

19. Shaw *op.cit.,* p. 137.

20. A term used by Shaw in his 'Back to the Maginot Line: Harman's New Gramsci', *International Socialism,* series 2, No. 1.

21. For a full account see J. Deason, 'One Year of the Right to Work Campaign', *International Socialism* 93.

22. Shaw, 'The Making of a Party?', p. 129.

23. *Socialist Worker,* 13 March 1976.

24. Shaw, *op.cit.,* p. 137.

25. 10 June 1978.

26. Martin Shaw's *Marxism versus Sociology,* Pluto Press, 1974—a very useful bibliography of Marxist writing—was able to muster only twelve items on women and the family (as against nineteen on religion and twenty-five on culture). He does not have a single reference to the gay question. Shaw, *Marxism and Social Science,* Pluto Press, 1975, has no index entries for 'family', 'feminism' or 'women'. This is not meant as a debating point; but it does suggest that it might be better to approach the problem of Marxism and sexual politics in a spirit of self-criticism rather than using it as a stick to beat the 'leadership'.

27. Shaw, 'The Making of a Party', p. 131.

28. *Gay Left* 3.

29. Not entirely accurate, however. Discussing the IS National Committee statement on Gay Work adopted in autumn 1973 Cant says: 'It fell into the old Stalinist trap of assuming that all gays are middle class, and, therefore, a bit perverted.' My copy of the document (originally drafted by Roger Protz) says no such thing. It in fact states that the Gay Liberation Front contains 'people of widely differing class backgrounds' and explicitly refers to 'male homosexuals on the production line at Ford'. What it does argue is that the Gay Liberation Front has middle-class political leadership.

30. Shaw, *op.cit.,* p. 117.

31. *Socialist Worker,* 21 August 1976, 8 July 1978.

32. Shaw, *op.cit.,* p. 137.

33. *Socialist Worker,* 26 August 1978.

34. Shaw, *op.cit.,* p. 145.

35. Shaw refers, rather patronizingly, to the SWP's 'severely depleted intellectual forces'. It is hard to know how to reply; how does Shaw

quantify 'intellectual forces'? Are there only a few intellectuals left, or are those who remain feeble-minded? The nearest I can get to a quantitative answer is to point out that in Shaw's bibliography *Marxism versus Sociology* Tony Cliff and Nigel Harris have more entries than any other thinker apart from Marx, Engels and Trotsky. Both are still members of the SWP.

36. Shaw, *op.cit.*, p. 130. (On a strict point of fact, there had been exactly *one* long-distance march.)

37. *Socialist Worker,* 12 June 1976.

38. Shaw, *op.cit.*, pp. 108, 142.

39. Shaw does pick on the 'rapid exit of the "Black caucus" shortly after it was formed in 1976'. (*op.cit.*, p. 131). This was an unfortunate loss, arising from organizational as well as political disagreements. For the record, a new Black caucus was formed, and in April 1977 the SWP held a Rally for Black Revolutionaries which attracted 130 black workers. (*Socialist Worker,* 7 May 1977.)

40. *Socialist Worker,* 2 October 1976.

41. Admittedly Shaw's narrative ends in 1976. But surely one's account of a funeral must be conditioned by knowledge of a subsequent resurrection. Shaw's article was completed after the successful ANL Carnival of 30 April 1978 which attracted 80,000 people. (Cf. footnotes 81 and 82.) Yet he makes no mention of the ANL, despite the fact that he has strong feelings on the question: three months earlier he had described it as part of the SWP's 'blatant attempts to bypass the united anti-fascist movement'. (*Socialist Challenge,* 2 February 1977.)

42. 4 May 1978.

43. A detailed study of the election results reveals some interesting and contradictory factors. The sharp decline in the vote of the National Front (which often fell by more than half in some of its strongest bases) is an encouraging fact. Undoubtedly this is at least partially attributable to the persistent and vigorous campaigning of the Anti-Nazi League, and confirms the SWP view that this was a crucial area for revolutionary socialist activity. On the other hand the finding of the BBC/University of Essex election-day survey (*The Economist,* 12 May 1979) that there was an 11 per cent swing to the Tories among skilled workers suggests that the ideological struggle against craftism will have continuing importance in the years to come.

44. Shaw, *op.cit.*, p. 101.

45. In many constituencies Labour candidates increased the number of votes they received despite the percentage swing to the Tories.

46. Shaw, *op.cit.*, pp. 141, 145.

47. In the general election no Socialist Unity candidate obtained more than 500 votes. (This can be compared with 642 votes for the Silly Party in Dover and Deal.) There is little likelihood that the SWP would have fared significantly better if it had decided to stand candidates; the results seem to confirm the decision that the time was not yet ripe.

48. On 28 April 1979 fifteen thousand people—members of the Indian Workers Association, the Labour Party, the Communist Party, of most of the revolutionary groupings as well as thousands who belonged to no organization—demonstrated in the streets of Southall in protest at the murder by police of anti-fascist demonstrator Blair Peach. It was a dignified but militant demonstration against state defence of racists. The following Thursday Tariq Ali, Socialist Unity candidate, polled 477 votes in the Southall constituency. Any strategy towards unity must begin with the fifteen thousand, not the 477.
49. London, 1977.

Acknowledgement

I should like to thank Duncan Hallas and Norah Carlin for valuable comments during the preparation of this article.

SOCIALISTS AND THE LABOUR PARTY:
A REAPPRAISAL

by Leo Panitch

In the 1973 *Socialist Register*, Ken Coates produced a timely and brilliant defence of socialists working within the Labour Party. The argument was largely cast in terms of the absence of any alternative agency capable of maintaining a full scale political presence outside the Labour Party. But at the same time Ken Coates provided a positive case for working within the Party, stressing the critical role it plays in defensive struggles, the importance of parliamentary activity, and the possibilities for change in the Party contained in the radicalization of the unions in the late sixties and early seventies. The article was notably free of illusions on the radicalization of the Parliamentary leadership of the Party, but it contended that the 'cardinal tenets of late fabianism have been refuted by events' and therefore that the ideas of the leadership could no longer dominate the labour movement, 'since the integrating force of their dogma has rotted away'. The changing balance of forces in the movement would come to be reflected in its political councils: the Parliamentary Party would have to elect a new leader acceptable to the unions or face a 'shattering rift', indeed, 'a candidate with the insight and skill to present a platform of socialist change [was] very likely to win'. The idea that the *status quo* pragmatism of Wilsonism 'might be botched along for another parliamentary term [was] not completely absurd', but the consequences of this for Labour would be immense:

> Another Wilsonite government would split the labour movement into irreconcilable camps, the vastly larger of which would be in sharp opposition to it ... if this scenario is plausible, where must the socialists engage themselves? There can hardly be a moment's doubt. Another Labour Government offers socialists the chance to do well the work they botched up last time: to force the imposition of socialist policies, or to isolate and defeat those who oppose them. While external critics might aid in this process in its essentials it will either be an inside job or it won't get done.

51

The challenge Coates presented to socialists outside the Labour Party has not stood alone. Despite the actual emergence of another 'Wilsonite' government similar arguments directed to, or at least against, the extra-Labour left have continued to be advanced, most notably by Geoff Hodgson, Peter Jenkins and Frank Ward.[2] And most recently, Lewis Minkin's monumental study of *The Labour Party Conference,* while meticulously uncovering the organizational bases of leadership control over the Party, has also sought to challenge the orthodox view that intra-party democracy is ineffectual or inconsistent with parliamentary government, and to show that the unions' policy commitment to extensive public ownership never waned, but was only temporarily concealed by the Party leadership. On both counts he clearly identifies the Labour left of the 1970s with the forces 'which Party tradition nourishes' and contends, albeit more circumspectly than Ken Coates, that the alignment between the left and the unions on the floor of the Party Conference which emerged in the late 1960s was 'bound to have long-term consequences for the distribution of power in the Party as a whole'.[3]

Taken as a whole these writings may be seen as a regeneration in the 1970s of what Ralph Miliband has called 'the belief in the effective transformation of the Labour Party into an instrument of socialist policies [which] is the most crippling of illusions to which socialists in Britain have been prone'.[4] It is the purpose of this article to reassess the case for working within the Labour Party not only in the light of the record of the 1974-9 Labour Government, but of the behaviour of the trade unions and the Labour left since the late 1960s. As the labour movement moves into a period of opposition against a clearly reactionary Tory Government, as the actions of the Labour Party leadership against the working class recede from centre stage, as the appeal for defensive solidarity re-emerges with urgency and cogency, the pull to join the Labour Party will gain renewed strength. And with it the illusion that Labour can be transformed will cast its shadow over many dedicated socialists. As it does the argument that there is no viable alternative to the Labour Party is liable to take on the hue of a self-fulfilling prophesy.

1

It has always been its unique relationship with trade unions that has drawn socialists to the Labour Party. To a large extent this has simply reflected the perception that it is necessary to locate one's political work on that terrain where the working class is itself engaged. But more than this is involved. Precisely because the Labour Party is *part* of the labour movement, this means that the development of class struggle even if not initiated by the Party, is bound to affect it considerably from *within*. The great paradox of the Labour Party, and the source of the continued renewal of the belief that it can be changed, lies in this fact. The 'class harmony' ideology which has dominated the thinking of the leadership since the founding conventions rejected the concept of class struggle, is consistently challenged not merely by external events and by socialist currents in the Party, but by the direct expression of working-class struggle within the Party, above all on those occasions when the trade unions act as immediate agencies of working-class defence against the actions of Labour Governments.

The central factor underlying the belief in the 1970s that the Labour Party was ripe for socialist change may be located in the specific manifestation of this contradiction in the late 1960s. The action of the 1964-70 Labour Governments, not just in terms of disappointing the promise on which they had been elected, but in terms of directly challenging the basic material and organizational interests of the trade unions, would itself have strained considerably that 'bond of mutual confidence between the Parliamentary leaders and a preponderant part of the trade union leadership which is the essential key to the understanding of the functioning of the Party'[5] and the mechanism whereby the contradiction had been contained for most of the post-war years. But it was combined with developments within the union movement which strained the relationship further. The broadening and deepening of militancy at the base and the increasing decentralization of collective bargaining began to come to fruition in the mid 1960s and resulted in a greater radicalization of union conferences and delegations to TUC congresses and Labour Party conferences, and in the election of left-wing leaders in some major unions. After the enormous political loyalty and material sacrifice shown by the union movement from 1965 to 1967, and as a direct reaction against it, there ensued a period of sustained conflict within the Labour Party which was unparalleled in the Party's history. To Minkin these developments proved that ' "the bond of mutual confidence" was a contingent and not an endemic feature of the pattern of power within the Party'.[6] Coates was more emphatic:

... Wilson injected an unprecedented scepticism about Labour politicians into nearly all the unions, which serum took effect from top to bottom. At the same time, the reaction produced a notable democratization of the main unions, which process has adamantly resisted the Industrial Relations Act, and shows not the slightest sign of recession. No new leader of the Party can avoid coming to terms with this profound development, which already carries the problem of accommodation far beyond the scope of the kind of bureaucratic intrigue which was open to leaders of the Gaitskell era. Unlike Lawther and Williamson, whose capacity to uphold conservative policies rested on widespread mass lethargy, Jones and Scanlon can only lend their weight to policies which carry support in an active and self-assertive rank and file. Of course, they could always theoretically abandon the rank and file; but if they ever did, they would be of little value to the establishment without it. All this means, quite plainly, that the unions will not be easily diverted from the pursuit of serious social change.[7]

Indeed, in the 1970-74 'interregnum' the unions supported policies which, while not amounting to a socialist programme, certainly went as far in proposing to test the limits of reforms within capitalism as any in Labour Party history. Suffused in the spirit of the greatest period of class confrontation in Britain for fifty years and encouraged by the alliance between the TGWU and AUEW and the Labour left forged in the late 1960s, Party Conferences breathed the rhetorical fire of socialism with uncharacteristically little intake of the reformist smoke that is inevitably present on these occasions. The National Executive Committee's 1973 *Programme*, while going nowhere near as far as some successful conference resolutions of 1971 and 1972, nevertheless promised a major extension of public ownership and control, above all through the proposed National Enterprise Board's acquisition of 'some twenty-five of our largest manufacturers', and through a system of Planning Agreements with the top 100 companies, both backed up by extensive compulsory powers in a new Industry Act.[8] When combined with the commitments established in the TUC-Labour Party Liaison Committee's 'Social Contract' on repealing the Industrial Relations Act, 'real moves' towards industrial democracy, extensive wealth and income redistribution, and statutory price controls, socialists in the Party could with justification claim to have made major gains. It was all summed up in Coates's challenge to sceptics: 'If the unions decide to support real socialist options, why should the socialists need to split away?'[9]

Yet if the events of 1968 to 1974 were indicative of the extent to which the Party is internally affected by major periods of class struggle, they by no means disposed of the question of whether the Labour Party can actually be transformed into a socialist party by struggles on its own terrain. On the contrary the intra-party conflicts of this period were subject to specific limitations which considerably undermined their potential for change. In the first place, the shift to the left in the unions was not nearly as pronounced as was sometimes imagined. As Minkin himself has shown ' ... in spite of the move to the left evident in the resolutions submitted and votes cast there was no major change in the leadership of the largest unions between 1970 and 1973. Those changes which did take place in fact reinforced the position of the right ... thus it was still the case in 1975 that most of the senior officials of the ten largest unions were to the right of the Party's political centre of gravity.'[10] Secondly, the extent of the rift between the left-wing union leadership and the Party leadership was often exaggerated. Both the left-wing union leaders and the Parliamentary left had a consistently great regard for Harold Wilson's 'tolerance' of minority opinion in the Party and a marked tendency to put real stock in the (re)conversions of their erstwhile Bevanite colleagues. This did not apply to the Jenkinsites both because they showed less tolerance and less readiness to employ socialist rhetoric to conceal their orthodoxy, and because they never fully appreciated as did Wilson (and Callaghan) that without the unions the Party would be 'uneasily poised between the Liberals and the Bow Group' without a mass base.[11] To be sure, the establishment of the Liaison Committee and the absorption of Michael Foot into the leadership specifically to act as what Tony Benn called 'the link and buckle with the industrial wing of the movement',[12] greatly facilitated the accommodation between Jones and Scanlon and the leadership. But apart from the stipulation that a Labour Government never again impose statutory penalties on collective bargaining, this accommodation was much more 'endemic' and much less 'conditional' than Coates or Minkin allowed.

Thirdly, the force of union solidarity and tradition, which had been a source of the cleavage regarding the issue of state intervention in collective bargaining, was at the same time a source of continuity and conservatism in terms of maintaining the dominance of the Party leadership. Again as Minkin admirably has shown, even the left-wing unions continued to cast their votes for the Conference

Arrangements Committee and the NEC largely on the basis of traditional arrangements and understandings, leaving right-wing sitting tenants in place. Although these committees were more responsive to delegate pressures in the early 1970s, it was significant that CLP resolutions which would have required MPs to abide by conference decisions were either kept off the Agenda or remitted to the Executive. Similarly left-wing union leaders refused to countenance the idea of instructing their union's sponsored MPs on how to vote. The Party leadership were still able to draw substantially on the union leadership's feeling, gained from experience in managing their own union conferences, that a 'good conference' was one that did not go too far towards divisiveness, and their sensitivity that unions should not be seen to be 'running' the Party. All this was reflective of the 'typically limited role' which Ralph Miliband identified the union leaders as playing in the Party, whereby they see themselves as 'representatives of organized labour, involved in a bargaining relationship, notably over industrial and economic issues, and their political colleagues in the Labour Party, and not in the lead as political rivals intending to capture control of the Party for purposes radically different from those of the men who now control it'.[13] This is not so much a matter, as Ken Coates seemed to think in challenging this view in his 1973 article, of union leaders failing to put themselves forward from time to time as political leaders or even acting as policy initiators; it is rather the unions' maintenance of traditional practices *vis-à-vis* the party leadership which inhibits them from throwing the full weight of their organizational strength in the Party behind the forces for change, even when their differences with the leadership on major policy issues is significant.

But far the most important factor prohibiting change in the Party, what in fact reproduces the unions' 'limited role', is the very commitment of the unions to maintaining the Labour Party as a 'viable' political force, both out of immediate defensive and electoral considerations and out of overwhelming loyalty to the Party as an institution. The very process that suggested to Coates that the Party 'might possibly recover from a whole succession of Wilsons'—the threat of a Conservative Government to the interests of the working class and the lack of any ready alternative to Labour's political machine—is the same process which all but guarantees that the Party *will* actually have to face a whole succession of Wilsons, however 'implausible' Coates finds this prospect. For to carry intra-party conflict to the point of forcing the imposition of socialist policies, or isolating and defeating those who oppose them, entails too great a risk to Party unity in terms of the primacy of immediate electoral and defensive campaigns. It is Party unity, not change, which is ultimately paramount from the union's perspective when intra-party conflict emerges. There may be some good defensive reason for this, but it is not the basis for the kind of transformation entailed in changing the Labour Party.

What Coates called the 'barely concealed civil war' between the Party and union leadership in 1968 and 1969 is particularly illustrative in this regard. The 'Solemn and Binding Agreement' between the TUC and the Government, which resolved the immediate controversy over *In Place of Strife,* may be seen from one perspective as a sterling victory by the labour movement over a Labour Government. But from another perspective, the long and abrasive negotiations between Wilson, Barbara Castle and the General Council was not only about avoiding the proposed legislation, but about avoiding an actual 'civil war' in the Party. The union leadership, no less than the Party leadership, were reaching for some political formula to heal the immediate scission and were for that reason anxious that 'extraneous' issues (such as those which were at the source of the division) should not be raised. What stood out about the victory over *In Place of Strife* was its purely defensive character: it involved neither a change in Party leadership or ideology, indeed it did not even address the question of the Government's continuing commitment to a statutory incomes policy. Although it did not by any means re-establish a consensus between the unions and the Government, it certainly left the latter in a much stronger position *vis-à-vis* the Labour Party than it had been a year earlier. Whereas the leadership had been defeated in five major policy issues at the 1968 conference, the 1969 Conference left the TGWU and AEU in virtual isolation amongst the unions in opposing the leadership on incomes policy, and the delegates were treated to the sight of Hugh Scanlon moving fulsome support for the Government, without the reservations he had insisted on (and obtained) a year earlier.

It can, of course, be said of 1968 (as Coates said of 1973—and is being said of 1979) that the 'battle-lines are just beginning to form'. But in the 1970-73 period again the very factors that Coates identified as ensuring that 'the whole alliance did not fall apart'—the common struggle against the Tory Government and the necessity of maintaining Labour as a viable political force to fight the next election—also ensured that the battle would not go so far as to risk Party unity. This was most critically evident with regard to Harold Wilson's successful opposition to the NEC's '25 companies' proposal. As Minkin has put it, the 'triumvirate' of Foot, Jones and Wilson 'acted as a reconciling force between the Party's factions and a restraint upon the leftism in the Programme. Thus in 1973, the advantages of this link went to the Party as both large union delegations responded to the call for moderation and pre-election unity. There was no concerted attempt to push the more radical interpretation of the role of the National Enterprise Board.'[14] In these circumstances, Harold Wilson did not actually have to use his threatened 'veto' by the Shadow Cabinet against including this proposal in the Manifesto. But his view that 'it was inconceivable that the party would go into a general election on this proposal, nor could any incoming Labour Government be so committed',[15] was overwhelmingly confirmed by the 1973 Conference.

The result was that the Labour Party emerged out of its period of opposition with a most ambiguous programme. The NEC's *Programme* itself had already exhibited considerable ambiguity by noting that the proposed Planning Agreements System as 'developed from those already in operation in France, Belgium and Italy', thus inviting the question of whether this was in fact to be the centrepiece of a socialist economic strategy or of a modernized state capitalism. Similar questions could have been raised about the resemblance between the NEB and Italian state holding companies. Precisely because it could have been argued, however, that the way that these new policies would be used by a Labour Government would depend on the balance of forces in the Party and the State, Wilson's pre-election victory on this question was so significant. For it indicated how easily openings for change in the Party are closed in the face of immediate pressures of Party unity. Insofar as the unions were concerned in 1973, the battle-lines for change were hardly being drawn. On the contrary, the hatchet was being buried.

2

The limitations which the requirements of defensive and electoral unity place upon changing the Labour Party entail consequences which by no means can simply be measured in terms of the ambiguity of Labour's Election Manifestos or even the failure of Labour Governments to implement those reforms which the Manifestos do explicitly promise. For the problem with the Labour Party is not simply that in the absence of a better alternative, the working class has to make do with a reformist rather than a revolutionary party. It is that the Party itself plays an active role as an agency of social control *over* the working class. Ken Coates was indeed right to explain the importance of Parliamentary politics and the stability of the Labour Party on the grounds that no alternative socialist grouping can become an alternative vehicle 'for the development of the outlook of a whole social class until they can be seen to have the potential to enable that class to speak for itself at every political level on which its interests are, the object of contention. Even the corporate interests of the subordinate class cannot be safeguarded without organization on this scale.' But when he immediately went on to maintain that 'it is manifestly silly to speak about "hegemonic aspirations" developing within such a class unless it has safely passed the point at which its self-defence is relatively assured',[16] it was he who was being unrealistic. This is not only because self-defence entails a constant struggle and is never 'assured'; but more importantly because continued subordination may be inscribed within the very process of self-defence. In the case of the Labour Party, self-defence takes place *at the expense* of the hegemonic development of the working class.

This is not just a matter of Labour Governements introducing reforms which are specifically structured to integrate the working class in the existing social order, reforms which constitute real gains for the class—but are designed to close rather than open room for further struggle.[17] Nor is it just a matter of leaving a Party leadership in place which proclaims and maintains those 'national' values which *prescribe* subordination of the working class and which treat the *whole class* as a mere *sectional* group in the society. (In periods of mass quiescence this may not entail misrepresentation; but it certainly will greatly reinforce the quiescence.) It is also a matter of Labour Governments employing the loyalty and solidarity inherent in the movement actually to *demobilize* the working class at critical junctures in its development and to secure real material sacrifices from the working class at those very moments when economic militancy threatens profitability. The very self-confidence and self-awareness of an active working class, which is the force behind the election of Labour Governments, becomes the very *object* of the attempt to subdue and extirpate this energy. Although these attempts are only partially and temporarily successful, they nevertheless mean that it is never quite a matter of just picking up where one left off when class conflict re-emerges again.

The 1974-9 Labour Government has to be seen precisely in this light. It was composed of a Party leadership which in Coates's words, 'inspires no sacrifice, blazes no trails, bodes no fundamental changes, and meets no spiritual needs'. But this is too negative a view. It was a leadership which continued to see itself playing, and did play, an active and indispensable role in the British political system—above all the role of tempering, containing and channelling into 'responsible' outlets the industrial militancy of its time. The Labour leadership's part in the defensive campaign against the Industrial Relations Bill was not merely that of fighting the battle in Parliament, but of urging the unions not to take the very industrial-cum-political action which in the end scuppered the Act. A prime basis of Wilson's opposition to the Act was that it fostered revolutionary tendencies in the working class, that it was a 'militants' charter', that it treated industrial relations as part of 'a wider political conflict'. Throughout its years in opposition the Labour leadership remained committed, moreover, to one fixed ideal—resurrecting union agreement to wage restraint. Wilson and Callaghan did come to appreciate that a statutory incomes policy was unacceptable to the unions; indeed, this was the one genuine 'conversion' they experienced while in opposition, the one real lesson they learned from Michael Foot and Jack Jones. But this did not dampen their enthusiasm for wage restraint. On the contrary, they continued to hold to the view, first elaborated in the early 1960s, that the Labour Party's ability to promise this was its major electoral asset. Although they could not obtain from the unions the kind of fulsome commitment to incomes policy than they had engineered in 1963, they continued to press for it *via* the Liaison Committee and in the drawing up of the Manifesto, right through the industrial crisis of December 1973 and January 1974. The Labour left were able to convince themselves, as they had done from 1959 to 1964, that what was involved was a 'socialist incomes policy', in which wage restraint was not the object of the exercise but an inevitable part of socialist planning. The Labour leadership, however, clearly accepted the more radical elements of the Social Contract only to the extent that unions insisted that, as the February Election Manifesto put it, 'only deeds can persuade ... that an incomes policy is not some kind of trick to force [the worker] ... to bear the brunt of the national burden'. If it turned out that such persuasion was possible without too many such deeds, so much the better.

And what happened? Within a year of the February 1974 election, incomes policy became the centrepiece of the Social

Contract, and the unions responded with an exercise in voluntary wage restraint unparalleled in modern British history. Increases in gross money earnings for the average worker fell from 25.5 per cent in 1974-5 to 12.4 per cent in 1975-6 to 8.8 per cent in 1976-7. As the rate of inflation fell more slowly (from 25 per cent to 14 per cent over the three years) real wages fell considerably. Even taking into account the compensatory tax concessions offered by the Government, real wages fell by 5.5 per cent, 1.6 per cent and almost 1 per cent in the three respective years.[18] The real weekly net income of the average male worker, married with two children, if calculated in terms of October 1978 prices, had stood at £68.90 in September 1970, risen to £74.50 in September 1972, and maintained that level until September 1974; it fell by September 1977 to £68.10—i.e., by over £6 per week. In 1977-8, with a less restrictive pay norm, a rate of inflation of 8 per cent, additional tax concessions, and the first instances of breakdown of union co-operation, real net earnings recovered substantially (increasing by 9 per cent). But this still left the average worker with a real weekly take home pay in September 1978 which was £3.50 less than in 1974 and almost £1 a week less in terms of real net weekly income (i.e., taking account of increased transfer payments of 1977-8).[19]

It would of course be absurd to attribute these losses to the Labour Government's wage restraint policies alone in abstraction from the economic crisis. But the sacrifice entailed in wage restraint would have been one thing had it been inspired on the basis of Tony Benn's promise to the 1973 Conference (broadly incorporated into the 1974 Manifesto) that 'the crisis we inherit when we come to power will be the occasion for fundamental change and not the excuse for postponing it'.[20] Instead the crisis became the basis for maintaining the existing balance of wealth and power in British society by increasing the exploitation of the working class. Wage restraint was secured and maintained: while the statutory price controls and food subsidies introduced in 1974 were weakened and phased out; in the context of massively deflationary budgets and an increase in the unemployed, once school leavers were included, by almost one million; and while public expenditure programmes were cut and subjected to cash limits so that instead of the promised 13 per cent growth there was no growth at all in real terms from 1974 to 1978. As Stuart Holland put it in commenting on the Thatcher Government's Budget of 1979: 'Certainly, the edge of Mrs Thatcher's axe was first ground and then fell under successive Healey Budgets.'[21]

As for the Industrial Strategy, the true basis of the case for a 'socialist incomes policy', the wage restraint programme was launched *after* Tony Benn had been dismissed from the Department of Industry, an act which Jack Jones, speaking for the TUC as a whole, warned at the time would constitute 'a grave affront to the trade union movement'.[22] The Industry Bill was shorn of its compulsory dimensions, and the singular Planning Agreement entered into with a private company occurred in the context of the Government sanctifying in this way the bail-out of Chrysler. As for the NEB, it was largely absorbed into the role of traditional state fire-fighting on closures and in any case operated, as its intellectual progenitor put it with great dismay, 'purely on commercial rather than public, or social criteria'.[23] In these circumstances, the locus of the Industrial Strategy shifted back to the NEDC and the tripartite sectoral working parties established under its auspices in 1975. It was all summed up in 1977 by Jack Jones: 'Somehow, somewhere, the Goverment's objectives seem to have been hijacked off course, and I mean "hijacked" ... an industrial strategy which relies only on deliberation of sectoral working parties, on polite talks with industrialists and trade associations ... is not a strategy at all, but an excuse for one.'[24]

Why then did the unions display such loyalty? One explanation, which is fairly common on the Labour left, was expressed in Ian Mikardo's early admission to the 1975 Conference: 'We were all conned'[25]—with the implication that the unions were simply conned for a longer period. This is an attractive explanation for the Labour left for it carries within it the premise that you can't fool all the people all the time and that at some point the party will rise up against the charlatans. But this will not do as an explanation of the unions' loyalty. Jack Jones's own account of the Government's behaviour, that they were 'hijacked', already indicates a very different perspective: the Government were themselves unsuspecting 'victims' of the 'hijack'. This was indeed the dominant view among the union leadership and was reflective of the strength of the 'bond of confidence' established in the pre-1974 period.

This bond was in fact *strengthened* by the precarious parliamentary position of the Government and the constant spectre of another Tory Government (which would have of course acted as even less of a buffer against the worst effects of the crisis than Labour was doing). And no less important was the fact that this Government, far more than had been the case in 1964-70, showed a sanguine understanding of the unions' own priorities—that when push came to shove, the unions would insist on those policies in the Social Contract that pertained directly to industrial relations, and would exert less pressure when it came to the economic strategy. This order of priorities stemmed not only from narrow organizational interests, but also from the unions' own fears and frustration with the effects of economic militancy and high inflation on real wages and employment. It also stemmed from the union leadership's own lack of confidence in the alternative economic strategy they and the Labour left advanced in the face of the harsh 'economic realities' put forward by the Government, the Treasury and foreign 'experts' from the IMF. The fact that Michael Foot allowed the TUC to write its own ticket on industrial relations legislation served, in terms of the unions' own priorities, to cement the ties between the unions and the Government at the same time as reactionary economic policies were pursued. Moreover, the Government proved amenable to introducing wage restraint in the form advanced by Jack Jones, i.e., the £6 across-the-board norm so that the low paid would suffer less. And the very fact that the Government was seen to be resisting strong Treasury pressures to institute a statutory policy,[26] confirmed the unions' resolve to meet their 'obligations' to the Government.

The *defensive* priorities of the union movement in the context of the crisis were secured, in other words, at the *expense* of insisting on alternative, let alone socialist, economic policies. The question remains, however, of whether the defensive gains were so great as to be worth the sacrifice. The egalitarian thrust of the £6 norm, such as it was, certainly struck a responsive chord in the labour movement, at least temporarily. But this cannot obscure the fact that it mainly concerned redistribution within the working class (involving Labourism's new twist on socialism—what I have called before its 'socialism in one class'[27]) in a context of a policy which reduced the proportion of the national income going to the class as a whole. Much more of a case can be made for the industrial relations legislation of 1974 to 1976. Yet it is certainly questionable how much the unions have benefited from this in concrete terms. The Tory Industrial Relations Act had before its repeal been rendered more or less impotent by the unions. The role that ACAS has been able to play in extending union recognition under the legislation has been very limited, particularly when conciliation has failed. As a number of long and futile recognition strikes have shown, moreover, employer intransigence and an anti-union judiciary are able to render the new procedures useless. In other areas—disclosure of information, job security, equal pay for women—the laws are not only deficient in certain respects, but are only effective when unions are already strong enough to advance their members' interests beyond minimum legal guarantees. Above all, there is a real danger, that litigation of issues (e.g., unfair dismissal) undermines shop floor struggle and saps the time and energy of officials who become embroiled in the legalistic procedures. In two internal TUC reassessments of the legislation at the end of 1978, all this was being admitted, although little was said publicly lest it be used by the Conservatives to remove the advantages the laws do give. But this should not conceal what the TUC's own counsel, Lord Wedderburn, has called the unions' own

> ... self-doubt as to the degree to which the trade union movement should in future come to rely upon machinery provided by the State to achieve that which in the past it has collectively won largely without the help of—often despite—the State's laws. Already the movement has been disillusioned by the operation of some of 'its' laws and has realised afresh the limitations that inevitably fall upon trade unions who trust in the regulation of industrial relations by the law. Even the floor of *individual* laws is often found to be ineffective without industrial strength to support them, especially in the case of equal pay for women. What the law gives the law can take away.[28]

The point to be drawn from this, however, is that the Labour leadership can hardly be accused of 'conning' the unions on this question—they were fulfilling 'their side' of the Social Contract. Indeed what Ken Coates did not foresee in predicting the scission that another Wilsonite Government would produce in the movement was that this was another Wilsonite Government with one major difference from the last ones—it was bent on ensuring that it was not the Labour leadership that would become isolated from the union leadership, but the Labour left. (As indeed occurred over public expenditure cuts and wage restraints in 1976.) To this end, the Government even maintained the form of the rest of the Social Contract while violating its spirit in most respects. Unlike the 1964-70 Government's abandonment of the Economic Plan, this Government never rejected the Industrial Strategy. All its constitutive elements—the Industry Act, statutory prices controls, the NEB, even the concept of Planning Governments—were retained. Even the public expenditure cuts were defended, both by Labour and union leaders,[29] in terms of the industrial strategy, as freeing resources for investment in manufacturing industry. Even while union leaders recognized that the brunt of policy was in the opposite direction from what they had intended, the fact that the formal structures were in place (as was also the case with the Royal Commission on Income and Wealth and the Bullock Inquiry on Industrial Democracy) allowed them to expect that a new spirit might be injected into them once the immediate crisis passed. Above all the Government did maintain close consultation with the union leadership. The accommodation between them, which Ken Coates believed could be secured only on the basis of socialist policies, was in fact reached on the basis of corporatist ones. Only occasionally did a union leader admit the reality of the situation to the movement, as did Alan Fisher at the time of the TUC's twenty-to-one endorsement of wage restraint in 1976:

> ... we in the movement should understand the nature of bargaining at the national level between the TUC and the Government ... it is possible that we will become mesmerized by the process itself rather than considering the results that it achieves ... capital will not hold back from using its power to influence these negotiations. One example we have is by pushing down the value of pound. In that context, it is dangerous for the movement to accept incorporation in the apparatus of the State, articulated through what may be a loyalty to a Labour Government and the test for the trade union movement is to develop effective bargaining power at this level, if necessary through new procedures and new institutions, and not to regard the State as in some mysterious way a neutral body. It never has been and it never will be.[30]

The big question, of course, remains why the rank and file went along with the leadership. Coates's confidence rested after all on the 'active and self-assertive rank and file' without whose continuing support Jones's and Scanlon's 'theoretically possible' about-face would be of little worth to the establishment. It was in fact worth a great deal. As Steve Jefferys has pointed out ' ... "left" union leaders either led or were prominently placed in four of the five most strike-prone industries. Despite the fact that the five only employed 6 per cent of the total labour force, they accounted for 47 per cent of the working days lost in 1969-74; by 1975-6 this figure had declined to 22 per cent, in a period of falling strike statistics.'[31] The level of resistance to Phases I and II of the Social Contract was simply minimal. Both the deep reserves of loyalty to a Labour Government among activists and the same fears and frustrations that beset the union leadership must surely have been factors in this. Just as there was a mistaken tendency among some of the Trotskyist left in the early 1970s to assume that the shop stewards of today are the revolutionary vanguard of tomorrow, so it must be said that many on the Labour Left vastly overestimated the staying power of economic militancy and the political effects which an 'active and self-assertive rank and file' would have as a force for change within the Labour Party. In order to forestall criticisms of being wise after the fact, it might be permissible in this instance to quote something I wrote in 1974:

> It is true that industrial militancy does have a clear political character. The dissatisfaction with existing social relations is inherent in wage claims of 25, 30 or 40 per cent; in the expectation by dockers or car workers or miners that they be paid as much or more than groups high above them in the status hierarchy; in occupations of factories shut down in accordance with the law of profit; in the large number of strikes challenging managerial prerogatives. But this militancy retains a non-political veneer by virtue of the fact that it arises from separate segments of the working class at different times, and arises moreover in the absence of a generalized and explicit rejection of the economic and political structures in which these social relations are embedded. This is indeed an inherent limitation of trade unionism; demands for a 40 per cent increase in the income of the working class as a whole, and for workers' control over production, cannot be effectively expressed industrially but only politically, and although we have seen in recent years a number of overt and official political strikes for the first time since the TUC left Trafalgar Square for Whitehall in the aftermath of the General Strike, these actions have been hesistant, sporadic and defensive. Without a political party which would maintain and give focus to industrial militancy, it is not unlikely to be dissipated in yet another phase of quasi-corporatist policies, or, if not, to be met by a more fully authoritarian challenge than the British labour movement has yet faced.[32]

That this militancy was indeed dissipated from 1975 to 1977 has a great deal to do with the inability of the Labour left, *no less than the various socialist groupings outside of it,* to capture the political imagination of rank and file activists. The fact that the Labour vote continued to drop in 1974 despite Labour's more radical programme was proof of this, and suggested that the 'unprecedented skepticism about Labour politicians' which Coates identified, was by no means highly discriminating between right and left and not necessarily an entirely positive force for social change. Steve Jeffery's admission, from an IS/SWP perspective, that 'in the face of the crisis there appeared to be no "practical" alternative' as far as most workers were concerned, and that 'when the general conviction was that there was little you could do, you just had to put up with the Government's pay policy; then this is what the shop stewards generally felt as well,'[33] is a damning testament to the ineffectiveness of the IS/SWP in the previous period. It is even a more damning testament to the failure of the Labour left, whose alternative might be thought more 'practical', to touch the roots of the movement for all its visibility at the national level in the 1970s.

Of course the forces that originally produced this militancy were not themselves dissipated during this period, and, as had been the case with the wage restraint policies of both the 1945 and 1966 Labour Governments, the breakdown of restraints occurred not *after* Labour was defeated at the polls, but *before*. This indicated once again that while Labour remains able to foreclose class struggle for a certain period, it is unable to quash for too long the class antagonisms of British society. Callaghan's cynical manipulation of the 1978 Congress, encouraging it to pronounce its opposition to the 5 per cent guidelines only in faint whispers by giving it the impression that a general election was imminent, may have looked like a brilliant political manoeuvre at the time, but it proved to be a major blunder. For the union leadership by this stage could simply not hold back the rising tide of economic militancy that had begun to surface spontaneously as early as a year before. (Indeed to some extent they may have encouraged it, despite their effective co-operation in wage restraint until 1978, by their verbal recommitment to full collective bargaining and by their more open criticisms of the Government's policies from 1977 onwards.) As a result the class collaboration dogma of social democracy faltered again on its own terms: Labour's claim that it was the governing party of 'consensus' while the Tories were the party of 'confrontation' lost a good deal of its electoral credibility.

The resurgence of economic militancy in the winter of 1978-9 certainly reflects the resilience of the working class and its continuing ability to impose severe barriers to the strategic options of capital and the state. But in terms of the question of changing the Labour Party, there is little comfort to be drawn from it. It most certainly does not conform to Coates's scenario of an irreconcilable split between the vast proportion of the labour movement and the

Labour leadership. There has been renewed friction, but what is remarkable is how the conflicts within the movement were politically contained in the last years of the Government. Both the NEC and the Party Conference were certainly much less the mouthpieces of the leadership throughout this Government, but their ability to control or even influence its actions showed no marked increase. On the contrary, the existence of the Liaison Committee has allowed the leadership to by-pass conference resolutions without openly flouting them by promising to work out policy disagreements at a higher level. The Liaison Committee's policy statements have invariably turned out to be much less radical than those of the NEC or than conference resolutions. And even when conflict with unions broke into the open, as they did on the first day of the 1978 Conference, when the unions defeated the leadership on both the 5 per cent guidelines and economic policy as a whole, the unions refused to widen the conflict. On the very next day, enough union votes were available—including the TGWU's—to defeat the constitutional amendment for an electoral college, encompassing both the extra-Parliamentary and Parliamentary Party, to elect the leader. The fact that this was combined with the defeat, on the basis of Hugh Scanlon miscasting the AUEW vote, of mandatory reselection of MPs, made Coates's burial of 'bureaucratic intrigue' in the Party look very premature indeed.

Nor did matters change as the industrial conflict of the winter gained momentum. In order to protect the Government, as far as they could, from the electoral consequences of the media rampage against its 'weakness' in the face of anarchy, the General Council was drawn into producing, with indecent haste, a new Solemn and Binding Agreement, the so-called 'Concordat', in which they agreed to undertake voluntary control on picketing, the closed shop, inter-union disputes and (eventually) wage demands. Even seen as a symbolic electoral exercise pure and simple, it was nevertheless significant how purely *defensive* a document it was. It was accompanied moreover by a policy statement by 'moderate' union leaders which endorsed the economic policies of the leadership. With no little justification, and in the midst of the winter's industrial strife, Shirley Williams could observe that the unions were 'moving clearly back to the centre' and scorn earlier suggestions that the social democrats in the Party were politically 'dead'.[34] Not surprisingly, the hopes of the Labour left in the fall of 1978 that the postponement of the election would give them the chance to avoid the Election Manifesto 'watering down' the NEC's 1976 *Programme,* were entirely frustrated.[35]

3

To be sure, the battle is not over. It is in the nature of the Labour Party that the battle-lines will continue to be drawn up to and including the Day of Judgment. But given the experience of the last dozen years, what foundation remains for the argument that the Party can be changed? The NEC has once again put the issues of election of the leader and mandatory reselection on the Agenda of the 1979 Party Conference, and despite considerable noise from 'moderate' union leaders against friction in the Party, it is by no means certain that these proposals will be defeated. But even if these proposals were carried, would they constitute an effective basis for changing the Party? It was certainly clear from Callaghan's election that a leader who is 'acceptable to the unions' is not necessarily one who is committed to socialist policies. And if a Michael Foot or even a Tony Benn were elected, and setting aside all doubts as to their socialist 'credentials', how fundamentally different a tack could they take, given the fine array of upstanding gentlemen that numerically dominate the PLP?

The mandatory selection procedure is presumably designed to obviate this problem. But the Parliamentary left is itself divided on this issue; the unions are concerned about its effects on sponsorship; and it is unlikely that those constituency parties that are presently moribund will suddenly spring to life just to turn out a sitting MP. As a theory of an inevitable fall from grace of socialist parties, the 'iron law of oligarchy' may have little to recommend it. But as an account of how MPs will be able to use considerable organizational and psychological resources to maintain their position *vis-à-vis* their constituency parties, mandatory reselection or no, it is discounted only by the naive.

But what about 'forcing the imposition of socialist policies'? This, as Coates made clear, will depend on the unions. Minkin's identification of a steady undercurrent of union support for public ownership, despite the revisionist machinations of the Party leadership, says nothing about the efforts they will make to force its imposition on the Labour leadership. If anything the 1970s provide rather strong evidence that too much stock should not be put in union conference resolutions on public ownership.

This may be especially seen with regard to the unions' reaction to the NEC's 1976 statement on 'Banking and Finance', which proposed taking over the biggest four clearing banks, a merchant bank, and the top seven insurance companies. Like all NEC proposals of this kind, it was primarily defended as a means of facilitating investment in manufacturing industry and specifically drew its inspiration from the publicly owned financial institutions of Britain's capitalist competitor countries (in this case, France, Japan and Italy). Nevertheless for the Labour Party it was a very radical proposal indeed. Although it drew screams of anguish from the City and strong public opposition from Callaghan and other Labour Ministers, it did not come out of the blue (having stemmed from a Conference resolution passed in 1971 and revived in 1975). Nor was it without apparent support from the unions directly involved—at least those affiliated to the Labour Party. USDAW's annual conference, which Minkin describes as 'that weathercock of the British trade union movement', passed resolutions in 1973 and 1974 proposing to 'eliminate the capitalist system' and specifically endorsing the takeover of the banks, the Stock Exchange and the insurance companies.[37] But while the 1976 Party Conference endorsed the statement by an overwhelming majority of 3,314,000 to 526,000, it turned out the unions weren't too keen on the idea. The total votes cast already indicated a substantial number of abstentions; the TGWU had reservations about 'timing'; and the unions in the field of banking and insurance demanded 'further consultation'. When nine relevant TUC unions were consulted by an NEC working party, they were found to be 'to varying degrees, hostile to the proposals on nationalization'. Fears of redundancy and loss of overseas earnings were apparently involved, but most interesting was the fact that both USDAW and ASTMS, while agreeing that 'some reform was necessary ... questioned the conclusion that ownership was the best means of exercising control'.[38] Despite the conference decision, it was clear that the issue was now a dead letter. The 1978 Liaison Committee Statement, 'Into the Eighties', and the 1979 Election Manifesto made this abundantly clear. It will be less easily resurrected than mandatory reselection.

This critical episode suggests that a concerted push by the unions *against* the Party leadership on socialist policies is less of a possibility than the Labour left would like to think. There remains, however, one other prospect suggested by Coates (although he was none too keen on the idea): that if the Party could not be won over, it might be divided with the left retaining a considerable hold over 'the apparatus ... necessary to meet the demands of full participation in political life'.[39] Yet the likelihood of such a division being initiated by either of the major groupings on the right or the left must be counted as remote in the extreme. The leadership as a whole understands only too well the importance of retaining their hold over this apparatus; a Prentice or a Taverne may go from time to time, but attrition at this rate is not going to matter much. A resurrection of 1931 is perhaps more likely, but this would leave the Party composed of much the same forces as before. One would still have to ask whether, apart from a temporary hiccup, the Party could be changed against 'those who helped to sustain MacDonald's supremacy and Snowden's economics to the eleventh hour of the last day',[40] but who had the sagacity to stay.

As for the Labour left, it must surely be recognized that whatever else it is about, it is not about dividing the Labour Party. Precisely because it identifies itself with Party Tradition, the thought of dividing the Party is particularly abhorrent to it. (It must be said that to the extent it makes this identification unambiguously, it is either hypocritical or mistaken. In terms of the class harmony ideology, the policies effectively pursued, and the absence of mass socialist education *via* the Party at the base, the task of changing the Labour Party surely invovolves wrenching it *out of* its tradition.) The left has always taken the burden of Party unity on its shoulders and has been far more ready than the right to compromise its principles to this end.

What then *is* the alternative for Socialists? In a number of respects, Coates cannot be faulted. The issue is not about 'parliamentarianism versus insurrectionism'. The question of whether Parliament can be the effective vehicle for implementing a socialist programme will indeed 'only be answered when it has been tried' (which it never has in Britain or any other major capitalist country), and tried, moreover, on the basis of the crystallization of the kind of socialist consciousness 'in the whole active part of the subordinate class' which Coates envisages [41] The point about the Labour Party is that it has always been dominated by a leadership which, with the support of most of the movement, has not only been unable or unwilling to develop a coherent socialist programme, but has not seen its task as one of instilling such a consciousness. It has lived off the existing consciousness of the working class, it has even represented it, but rather than attempting the difficult task of securing working-class support by undermining those values of national unity and moderation which encapsulate class subordination, it has chosen the easier route of engaging working-class allegiance by associating itself with those values. The problem with the Labour Party is not that it has sought to bring the working class to power by peaceful means. Rather the fact that it has not seen its task as bringing the working class to power has determined the *kind* of parliamentarianism which it practices.

Coates was also right in his assessment that existing revolutionary groups will not stand serious scrutiny as viable alternatives to the Labour Party, not least because of their doctrinaire refusal to allow any 'equivocation' on a parliamentary strategy.[42] And however one might applaud certain changes in the Communist Party, the vast historical weight under which it staggers, no less than the transparency of its illusion that the Labour Party might be remotely interested in an alliance with it, suggests that it will continue to fail to make much progress as a viable alternative.

To sum up: the Labour Party will not conveniently fall apart; a good measure of parliamentary success is indeed essential; the present alternatives hold out little hope. It is scarcely surprising that many socialists cling to the illusion that the Labour Party can be changed although one might expect from them greater candour about the costs involved—i.e., that by continuing to work within the Labour Party, they necessarily do their bit to sustain Labourism's strangling hegemony over the politically active working class. But given the Sisyphus-like task they appear to be engaged in, it is by no means inappropriate to ask whether it is not indeed worth the candle for socialists in Britain to come together to 'try again' in the 1980s: to make a start at building a mass socialist party. Certainly such a party would have to detach many activists, and perhaps eventually some major unions, from the Labour Party. But it need not inherit by this token the same structure or all the burdens that come with the Labour Party tradition. With different leaders, a different ethos and with a positive attitude to Marxism, these elements would necessarily combine in a different way. Even if a federated structure were adopted, it need not carry with it the same separation between parliamentary and extra-parliamentary activity, and the same division of labour between industrial and political leadership. One important reason for making the attempt is that even a remotely viable alternative would act as pole of attraction for those socialist elements within the Labour Party to break out of the vicious circle of both trying to change the party *and* maintain its defensive unity, and put their energy, their talents, and the respect and legitimacy they enjoy in the eyes of many trade unionists to more positive use.

The fact that what is entailed in creating a mass socialist party today is not the political mobilization of the working class, but its *remobilization,* is indeed what makes such an attempt seem so Herculean. That there is little historical evidence for such a successful remobilization is true. But where are the examples of a transformed social democratic party? With no less justification, indeed with rather more in light of the experience of the past six years, one might indeed launch such an attempt at remobilization by quoting Coates's own concluding call to arms: 'The work will be arduous and intricate, daunting indeed. It will need all the socialist forces we can muster, and, indeed, it needs them now.'[43]

NOTES

1. Ken Coates, 'Socialists and the Labour Party', *The Socialist Register 1973*, p. 174.
2. Geoff Hodgson, *Socialism and Parliamentary Democracy*, Spokesman, 1977; Peter Jenkins, 'The Labour Party and the Politics of Transition', *The Socialist Register 1977*; Frank Ward, *In Defence of Democratic Socialism*, Rye Express, 1978.
3. Lewis Minkin, *The Labour Party Conference*, Allen Lane, 1978, p. 322.
4. Ralph Miliband, 'Moving On' *The Socialist Register 1976*, p. 128.
5. Robert McKenzie, *British Political Parties*, London, 1963, p. 505.
6. Minkin, *op.cit.*, p. 321.
7. Coates, *op.cit.*, pp. 176-7.
8. See *Labour Programme 1973*, esp. pp. 13-39.
9. Coates, *op.cit.*, p. 176.
10. Minkin, *op.cit.*, p. 344.
11. Harold Wilson, quoted in *Fianancial Times*, 16 and 31 May 1968.
12. Tony Benn, *A New Course for Labour*, IWC, 1976, p. 10.
13. Ralph Miliband, *Parliamentary Socialism*, Merlin, 1972, p. 375.
14. Minkin, *op.cit.*, p. 344.
15. Quoted in Michael Hatfield, *The House the Left Built*, Victor Gollancz, 1978, p. 199.
16. Coates, *op.cit.*, p. 156.
17. When Hodgson (*op.cit.*, pp. 60-61, 129) and Jenkins (*op.cit.*, pp. 21-2) use the examples of the New Deal to argue that legislative reforms are possible even in a period of capitalist crisis and can have a 'galvanizing effect on large numbers of workers', they ignore the longer-term role that industrial relations legislation has played in the United States in containing, juridifying and deadening autonomous working-class struggle. The 'right to belong to a union' sanctioned by the state against the wishes of the employers in the 1930s was by no means an entirely unmixed blessing given the package it became enveloped in.
18. See Ralph Tarling and Frank Wilkinson, 'The Social Contract: Post War Incomes Policies and their Inflationary Impact,' *Cambridge Journal of Economics*, Vol. I, no. 4, December 1977. The figures for each year have kindly been supplied by the authors in personal communication.
19. The quarterly figures for real weekly income from 1970-78 at October

1978 prices, are presented in tabular form in Written Answers by Robert Sheldon in *H.C. Debates*, Vol 960, 15 December 1978, and 19 January 1979, cc. 519-20 and cc. 969-70.

20. *Labour Party Annual Conference Report (LPACR)* 1973, p. 187.

21. 'Budget That Sells Seed Grain For a Decade', *The Guardian*, 18 June 1979.

22. Quoted in Hatfield, *op.cit.*, pp. 148-9.

23. Stuart Holland, 'Planning Agreements: A Case Study of Industrial Suicide', *Tribune*, 19 September, 1978, p. 3.

24. TUC, *The Trade Union Role in Industrial Policy*, report of a conference of Affiliated unions, October 31, 1977, p. 33.

25. *LPACR*, 1975, p. 323.

26. See Joe Haines, *The Politics of Power*, Jonathan Cape, 1977, ch. 3.

27. See my *Social Democracy and Industrial Militancy*, Cambridge University Press, 1976, p. 124.

28. Lord Wedderburn 'The New Structure of Labour Law in Britain,' *Israel Law Review*, Vol. 13, No. 4, October 1978, p. 457.

29. See Scanlon's speech in *LPACR* 1973, p. 167.

30. TUC, *The Social Contract 1976-77*, Report of the Special Congress, 19 June 1976, p. 39.

31. Steve Jeffreys, 'Striking into the Eighties,' *International Socialism*, Series 2, No. 5, Summer 1979, p. 33.

32. *Social Democracy and Industrial Militancy*, *op.cit.*, p. 253.

33. Jeffreys, *op.cit.*, pp. 33, 35.

34. *Financial Times*, 21 February 1979.

35. See Eric Heffer, 'Conference gives Labour the lead on the election manifesto', *Tribune*, 29 September 1978, p. 5.

36. The Labour Party, *Banking and Finance*, 1976.

37. Minkin, *op.cit.*, p. 325.

38. *LPACR 1978*, Appendix II, pp. 450, 453.

39. Coates, *op.cit.*, p. 171.

40. Michael Foot, *Aneurin Bevan*, Vol. I, Paladin, 1975, p. 136.

41. Coates, *op.cit.*, p. 158.

42. See Duncan Hallas's reproach to Ralph Miliband in 'How can We Move On?', *The Socialist Register 1977*, p. 10.

43. Coates, *op.cit.*, p. 177.

OFFICIAL SECRECY AND
BRITISH LIBERTARIANISM

Duncan Campbell

The United Kingdom has had laws providing for Official Secrecy for ninety years. The two main Acts now in force were both passed in the first quarter of this century, and their essential provisions have been reflected in legal statutes of similar names adopted into the penal codes of most present or former commonwealth countries —notoriously including South Africa and Rhodesia. In contrast to the United States libertarian tradition flowing from its plural democracy and federalist government, British official secrecy legislation has provided much of the Anglo-Saxon world with a legacy of fundamental state secrecy, supported by the potential criminalisation of persons inside or outside the civil service who indulge in disclosure.

The argument is not fundamentally about the provisions made by states for *bona fide* foreign espionage, if that is the correct term. (Although the definition of just what constitutes espionage is capable of considerable bending; I return to this point later.) It is about subsidiary provisions—specifically those made under Section 2 of the British Official Secrets Act—which crimininalize any unauthorized transaction in official information.

It is now widely accepted that this provision is overdue for complete reform, although the motives and benevolence of some of the reform lobby is entirely suspect. Section 2 is in effect the antithesis of proposals for Freedom of Information. (A more apposite title would be the right of free access to official information, although the title of the US legislation has stuck.)

The purpose of this article is to recount the circumstances of, and report the lessons for the left from, a two year case under the Official Secrets Acts, which ended in November 1978. It became known as the ABC case; this derives from the surnames of the three accused: Crispin Aubrey, a journalist for the 'alternative' London weekly *Time Out,* John Berry, a former soldier in the Intelligence Corps, and the present author. From arrest to the end of a trial at the Old

Bailey, the case took almost twenty-one months. It ended in convictions under Section 2 for each of us, but with negligible penalty—in the case of myself and fellow journalist Aubrey, no penalty at all. During the course of the trial, those involved directly, legally, or in defence campaigning had the opportunity to learn a great deal about the intelligence organizations operating in Britain, internally and externally. Although the direct effects of the case were hard to measure, there has been a clearly perceptible undermining of the national security myths which are the civil servants' and politicians' handy blank walls behind which illiberal activities can be screened. In particular, an anonymous army intelligence witness in the case ('Colonel B') rapidly achieved the position of a national figure of ridicule.

It is also probable that the case, with the barrage of criticism which followed for the government, was responsible in large measure for the decision by the Liberal Party, on the fortuitous winning of the ballot for first place in presenting private member's Bills by Clement Freud MP, to select a Freedom of Information Bill. Although muddled and unsatisfactory in many ways, Freud's Bill—which lapsed with the collapse of the Callaghan administration—achieved a wholly unopposed second reading in the House of Commons, reflecting a considerable change in the general attitude of British parliamentarians.

The political context of the creation of the Official Secrets Acts is well reported and analysed from a committed socialist point of view in Tony Bunyan's *The Political Police in Britain*[1]. He notes that the OSAs 'represent the last resort in suppressing public knowledge of the workings of the state'. They are one of 'a number of overtly political laws drawn up to protect and preserve the state in a capitalist society'. It should be noted in passing that provisions at least as harsh apply in Eastern European Socialist states, as in other capitalist states.

The last airing of Section 2, which ironically but not unsurprisingly was an attack on the *Conservative* pro-Biafra lobby launched by the Wilson administration in 1970, resulted in a wholesale acquittal and the appointment of a Committee of Inquiry (Franks[2]) to investigate the workings of Section 2. (See Bunyan, *op.cit.*, p. 5, and Aitken[3] for details.) Nothing save a stream of empty promises flowed from the Franks Report, however.

The origins of the ABC case have their roots entirely elsewhere, in a counter-attack by the British intelligence and security services against the importation from the United States of post-Watergate investigative journalism, which had been adopted by radical and left journalists at a considerable speed during 1975. It was a logical outcome of the dramatically changed US popular perception of 'national security'—Nixon's ready phrase when a cover-up was needed—and of the US intelligence agencies themselves, whose part in the affair led eventually to the stream of investigations and reports in the US press and in the Senate and Congress. Although there have been past major initiatives against the British internal repressive agencies, particularly associated with the Committee of 100 (and in particular the 'Spies for Peace' who in 1963 disclosed the extensive network of secret emergency wartime headquarters), what had come from the United States was a new legitimacy for the idea that the secret agencies should become the subject of watchful press reporting and close democratic scrutiny.

The British left had a figurehead ready to hand for this new current in the person of ex-CIA agent Philip Agee, then domiciled in England whilst writing a major account of his CIA work in South America, *CIA Diary*.[4] He became the CIA's first serious, 'whistle-blower' of the seventies, who renounced and denounced his own repressive activities. A good number have since followed; at the time too, a serious intellectual and factual study of the US intelligence community was written by Marchetti and Marks[5] which provided a useful stimulus to disclosures and investigations about the role of the CIA in Britain.

Agee became and remained, despite suspicion on the left about his book which was an admitted reconstruction, the figurehead of the movement to 'name names' of CIA agents; a philosophy based on the unexceptional idea that those personally engaged abroad by the CIA on covert and subversive work should be called to account by the peoples whose liberties, as often as not, they were a party to destroying.

Agee was not of course involved in the ABC case, or with the Official Secrets Act. But it was he whom—with another American Mark Hosenball—the Security Service targeted for their counter-attack. And it was from the Agee-Hosenball deportation case that the ABC arrests arose. Deportation orders against both men were announced by Home Secretary Merlyn Rees in November 1976, citing powers to deport 'aliens in the interests of national security'. The reasons given were vague in the extreme; in both cases, the preparation of material for publication that was 'harmful to the security of the United Kingdom' and in Agee's case the allegation also included alleged contact with 'foreign intelligence officers'. No

evidence to support charges against either person was ever
produced; it may be assumed that, in all probability, no evidence in
the judicial sense ever existed. I do not think it would be too harsh to
say that Agee was selected because, as an alien, he could be
punished by executive action; the signature of Labour's Home
Secretary sufficed.

Hosenball's case was separate and appeared rather more trivial.
He had worked on a series of articles in *Time Out* which dealt with
the activities of CIA front organizations in Britain, notably the
Forum World Features syndication agency. Subsequently, an anonymous informant from the Institute for the Study of Conflict, to
which some of the feature agency's personnel had transferred,
provided extensive files revealing the Institute's programme for
setting up a subversive right-wing network of contacts within the
intelligence agencies, police, military and civil services. Hosenball
had been involved in that exposure, and in 1976 jointly worked with
the present author on a two-page study of British and US electronic
espionage operations in *Time Out* ('The Eavesdroppers'[6]).

'The Eavesdroppers' was to feature prominently in a hearing in
which Hosenball appealed against his deportation order[7]; the
publicity given to the case drew the attention of John Berry, a social
worker and former employee (indirectly) of the massive Anglo-
American electronic espionage organization, run by the US National Security Agency and Britain's Government Communications
Headquarters (GCHQ) in Cheltenham. Berry contacted the
Defence Committee to offer his assistance, and to offer to go public
with his own view of the intelligence work with which he had been
involved. Until the Agee-Hosenball case arose, he had not tried to
relate his own socialism to the work he had formerly carried out in
military intelligence.

From events at the time and later, there is little doubt that Berry's
contact with the Defence Committee came at a time when much of
the Committee's work was under the direct surveillance of MI5, the
Security Service, whose proposal the original deportation orders had
probably been. They intercepted letters and telephone lines, and
they seem the only likely culprits for a series of disturbances early in
1977 involving thefts of papers and documents from Agee-
Hosenball and ABC Defence Committee members.

As a result of Berry's contact with the Defence Committee, *Time
Out* reporter Crispin Aubrey and I visited Berry for a three-hour
conversation on 18 February 1977. Immediately thereafter, we were
arrested, and charged later with offences under Section 2 of the

OSA. Although we were arrested by the Special Branch of the Metropolitan Police, it is clear that they were acting only in their accustomed role as fetchers and carriers for the secret agencies who lack police powers[8]; either MI5 or the security and intelligence overlords, the Cabinet Office's Joint Intelligence Staff.

Following the arrests, we went successively through a preliminary hearing (committal) and a long trial at the Old Bailey. Although the facts of the case were well reported, there were a number of important events of a political rather than judicial character.

One of the first, and most significant, was the exercise by the Labour administration of the powers of oversight and veto which they possessed. Although the Home Secretary could (and, reportedly, did) claim to have been caught unawares by the precipitate action of the security services in making arrests, the reverse was true of the Attorney General Samuel Silkin, whose written consent is statutorily necessary for any OSA trial to proceed. At this stage, therefore, the Labour government, through its law officer, had the opportunity to fulfil its promises to reform the OSA, by acting accordingly in the circumstances of the case. A veto on prosecution would also necessarily have served as a rebuke to the security services and as notice to rearrange their priorities.

No such veto was applied. Despite the instinctive distrust of the security services felt and indeed often expressed by many in the Labour Party, the political appointees have historically lacked any ability or will to manage them effectively. This had been clear in the same administration from a costly earlier débâcle when fourteen pacifists campaigning on behalf of the British Withdrawal from Northern Ireland Campaign had unsuccessfully been accused of conspiracy and incitement to disaffection under another notorious political statute. In our case, the Attorney General not only sanctioned the continuation of charges under Section 2, but permitted extensive and far more serious charges under the 'espionage' Section 1 of the Act. In all, nine charges were eventually brought; in the end, all the Section 1 charges were dismissed without going before a jury, and we were convicted on one Section 2 charge each, largely on a legalistic basis.

The Attorney General had later to defend his conduct in the forum of the Parliamentary Labour Party; he did so without allowing debate, spoke mostly bluster, but did tacitly acknowlege that he had been led up the garden path about the significance of the information involved in the case. He had allowed himself to be used as a patsy for the security services to try to rearrange the law of official secrecy to their choosing. Several initiatives from that quarter had become apparent during the case.

The charges under Section 1 of the OSA had normally previously been confined to cases of espionage. However, the wording of the law, in alleging for example that Berry provided 'for a purpose prejudicial to the safety or interests of the state ... information which might be useful to an enemy', is enormously flexible. Although the statute is clearly capable of extensive use for repressing political dissent, its implications have generally gone unnoticed by both libertarian and socialist groups. The requirement of a 'purpose prejudicial' to the state is almost invariably deemed to be the case in the circumstances of an arrest, and the accused has to prove his or her innocence; the 'information' concerned need not, unlike Section 2, be official or classified information obtained from a state employee; and the 'enemy' may be 'external or internal, potential or actual'. Like any similar repressive political legislation, it can only be successfully applied when the state can legitimate such activities, usually with reference to a popularly perceived threat, such as an 'internal ... potential ... enemy'. For this reason, the Section 1 charges in the ABC case wholly failed, as there was no involvement in the case of any subversive or terrorist group or foreign power. A related initiative under Section 1 *had* succeeded in 1963 against Committee of 100 activists who planned to sit down on a US Air Force nuclear bomber base. Their planned protest against nuclear weapons was held to be sabotage, and prison sentences were imposed after conviction of a Section 1 offence.

The ABC case did therefore reveal the intentions of the state security agencies towards the use of such political laws. In the end the initiatives failed, because there was no perceivable threat associated with ABC, whether a revolutionary organization or a foreign connection, and because the only consequences of a single conversation between two journalists and a soldier were hard to view as a dangerous event. (Compare for example the case of the Angry Brigade, where revolutionary anarchists were accused of a series of bomb explosions which *had* taken place.) ABC also benefited from the demystification resulting from the naming of 'Colonel B', and the consequent ridicule.

One of the new twists in official secrecy introduced in the ABC case was related, historically, to the Committee of 100 and the disarmament movement. The *Spies for Peace* exposure of the secret civil defence plans for nuclear war ('Regional Seats of Government') gave fire to the 1963 Aldermaston demonstration and has since created a steady interest in the state's 'home defence' equipment and installations. A major product of this interest was a book published in 1970, Peter Laurie's *Beneath The City Streets*,[9] which examined in some detail the nature of civil defence, and in particular deduced a great deal of useful information from open official sources, especially by observation. Major preparations by the state for internal or external warfare—and especially some of the arrangements made for emergency communications—proved amenable to analysis by detailed observation. Although *Beneath The City Streets* was a rather apolitical, journalistic tract, it attracted considerable attention on the libertarian left. It satisfactorily proved the thesis that 'civil defence is about the preservation of government' (the state) and not for offering succour to war survivors. Latterly, this point of view has been extended both in a revision of the same book, and elsewhere[10] to a discussion of the counter-insurgency and counter-revolutionary preparations of the British state. After the Irish experience—interpreted as classic colonial counter-insurgency brought back home—more attention was paid to military and other defensive preparations being made within Britain for a 'strong state'—required to enforce a reduction of democracy in a time of capitalist crisis. In 1972, the partial resurrection of civil defence with a new brief for 'peacetime emergencies' and crises of various sorts, provided satisfactory evidence for this view. Since then, military 'anti-terrorist' and counter-insurgency exercises have considerably increased in number and scope.

Following Laurie's book, I conducted considerable research into the secret provisions made for the 'strong state'; in particular the communications systems and the secret purposes of the Post Office network of radio towers. This material was seized together with all my papers during a Special Branch raid on my home immediately after our arrests. When the Attorney General allowed the OSA charges to proceed against us, this material was examined closely, and a charge of 'collecting information concerning defence communications … which might be of use to an enemy' was alleged against me.

I have explained at some length the background of the researches which formed this 'collection' charge. If I do not do so, the political significance of the charge and the evidence presented would be difficult to interpret coherently. For the evidence produced was a mishmash of files, photographs, cuttings and maps—it was clear that the security authorities had no clear idea what the research was leading to; they had however formed a very clear view that it was a threat to the state.

To this end they constructed their case very simply. A Major-General, in charge of defence communications, viewed a selection of the material and vouched his 'professional opinion' that it might be 'directly useful to an enemy'. Very simply then, the elements of a new political offence were created. It was sufficient to possess information, of itself neither illegal, improperly obtained, official or even secret, if it constituted a 'collection' or 'jigsaw' from which an incomplete picture of 'secret' activities could be assembled. Since agents of a hostile power can safely do this exercise at their leisure, the offence here resides in the political idea which motivates such research.

When the ABC case came to trial this charge in fact collapsed very quickly and embarrassingly. Since the prosecution, as mentioned above, lacked the legitimation which could be provided by the existence of a subversive or hostile threat, the presentation of their evidence rapidly became ridiculous. The information I had gathered, dealt with piecemeal, was of course readily available in public. As witness after witness conceded this point, the prosecution rapidly lost any sense of purpose. Well before the critical witnesses appeared, or the fundamental nature of the charge was argued out in court, the state withdrew its evidence.

The 'collection' or 'jigsaw puzzle' charge was a sideshow from the main course of the trial, although it was the most advanced (and disastrous) new twist in political law-making introduced during the case, and its political implications remain severe. But the remaining eight charges which we faced continued for some time into the trial; all were concerned solely with the interview we had held. In the course of the interview, which had been tape-recorded by Aubrey, Berry talked about his army life, joining army Intelligence, subsequent disillusionment, and later politicization. Between 1966 and 1970 he had worked at a Sigint (Signals Intelligence, i.e. electronic monitoring) establishment of some size and importance in Cyprus, monitoring Middle Eastern communications for Anglo-American intelligence[11]. During the conversation he discussed what he could recall of the work he had done, revealing little in the way of secret information that was not already known to those interested in the subject. The only contentious point to emerge (and which was revealed during the trial) was the apparent exchange of intelligence reports with SAVAK, the notorious secret police of Iran, arranged through the American agencies.

The significance of his remarks was not in their factual content but in the fact of his speaking at all, renouncing vows of (literally) 'indoctrination' which he and his comrades had had to take, over and above the normal provisions of secrecy. The indoctrination procedure was a necessary preliminary before being granted 'the need to know' about the Sigint organization and its activities.

Berry was, and intended to be, a whistleblower, and to encourage others to do so when their own consciences told them to speak out in the public interest. He did so specifically in the context of the repressive activities of the US intelligence agencies revealed during and after Watergate, and in the hope of making a positive contribution to the defence of Agee and Hosenball. The whistle-blowing tradition has not hitherto been culturally recognized or applauded in Britain. There always have been and always will be 'leaks' from within the state apparatus, both principled and self-seeking. There have also been British whistleblowers who have aired and exposed other matters in less sensitive areas, albeit braving the Official Secrets Acts to do so. The most noteworthy recent example was a former senior civil servant in the Environment department who quite boldly invited prosecution for the publications of a book revealing the disobedience of the department to government instructions.[12]

To find a real parallel to John Berry, however, it is once again necessary to go back twenty years to the nuclear disarmament movement. Two students who had worked during a period of national service in British naval Sigint revealed in a magazine how many of the frequent cross-border disputes and incidents during the Cold War were the result of Western provocation deliberately engineered. Prosecuted under Section 2, both received short prison sentences. We were left in no doubt at the end of the day that encouraging 'whistleblowing' by others whose consciences left them uneasy was the almost only subversive aspect left in the whole affair. Sentencing John Berry to a six-month suspended prison sentence, for giving information to us, the trial judge stated: 'the law will not tolerate … whistleblowers from our intelligence services who seek the assistance of press or other media to publish secrets'. (For our part Aubrey and I were given conditional discharges—in effect no penalty and no conviction, subject to review were we to commit a criminal offence during a two-year period.)

Here was notice that, although most of the prosecution had failed dramatically, the state institutions were determined to ensure that whistleblowing was not to become part of the British political tradition.

The course of the case against us in respect of the Berry interview was marked by many unusual measures—ostensibly required for and justified by 'security', in actuality simple and crude techniques to whip up prejudice. A transcript of our conversation was analysed by military intelligence experts, and at a preliminary hearing of the case, we heard the evidence of the anonymous 'Colonel B'. The anonymity of this witness proved to be a most inept move. It was ordered by the intelligence authorities who for long have regarded any request for information on their activities, even arising in the liberal democratic forum, as inherently naive and subversive. Colonel Johnstone ('B') had been the administrative head of British Army Sigint, and pronounced that the material revealed by John Berry contained secret and top secret information and that its disclosure could cause 'exceptionally grave ... damage' to the national interest. Later, forensically and legally, we destroyed this evidence almost totally. But that narrative belongs to the lore of the Bar rather than here. Some important political points do arise, however.

Forceful arguments were advanced and readily accepted for Johnstone's anonymity. When journalists on two magazines which had been prominent in supporting the ABC Defence Campaign, *Peace News* and the *Leveller,* revealed his name they were prosecuted, in the end unsuccessfully, for contempt of court. Significantly however, the revealing of the name did no harm whatsoever to the national interest, although it clearly damaged the credibility of the prosecution. When the case finally reached the Old Bailey for trial in September 1978, the prosecution indicated that they would need another, new, expert witness to extend Colonel Johnstone's no longer anonymous evidence. The person concerned, one of the Directors of GCHQ, was inevitably an even more secret figure, whose evidence could only be heard entirely *in camera* and whose identity needed to be masked as 'Mr C'!

It was a simpleminded, if Kafkaesque, extension of the ruse of 'Colonel B'. This time, however, Mr C was never to be seen. As the prosecution drew to its finale, the court decided that the bringing of the Section 1 'spying' charges was 'oppressive in the circumstances' of the case; in a round rebuke to Labour's Attorney, the judge had the prosecution withdraw, leaving only the three Section 2 charges on which we were eventually convicted.

Colonel Johnstone and his evidence gave a novel insight into the security and intelligence high command. Their operations and arguments were justified within a closed set of concepts which explicitly embraced a design for Anglo-American world hegemony, and an authoritarian internal model of the requirements of national security which allowed little challenge of *dictat* from above. John-stone found the very idea of even liberal democratic scrutiny or of interest in intelligence activities hardly comprehensible. He was unfamiliar even with the ready model of ministerial accountability to parliamentary democracy which normally serves civil servants and policemen as legitimation for their tasks.

Since the activities on which John Berry was engaged do not directly bear on internal repression in Britain or in other countries, the arguments about their political significance are not brief. I have tried to deal with them elsewhere.[13].

Public reaction at the end of the trial was almost exclusively concerned with the embarrassment of the Labour government, and it was anticipated that the Attorney General would have to justify his actions at length. (He had previously been shielded by the application of *sub judice* rules.) He did so only unwillingly and unhelpfully. It was also anticipated that pressure would mount for urgent reform of the OSA, at the very least.

There was no censure from the press or even the trial judge for the activities of the two journalists, myself and Aubrey. Berry's position was more equivocal but hardly unsatisfactory. To that extent, and despite our convictions, we regard the verdicts of the case as a victory.

We also had, we learned, the support of many of the jury that had convicted us. Four of them later apologized and explained the course of their decisions. The jury's views are important because they are the ultimate safeguard against a repressive regime and a vital product of libertarian radical tradition. The jury which convicted us had its sympathies firmly against the provisions of the Official Secrets Act. But they were unable on this occasion to escape from the immense authority which was impressed on them by the circumstances of Court 1 at the Old Bailey. In an almost satirical irony, the fundamental working-class sympathies of most of the members (to acquit) were overruled by the liberal instincts of a fore-man whose young middle-class university-educated background most closely resembled that of two of the defendants (myself and Aubrey).

This was the jury of the second trial. We had already had an abortive first trial, which had been stopped after the publication of details of our unsuccessful attempts to remove the foreman of *that* jury. The defence had discovered at the start of the first trial that potential jurors had been vetted through police and Special Branch files, 'for loyalty'. All the names on the jury list had been secretly made available six weeks early to the prosecution. It then strained coincidence, although coincidence it may be, when it was discovered that the foreman of that jury was a former member of the Special Air Service regiment, and had participated in counter-insurgency campaigns in Ireland and elsewhere. He made little secret of his strong views on the case, and intention to convict.[14]

The ABC case was directly responsible for exposing this practice of jury vetting, and eliciting official disclosures on the nature and previous extent of the practice—generally in the case of political or terrorist trials, or cases of organized crime. Increasing attention by libertarians to the nature of the present jury system, and its preservation and strengthening, is one of the positive gains from the ABC case.[15]

Throughout the case, the ABC Defence Campaign provided vital support, and organized fringe activity and protest to an extent which caused the Attorney General to comment that he had never previously experienced such a 'level of contempt of court'. The Campaign drew its strength mainly from those associated with radical or left journalism, and it did not attract the consistent support, as an issue, of the socialist left. Individual members of the SWP, Labour left and other groups gave strong support, but events such as local campaign meetings tended to be organized by libertarians. The National Union of Journalists gave unfailing and vital support from beginning to end, and twice took the case before the TUC obtaining (on the first occasion) its unanimous condemnation of the charges. Successful initiatives were taken within other unions, particularly those in the public sector, who already keenly appreciated the importance of the issues. The National Council for Civil Liberties organized a number of events around the issue, and has subsequently released studies of Official Secrecy and the jury system.[16] A particularly important question within the NUJ was whether the union should support John Berry, a non-member. Arguments about the complementary importance of sources to journalism won the point, which was vital to the solidarity of both the individual defendants and political campaigning on the issue as a whole.

An inviting trap, when recounting the history of the case, is to fall into the Watergate idiom. The *macho* loner journalist and his deep throats take on the Establishment and overthrow it. But Watergate, although it achieved important reforms and changes, some fundamental, did not alter the basic power relationships within US society—still less those operating internationally. The same is obviously true of the ABC case. But it did further the awareness of the need to control the secret apparatus of the state.

The most immediate example of this has been Tony Benn's formation of a Labour NEC sub-committee to study the workings of the intelligence services. The committee, however, because of the exigencies of Labour's recent history has not met or reported at the time of writing.

The ABC case served to bolster, and eventually hearten, the libertarian cause. It has drawn attention and concern, as recounted above to matters of the reform of the OSA, 'Freedom of Information', the role of the government's Attorney, the vital importance of independent juries and open justice, without anonymous witnesses and secret hearings. The relationship to traditional socialist concerns is more tenuous. The labour movement continues to rely on basic industrial strength as its ultimate weapon, and is generally insensitive except at times of crisis to the subversive effects of the activities of secret police. Trade union leaders and Labour luminaries still subscribe to the notion of national security, with little, if any appreciation of its inherent requirement that individual civil rights and competing class interests be sacrificed to those of the dominant class. That, almost invariably, is what the 'national interest' is about. If an understanding of that can spread within the Labour movement, it will be a worthwhile ending to our encounter with the secret police.

NOTES

1. Tony Bunyan, *The Political Police in Britain*, Julian Friedman, 1976.
2. *Departmental Committee on Section 2 of the Official Secrets Act 1911*, Chairman Lord Franks, HMSO, 1972. Four vols.
3. Jonathan Aitken, *Officially Secret*, Weidenfield and Nicolson, 1971.
4. Philip Agee, *Inside the Company—A CIA Diary*, Penguin Books, 1975.
5. Victor Marchetti and John Marks, *The CIA and the Cult of Intelligence*, Cape, 1974.
6. Duncan Campbell and Mark Hosenball, 'The Eavesdroppers', *Time Out*, 21 May 1976.
7. Duncan Campbell, 'Hosenball: The Ex-Directory Evidence', *Time Out*, 28 January 1977.
8. Bunyan, *op.cit*, p. 152.
9. Peter Laurie, *Beneath The City Streets*, Penguin Books, 1972.
10. See, for example, Ackroyd *et al*, *The Technology of Political Control*, Penguin Books, 1977.
11. Leslie Chapman, *Your Disobedient Servant*, Chatto and Windus, 1978.
12. For an extended discussion of the British and US Sigint agencies and their political significance, see *The Eavesdroppers*, *op.cit*, and also

Duncan Campbell, 'Threat of the Electronic Spies', *New Statesman*, 2 February 1979.

13. See *New Statesman, op.cit.*

14. An account of the affair of the first jury is given by Anna Coote, 'The Loyal Jury and the Foreman with Firm Opinions', *New Statesman*.

15. National Council for Civil Liberties, *Justice Denied*, NCCL, 1979.

16. *Justice Denied, op. cit* and James Michael, *The Politics of Secrecy*, NCCL, 1979.

THE NINETEEN THIRTIES:
A REVISIONIST HISTORY

Alan Howkins and John Saville

John Stevenson and Chris Cook published in 1977 *The Slump: Society and Politics during the Depression:* a volume whose purpose was to assess what the first chapter headlined as 'Myth and Reality: Britain in the 1930s'. This is how the authors begin:

> Of all periods in recent British history, the thirties have had the worst press. Although the decade can now only be remembered by the middle-aged and the elderly, it retains the all-pervasive image of the 'wasted years' and the 'low dishonest decade'. Even for those who did not live through them, the 1930s are haunted by the spectres of mass unemployment, hunger marches, appeasement, and the rise of fascism at home and abroad.

These sentences preface a text which provides a markedly uneven treatment of the decade, in that it omits much that is relevant to its theme; which is altogether lacking in intellectual rigour; and which, for two young historians of the 1970s, is notably old-fashioned in its approach and techniques. The book, moreover, is a cobbling together of a good deal of material already published, by both authors. The social history chapters for example, which offer the central revisionist thesis of the volume, are no more than an expansion of John Stevenson's chapter in *Crisis and Controversy, Essays in Honour of A. J. P. Taylor* (1976) edited by Alan Sked and Chris Cook. He uses the same quotations and the same sources; if new research has been undertaken, it is not evident. There would therefore be no point to a comment on this present volume were it not for its uncritical reception by some of its reviewers, to whom certain of its elementary points appeared to come as a blinding light of revelation; and also, because the book does raise some questions that need to be taken further.

What apparently came as a surprise to some reviewers was the discovery that the thirties were not a decade of unrelieved gloom,

89

but that for those who remained in work real wages were higher than ever before. These facts, it must be said at once, have been the stock in trade for many years for both economists and historians. C. L. Mowat, in 1955, in *Britain between the Wars,* was fully aware of the position and Sidney Pollard in *The Development of the British Economy 1914-1950* (1962) provided detailed statistical information. And all this before Aldcroft and Richardson began writing. Popular belief, including the understanding of many within the British labour movement, has accepted the mythology of crisis and unrelieved depression; and for these misconceptions socialist historians are no doubt especially to blame. The uneven, but unmistakable upward trend of working-class living standards, during the inter-war years were part of the secular improvement in the material basis of ordinary life characteristic of all mature industrial societies in the twentieth century since 1914; but one must always accept the qualification of unevenness as between different social strata and different social groups within the working class. The causes are well known: among them, the rise in output and productivity; technological change and occupational differentiation, particularly the shift away from wholly unskilled jobs in the manufacturing sector; the emergence of a large tertiary sector—with a large unskilled component; the increase in the propensity to consume; the decline in family size. How much improvement there was in different countries down to the beginning of the Second World War partly depended on the poverty levels and national income *per capita* in earlier periods, partly upon the course of economic change in the inter-war years and not least upon the incidence of world crisis and depression at the end of the 1920s. For Britain between the wars there were factors on both sides of the equation. After 1920 the economy suffered from an 'over commitment' to certain staple export trades in the nineteenth century, with the processes of adaptation to a new world situation being long drawn out and very painful in terms of human costs; hence the depressed areas with their permanently higher than average levels of unemployment. The 1920s saw the economy labouring under the additional burden of an over-valued currency; but after the low point of the slump in 1932 the combination of a housing boom and the growth of the 'new' industries (electrical engineering, motor vehicles, food products and a range of consumer goods marketed through the growing distributive trades) led to a considerable expansion of the economy with its high point in 1937—in which year official unemployment was still above the million mark. There had also taken place a significant

and favourable change in the age structure of the population, with
a now larger proportion in the producing age groups of fifteen to
sixty-four. But it was the dramatic fall in food costs which
contributed most to the improvement in real wages in the thirties,
given the high expenditure on food in relation to total income
among all working-class groups compared with forty years later.

To underline the improvement in real wages and real standards of
living over the 1913 levels requires, however, important qualifica-
tions if we consider the working population as a whole. There are
different measures of this improvement—between ten and fifteen
per cent in the 1930s for those who remained throughout in
full-time work; but it is difficult to be precise about exactly how
many did in fact remain continuously employed. If for example the
earnings of men in work were spread over the whole of the working
population—employed and unemployed—the position in the thirties would compare far less favourably with that of pre-war: the
improvement by 1937 would only be around five per cent. But the
most significant factor—and one which it is very difficult to be at all
precise about—is the much greater seasonality of employment in the
inter-war years. Set aside for the moment the matter of the cyclical
fluctuations in demand for labour, and their consequences; and
recognize that seasonal fluctuations, in the best years, have always
been built into the labour markets of industrial capitalism until the
post-1945 period. The building industry has always known seasonality, as did motor car workers in the years between the wars. The
statistical calculation of the impact of seasonality upon real
standards of living is rarely if ever made. It has been largely ignored,
for example, in the Hobsbawm-Hartwell standard of living debate
for the first half of the nineteenth century, among other reasons
because of the absence of much of the relevant data. What kind of
guesses can be made, for instance, about the largest working group
before 1850, the agricultural labourers, divided between fully
employed workers throughout the year and those on a casual basis,
which could be daily or weekly or sometimes longer but short of an
annual contract? Similarly for the 1930s. Casual, semi-casual,
seasonal work entirely alters the calculations of real wages and real
standards. Building workers, even in the best years, could nearly
always expect at least the equivalent of a month's loss of work
through weather conditions or days lost in changing jobs or
hold-ups of materials. And this in addition to almost all unskilled
workers who are only rarely on permanent contract. As for those not
subject to seasonality of employment in the 1930s, how do we

calculate the improvement in real standards of living as against real wages? A comparison of the average real wage of a skilled engineer in 1913, 1929 and 1937 gives results which have been eagerly seized upon by conservative historians; and of the improvement over time there is no doubt; but by how much? Real wages and real standards of living are different matters. If a skilled engineer was unemployed for three years between 1930-1933, and then remained in work until the outbreak of war, had his standard of living risen by fifteen per cent by 1937-8? It is to be doubted. Jürgen Kuczynski's work on labour conditions has either been rejected, because of ideological bias, or more commonly, ignored; but the questions he asked, and tried to answer in his statistical calculations remain important and significant; and there is here a major area of work for statisticians not crabbed and confined within conservative assumptions.

If we move from an assessment of material standards to the quality of life, the calculations become more complex. As E. P. Thompson wrote:

> ... the term 'standard' leads us from data amenable to statistical measurement (wages or articles of consumption) to those satisfactions which are sometimes described by statisticians as 'imponderables'. From food we are led to homes, from homes to health, from health to family life, and thence to leisure, work-discipline, education and play, intensity of labour, and so on. From standard-of-life we pass to way-of-life. But the two are not the same. The first is a measurement of quantities: the second a description (and sometimes an evaluation) of qualities ...
>
> It is quite possible for statistical averages and human experiences to run in opposite directions. A *per capita* increase in quantitative factors may take place at the same time as a great qualitative disturbance in people's way of life, traditional relationships, and sanctions. People may consume more goods and become less happy or less free at the same time ...
>
> (*The Making of the English Working Class*
> Penguin, 1968, pp. 230-1.)

A question of human experiences. Thus, to give one example from the 1930s, many of the car workers in the inter-war years—in one of the growth industries—were migrants from South Wales and other depressed areas. They left behind them family relationships and a way of life, a culture, which was not to be reproduced in their new environment. They also left behind unemployment; but like their forefathers in the 1830s, and the comparison is not far-fetched, they moved into a situation of social alienation. The Welsh migrated to Oxford and Slough: despised by the local inhabitants, they lived in social isolation in lodgings until they developed their ghetto communities. In work they moved into factories which were almost always non-unionized, often on piece rates and the conveyor belt. Arthur Exell was a young twenty-year-old Welshman who went to become a car worker in Oxford. His experiences have been published in *History Workshop* (Autumn 1978):

> Mr. Kendrick was the top man for all the factory and he was the most hated man of all. He was *terrible* to work under, but we were frightened of him, and he was the boss of the factory. If you were one minute late in the morning he would send you back home ... I remember what happened once to Dickie Yates. He lived at Burford, which is about twenty miles away. And one day he got a puncture. He rode his bike all the way—even though it had a flat tyre—and there was Mr. Kenrick standing. He said, 'Look Mr Kendrick, I had a puncture, I couldn't do it.' 'Have another two days off to mend it' said Mr. Kendrick. That's the sort of pig of a man he was ...
>
> I remember one day I had completed my five radiators, just before the first hour was up. The inspector tapped the badge with his knuckles and shouted over to me, 'Exell, all your cows have calved', which meant the enamel of the cow had chipped out. This meant I had to take them all apart and rebuild them. The badges chipped very easily if you screwed them too tight, and would spin around if not tight enough. One man put cochineal in where the red had chipped; he was found out and got three day's suspension. Because we were only allowed to work the number of hours specified for the job, I earned no money that day and when I got home to my digs I just sat down and cried. Things were very hard.
>
> (pp. 53, 73)

Arthur Exell as a unit in calculations of statisticians belongs to the positive side of the standard of living equation in the 1930s, for all the material indices in his Oxford situation would show an improvement on those of an unemployed young worker in South Wales; but then, there is no good statistical measure by which to assess, in imaginative as well as rigorous fashion, a bullying foreman with seigneurial rights of hiring and firing; and in the absence of imagination and rigour, let us pass on the other side, holding firmly our pocket calculators, determined always to ignore all but the facts that Gradgrind himself would have recognized.

*

The old-fashioned character of the work under discussion is surprising. Women, for example, are subsumed under the discussion of men, and among many omissions Margery Spring Rice's volume, one of the important sources for women's condition, is not mentioned either in the text or the bibliography. Its absence fits the general approach. This is a book about an economic catastrophe which affected millions of working-class people. Their experiences have been written down in many places and in the past decade oral historians have begun to recover the tone, the feeling, the sentiment of life in the depression. But not in the Stevenson and Cook volume where the evidence is almost entirely based upon outside observers and where the poor are nowhere to be heard. Their voice is subjective; some things of what they are now saying about the past may be the product of forty years living with myth and illusion; but their testimony has a power and resonance which historians must assess and evaluate and which cannot be ignored, as it is ignored here.

It is not, however, only for its many lacunae that this volume is so unsatisfactory. The use of evidence is too selective, often dubious and sometimes wholly wrong and misleading. It is, in the final analysis, the authors' scholarship which is in doubt. Here are a few examples. The first is taken from chapter five headed 'The Impact of Unemployment' which on its second page (p. 75) offers a critical contemporary quotation from a leading conservative historian, Arthur Bryant, on Orwell's *Road to Wigan Pier*. Bryant dismissed Orwell's account as propaganda. 'Thus', say our authors, 'even for contemporaries, the picture was by no means clear. The true impact of unemployment upon social conditions was often obscured by the more emotive and committed writings on the subject.' The contrary is the case. For the majority of middle-class contemporaries, certainly the majority of those who had access to the media—even more for those who owned the media—the position was all too clear: the unemployed were deemed to be work-shy, the dole was the scrounger's charter, those who worried about the poor were soft-centred do-gooders. We hear these opinions again today, in the 1970s; but never in the volume or with the absolute certainty of the middle and upper classes of forty years ago. Historians who can write 'even for contemporaries' are not just naive: they have clearly failed to appreciate the range of opinion, to say nothing of the tone, of their chosen period. Nor is the reader helped by the ·slippery method of selective quotation. Dr M'Gonigle, for instance, was a well known medical authority who produced what became a famous report on the differential mortality between the employed and the unemployed in the early 1930s in Stockton-on-Tees; and the results were true for the standardized death rates as well as the crude. Our authors continue (p. 79):

> This result, however, was based upon a relatively small sample and not all commentators were prepared to accept its validity.

Now the reference to this sentence could be expected to reveal a source critical of the M'Gonigle results. It was in fact to G. D. H. and Margaret Cole's *The Condition of Britain*, published in 1937. On p. 95, under the heading 'Death Rates in Different Areas' there is a discussion, among other work, of M'Gonigle's researches, and after stating the results of the crude death rates analysis, they comment:

> These results, though they are based on quite small investiga-tions, are of real significance.

and after noting the revised figures based upon standardized death rates (that is, allowing for the age and sex composition of the employed and unemployed groups) the Coles add (p. 98):

> It is greatly to be regretted that many more investigations of this sort have not been made. The Stockton results are not put forward as yielding conclusions liekly to be valid for the whole of the unemployed, for many unemployed persons have been out of work continuously only for short periods. Nevertheless what is true of Stockton may well be typical of a considerable section of those families whose breadwinners have been out of work continuously or nearly so for a stretch of years; and this question of the incidence of mortality among the families of the chronical-ly unemployed especially deserves fuller study at the present time.

This is not quite what Stevenson and Cook told us, and the way in which they misleadingly summarize a careful argument is typical of their approach.

There are several political chapters, mostly of a psephological character, the work, we assume, of Chris Cook. In the first of these, 'Labour and the Working Class; the General Election of 1931', it is argued that the common belief of the catastrophic defeat of Labour being the result of the defection of MacDonald and his senior colleagues, is wrong. 1931 was not apparently a Red scare: the electoral defeat of the Labour Party was the inevitable consequence of first the general disillusionment of the voters with the record of the 1929-31 Labour Government, there having already been a series of by election defeats to underline the argument; and second, there was a desertion of the Liberal vote to the Conservative Party. There is some truth in both points, but typically of this volume, it is not the whole truth and indeed this sort of argument is fallacious in terms of an explanation of the landslide that occurred. Certainly the Labour Government had a miserable record, and the Labour Party would have lost any future general election, even without abnormal circumstances. But the situation was not normal from August 1931 until the polling day of 27 October. The break up of the Labour Government, the formation of a National Coalition and the appeal to the country at the end of October were parts of a political crisis that involved a pattern of misrepresentations, lies and abuse already well tried out in the previous coupon election of 1918 and the Zinoviev letter election of 1924. The Conservative vote in 1931 rose by over three millions; the Liberals' fell by nearly three millions. The Labour Party dropped by two millions, their seats falling from 287 in 1929 to 46. It was a landslide victory for the National Government which had an enormous majority of 497 seats, with the Conservatives alone having 472 seats. But it was not, according to the authors, a panic election, and in three short paragraphs they exorcise the panic theory (pp. 101-2). Their last paragraph reads:

> The whole assumption of a panic election has rightly been disputed. Bassett, for example, cites a comment from the *Manchester Guardian* of 29 October to the effect that 'it has been a remarkably quiet election' and though there were some reports of rowdyism these were very much isolated incidents.

It is typical that no page reference is given for this comment by Reg Bassett from his *1931: Political Crisis,* published in 1958. It will be found on p. 312 at the end of a short quotation from the *Manchester Guardian* which puts the 'remarkably quiet election' into a very different context from that suggested by Stevenson and Cook. Here are the three sentences from the *Manchester Guardian* quoted by Bassett:

> There is agreement that it was panic, but the panic had not

manifested itself beforehand in any open way. There had been no turbulent terror, none of the exasperation of temper in which panic often makes itself manifest. It has been a remarkably quiet election.

There was, in fact, a good deal of rowdiness on both sides, as Mowat noted; but elections in general became steadily less noisy and rowdy as the twentieth century moved along; and compared with most elections prior to 1914, that of 1931 was relatively quiet. But a landslide has to be explained with the shift of the Liberal vote on a massive scale to be analysed; and as Mowat again emphasised: 'The most powerful weapon against the Labour Party was fear' (p. 410) to which Philip Snowden and MacDonald made their considerable contributions. The former's famous speech 'Bolshevism run mad' —not mentioned by Stevenson and Cook—and the Post Office scare were important ingredients in the development of a desperate mood which swept the electorate into its remarkable support for the Conservative Party and the National Government.

*

One of the ways in which any political analysis of the 1930s must be judged is the approach and attitude towards the Communist Party, and more generally, towards the radicalization of sections of the British people during the decade. An adequate political sociology of British Communism has yet to be written, and whoever publishes it need not read this present volume for enlightenment. 'The typical recruit of the mid-1930s tended to be young, middle-class and attracted by the appeal of the Left' they write. But this is incorrect. It is true, of course, that one of the social components of the radicalization of the 1930s were university students, an important minority of whom joined the Communist Party. But to suggest that the radicalized student was the 'typical' recruit of the 1930s is to exhibit a wilful ignorance of social and political trends. The misconception is on a par with the common exaggeration of the part played by a coterie of radical poets around or associated with Auden; or the equally common failure to appreciate that the overwhelming majority of Britishers who joined the International Brigade were working class. John Cornford, Ralph Fox *et al* were tragic deaths of enormously gifted individuals; but it was the solid working-class core of the Brigade, many experienced militants among them, who suffered the main losses. But to return for a moment to the 'typical' recruit of the 1930s: precise data are not yet available, but we do know the social groups from whom recruits must have come in relatively greater numbers than from the population at large. The miners of South Wales and Scotland, for example, and the metal workers of the Manchester region and London. Busmen in both London and the provinces; print workers in London and possibly elsewhere. And there are some defined groups besides the students who were radicalized. The Jewish community is an obvious example, and here we must include the Jewish middle class as well as the working class. There was always in Britain, going back to the 1880s, a radical trend among Jewish people in Britain; but the coming of fascism in Germany encouraged a much wider participation of Jews in the anti-fascist movement; and undoubtedly in areas such as the East End of London, or Leeds or Manchester, there was a significant accession of Jews to the Communist Party.

The Communist contribution to the political and intellectual history of the 1930s was considerable. Inevitably, Stevenson and Cook do not understand the problem, brought up as they have been in a very traditional style of historical research to which A. J. P. Taylor has contributed a great deal. The interconnections and interrelationships to be made demand an imaginative perception which Taylor, for one, deliberately eschews; and yet there can be no serious attempt at understanding without a willingness to interview, carefully and patiently, the historical record. It is, however, not just the cultural and intellectual record; there are many hard facts to be established of many different kinds.

One such fact is the attendance at political meetings. In his 1976 essay Stevenson discussed the significance of the Hunger Marches in the 1930s; and almost word for word the argument is repeated in this present volume under consideration. Briefly the argument is (a) the unemployed were only effectively organized by the National Unemployed Worker's Movement, whose leader was the Communist Wal Hannington; and Communists formed the majority of the leadership throughout—agreed; (b) the unemployed in the 1930s were not 'disposed to become revolutionary' and (c) the great majority of demonstrations against unemployment were quite small affairs. The demonstrations and hunger marches organized by the NUWM 'achieved very little and soon faded into obscurity' (p. 194).

These last two points demand a more detailed analysis than can be given here. We are dealing, not with intangibles, but with phenomena that are certainly difficult to be precise about. The testimony that contemporaries were impressed or influenced by the national hunger marches—the Jarrow March excluded—is not examined by Stevenson and Cook, not least because they never consider how public opinion is formed or altered. In the case of the hunger marches, it is necessary to begin with the reactions of the labour movement in its industrial and political sections; and to chart the remarkable change in sympathy and support for the NUWM's marches between 1932 and 1934. In the latter year the local support for the marchers was considerable, and by 1936 this had reached the top levels of the movement, especially within the Labour Party. The London Trades Council officially backed the 1936 march, and at the demonstration in Hyde Park on 8 November 1936 a very large number of people gathered in Hyde Park to welcome the marchers. On the platforms, among Communist speakers, were Clem Attlee, Nye Bevan, Ellen Wilkinson and Edith Summerskill. It was raining most of the time, but everyone who was there thought it was a very large turn out; and so did most of the Press. Stevenson and Cook quote the police estimate at about 12,000, taken from the Metropolitan Police files in the Public Record Office. They continue: 'It was an impressive gathering, at which the NUWM attracted far more support from the Labour Party than ever before' (p. 189), but on the following page, when pursuing their argument that support for the Hunger Marches was really quite small and much exaggerated at the time and by later commentators, they quote the police figure of 12,000 without qualification. This is what Stevenson had already done in his article of 1976.

There are several matters here that require comment. First, we are given no evidence from the Press or contemporary accounts to support the 12,000 figure. Second, and most important, why should police reports be accepted as good reliable evidence? Stevenson thinks they can be. In his 1976 article Stevenson wrote of these police statistics: 'These figures appear reliable, coming from police records intended solely for internal circulation' (p. 100). A somewhat naive statement for any historian to make, it might be thought. It is rather like believing the accuracy of Sir Nevile Henderson's despatches from Berlin when he was ambassador to Nazi Germany. After all, his defeatist words were not intended for publication, but like the police statements, they were solely for internal consumption. This uncritical acceptance of police records and statistics, however, seems to be not uncommon these days; Skidelsky's biography of Oswald Mosley for example quotes internal police memoranda at length (in the chapter headed 'The Campaign in East London'). To have access to police records is of great value to the historian; but to accept them at face value, without check and counter check, is to abrogate the methods and techniques associated with serious historical research.

*

The debate on the 1930s in going to arouse much discussion, and socialist historians must not be absent from the controversies. What we need first of all is a much more detailed analysis of working-class living standards in all their complexities. We need as a first requirement to be able to quantify our results. How many?—is the central question that has to be answered when considering any statement about improvement or deterioration. There are immensely more data available than for the standard of living debate of the first half of the nineteenth century, and it is going to be possible to be fairly definite and precise about the material statistics of the argument. What socialist historians must not do is to allow the discussion to stop there. We are required to talk about attitudes, ways of life, social alienation and to present the whole man and the whole woman in the context of family life and class: and we must on no account allow ourselves to be bemused by those to whom the calculating machine and the computer offer substitutes for historical imagination.

SOCIALIST POLITICS AND THE
'CRISIS OF MARXISM'*

Elmar Altvater and Otto Kallscheuer

1. *'THE CRISIS OF MARXISM HAS ERUPTED AT LAST!'*

With this provocative challenge at the conference on 'Power and
Opposition in Post-Revolutionary Societies' organized by *Il Manifesto* during the Venice Biennale of November 1977 *(Il Manifesto,*
Quaderno 8, 1978), Louis Althusser introduced a wide-ranging
discussion which is documented in all essentials in the present
volume. In so far as it would be wrong to see this 'crisis of Marxism'
simply as a left-wing variant of the general decline of values in
late-bourgeois society—a kind of dance on the sinking *Titanic*—then
it must itself be explained, or indeed explain itself, in terms of the
material conditions of politics and the formulation of theory.
Althusser was quite right, therefore, when he continued his intervention: 'At last the crisis of Marxism has visibly surfaced, and at last
something new and living can be liberated in the crisis and out of
it!'

The contributions published in this volume are responses to
Althusser's intervention. When set against the discussion on Marxist
theory that has taken place in the Federal Republic, and is still
taking place today, particularly the discussion on the theory of the
state and its political implications, these responses do provide us
with the possibility of reflecting on the Italian debate from the
results of our own debates.

Marxism in the 'Opposition Culture'

The need for a reflection of this kind arises from the fact that the
discussion on the state among the West German left seems to have

* This text is a somewhat shortened version of the Introduction to the
German edition of *Discutere lo Stato,* a series of articles which first appeared
in *Il Manifesto* between April and September 1978, and which was
subsequently published in book form by De Donato, Bari, in late 1978. The
German edition is published by Verlag Aesthetik und Kommunikation
(West Berlin).

ended up in a blind alley. The differing approaches to an analysis of the form and activity of the bourgeois state have each been developed to a point at which a change of level and perspective seems the only way of escaping from merely philological exercises of the kind that so frequently fizzle out in senseless polemics. Analyses of the limits of the welfare state or of state intervention were of major importance in the phase of prosperity after 1968, when the bourgeois state was assumed, not only in general consciousness, but also in Marxist theory, to have an almost unlimited capacity to manipulate trends of social development and handle their contradictions. Habermas saw modern state intervention as giving the possibility of overcoming economic crises, even though the price of such intervention was a decline in legitimation. It followed from this that the interest of the state in reform could be viewed as having a basis of its own, so that only minimal attention was consequently paid to the contradictions resulting from the system of capital accumulation. Finally, in the theories of state monopoly capitalism, the idea prevailed of the state being able to steer society in the interest of the monopolies, with the burdens involved in the securing of monopoly profits being shifted onto the non-monopoly strata and the working class. These assumptions as to the role of state intervention typical of the highly developed capitalist societies ('late capitalism' or 'state monopoly capitalism') deserved a fundamental critique, and the Marxist discussion on the 'derivation of the state' devoted itself to this task,. State theory thus came to be understood primarily as the analysis of the limits of the state, this in turn providing its political significance, as was shown above all by the broad reception that the state theory of Blanke, Jürgens and Kastendiek enjoyed among the Young Socialists and the SPD (and of course among the new left as well). In these circles, of course, the limits of the state's system and activity could provide ammunition for a criticism and struggle against both the government policy of the Social-Democrats and the illusory position of the 'Stamokap' (state monopoly capitalism) tendency. In the theoretical context of the late 1960s and early 1970s, the discussion on the derivation of the state was essentially destructive, in the sense of a critique of ideology.

This destructive character rested on the fact that the West German left which produced theories of the state, and gave them an astonishingly broad currency, at least in the universities, had no political responsibility and hence did not need any positive conception of politics. To use a concept developed in a different context—one of a quite different 'order of magnitude'—as a reason for the crisis of policy affecting the Italian Communist Party, this discussion on the state developed completely within the 'opposition culture', i.e., in an attitude of opposition to the prevailing system, and was never forced even to begin to confront the requirements of a 'governing culture' (Duso, 1978, on the PCI). The relations of political power in the Federal Republic have not permitted anything else. But this position of exclusion from the system of political power was hardly understood within the West German left after 1967 as something negative, being rather interpreted as an advance made against the integration tendencies of the bourgeois state (the 'social state'). The rise of the student movement, followed by the extra-parliamentary opposition (APO), appeared to confirm a theoretical view in which the new political subject had to be discovered outside the domain of the existing political system. West German Marxism accordingly developed exclusively within the anti-institutional opposition, and to a large extent bore the marks of this fact. The Marxian thesis of *Capital* as the 'most fearsome missile ever slung at the heads of the bourgeoisie' was translated into the slogan of a 'struggle against bourgeois science', at least in the universities. It is not our task in the present essay to demonstrate the undoubted subtleties of Marxist debate with bourgeois science that were sometimes concealed behind this rather vapid slogan, and we only want to stress how this Marxism, as a science of the forms of bourgeois socialization in the Federal Republic, found its characteristic limitation in the political fact that it never reflected any effort to escape from the 'opposition culture' into the 'governing culture' (and by this we do not mean simply in the sense of a parliamentary shift). As long as the opposition movement was on the rise, this hardly seemed a weakness. But once the opposition fragmented into tiny grouplets, tendencies and factions, and received some hard blows from the repressive power of the state (*Berufsverbot*, anti-terrorist legislation, proscriptions, etc.), it was inevitable that West German Marxism should come into crisis.

A second relevant aspect to be borne in mind here makes Marxist theory, including its theory of the state, appear 'economically reductionist'. In the crisis of the mid 1970s, experience confirmed what had already been partly established by theory, i.e., that bourgeois rule does not 'collapse' with economic crisis, so that there are necessarily domains, institutions, relationships and mechanisms in bourgeois societies which produce a social hegemony of the bourgeois class going beyond the securing of its rule that results from economic reproduction. The 'reconstruction of the critique of political economy' in West Germany applied itself first and foremost to the theory of the economic reproduction of bourgeois society, and subsequently either referred its theory of the state to this or even derived it from it. This gave rise, however, to several kinds of reduction, since those aspects involved in the securing of bourgeois rule that could not be subsumed under the concept of 'mystifications' simply remained outside the field of vision. In this way Marxism suffered a loss of plausibility, and had to yield ground to psychologizing and totalizing theories of power, or to political theories which, while opposed to 'bourgeois science',♦ were also divorced from the 'critique of political economy'. In general, this amounted to a 'subjectivist turn', as against the intended objectivism of Marxism. These two interconnected reasons, together with the dimensions reached by the 'academization' of Marxism (cf. Blanke, 1979), are what cause us to speak of a 'crisis of Marxism' in the Federal Republic, too, and to reflect on this via the discussion that has taken place in other countries. This reflection, however, means ascertaining the different conditions of policy formulation and theoretical tradition that obtain in the countries concerned. Whereas in West Germany Marxists also discuss the question of a 'translation' of economic developments and political structures into social action, i.e., cautious attempts are made under the prevailing conditions of political power to set foot in the established political system (and this is only true, moreover, for one wing of the left, another wing preferring to withdraw into the 'opposition culture' in the form of an alternative subculture), the Italian workers' movement today faces the question of the limits that have so far prevented it 'translating' its political strength into a change in relations of social power and model of economic development, the question of the economic and social developments that undermine a stabilization of its political strength (cf. Donolo, 1978).

The 'crisis of Marxism' today, therefore, does not indicate simply a theoretical incapacity (cf. Blanke, 1979)—there has always been this factor, without it creating any 'crisis'—but rather a crisis of working-class policy in those Western countries with a strong Marxist workers' movement, which must be clearly distinguished from the situation in the Federal Republic with its principally academic left. It is in no way paradoxical that the crisis of capitalism and the crisis of Marxism have broken out simultaneously in the mid 1970s. For it is precisely the traditional models of theory and strategy that have become obsolete, through the requirements of social transformation, or better: this obsolescence is threatening, and can no longer be dismissed. The set of problems that has to be considered anew does not include only the theory of the state that is under discussion here, but also the theory of classes. For with 'new social subjects', the traditional alliances that are suggested by a class theory focused on the working class are also put in question. Ultimately, even such general categories as that of social progress based on the development of the productive forces must be reconsidered afresh in the light of the destructive and even life-endangering effect of modern technology (e.g., nuclear power). Theoretical deficiencies of this kind find their expression in politics. Is it possible, for example, to whitewash the great defeat of the French (and West European) left in March 1978, a defeat resulting from the self-induced collapse of the Union of the Left, with the old triumphalist rhetoric, or to overcome it by a separation of the PCF from other Socialist forces? Is it possible to overlook the problems that the PCI has had in relation to state power after its electoral victory of June 1976? Do we not also have to see the (repressively supported) consolidation of a reformist Social-Democratic regime in the Federal Republic of Germany, in the face of the Marxist offensive with its critique of reformism, as a sign of the 'crisis of Marxism', and a challenge to new efforts in theory and political strategy? And does not the development in the countries of 'actually existing socialism' give sufficient occasion for the Western left to reconsider its ideas about socialism and its attitude towards basic 'bourgeois' liberties? Has not the drifting of isolated left-wing grouplets into the sphere of terrorism produced evil consequences for Marxism, as well as for Marxists? And last but not least, we should not forget in this enumeration of the aspects of the crisis, the precarious position of academic Marxism and its representatives in the universities today.

But this is a long enough list. The central theme of the contributions in this volume is Althusser's thesis, as expressed in Venice and later developed in reply to Rossanda's questions, that the present crisis of Marxism is essentially attributable to the fact that Marx did not elaborate any theory of the state. In contrast to his theory of the economic reproduction of bourgeois society, as developed in *Capital,* there is no corresponding theory of the state, of the politically mediated framework of domination under capitalism. This 'gap', or 'blind spot', is then responsible for the way in which the traditional ideas of the overcoming of capitalism and the transition to a 'higher' social formation appear inadequate. We shall go on to see, in the course of our present discussion, that the contention implies a specific conception of Marxist theory, i.e., that there are two distinct modes of approach, or logics, for the economic and the political. In the West German 'reconstruction of the critique of political economy,' however, it was always taken for granted that the state could precisely be 'derived' as a further development of the systemic logic of Marx's critique of political economy. We are thus faced with two differing conceptions of Marxian theory, each able to criticize the other. Critique, however, in no way necessarily means crisis, so that the cause of the crisis must rather be sought in the problems of strategy.

A Contradiction between Party and Social Movement?

That the 'crisis of Marxism' is not simply a theoretical crisis is shown by the fact that the major working-class parties, and not least among them the PCI, are experiencing a crisis of identity, affecting their membership, their voters, the political self-conception of their intellectuals and their responsible leading groups (cf. Kallscheuer, Rafalski and Wenzel, 1978). In the course of the crisis, social movements have developed outside the traditional organizations of the workers' movement, in part even against these organizations; and these new movements radically question both the traditional form of working-class politics and its organization in the trade union and party. The political party is fundamentally criticized as a form of political organization expressing a specialization of politics and the separation between different spheres of human reproduction. Thus it is not just the particular present line of the party that is at issue, but the actual form of the party as such. This history of the workers' movement shows a permanent critique of this kind, from the anarchists, via the council communists in their opposition to the Leninist party, through to the students', women's and youth movements of today. This time, however, the critique is a mass one, with a mass influence, and presents both an opportunity and a great danger: the danger of a split between the traditional workers' movement with its organizations, and the *movimento,* so that the workers' parties may come to find themselves, once more, as the Social-Democrats have long done, in the realm of state power, while the *movimento* breaks up into a plethora of groups and grouplets that are incapable of action and devoid of further perspective, but still able to represent their interests at the corporate level, so that they can be manipulated in the political system as a subject, either in a meaningless or an actually regressive fashion.

This possible danger lies at the root of Althusser's arguments, when he warns the Communist party against getting transformed into a governing party. There could then be a split between those within the state apparatus and those remaining outside of it, yet unorganized and devoid of perspective—a split that could lead to defeat. Formulae such as the 'entry of the masses into the state', interpreted as meaning that the Communist party should make policy in the field of the state are no solution for the contradictory relation between party and masses in the present crisis. And we have now arrived at a further aspect that is made responsible for the 'crisis of Marxism', i.e., the problem of the establishment and reproduction of political power, which has up till now been inadequately conceived.

Do We Lack a Theory of Political Power?

The categories of power and the state are not of course identical. Any 'theory of power', however, is dependent on the conception of the state, and vice versa. On this subject, there are very differing conceptions, ranging between the view that political power is completely dependent on the conditions of economic reproduction ('orthodoxy'), and the view that the development of political power is determined not by economic law but rather by political 'will' and the political organization of class blocs ('revisionism'). Position in this spectrum also determines the view taken of the state, its form, character, functions and the barriers to its intervention. In his early writings (e.g., *The German Ideology*), Marx conceived the state as expressing the duplication of bourgeois society into society and state. This dual relation of state and society, however, is not confined to Marxism and post-Marxian theories, but also underlies the bourgeois idea of the *Rechtsstaat:* the state as a separate institutional system, linked to society through law and hence guaranteeing a state-free space for free exchange between citizens. In this way, legal ideology is constructed, though—as against Althusser's conception—this is in fact not only ideology but also repression, providing in addition the institutional framework for the processes of circulation (i.e., commodity exchange, circulation of capital, relations between classes, labour market), and today ever more the framework also for processes of production (enterprise constitution, economic planning, and all kinds of preventive legislation). According to the conservative doctrine of constitutional law (cf. for example Forsthoff, 1971), this dual relationship should be maintained, and disrupted neither by the 'statification of society' (in the sense of authoritarian relations) nor by the 'socialization of the state' (in the sense of its 'corporative' use by 'group interest').

The thesis can now be put forward that this same dualism is precisely reproduced in traditional Marxism, with the state being understood only as something negative, i.e., as counterposed to society and its classes and hence as only of instrumental use. (Nor is Althusser completely free of this idea.) Bobbio is thus partly right in reproaching Marxists for having developed only the idea of how to conquer and smash the state (Third International), or alternatively of how to use it instrumentally for reform (Social-Democracy). This concept, which takes concrete form on the one hand in the dictatorship of the proletariat as the negation of the bourgeois state (hence without the positive achievements of civil liberties, for example), on the other hand as a fetishism of the democratic form of the state (hence without any vision of the regressive and authoritarian tendencies immanent within it), is neither analytically nor politically apposite to the 'modern state'. The distinction made by Gramsci, and in recent years widely accepted, between *società politica* (as the state in the narrow sense, the apparatus of state power), and *società civile* (as the system of state institutions that 'extends' into society, together with the para-state formations and non-state or rather privately organized institutions of reproduction of class hegemony), has led to an overcoming of this fatal dualism being at least attempted, as also has the concept of the 'expanded state' *(stato allargato)*, the form of which has undergone changes in the process of capitalist development, that a series of authors in this volume place in the centre of their discussions. This negatively defined sense also involves a shift in the concept of the political. Colletti (1979) criticizes this concept of the state for its inability to develop any theory of the political, something that again has fatal consequences for working-class strategy. According to traditional Marxism, the withering away of the state also means the withering away of politics, or at least that politics is reduced to the mere 'administration of things'. This simplification, however, is extremely dangerous for strategies of transition, as is shown by developments in the post-revolutionary societies. Even if the justificaton of this charge is not contested, however, it is still possible to draw different theoretical conclusions.

The problem of power, however, is not so easily settled. In Marx himself, for example, we find (particularly in *Capital* Volume 1, chapter 23), the first approaches to a theory of the reproduction of social power, when Marx states that the worker reproduces by his labour both the material conditions of society and the capital relation, i.e., the economically mediated power of the capitalist class. In the revisionism debate, and expressly for example in the controversy over the 'political wage', the question was the extent to which the organization of the immediate producers (in party and trade union) could establish a countervailing power, thus invalidating politically the laws of capitalist reproduction. In this perspective, power was understood simply as a quantitative complex concentrated at two poles, its 'balance of forces' being responsible for the outcome of the struggle between the complexes of class power. How many justifications for a mistaken or even catastrophic policy in the history of the workers' movement have subsequently been based on an 'unfavourable balance of forces'! In this way, there is no understanding of power as a 'capillary' system (cf. the 'molecular diffusion of politics'—De Giovanni), based on complicated mechanisms of economic policy, social and psychological mechanisms. The power that actually 'passes through us', and is reproduced in the institutions of both 'political' and 'social' society, demands reflections on the forms of politics, and political solutions to both these and to the organization of political action, that go beyond the antithesis between 'power' and 'economic law'.

But the problem is not yet exhausted. For with respect to social power, the question also arises as to the political institutions that limit power, i.e., political freedom, democracy and pluralism. All these concepts have been abominably treated in the history of bourgeois society, with the result that they sound hollow and false. But assurances that only under socialism will 'true' democracy be established, 'material' freedoms guaranteed and the 'genuinely' plural development of interests be possible, have lost their credibility with Stalinism, with conditions in the 'Peoples' Democracies' after the Second World War and most recently since 1968 (the invasion of Czechoslovakia and the defeat of 'socialism with a human face'). Even the belief that socialism at least ensures the preservation of peace has been proved untenable by China's 'punitive expedition' against Vietnam. Along with the re-evaluation of 'actually existing socialism' that has thus become necessary (as undertaken by Bahro, 1977), we also require a new definition of the relationship of the left to the 'bourgeois' institutions of freedom, democracy and pluralism, and hence a new definition, too, of the revolutionary road, which can no longer be simply described as the dictatorship of the proletariat (quite apart from the difference in class structure between the Soviet Union of Lenin's time and the developed capitalist countries of today). Thus the elimination of this concept from the programme of the PCF (the PCI had already not used it for a long while) does not just mean an opportunist adaptation, but rather corresponds to a political necessity.

We can see, therefore, that the 'crisis of Marxism' is in no way simply a theoretical crisis. Quite independent of the changes in the political tasks facing the left in the present crisis, theoretical development would anyway have advanced via a process of reciprocal critique. The sharpening of the crisis of Marxism is a result of the social crisis, which requires the elaboration of theoretically based strategic responses. The opportunity given by this crisis, and this is what Althusser had in mind with his challenging intervention at Venice, is that the crisis, more than the critique, can lead to a productive new development of theory in the direction of an improved understanding of the reproduction of the conditions of domination in bourgeois societies, and how this can be overcome by the workers' movement.

2. HISTORICAL PREMISES AND POLITICAL NODAL POINTS OF THE MARXIST THEORY OF THE STATE IN WEST GERMANY AND ITALY

In the first section, we attempted to indicate the political implications of the discussion of the 'crisis of Marxism', particularly for the Italian left. It was already apparent here to what extent any approach to the theoretical problem areas of the Marxist conception of the state is marked by historical premises. This is particularly true of the question under debate here as to the relationship between democracy and socialism, which—as N. Bobbio quite rightly maintains in his summary of the polemic between Communists and Socialists over 'Marxism and the state'—necessarily leads to the question of 'which socialism?' (Bobbio, 1976).

The PCI as Part of the Italian Political System

The first of these premises lies in the fact that in Italy the workers' movement has become a decisive element of the political system within the 'rules of the game' of parliamentary democracy—though in no way as a simple result of these rules—yet without abandoning its anti-capitalist goals. Secondly, this development was only possible on the precondition (necessary but not sufficient) that the movement of the Italian working class had accepted the democratic freedoms as an integral component of its definition of socialism. These two premises, the political strength of the Italian workers' movement and its democratic culture, cannot be divorced from the specific tradition of Italian communism, beginning already with the 'translation' that the Leninist conceptions of the party and politics underwent for the capitalist West at the hands of Antonio Gramsci (Telò, 1976), though this only became historically effective after 1956, in the 'Italian road to socialism', i.e., in the new definition of the PCI's politics and identity made by Palmiro Togliatti and others—1956 being the year of crisis for both the world Communist movement and for the strategy of the Italian Communists (see Ingrao, 1977, pp. 101-76).

From the 8th party congress in 1956, at the latest, the political practice of the PCI was determined both by a positive (i.e., no longer purely 'tactical') relationship to republican and parliamentary institutions, and also by an active and autonomous mass work by the 'new party' within social conflicts and areas of alliance (see Priester, 1977b). The PCI was also able, in contrast to the French Communist Party, for example, to accept into its institutional strategy from the late 1960s onward the working-class movement of 1968-9 and certain basic aspects of the 'cultural revolutionary' movement and the other new mass movements based on grass-roots democracy. This makes it possible for the Communist A. Asor-Rosa (1977, p. 20), to describe his party as 'at the same time the most authentic heir of the reformism of the Second International ... and the most authentic heir of the Leninist tradition in Italy'. The fact that 1977, the same year that the integration of the PCI into the political system was officially completed by its passage into the government majority, also saw a crisis of identity, for the party and for Communist mass culture, is what gives the 'crisis of Marxism' its historically specific and party-political character in Italy.

Whereas in the West German debate on the state, the question of political democracy remains analytically in the background, being treated at most in terms of a critique of ideology or as the functional equivalent of 'simple circulation', an 'abstract surface' of the overall capitalist process, this is the decisive starting-point for the Italian debate. All this, of course, is impossible to understand without the historical background of the Italian workers' movement, its mass anti-fascist and democratic tradition, the role of the PCI in the founding of the parliamentary republic and its strategy of the Italian road to socialism. In this respect, the present set of problems facing the Italian workers' movement has certain similarities to the situation of the Social-Democratic parties of Germany or Austria after the First World War (as pointed out in Italy by Marramao (1977, 1978) and Rusconi (1977), among others).

The working class see the republic as their work, they are the agent of this form of state, which would have been impossible without their passionate support and defence ... It is not the democratic state that now appears to the workers as an obstacle, but rather social influences, and mental influences dependent on these. Their attitude towards the state is therefore a new one.

These words of Rudolf Hilferding, in introducing the journal *Die Gesellschaft* (1924, p. 13), can also serve to characterize the approach of the PCI theorists in particular, though not them alone. The question therefore is how, under the conditions of political democracy, the 'factors of social power' (Bauer, 1920, pp. 345 ff.) of the organized working class can be developed in the direction of a growing 'hegemony' of the working class, and in what relationship to this 'hegemony' the 'autonomy' of new social movements can develop. Both old and new left in Italy are today in broad agreement as to these questions, though they differ in the responses that they give.

Three Central Questions

We shall now introduce three key points, which also indicate certain 'nerve centres' of the Italian political system. The order in which we introduce these questions—leading from the immediate (party-) political problem through to the question of the overall social dynamic—is also characteristic of the political approach to the problem area of the state in the Italian left.

1. What is the significance of the integration of the Italian Communists into their country's political system, as deliberately pursued from their collaboration on the Constitution, in particular after 1956, and now advanced to a new level, as from 20 June 1976, with the formula of the 'entry of the workers' movement into the state'?

—Does it mean a democratization (at least potentially) of the Italian state, a broadening of democratic space, progress in the direction of a ' democratic socialism, as many PCI theorists maintain?

—Or does it imply (the danger of) a de-democratization of the workers' movement, i.e., the first step towards a new 'corporate and authoritarian' state? (Cf. Frederico Stame, 1977, Danilo Zolo, 1978.)

—Alternatively again, is it the expression of a regressive mastery of the social crisis? (Donolo, 1979.)

While the Italian Socialists may well have cultivated the fear of a new 'regime' arising from the direct agreement between Christian Democrats and Communists out of party-political reasons (cf. again Stame 1978), the theorists of the new left represented in this volume rather proceed largely from the danger that the policy pursued by the PCI since 1976 will lead to a weakening of the 'factors of social power' of the working class, and thus indirectly pave the way for a complete restoration of the 'DC regime' which has by no means been broken as the centrepiece of Italian state power, in the way that a creeping defeat of the workers' movement can often prepare the ground for a direct defeat.

2. What is the relationship between the organized workers' movement and the new movements of social liberation, and to what extent is this relationship changed by the 'entry of the workers' movement into the state'?

—Is an 'organic' (and organized) relationship between them needed, as the PCI maintains, so as to prevent the 'marginalization' and destruction of autonomous anti-capitalist conflict potentials and movements?

—Or is a 'separation between state power and collective needs' (Melucci, 1978, p. 17) necessary, so that the liberal freedoms and free space for the development of social movements have now to be defended also against the class parties of the workers' movement?

The concluding contribution to this volume by Rossana Rossanda shows the way in which the axis of the theoretical discussion has shifted under the impact of the political development itself: how the 'hegemonial' optimism of the PCI within the state power has come up against the 'wall' (De Giovanni) of the socio-economic limitations of the existing system, in addition to the political resistance of the Christian Democrats.

In this way, however, the entire horizon of debate is shifted. Without abandoning an iota of the positive value of political democracy for the workers' movement, or of the positive regard for individual and collective liberties (as well as for movements of social liberation), these theoretical parameters are sufficient neither to determine the space of action available to the workers' movement and other 'collective movements', nor to analyse the specific developmental logic of democratic systems in developed capitalist societies—the dangers of an 'involution of democracy'. (It is precisely against the background of these questions that Italian Communists are today making a new theoretical study of the historic collapse of German Social-Democracy in the Weimar period

(Rusconi, 1977; Marramao, 1978; cf. also Blanke, 1978).) The final question, then, is:

3. How is the relationship between social movements and political system evolving in the conditions of economic crisis? Indications of a change in Italy are visible,

—in the shift of emphasis in the PCI strategy from 'historical compromise' to 'austerity' (Berlinguer, 1977; cf. below, section 4), which has been described by a trade unionist independent of the left as the supplementing of political strategy by a 'social philosophy': 'the line of broad agreement at the political level thus found its justification, and not merely a tactical one, in a social package at the level of production' (Lettieri, 1978, p. 7);

—in the crisis of the capacity of the social movements to affect the political system (Donolo, 1978; Melucci, 1978);

—in the growing difficulties of the trade union movement, among other things in the crisis of the factory councils (Trentin, 1978a, 1978b).

These processes find differing theoretical explanations in the Italian discussions. Yet there is a certain common ground shared by the Italian Marxists, which we shall briefly indicate here before dealing with the particular theoretical 'schools'. Almost all the contributions to this volume assume, in discussing Western capitalism since the 1920s, a relationship between economics and politics that has been changed by state intervention into the economic process, and assume also a transformed relationship between the masses and the social institutions. The concept of the 'expanded state' embraces both aspects (see section 4 below). The analysis of the 'change in the form of crisis' (Marramao) thus implies the controversial question as to whether this 'expanded state' is now itself in crisis (through the failure of economic interventionism and the democratizing attempts of the organized masses who have 'entered into the state'), or whether the social and political opposition movements are themselves brought into the crisis through the mechanisms of the 'expanded' presence of the state in society, being 'corporatized' and deprived of their system-changing dynamic. Naturally, these two responses are not mutually exclusive (for the first, see Minucci, 1979, for the second, Zolo, 1978).

3. THEORETICAL APPROACHES TO THE ANALYSIS OF THE BOURGEOIS STATE

Althusser's formulation of the problem

Before we go on to indicate some of the various strands in the Italian discussion of the state, we must refer briefly to Althusser's position, his works having enjoyed a wide reception and discussion in Italy (as also in the Anglo-Saxon and Scandinavian countries) since the early 1960s, in complete contrast to West Germany (see the detailed *Dossier,* 1973). For the echo that the theses of Althusser find throughout the Italian left is understandable only against the background of the role that his works have played in the Italian debates on Marxist theory for the last fifteen years, these having quite pertinently been described as a 'new orthodoxy' (Rovatti, 1974; cf. also Rancière, 1975). In February 1968, for example, the PCI's daily paper already published an interview with the French philosopher (see Althusser, 1968, pp. 203 ff.) by its then Paris correspondent, M.-A. Macciochi, which is moreover well worth reading as a contrast to his contribution in the present volume.

This quite striking distinction—broad discussion already of the first (and best!) works of Althusser's (1969, 1970) in Italy, as opposed to their almost complete neglect in the West German Marxist debate—has very diverse reasons, including those of theoretical history (see Kallscheuer, 1974). It can be at least partly explained, however, in terms of the political problem facing a non-Stalinist Communist theorist after the Twentieth Congress of the CPSU, i.e., in the years of a 'de-Stalinization' that was substantially delayed in the PCF, as opposed to the PCI. Althusser's purpose at this time (the early 1960s) was to remain a Communist in theory, and to do so on a double front: both against the dogmatic doctrinal edifice of domination of Stalinist 'dialectical materialism', and in opposition to the 'humanist' philosophical tendencies that prevailed in that section of the French left intelligentsia who had ceased their collaboration with the PCF after the crushing of the Hungarian uprising (and the justification of this action by the PCF): an existentialist (Sartre) or phenomenological (Merleau-Ponty) inter-pretation of Marx. In his quest for a sure basis for Marxist theory and politics, a quest which set an example for many French Communists of this time, Althusser was seeking an epistemological foundation for Marxism, linking up with certain traditions in French philosophy of science, and with elements of structural linguistics and ethnology, and leading to a new and (in part justifiably) scholastic Marxist conceptual vocabulary in the French universities (which all had a strong influence on Marxist discussion in Italy). In certain of its aspects, therefore, Althusser's theoretical approach in the 1960s was comparable to the concern of a section of the West German left after the student movement with a 'reconstruc-tion of the critique of political economy'—though with the basic distinction that in the Federal Republic both positive and negative theoretical reference points were quite different: the Frankfurt school, the Marxism of Lukács and Kòrsch, etc. Althusser attempted the epistemological renovation of 'Marxism-Leninism' via a theoretical critique of Stalinism, hoping by the same argument to dispatch the French existentialist and phenomenological philosophy oriented to subjective 'lived' experience by stressing the scientifically 'objective' character of historical materialism as a 'theoretical anti-humanism' (Althusser, 1969, pp. 229 ff.). Later, after May 1968, Althusser criticized in particular the epistemological aspects of his earlier works as 'theoreticist'. Yet this in no way meant that he had abandoned his 'neo-Leninist orthodoxy' (as Giuseppe Vacca describes it in this volume). On the contrary, his fastidious epistemological arguments were rather poorly replaced by a supposed 'new practice of philosophy' (as immediate political intervention) founded on borrowings from Lenin's *Materialism and Empirio-Criticism*.

Almost all the writers represented here have already engaged in intensive debate with the Althusserian school in the past. (See Luporini, 1967; Vacca, 1968; De Giovanni, 1970, pp. 7 ff. and 46 ff.; De Giovanni, 1976, pp. 243 ff.; Rovatti, 1974; Zolo, 1976, pp. 105ff.) And it is against this background that we must understand how provocative it is for precisely Althusser, formerly one of the chief representatives of a 'scientific Marxism' (with the stress on science!) now to come forward to proclaim the crisis of Marxism. It is precisely this 'pope of theory' who today proclaims that the political crisis of the workers' movement has its underlying cause in a crisis of theory. Danilo Zolo draws attention to the fact that the final result of Althusser's critical overcoming of Marxist orthodoxy is simply that he makes such 'central components of classical Marxist-Leninist doctrine' as the 'conquest' of state power, the 'withering away of the state', the 'dictatorship of the proletariat', etc., rise again like a phoenix from the ashes of the crisis of Marxism. Biagio de Giovanni and Giacomo Marramao see in Althusser's demand for a *'movimento'* politics quite outside of the state, and his definition of the revolutionary party as 'anti-state', a continuation of the Third International's theory of revolution, which frontally counterposed 'the class' to the state to be 'smashed', and thus remained theoretically blind and politically incapable of action in the face of the new dimensions of politics in the 1920s and 1930s.

A Radically Opposed Theoretical Position: Cesare Luporini

The discussion of the state in West Germany has also sought to go beyond the traditional solutions to the base-superstructure problem. It has however proceeded quite differently in this than Althusser, which also helps explain why, in contrast to literary theory, for example, Althusser's reconstruction of historical materialism has not played any role for the theory of the state in West German Marxism. The basic category of the West German debate was the 'duplication of society into society and state', which the so-called analysis of form was designed to delineate conceptually, so as to develop theoretically step by step at least the 'general concept' of the political structures of those societies which were conceived as capitalist on the basis of the economic determinations.

This premise, however, of going beyond the traditional schema of base and superstructure so as to reconstruct theoretically the relationship of society and state according to a unitary logic, has recently been challenged by an Italian Marxist philosopher, in the contribution that Cesare Luporini presented to the most recent Gramsci Congress, intended also as a response to the Althusserian diagnosis of the crisis of Marxism. (Luporini, 1977, 1978; see also the articles by Luporini and Rossanda in the present volume.) His theses deserve a brief summary here, as they clearly show also the specificity of Italian Marxism in the tradition of Antonio Gramsci.

In Luporini's view, Marx operated with two parallel conceptual registers in his analysis of capitalist society, which are not theoretically integrated even in his mature works.

—The first conceptual pair, *economic base* and *superstructure*, underlies Marx's theoretical analysis in *Capital*. Here we find a theoretical conceptualization designed to analyse the economic forms, the forms of law and the form of politics (of class struggle), but no conceptual basis for the analysis of the state (as was implicitly assumed in the West German 'derivation' discussion).

—In Marx's political writings, on the other hand, a second conceptual pair prevails that is older than historical materialism: *civil society* [*bürgerliche Gesellschaft*] and *political state*. This pair is in no way identical with the former. (*Capital,* as the analysis of the economic structure, is an analysis of the 'anatomy of civil society', not the depiction of civil society itself.)

The 'theoretical paradox', then, according to Luporini, is that no integration of the two conceptual pairs is possible, by virtue of their logical heterogeneity. In *Capital* the concept of 'civil society' vanishes, being incongruent with the conceptual framework of that analysis. With it, too, vanishes any explicit thematic reference to the state. True, law and politics are both organically present in *Capital*, but in the field of politics—the class struggle—we do not find the state as a theoretical concept. In *Capital,* a theoretical conceptualization of the state is in fact prevented and blocked.

In the theoretical model of *Capital,* the capitalist mode of production has to function 'of itself'. There is no theoretical concept expressing the fact that the bourgeoisie needs the 'political state' and its development into the 'modern state', i.e., an extra-economic compulsion, in order not only to establish its class domination, but also to maintain and reproduce it (Luporini, 1978, p. 44).

Law as a form of social organization, and politics (the form of 'class behaviour' for both bourgeoisie and working class) can be conceived in *Capital* in terms of the 'economic base' for the precise reason that in radical contrast to all previous forms, the ensuring of social reproduction is no longer the task of specific social organizations (such as tradition, custom, law, political compulsion), but rather of the economic mechanism itself: the valorization of capital. Thus the economic mechanism is *eo ipso* also a social mechanism, without being directly visible in the social characters that it presents ('economic mystification'). In the form of social reproduction specific to the capitalist mode of production, extra-economic compulsion is replaced by economic compulsion and legal relations (Luporini, 1978, pp. 37-40).

Marx and Gramsci

No direct 'translation' of the Italian debate on the state into the terms of the German debate on the derivation of the state is thus possible, for reasons of method. In their attempt to explain the 'duplication of society into society and state', the West Germans focused (to put it schematically) on the relationship between economics and politics. The Italian Marxists, on the other hand, operate with the relationship between *società civile* and state. The Gramscian concept of *società civile,* however, as Bobbio (1967) has shown in particular, is not identical with the Marxian concept of *'bürgerliche Gesellschaft'* (cf. Priester, 1977a): 'Between the economic structure and the state with its legislation and compulsion, there is the *società civile'* (Gramsci, 1975, p. 1253). Here Gramsci partly adopts the Hegelian concept of *'bürgerliche Gesellschaft',* which in a certain respect is broader than the sense given the term by Marx and Engels, in as much as for Hegel it not only embraces the economic relations and class structure, but also the judicial system and the organization of administration and associations (i.e., subjects that traditionally fall into the sphere of constitutional law). 'For Hegel, *"bürgerliche Gesellschaft"* includes the sphere of economic relations and their external regulation according to the principles of the liberal state, thus combining bourgeois society and bourgeois state. It is this concept that Hegel uses for his critique of political economy and his critique of the science of politics ... ' (Bobbio, 1967, p. 25).

In Gramsci's own analysis of the 'expanded state', the Marxian critique of political economy is supplemented by elements of an analysis of social institutions *(società civile)*, and of the state functions which adapt the *società civile* to the changed economic structure. It is only against this theoretical tradition that we can understand the majority of contributions to the problem of the state by Italian Marxists (especially the PCI theorists).

The theoretical 'expansion' of the concept of the state by Gramsci must thus be seen in connection with a real historical development, which has changed in the West the relationship between economic mechanism and political institutions. Through the 'organic' presence of the state in the process of accumulation, we have had a 'diffusion of the superstructure into the base', while at the same time the comprehensive re-combinations of the economic and social process in the 1920s and 1930s had profoundly changed the relationship between masses and institutions, leading to new forms of the 'expanded' presence of the state in the *'società civile'*.

The varying theoretical emphases that differentiate the PCI theorists on the state are also connected with their specific political interpretations of the present Italian historical situation—more precisely, of the phase between the parliamentary elections of 1976 and the entry of the Italian Communists into the government majority. The 'neo-Gramscian' tendency, for example (e.g., Vacca, De Giovanni, Gerratana, Ingrao; see their contributions to the Gramsci Congress of 1978), taking up the Gramscian conception of hegemony as well as his conception of the 'historic bloc', see in the present political phase an 'entry of the masses into the state', bringing with it a 'political re-combination of the entire social body' as well as a 're-combination of technique and politics' in the representative organs of the Italian republic, in administration and the sphere of reproduction (Vacca, 1977, cf. Kallscheuer, Rafalski and Wenzel, 1978). This tendency, however, is itself differentiated, according to whether greater emphasis is placed on the primacy of politics (Vacca, De Giovanni), i.e., among other things the consensus between the democratic parties, or alternatively on the need for a socialization of politics (Ingrao, Trentin), requiring not just the parties, but also the autonomy of the trade unions and other forms of grass-roots democracy and participation.

The 'Centrality of the Workers' and the 'Autonomy of the Political'

A quite different theoretical approach to the question of the modern state, with a corresponding political approach to the relationship between the workers' movement and the institutions, is to be found in the theorists of the so-called 'autonomy of the political', in particular Mario Tronti, Alberto Asor-Rosa and Massimo Cacciari. Since this analytical approach, and in particular its normative implications for PCI politics, is directly or indirectly referred to in several contributions to this volume, though none of this tendency's representatives took a direct part in the debate organized by *Il Manifesto*, a few short comments are again required. (See Napolitano and others, 1978.) While the majority of contributions collected in this volume refer to the Gramscian theoretical tradition, the theorists of the 'autonomy of the political' come from a quite different tradition in Italian Marxism, the 'workerist' attempts, linked with the journals *Quaderni Rossi, Classe operaia* and *Contropiano*, to give Marxist social theory a new foundation as a 'workers' science', involving also a new reading of the history of the workers' movement as a 'class history' (as distinct from an 'organizational history'). This tendency in Italian Marxism has however found only a very belated and abridged reception in West Germany, i.e., in the version of Toni Negri (the former spokesperson of the *Potere Operaio* group) as the 'mass production workers thesis' and the 'plan state theory' (Negri, 1973, 1977), publicised in particular by Karl Heinz Roth (1976). In presenting the theoretical and political hypothesis of the 'autonomy of the political', therefore, we must show at what point in the theoretical development of 'workersism' it emerged, what are its basic methodological assumptions, what concrete problems of the Italian workers' movement it seeks to answer, and what makes for its political emphasis within the spectrum of PCI discussion.

The starting-point of the 'workerist' conception—see in particular the now 'classical' work of Tronti (1974)—was the reversal of the relationship between capital and labour-power, as a theoretical paradigm for the analysis of capitalism, but also as a political programme (cf. the special issue of *Aut...Aut*, 1975). In this way, Marxian theory was 'politicized' in a very direct sense, as is clear from Tronti's definition: 'Labour is the measure of value, because the working class is the condition for capital.' (On the following discussion, see also Cacciari, 1978.) Just as labour-power can be conceived theoretically as the condition for capital, so capitalist development should be interpreted in its totality (its technical, economic and political aspects) as a directly political development, through the movements of the working class. These movements of the working class determine the form of capitalist 'command', the 'government' of capital in the production process and beyond this. 'Factory → Society → State' is thus the theoretical key that the 'workerists' bring to bear on the analysis of capitalist development, and the political path for a 'renovation of the workers' movement' should also be from the factory to society to state power, as prefigured in the 1960s by the movements of the 'mass production workers' of the great factories of northern Italy. The central mediating category between factory and politics was applied in a very reductionist sense, related simply to the immediate relationship between capital and labour in the production process. 'Everything that was not reducible to this level was seen by *operaismo* as functioning as ideology, as a distortion of the class "interest" that proceeded from the immediate relationship of capital and labour', in the self-critical analysis of Cacciari (1978, p. 51).

The further development of this theoretical paradigm led politically in two opposing directions:

The first led from *Potere Operaio* to 'organized autonomy' in which the totality of social relations was seen as the direct expression of capitalist factory despotism ('factory society'), which the 'class autonomy' of the 'mass production workers', and latterly of the 'marginalized' social proletariat, has to confront immediately and quasi-militarily. Politics is thus reduced to direct conflict, to war.

The second path was that taken by the group around the periodical *Contropiano*, leading politically back into the PCI, and theoretically to the conception of the 'autonomy of the political'. Here politics was understood among other things as *mediation*.

The conception of the 'autonomy of the political', amounts to a radical about-turn from the former 'monotheistic conception of capitalist society' upheld by the 'workerists'—the capital relation as motor of capitalist society, and the working class as motor of the capital relation (see Tronti, 1977a, pp. 54 ff.). The development of capitalist society is now separated into two parallel developments, the history of capital (or the history of the workers' movement) on the one hand, and the history of 'the political', of the state or state power, on the other, which in contrast to what Marxism traditionally sees as the foundation of state power (*ibid.*, p. 9), now conceived social classes or relations of production as 'autonomous'. The 'political' in this sense embraces two realities: an objective structure of power, embodied in specialized institutions, and a 'political leadership stratum', the subject of 'policy-making', which develops its own system of mediation, with privileges and dysfunctionalities, *vis-à-vis* the social classes. The history of the working class and capital is the history of Marxism, while the history of 'the political', of the modern state and the 'art of politics' is a quite different history, outside the scope of Marxian theory. Thus at the present moment, when the working class is approaching state power, the theoretical question is to read this history of the modern state anew, beyond the sociology of the two great classes. In practice, the class struggle in this field of the political presupposes an 'emancipation of the party from the working class'. The form and content of the 'class combination', the working class and its organization, no longer directly coincide, as they did in classical 'workerism', they are on the contrary completely divided: 'The modern state ... is nothing other than the modern form of the autonomous organization of the working class' (p. 14, see also Tronti, 1978a, 1978b).

This theoretical development of 'workerism' which is at first sight so very striking—from the 'autonomy' of working-class struggle that forces the development of capital, hence producing a revolutionary situation, through to the 'autonomy of the political' *vis-à-vis* both capital and the working class—can be only understood politically against the background of the concrete problems of the Italian workers movement in its present phase.

The first problem, as Asor-Rosa has very clearly expressed it (1978, pp. 197 ff.), lies in the reduced room for manoeuvre that the working class disposes of during the economic crisis. Classical workerism was itself a product of boom conditions, 'in the sense that the acceleration of the accumulation process brought a whole series of working-class struggles that were directed towards checking the newly created profit margins'. But this also 'accompanied and influenced the development of Italian capitalism in the sense that the intensified dynamic of conflict threw the former model of accumulation into crisis and hence forced capital to a renewal and emphasis of its own internal dynamic—in the political aspect as well' (*ibid.*). In the crisis conditions, the balance of forces between capital and labour has been reversed, and the 'centrality' of the working-class struggle itself threatened by this: 'Today the theme of workers' "centrality" is raised in a situation of an evident and far-reaching crisis of capitalist development. We can no longer expect the mechanism of accumulation to start up again automatically, in such a way that working-class struggles will again become as political as they were before. But just as little can we demand that workers' struggles should again simply function as the driving wheel of capitalist development' (p. 197). The centrality of the working class, which no longer comes about 'economistically', must therefore be achieved politically: the classical formula 'Factory $\longrightarrow$ Society $\longrightarrow$ State', 'in which the party provides not a mediation between different social strata ... but rather the element of leadership (or to put it better, one element of leadership), the vector of specific social and class interests in the heart of the state'. The Communist Party thus becomes for Asor-Rosa 'the concrete subject of working-class centrality' (p. 198; a somewhat different emphasis on the party as political 'filter' of the social crisis is given by Tronti, 1978b).

The second concrete problem that underlies the theory of the autonomy of the political lies in the changed composition of the working class itself, which, as a result of a capitalist 'dismantling' of the labour market, has extremely weakened direct trade union industrial action (as this was waged in the 'hot autumn' by the assembly-line workers in the big factories of the north Italian 'industrial triangle'). (See Genth and Altvater, 1977; Accornero, 1978b.) Capital in these sectors reacted to the 'rigidity' of the defence of wages and levels of employment by those workers with strong trade union organization with a so-called 'turn over', the rotation of industrial employees without the creation of new jobs. In parallel with this, a 'secondary sector' of the labour market has developed in the course of the last ten years, alongside the strongly trade-unionized primary sector, as a result of the extreme decentralization of entire branches of production, this secondary sector being characterized by a low level of trade union organization and the absence of a guaranteed basic wage ('precarious work', domestic work, illegal work, seasonal work, under-employment, etc.). Alongside the classical danger of a split between employed and unemployed, there is also in Italy the danger of a split between the 'strong' sector organized in trade unions and the 'weak sector' irregularly employed in the 'dispersed factory' (particularly in central Italy, see Graziani, 1978 and Bagnasco, 1977). This also gives rise within the trade union movement to an attempt to compensate politically for the weakening of the unions' direct powers of struggle, and make up for the 'social centrality' of the working class in large-scale industry that has been put in question, by the 'political centrality' of the PCI in the institutions (see Accornero). The theory of the 'autonomy of the political' provides a theoretical foundation for such a transformation of political structures, leading to a greater emphasis on centralism, though also to a stronger competition of party-political orientations within the trade union movement.

In the words of Mario Tronti:

> There are two conditions for the centrality of the working class to function politically. The first necessity is that the factory workers are surrounded by a large penumbra of social consensus, the second that their effect on the political and their relationship to the institutions remains stable over a long period. It must be made evident and perceptible, with practical actions, that this state must be simultaneously defended and changed. What must be defended are the formal guarantees, the constitutional mechanisms of equilibrium and the significance of the political agreement between the democratic parties. What has to be changed is the significance of power, the functioning of the decision-making mechanisms, the guidance of the economy, and the control, consumption and application of social wealth. (Tronti, 1978a, p. 24.)

As against this understanding of party politics as politics in the institutions, which is gaining strength within the PCI—and thus also against the corresponding subordination of trade union strategy to the space of compromise defined by the political system—the trade union and inner-party criticism is voiced that is is not the party but rather the working class itself that should be the 'concrete political subject' of social change. The 'hegemonial force' of the working class, in this conception, cannot be delegated to a party or institution, or to the state, it must rather be realized by way of 'the instruments that the working class is able to develop historically and combine in a dialectical relationship: one or more parties, trade unions, other forms of participation, whether these are temporary or permanent', which must all be developed in the direction of the 'self-government of the producers' (Trentin, 1979, p. 9).

4. THE INTERVENTIONIST STATE AND SOCIAL CONTRADICTIONS

In its fundamental aspects, this conception of politics as institutional in the realm of the state and 'social' on the part of the various movements, is dependent on the idea of the 'interventionist state', and on the development of political alternatives to the interventions of the bourgeois state directed at maintaining the status quo. The first question to ask, therefore, is that of the reasons for the crisis of the interventionist state, before we go on to deal briefly with the contents of politics, having already discussed the changed forms of politics in the crisis.

Keynesianism as Political Compromise

The modern interventionist state grew up as the result of a social and political compromise, and not simply on the basis of the contradictory tendencies of capital accumulation. Keynesianism can thus be understood as the result of a social and political compromise between the classes. In as much as it promises full employment, it takes into account the interests of the working class. The need for a compromise results from the redistribution effect between the tax burden and the consumption of state expenditures. The distinction between 'right'- and 'left'-wing Keynesianism indicates that the zone of compromise is itself wide enough for different political options to be fought for and carried through. This compromise, however, is not simply the result of the temporary balance of class forces at the time, but is far more complex in its composition. Firstly, it is dependent on the conditions of accumulation. In times of prosperity, it is possible for profits and wages to rise together, with a simultaneous expansion also of state expenditures, i.e., a shift within the zone of compromise in favour of the working class, whereas in time of crisis this is precisely not possible. Compatibility between working-class and capitalist interests is thus dependent on accumulation. Secondly, the particular form of the political system is itself significant for the applicability of Keynesian perspectives. (Cf. in particular Blanke, Jürgens and Kastendiek, 1975, chapter 10.) This is true first of all in a quite trivial sense, i.e., that the political system must itself be rationalized, if it is to react in Keynesian fashion to the demands placed upon it. If the political and social compromise has to be newly reached for each major intervention decision (e.g., between the different clienteles of the political leaders), then it is generally impossible to reach any harmony between the time co-ordinates of economic trends and the modalities of political action and reaction. On top of this, considered from the point of view of the social system as a whole, the political system, as the 'cervello sociale' (social brain), is committed to systemic rationality, though it in no way need itself satisfy the Weberian criterion of formal bureaucratic rationality. Precisely because the state is not a 'plan state' and not institutionally divorced from society (corresponding to the idea of the dual structure which we discussed in the first section), all social contradictions resurface within it as internal bureaucratic contradictions between factions in the administration. The rationalization tendency of the social system is thus not automatically accompanied by an internal rationality of the political system. On the contrary, the difficulties of getting the state authorities to introduce quick and efficient programmes of Keynesian deficit spending are an index of this problem, as are also the ossified programmes of public works in the south of Italy, the famous 'cathedrals in the desert'.

The third point here is the already discussed institutional form of the relationship between masses and power, between participation in the state power and exclusion from it, which now becomes fundamental. The possibility of a 'left', i.e., socially oriented Keynesianism, is greater in a democratic republic than in an authoritarian state, which will tend rather towards a 'right'-wing Keynesianism. How does this state intervention get into crisis, how is this expressed, what consequences result from it, and how does the workers' movement react?

The crisis of the interventionist state is generally due to the contradiction between the rising need for intervention and the limited means available for this. This limit is expressed first of all in the material 'triviality' that revenues are not adequate to meet the needs arising from the functional mechanism of social development. This becomes particularly clear in times of economic crisis, when incomes fall or increase less quickly as a result of unemployment (falling wages), a decline in profits (falling revenue from corporate taxation), etc., while the functional requirements rapidly overtake fiscal capacity: i.e., unemployment benefit and other welfare-state provisions, these being hard-won social rights that can as yet scarcely be revoked, as well as higher subsidiary means of economic incentive (subsidies, etc.). The state taxation system experiences a fiscal crisis (O'Connor, 1974; Grauhan and Hickel, 1978). This can at times be avoided by government borrowing, but there are given economic limits to this, which are today imposed on the national state especially by world market conditions.

A vicious circle thus comes into existence, which is basically responsible for the non-functioning of bourgeois state intervention-ism. Given the requirements of the accumulation process, the political system develops into an interventionist state without the internal structure of the state administration and the political sphere (the expanded state) having been rationalized. It is impossible therefore to establish the preconditions for the satisfaction of functional requirements. As a result of its internal contradictions, which cannot be reduced to nothing, interventionism does not function to maintain or establish the rationality of the social system, and the interventionist state runs aground. Fundamentally, however, this results from the form of the state in bourgeois society as a state based on taxation. The political system cannot itself produce the means of its existence, and must consequently collect these in the form of taxes and government debt. This is a characteristic determined by the system itself, deriving from the fact that capitalist valorization can only take place as private appropriation, and while this can certainly be supported by the state, it can in no way be taken over by it. It also follows, therefore, that the securing of the state's material basis is linked to the accumulation of capital, which is a sure condition for politics having only a limited autonomy. Paradoxically, this is all the more true, the greater are the institutional apparatus of the state and its personnel, and the more comprehensive its potential for ensuring 'political primacy', since the costs of supplying it are correspondingly greater.

The Difficulties of the PCI's Transition Strategy

The functional requirements of a rationalization of the system can thus not be accomplished by way of the primacy of politics. This has precisely been the experience of the highly developed capitalist societies in the present deep economic crisis, since the situation has now arisen in which Keynesianism has been put to the acid test. The direction of retreat is back towards the primacy of economics, the rebirth of neo-classical and neo-liberal doctrines, the stemming of state intervention (which can be particularly clearly seen in the advice of the West German council of experts on economic development) and the abandonment of the social and political compromise which has been the content of Keynesianism. The withdrawal of the state from the economy and its 'surrender' to capital is simultaneously a political and economic attack on the workers' movement, even if certain basic achievements of the welfare state remain in existence.

From the standpoint of the PCI's transition strategy, at least, this situation means an unambiguous defeat. For the adversary is shifting the terrain of political struggle from the political sphere back into the economic, precisely where it is not possible to carry through the policy of 'homogenizing' a society that has been particularly torn apart and divided by the crisis, and instead of the 'great offensive of ideas' (Vacca, 1977, p. 309), the organizations of the workers' movement are compelled to act politically as a 'corporate power' (ibid.), i.e., as a group defending their special interests. (We should indicate here the difference from the Anglo-

Saxon debate on corporatism, which is rather about an orientation to overall interests.) The political offensive of the workers' movement is now blocked by the 'specific economic laws' of 'industrial society', which has to remain competitive on the world market, so that attempts to take over general social responsibility under the sign of the primacy of politics (cf. here the important theoretical investigation of Jaroslawski, 1978) are barred in such a way as to prevent social rationality or a synthesis being established politically by the organization of the workers' movement. In the light of these economically mediated political constraints, the concept of hegemony is itself placed in question, and again Vacca notes how, under these conditions, which aim at a 'contraction in the sphere of working-class hegemony', elements of 'passive revolution' are clearly introduced into the Italian situation (Vacca, 1977, p. 310). By passive revolution, Vacca means here the passive binding of the workers' movement to the state, which it had sought actively to change in the direction of its own rationality, according to the concept of hegemony. The binding of the working class into a tripartite system of state, employers' associations and working-class organizations contains great dangers, particularly when the organizations of the workers' movement—and this is true also for the PCI after the high point of 1976—have lost their offensive dynamic. The inseparable connection between austerity and corporate political structures, as the content of the relationship between economic and politics in the present crisis, raises a problem to which strategic responses must be found, if the working class is not to lose the initiative to the bourgeoisie, i.e., on the question of a solution to the crisis, or to win this back, if it is already lost.

The Need for Alternatives in the Form and Content of Politics

The dual line of attack—authoritarian structuring of government policy, which no longer seeks social and political compromise with the workers' movement, and the release of the economy to market forces—presents the workers' movement with a historic challenge, and will gradually compel the formulation of alternatives to the prevailing policy. A retreat to the anticipated de-legitimizing effect of a social and welfare-preserving opposition movement ('the Achilles heel of late capitalism is not its functional structure, but rather its crisis of legitimation', Zolo, 1978, p. 150; cf. also Ferrajoli and Zolo 1978; Stame, in Berlinguer and Bolaffi 1977; Stame 1979) would be setting its sights too low. It could no more lead to a strategy of transition than could the hope for an 'entry of the masses into the state' effected by the PCI in the form of its participation in government (cf. Barcellona, 1978). A social adaptation to the economic restructuring demanded by the world market, in view of the new division of labour between the 'Third' world and the industrial centres, and especially in the light of the results of the oil price rise (cf. on this the discussion between Chiaromonte, La Malfa, Signorile and Trentin, in *Rinascita* 44, 10 November 1978), may well be achieved (a so-called *'mutamento'*), but not the perspective of a changed and new society (*'transizione',* cf. Donolo, 1977). The danger of a split in Italy between the party and the trade unions, with the party 'going into the state' and functioning as a transmission belt to the working class for hypothetical 'common interests', while the trade unions seek with greater or lesser militancy to promote merely corporate special interests, quite apart from the tendency that new and chiefly corporate operating groups will form and become active outside of the traditional organizations, could have the result that the bourgeois class will succeed in handling the social contradictions by itself and work politically to maintain its own hegemony (in the sense of a *rivoluzione passiva*).

If the 'relations between the process of economic development and the stabilization and legitimization functions of the state' (Stame 1979, p. 11) are not to be settled in the sense of a rationalization and consequent reinforcement of bourgeois domination (as a *rivoluzione passiva*), then the workers' movement cannot abandon the attempt to develop concrete initiatives of changing social relations. Alternatives are thus developed especially against the government's economic policy, which aim not only at a more effective economic policy for overcoming the crisis more rapidly, as well as paying greater attention to its social components (cf. *Memorandum,* 1978), but rather to compel or induce the bourgeoisie, by an appropriate political initiative, to remake the abandoned social and political compromise with the working class and the other subaltern strata. An alternative economic policy in this sense, therefore, while not demanding a revolutionary change in the system, does demand for a start the re-establishing of the status quo that prevailed before the crisis, adjusted to a certain extent for the needs of the time. This already indicates, however, that alternatives of this kind can in no way be designed first and foremost as better instruments of economic policy for re-establishing a lost 'governability', but rather as a political pressure to regain lost positions. These may be expressed economically in the deteriorated position of the working class in the relations of national income distribution but fundamentally the question is one of political action against 'austerity'.

There seem to be two points of departure on this question. The PCI is attempting, with a very fine distinction between 'austerity' (the bourgeois form, which adopts the English term) and *'austerità'* (as its Communist alternative), to find a road (cf. Soriente, 1978) which on the one hand concedes certain economies and restrictions in the gains made by the working class after 1968, but on the other hand demands from the governing Christian Democrats the granting of such reforms as a democratization of the state apparatus, investments in the South with a view to stimulating employment there, reform of taxation and of parliament, etc., with the goal of restricting the monopoly power of the Christian Democrat party. A political formula of this kind, however, no matter how attractive it appears at first sight, has to reckon with the sitting tenant, i.e., the Christian Democrats themselves, and what this means has been tragically shown in Naples where the PCI has held the mayor's position since 1976, and ever since been entangled in a constant war of position with the Christian Democrats, losing political support in the region as a result of its inability to carry through its electoral promises (cf. De Giovanni and others, 1978). On top of this, however, such a line requires the ability to keep in balance a complicated equilibrium between different interests within the working class itself: between those in employment, whose wages and working conditions may well be frozen, the unemployed in both South and North, regional and central interests, etc. A policy of political reforms at the price of economic retreat always hangs ultimately on the alliance between the workers' party (PCI) and the trade unions. Since 1977, this has become more than clear in Italy. The PCI's 'offensive of ideas' has come up against the (justifiably) 'corporate' trade union interests.

Before we come back to the problem that this involves, the second approach should be mentioned, as it is formulated for example in the *Memorandum*. Here, with little attention to projects of political reform, an economic alternative for government revenue and expenditure is formulated against the present economic policy. Taxes should be drawn more from profits, especially monopoly profits, and less from wages, while government spending should be directed less into profits by way of subsidies and contracts, and more to meeting the social needs of the population. Since economic activity is generally reduced in time of crisis and depression, there is also the question of achieving an overall expansion of demand by appropriate government policy. Even if the *Memorandum's* alternative cannot be called Keynesian in the traditional sense, we should not fail to notice that it demands both a stronger regard for the social and political interests of the working class in economic policy, i.e., the re-establishment of the compromise, and also an expansion in the zone of this compromise.

We cannot deal in any comprehensive way here with the key points in the conception of an alternative economic policy in the Federal Republic (cf. on this subject Altvater, Hoffman and Semmler, 1979a, 1979b). Two brief remarks, however, must still be made, which apply also to the conception of an alternative 'austerity', even if the consequences for wages of *'austerità'* and the *Memorandum* are opposed to one another.

Firstly, it is important that the policy proposed and carried through by the government should confront an alternative. But such alternatives alone are not enough, if they remain mere models without a political subject able to implement them. The political subject is not simply the party (PCI) as an organization, or the trade union apparatus, but rather the broad base of the social movement. The point is, therefore, to take up and articulate the demands developed by the mass movements in the phase after 1968, integrating these into a concept of social synthesis without thereby displacing the movements themselves. The Keynesian compromise was agreed between capital (and its political associations) and the organizations of the workers' movement. We believe that it can no longer be established in this way, and that alongside the 'traditional' workers' movement a broad social and political movement has arisen that neither can nor will be brought any more into the Keynesian compromise. (We have attempted to show this in our discussions of the crisis of Marxism.) This is true for the women's movement, and equally so for the movements of young people, students and unemployed. In order to overcome the crisis of working-class strategy, which is what the 'crisis of Marxism' actually indicates, it will prove more necessary than it has been in the past to take account of these 'new' demands, though without abandoning the 'centrality' of the workers' movement. These needs are no longer simply centred on and around the labour process (the demand for jobs, ensuring the conditions of reproduction of labour-power, leisure time, etc.), but rather arise on new paths of political socialization, being no longer unconditionally work-centred (we do not see Badaloni's distinction between productive and unproductive workers, as applied in this connection, as very adequate to the problem; cf. Asor-Rosa, 1978a). The problems that have thus arisen require a solution (cf. also the interview with Trentin 1978a), if alternatives in economic policy or a 'left' austerity are to become really effective.

Secondly, alternatives in economic policy are directed at the state. The state is the central subject of economic policy, and this also has its problems. For in many fields of policy, the state now acts in a compensatory way, but one that is problematic. Given the level of socialization of the reproduction process, the effects of the private sector have ever more ravaging effects on society. This can be seen both in the field of health, and in the ecological effects. The quantitative dynamic of capitalist accumulation does not yield to the qualitative requirements of individual and social life. To stem its course is one goal of the social movements that we mentioned in the previous section. We have still to show here, however, how new approaches for the discussion of alternatives follow from this situation. For it is questionable whether the destructive effects of highly developed capitalist production can still be stemmed or cancelled by a policy of state compensation, or whether the point of application for alternative measures does not need to be sought in a new organization of the production process itself, starting with new technologies that are benign towards workers and their environment, through to new dispositions of (shortened) working hours and changed organization of work, as well as alternative raw materials and products.

In this way we can link up with an antithesis that determines the discussion on the state: the politicization of society or the socialization of politics. Here the fact is expressed that it is already necessary under capitalism (and not just 'after the revolution') to develop approaches for taking the formulation, decision and execution of policy 'back into society'. The alternatives raised by the workers' movement in the present crisis, therefore, which always and necessarily develop as a force against the primacy of economics that the bourgeoisie seeks to reactivate, must consequently aim at politicizing the economic base of social domination (and hegemony), and not just the 'political superstructure'. The socialization of politics embraces the production process just as much as it does the realm of state activity in economic policy.

Translated by David Fernbach

REFERENCES

Accornero, Aris (1978 a), 'Operaismo e sindacato', in Napolitano, Tronti, Accornero and Cacciari, *loc.cit.*, pp. 27-43.

Accornero, Aris (1978 b), 'La classe operaia non basta immaginarla', in *Rinascita*, 7 April 1978.

Agnoli, Johannes and Brückner, Peter, *Die Transformation der Demokratie*, Berlin, 1967.

Agnoli, Johannes, *Uberlegungen zum bürgerlichen Staat*, Berlin, 1973.

Albers, Detlev, 'Inhalt und Perspektiven des historischen Kompromisses für Italien und Westeuropa', in Albers (ed.), *Demokratie und Sozialismus in Italien*, Frankfurt/M and New York, 1978, pp. 9-121.

Alf, Sophie G., *Leitfaden Italien*, Berlin, 1977.

Althusser, Louis, *For Marx*, London, 1969.

Althusser, *Reading Capital*, London, 1970.

Althusser, Louis, 'Ideology and Ideological State Apparatuses', in *Lenin and Philosophy*, London, 1971.

Althusser, Louis *Essays in Self-Criticism*, London, 1976.

Altvater, Elmar, 'Staat und gesellschaftliche Reproduktion. Anmerkungen zur Diskussion um den "Planstaat" ', in Brandes, Hoffmann, Jürgens and Semmler (eds.), *Handbuch 5, Staat*, Cologne, 1977.

Altvater, Elmar, 'Politische Implikationen der Krisenbereinigung—Uberlegungen zu den Austerity-Tendenzen in Westeuropa', in PROKLA 32, 1978, pp. 43-72.

Altvater, Elmar, Hoffmann, Jürgen and Semmler, Willi, *Vom Wirtschaftswunder zur Wirtschaftskrise*, Berlin, 1979.

Altvater, Elmar, Hoffman, Jürgen and Semmler, Willi, 'Notwendigkeit und Schwierigkeit eines Programmes alternativer Wirtschaftspolitik—Zur Kritik des Memorandums', in *WSI Mitteilungen*, March 1979.

Altvater, Elmar, 'Internationalisierung der Austerity-Politik durch das Europäische Währungssystem (EWS)', in *Wiener Tagebuch*, January 1979.

Arbeitsgruppe 'Alternative Wirtschaftspolitik', *Memorandum, Alternativen der Wirtschaftspolitik*, Cologne, 1978.

Arbeitskreis Politische Okonomie, 'Der Arbeitsmarkt in der BRD—Plädover für eine kurzfristige Beschäftigungs-politik', in Leviathan 3/1978, pp. 415 ff.

Asor-Rosa, Alberto, *Le due società, Ipotesi sulla crisi italiana*, Turin, 1977.

Asor-Rosa, Alberto (1978 a), 'Die zwei Gesellschaften', in *"Zwei Kulturen?" Tunix, Mescalero und die Folgen (Aesthetik & Kommunikation akut Nr. 2)*, Berlin, 1978, pp. 37 ff.

Asor-Rosa, Alberto (1978 b), 'Intervento', in Napolitano, Tronti, Accornero and Cacciari, *Operaismo e centralità operaia*, Rome, 1978, pp. 179-210.

Asor-Rosa, A., Colletti, L., Salvadori, M. and Spriano, P. *Il socialismo diviso*, Bari, 1978.

Aut Aut—*Sonderheft, Raniero Panzieri e i "Quaderni Rossi"*, with contributions by M. Cacciari, E. Masi, A. Negri, P. A. Rovatti and others), No. 149-50, Sept.-Dec. 1975.

Bagnasco, A., *Tre Italie,* Bologna, 1977.

Bahro, Rudolf, *The Alternative in Eastern Europe,* London, 1978.

Barcellona, Pietro, *La Repubblica in Trasformazione, Problemi istituzionali del caso italiano,* Bari, 1978.

Bauer, Otto (1920), *Bolschewismus oder Sozialdemokratie?* in *Otto Bauer Werkausgabe,* Vol. 2, Vienna, 1976, pp. 223-357.

Berlinguer, E., (1973), 'Der historische Kompromiss—Gedanken zu Italien nach den Ereignissen in Chile' (series of articles from *Rinascita),* in: *Extra-Dienst-Extra, Historische Wende in Italien,* Berlin, 1976, pp. 2338.

Berlinguer, E., 'Austerität—Gelegenheit zur revolutionären Erneuerung Italiens', in Barca and others, *Sozialismus für Italien,* Hamburg, 1977.

Berlinguer, Luigi, and others ' "Democrazia autoritaria", sistema delle libertè e transformazione sociale', in *Democrazia e Diritto,* no. 3, 1977, pp. 393 ff.

Biron, Daniel and Faire, Alexandre, 'Vers un système monétaire européen. Le Mark souverain', in *Le Monde Diplomatique,* November 1976.

Blanke, Bernhard, Jürgens, Ulrich and astendiek, Hans, *Kritik der Politischen Wissenschaft* (2 vols.), Frankfurt, 1975.

Blanke, Bernhard, 'Socizialdemokratie und Gessellschaftskrise. Hypothesen zu einer sozialwissenschaftlichen Reformismustheorie' in W. Luthardt (ed.), *Sozialdemokratische Arbeiterbewegung und Weimarer Republik,* vol. 2, Frankfurt, 1978, pp. 380-408.

Blanke, Bernhard, 'Krise der Linken—Krise des Marximus', in *Die Linke im Rechtsstaat,* vol. 2, Berlin, 1979.

Bobbio, N. (1967), *Gramsci e la concezione della società civile,* (speech at the Gramsci-Congress, 1967) Milan, 1976.

Bobbio, N., *Quale Socialismo? Discussione di un'alternativa,* Turin, 1976.

Bobbio, N. and others, *Sozialisten, Kommunisten und der Staat. Uber Hegemonie und Pluralismus,* Hamburg, 1977.

Bologna, S. and Cacciari, M., *Zusammensetzung der Arbeiterklasse und Organisationfrage, (Internationale marxistische Diskussion, No. 35),* Berlin, 1973.

Buci-Glucksmann, Christine, Interview (on the Situation of the French left in *Links,* No. 102, Aug.-Sept. 1978.

Cacciari, M., 'Problemi teorici e politici dell'operaismo nei nuovi gruppi dal 1960 ad oggi', in Napolitano, Tronti, Accornero and Cacciari, *op.cit.,* pp. 45-79.

Colletti, Lucio, *Tra Marxismo e no,* Bari, 1979.

Deutschmann, Christoph, *Der Linke Keynesianismus,* Frankfurt, 1973.

De Giovanni, Biagio, *Hegel e il tempo storico della societa borghese,* Bari, 1970.

De Giovanni, B., *La teoria politica delle classi nel 'Capitale',* Bari, 1976.

De Giovanni Gerrantana and Paggi, *Gramsci-Debatte 1, Hegemonie, Staat und Partei,* Hamburg, 1978.

De Giovanni, B. and others (1978 a), 'Il partito oggi. Il rapporto con le istituzioni e con le masse. (tavola rotonda)', in *Rinascita,* 6.1.1978.

De Giovanni, B. (1978 b), 'Teoria marxista e stato', in *Critica marxista,* No. 3/1978, pp. 3-17.

Gramsci, Antonio, *Quaderni del Carcere. Edizione critica dell'Istituto Gramsci. A cura di V. Gerratana,* Turin, 1975.

Donolo, Carlo, *Mutamento o Transizione? Politica e società nella crisi italiana*, Bologna, 1977.

Donolo, Carlo, 'Le forme della politica nella crisi sociale', in *Quaderni piacentini*, 67-68, June 1978, pp. 97-144 (also in Alberto Martinelli and Gianfranco Pasquino (eds.), *La politica nell'Italia che cambia*, Milan, 1979, pp. 329-350.

Dossier 'Althusser in Italia' (compiled by S. Pieri), in *Aut-Aut*, No. 135, May-June 1973, pp. 93-110.

Duso, Anna, *Keynes in Italia. Teoria economica e politica economica in Italia negli anni Sessanta e Settanta*, Bari, 1978.

Ferrajoli, Luigi and Zolo, Danio, *Democrazia autoritaria e capitalismo maturo*, Milan, 1978.

Forsthoff, Ernst, *Der Staat der Industriegesellschaft*, Munich, 1971.

Genth, Renate and Altvater, Elmar, 'Politische Konzeptionen und Schwierigkeiten der KPI in der Krise—ein Aufriss von Problemen einer Strategie der Arbeiterbewegung', part 1: PROKLA 26, 1977; part 2: PROKLA 27, 1977.

Gerstenberger, H., 'Zur Theorie des bürgerlichen Staates. Der gegenwärtige Stand der Debatte', in Brandes, Hoffman, Jürgens and Semmler (eds.), *Handbuch 5, Staat*, Cologne, 1977.

Giovannini, Elio, 'I contratti tra restaurazione economica e Crisi sociale' in *Sinistra* no. 5/6, October 1978, pp. 31-42.

Grauhan, Rolf Richard and Hickel, Rudolf, 'Krise des Steuerstaats?—Widersprüche, Ausweichstrategien, Perspektiven staatlicher Politik', in Grauhan, (ed.), *Krise des Steuerstaats, Leviathan*, Sonderheft 1/1978.

Graziani, A., 'Le tre Italie', in *Quaderni Piacentini*, No. 65-66, Feb. 1978, pp. 60 ff.

Habermas, Jürgen, *Legitimationsprobleme im Spätkapitalismus*, Frankfurt, 1973.

Hilferding, R., 'Probleme der Zeit. Ein Geleitwort', in *Die Gesellschaft*, 1924, vol. 1.

Hirsch, J. and Roth, R., 'Von der ökonomischen zur politischen Krise,' in *Links* 92, Oct. 1977.

Ingrao, Pietro, *Masse e potere*, Rome, 1977.

Jaroslawski, Jan, *Soziologie der kommunistischen Partei*, Frankfurt and New York, 1978.

Kallascheuer, Otto, ' "Anti-Hegelianismus" in der Arbeiterbewegung Hypothesen zur Althusser- und Della Volpe-Schule', in *Alternative*, No. 97, August 1974, pp. 164 ff.

Kallscheuer, Otto, 'Dossier Italien: Systemkrise und Krise der Linken' in *Der lange Marsch*, No. 21 (Berlin, April 1976).

Kallscheuer, Otto, 'Das "System des Marxismus" ist ein Phantom. Argumente für den theoretischen Pluralismus der Linken', in *Kursbuch*, No. 48, 1977, pp. 59-75.

Kallscheuer, Otto, Rafalski, Traute and Wenzel, Gisela, 'Italien: Gratwanderung zwischen Stabilisierung und Ubergangsprozess', part 1 in PROKLA 29, 1977; part 2, PROKLA 32, 1978.

Kastendiek, Hans, 'Konzeptionelle Probleme der Korporatismus-Analyse'. Referat für die 10. Arbeitstagung des Arbeitskreises 'Parteien

—Parlamente—Wahlen' der Deutschen Vereinigung für Politische Wissenschaft, February 1979 (Manuskript 8, revised in PROKLA, 1979).

Kostede, N., 'Die neuere marxistische Diskussion über den bürgerlichen Staat, Einführung—Kritik—Resultate', in *Gesellschaft*, No. 8/9, Frankfurt, 1976, pp. 150-96.

Krippendorf, E., 'Abriss der Geschichte der politschen Okonomie Italiens', in *Kritik der Politischen Okonomie*, No. 13, June 1977, pp. 2-26.

Leggewie, Claus, 'Von der Krise des Kapitals zur Krise der Partei—Zur Entwicklung der KPF seit der "historischen Niederlage" vom März 1978', in PROKLA 32 (1978), pp. 5-18.

Lettieri, Antonio, 'Lotte sociale e declino del compromesso storico' in *Sinistra* no. 5/6, October 1978, pp. 5-10.

Luhmann, N., *Soziologische Aufklärung*, Cologne, 1970.

Luporini, Cesare, 'Nota introduttiva', in L. Althusser, *Per Marx*, Rome, 1967, pp. vii—xxvii.

Luporini, C., 'Marx e Gramsci: le categorie strategiche' (speech at the Gramsci-Congress in Florence, 1977) in *Rinascita*, 23 December, 1977.

Luporini, C., 'Critica della politica e critica dell'economia politica in Marx,' in *Critica marxista*, 1978, No. 1, pp. 17-50.

Il Manifesto (Quaderno Nr. 8), *Potere e opposizione nelle società post-rivoluzionarie—Una disenssione nella sinistra*, Rome, 1978.

Marramao, G., *Austromarxismo e socialismo di sinistra fra le due querre*, Milan, 1977.

Marramao, G., 'Pluralismo corporativo, democrazia di massa e stato autoritario' in *Rinascita*, 8 December 1978.

Mattick, Paul, *Marx and Keynes*, London, 1971.

Melucci, A., 'Dieci ipotesi per l'anali si dei nuovi movimenti', in *Quaderni Piacentini*, no. 65-6, February 1978, pp. 3 ff.

Minucci, Adalberto, 'Crisi e terza via', in *Rinascita*, 26 January 1979.

Müller, Wolfgang and Neusüss, Christel, 'Die Sozialistaatsillusion und der Widerspruch von Lohnarbeit und Kapital', in *Sozialistische Politik*, no. 6/7, June 1970, pp. 4-67.

Napolitano, G., Tronti, M., Accornero, A. and Cacciari, M., *Operaismo e centralità operaia*, Rome, 1978.

Negri, Toni, *Krise des Planstaats, Kommunismus und revolutionäre Organisation (Internationale marxistische Diskussion, No. 33)*, Berlin, 1973.

Negri, Toni, *Staat in der Krise (Internationale marxistische Diskussion, No. 64)*, Berlin, 1977.

O'Connor, James, *The Fiscal Crisis of the State*, New York, 1973.

Offe, Claus, *Strukturprobleme des kapitalistischen Staates*, Frankfurt, 1972.

Panitch, Leo, 'Profits and Politics: Labour and the Crisis of British Capitalism', in *Politics and Society*, No. 4/1977, pp. 477 ff.

Parboni, Riccardo, 'Quanto ci sarebbe costato il "serpente" ' in *Rinascita*, 10 November 1978.

Poulantzas, Nicos, *State, Power, Socialism*, London, 1978.

Priester, K. (1977 a), 'Zur Staatstheorie bei Antonio Gramsci', in *Das Argument*, No. 104, July/August 1977, pp. 515-32.

Priester, K. (1977 b), 'Grundzüge und Probleme der Strategie des "italienischen Wegs zum Sozialismus" ', in *Beiträge zum wissenschaftlichen Sozialismus* 5/77, pp. 15-39.

Rancière, Jacques, *Wider den akademischen Marxismus (Internationale marxistische Diskussion, No. 54)*, Berlin, 1975.

Rieland, W., 'Die "Erneuerung der Arbeiterbewegung" und die neuen Bewegungen der Arbeiter in Italien'. Introduction to R. Alquati, *Klassenanalyse als Klassenkampf*, Frankfurt, 1974, pp. 7-38.

Roth, K.H., *Die "andere" Arbeiterbewegung*, Munich, 1976.

Rovatti, Pier Aldo, 'Filosofia e politica. Il caso Althusser, in *Aut Aut*, No. 142-143, July-Oct. 1974, pp. 61-94.

Rusconi, G.E., *La crisi di Weimar. Crisi di sistenza e scoufitta operaia*, Turin, 1977.

Schollinger, H. and Stöss, R., 'Bundestagswahlen und soziale Basis politischer Parteien in der BRD, II.' in PROKLA 26 (1976), pp. 111-49.

Soriente, Luciano, 'L'austerità è innanzitutto una politica di cambiamento', in *Rinascita*, 2 June 1978.

Spätkapitalismus und Klassenkampf. Eine Auswahl aus den "Quaderni Rossi", ed. Claudio Pozzoli, Frankfurt, 1972.

Stame, F. (1977 a), *Società civile e critica delle istituzioni*, Milan, 1977.

Stame, F. (1977 b), 'Lo stato contro i bisogni', in: *Aut Aut* (new series) No. 161, Sept.-Oct. 1977, pp. 19-27.

Stame, F., 'Oltre il bolscevismo per un'etica di liberazione', in *Quaderni Piacentini*, no. 67-68, June 1978, pp. 3-10.

Stame, F., 'I Processi di Socializzazione nello Stato moderno e la funzione politica e sociale del rapporto di autorità', in *Tendenze autoritarie del Capitalismo sviluppato*, Milan, 1979.

Telò Mario, 'Note sul problema della democrazia nella traduzione Gramsciana del Leninismo', in *Problemi del Socialismo*, No. 3, 1976, pp. 129-85.

Trentin, Bruno, (Interview) (1978 a), 'In der Krise haben sich die Prioritäten gewerkschaftlicher Politik verändert,' PROKLA 31, pp. 171 ff.

Trentin, Bruno, (1978 b), 'La crisi dei consigli e la linea del sincacato', in *Rinascita*, 7 April 1978.

Trentin, Bruno, 'Diskussionsbeitrag im Streitgespräch mit Asor-Rosa, Bufalini, Luporini über die "Thesen" für den XV. Parteitag d. KPI: "La terza via al socialismo" ', in *Rinascita*, 5 Jan. 1979.

Tronti, Mario, *Arbeiter und Kapital*, Frankfurt, 1974.

Tronti, Mario (1977 a), *Sull'autonomia del politico*, Milan, 1977.

Tronti, Mario (1978 a), 'Operaismo el centralità operaia', in: Napolitano, Tronti, Accornero and Cacciari, *op.cit.*, pp. 15-25.

Tronti, Mario (1978 b), 'Politica e potere', in *Critica Marxista*, No. 3, 1978, pp. 19-35.

Vacca, Giuseppe, 'Althusser: materialismo storico e materialismo dialettico', in *Rinascita*, No. 34/1968.

Vacca, G., *Quale Democrazia? Problemi della democrazia di transizione*, Bari, 1977.

Vacca, Giuseppe, *Quale Democrazia—Problemi della democrazi di transizione,* Bari, 1977.

Wahl, François, 'Die Philosophie diesseits und jenseits des Strukturalismus', in Wahl (ed.) *Einführung in den Strukturalismus,* Frankfurt, 1973, pp. 327-480.

Zeuner, B., 'Solidarität mit der SPD oder Solidarität mit der Klasse. Zur SPD. Bindung der SPD—Gewerkschaften', in PROKLA 26 (1976), pp. 3-32.

Zolo, Danilo, *Stato socialista e libertà borghesi. Una discussione sui fondamenti della teoria politica marxista,* Bari, 1976.

Zolo, Danilo, 'Democrazia Corporativa, Produzione del Consenso, Socialismo', in *Problemi del Socialismo,* 9 (Fourth Series), 1978, pp. 115 ff.

Zwei Kulturen? Tunix, Mescalero und die Folgen, Aesthetik & Kommunikation akut, No. 2, Berlin, 1978.

CONFLICTING CURRENTS IN THE PCF

George Ross and Jane Jenson

INTRODUCTION

The defeat of the left in the 1978 French legislative elections marked the end of an era for the *Parti Communiste Français.* The most extensive experiment into United Front politics in the PCF's history and fifteen years of strategic continuity had led to failure. The party's turn toward profound self-examination after the elections was therefore not surprising. What has come as a surprise, however, is the way—contradictory, confusing, often opaque, and sometimes brutal—in which the PCF has tried to re-evaluate its position. Basic aspects of the PCF's identity have been at stake. What should its strategy be? What should its relationship to socialist countries be? What kind of internal life will it have? Will it continue down the road of Eurocommunism? More than a year after the defeat of 1978, none of these questions have been answered. But the party's inability to chart its own future has simultaneously provided invaluable sources of understanding of what the PCF is now.

Anyone familiar with French politics knows that the PCF is not the paragon of scientific socialism governed by a truly democratic centralism in the service of a clear vision of socialist change which it claims to be. Nor is it the manipulative, autocratically-controlled, monolithic army of single-minded militants described by its enemies. The PCF's reality is both more prosaic and more subtle than either of these caricatures. As befits a political formation comprised of several hundred thousand members of very different political generations, with varied backgrounds, acting in countless different spheres of organizational activity, the PCF is very complex. This essay will analyse this complexity in a way which will, hopefully, illuminate the sinuous paths which the PCF has followed in recent times. The French Communist Party has, as we will see, a complicated internal political life due to the existence of different currents of strategic opinion. Its responses to the outside world follow from conflict and coalition between such currents as they act

139

within different spheres of party practice. These spheres of practice have evolved historically at different rates away from common Bolshevik-Stalinist roots, such that, in recent times, they have existed in relationships of contradiction one with the other. The defeat of 1978 was, in large part, caused by a knot of contradictions in a Eurocommunist vision of social change and practices of mobilization, alliance behaviour, and internal party life which made its implementation difficult. In response to this defeat, currents in the party, working in the context of contradictions, each proposed very different recipes for the future. Understanding what resulted from these processes is the object of our work.

1. *THE REALITIES OF MARCH 1978*

The failure of March 1978 revealed a number of truths about the PCF which the years of mobilization around the Common Programme of the Left had hidden from all but the most astute observers. For years, French Communists had pursued what seemed to be a realistic, if difficult, United Front strategy. In support of this they had worked a number of profound doctrinal changes away from their Comintern origins towards a genuinely democratic Eurocommunist vision of socialist transformation. The party's goals were easily summarized. It had wanted to make a Left coalition a majority in the country, install itself as the determining force in this coalition and thereby pull its Socialist ally away from its social democratic proclivities and towards genuine change. Objective number one had been reached. Alas, for the PCF, *Union de la Gauche* benefitted the PS much more than the PCF, especially electorally. In consequence, the Socialists, sensing that they and not the Communists would have the largest share of resources to shape the direction of any future Left government, slipped away from commitment to the kinds of changes which the PCF felt necessary. The split on the Left of September 1977 and the defeat of the divided Left in March 1978 followed.

For the PCF, the failure of 1978 was basically one of mobilization. The party had been unable to convince enough people to support its cause. When one asked why this had happened, however, the profoundly contradictory reality of the PCF became clearer. In its conceptualization of the transition to socialism and in its strategy, the party had taken its distance from the Bolshevik-Stalinist past. In its ability to *implement* this strategy, however, the PCF had 'modernized' in much less satisfactory ways. United Front strategy, designed to produce progressively more radical rounds of structural reform opening a 'democratic road to a socialism, in itself democratic' made sense. As befits the reality of France in the 1970s, the party had rejected the Soviet experience as model and committed itself to a *socialisme aux couleurs de la France,* to be constructed democratically out of French materials without reference to any *a priori* blueprint. Unfortunately for the PCF, modernization in one realm of practice had not automatically entailed change in others. Herein lay the drama.

For its strategy to work, the Party needed to accumulate new resources of support, in particular to expand its social base to appeal to sections of the new middle strata. This was no simple matter, for to do so it would first have had to demonstrate that it had come to grips with and broken with its involvement with Stalinism and the distortions which Stalinism had worked in the PCF during the years of Maurice Thorez's leadership of the Party. In fact, largely because of the monumental error of Thorez in 1956 in refusing to seize the opportunity of the Twentieth Congress of the CPSU to begin de-Stalinizing in France, the Party still had not fully faced such issues by the early 1970s. Thus it approached new groups not as a party which had reflected upon and learned from the mistakes of its past, but rather as one of heroic continuity. Moreover, it was also slow to provide members of new middle strata with a secure place and role in its vision of change. In theory, new middle strata were to have a place in a broad and complex anti-monopoly alliance which would respect their social specificity and their interests. In practice, traditional PCF *ouvrierisme,* dating from earlier party strategies and from deep French working-class reflexes, was the rule. Workers were the vanguard and main force for radical change, It was, therefore, the duty of non-working-class groups who wanted change to subordinate their own goals, their specificity, to those of the vanguard. This contradiction between the party's de-Stalinized, de-Bolshevized strategic position, which was based on an expected expansion of PCF support among new intermediary groups, and older mobilizational styles, was catastrophic. The Socialists had their own burdensome past, to be sure. Yet, through historical accident and political astuteness, the PS was able, unlike the PCF, to present itself to new middle strata as a party which had broken with this past. Beyond this, French social democracy had always been both middle class and reformist, less marked, as a result, by *ouvrierisme* than the PCF. Thus the Communists failed to produce the resources of support which their strategy demanded, while *Union de la Gauche* strengthened the Socialists.

Not unrelated to the PCF's general mobilization problem in 1978 was the contradiction which existed between the PCF's modernized vision of socialist transformation and the nature of its internal life. French Communists seemed determined to implement a Eurocommunist strategy with a party designed for a very different strategy. The general lack of internal democracy in the party was evidenced in numbers of PCF actions in the 1972-8 period. Abrupt about-faces on major political questions continually emanated from the party leadership, rarely with prior discussion in the party at large.[1] Moreover, the PCF's style of mobilization, intimately connected with its internal life, reinforced the problem. In good Leninist terms, Communists saw their task as one of bringing revolutionary consciousness to the masses 'from without'. Traditional methods for doing this, dating from the Thorez era, were unquestioned. The consciousness which was called for was to be conceptualized at the leadership level of the party, then to be forwarded to the people through PCF cells. Yet, the PCF's commitment to a democratic road clearly implied that the people should play a primordial role in deciding for themselves what they wanted. In the light of the party's vision of change, then, the Left Common Programme of 1972 ought to have developed profound connections with the people whose lives it was designed to change. In fact, however, the Common Programme was propagandized *to* the people, rather than emanating from, and therefore involving, them.

Thus far we have accounted for the failure of 1978 by suggesting that de-Stalinization and de-Bolshevization in different spheres of PCF activity had proceeded at varying rates. In the areas of PCF strategy and the party's vision of a transition to socialism substantial change, amounting to theoretical Eurocommunization, had occurred. Yet success at implementing this strategy and realizing this vision depended on commensurate changes in other realms of PCF practice which had not occurred at all or had occurred only partially. Insufficient democratization of the PCF itself, insufficient reflection of the party's history, antiquated notions of how to calculate risks in an alliance strategy for change, all undermined the success of what looked, on the face of it, to be a reasonable strategy. However, on its own, this picture of a party caught in contradictions created by uneven evolution of separate spheres of practice is incomplete. For these spheres or structures of practice were maintained and changed by political actors. In the PCF, central actors in recent times have been political *currents*.[3] The term current refers to an informal coalition around a particular strategic predilection. The mass bases of currents are found in the analyses made by large numbers of rank and file Communists, analyses which are almost always incomplete, sometimes little more than strong feelings. Leaders, by their positions and abilities, turn such mass analyses into coherent positions; they thus define currents in practice. But they represent currents as well. Currents have always existed in the PCF, so much so that they are enshrined implicitly in PCF vocabulary with its references to the 'sectarian' and 'opportunist' temptations between which the party must navigate to ensure its success. They have never been acknowledged openly, however. In the Thorez years, with the extreme centralization of authority in the party's Secretary-General, currents were submerged in a constant quest for Communist unanimity, a quest backed by the threat of expulsion.[4] Since Thorez, the internal life of the party has, *de facto*, been increasingly marked by the interplay of currents. Acknowledging their existence in public is still taboo, however. Thus the PCF's life of currents is carried on underneath a facade of unity. In the period which concerns us most, that of *Union de la Gauche*, two major currents coexisted and conflicted in the party. A third coalesced during these years and has only very recently become important.

The current which took the lead in defining the strategy of *Union*—which we will call the United Front/Eurocommunists—had honorable precedents in the party's past, emerging from the Popular Front politics of Maurice Thorez and from the political spadework of Waldeck Rochet, Thorez's successor, in the 1960s. Leaders of this current, Georges Marchais in particular, were responsible for pushing the party towards the 1972 Common Programme and later, after 1975, towards the important dose of Eurocommunism which culminated in the party's Twenty-Second Congress in 1976.[5] The United Front/Eurocommunist approach involved a quest for alliances with the non-Communist Left around agreed-upon programmes of reform to be enacted by the Left in power which would progressively work a transition to Socialism in France. For a number of reasons, the United Front/Eurocommunists focused much attention on the workings of the party's alliance strategy *at the top*, on the level of dealings with the leaderships of other organizations. They also tended to stress electoral mobilization above other forms of party activity in their calculations of how to succeed. In part because of the problems raised by these biases, and despite the powerful positions which United Front/Eurocommunists held in the party leadership, this current was never able to establish complete consensus within the PCF on its policies.

In fact, at every important juncture in the history of Left Unity, the United Front/Eurocommunists were opposed by a 'go-it-alone' current with a strategy of its own to propose. The 'go-it-aloners' believed that the crisis of French capitalism, together with the profoundly class-collaborationist nature of French social democrats, would eventually allow the PCF to gather important new strength, provided it maintained its radical identity in an uncompromising fashion. To this current, *Union de la Gauche* was a dangerous strategy. By granting the French Socialists a new certificate of honorably Left conduct—which they did not deserve—it allowed them new opportunities to reconstruct their sagging fortunes. It also led the PCF to compromise its identity in pursuit of alliance—hence the reticence of the 'go-it-aloners' to approve Eurocommunist changes. Finally, it would lead the Communists into an inevitable trap when the Socialists betrayed a united front alliance, 'turned to the Right', and followed their true vocation of managing the capitalist crisis.

The years of Left unity for the PCF were years of opposition between United Front/Eurocommunists and 'go-it-aloners' in which both had considerable resources. With recent party history, much rank and file support and the Secretary-General on their side, the United Front/Eurocommunists had the initiative. However, the need to maintain a consensus in the party on their policies obliged this current to accept limits on the changes which they desired to promote in order to reach a viable compromise with their strategic opponents. This need, plus the very real limitations in perspective of the United Front/Eurocommunists themselves, explains the development of the contradictions between practices during the *Union* years which we have discussed earlier. Because consensus was a problem and possibilities for change limited, the United Front/Eurocommunists focused their energies on the task of promoting strategic change. Taking on the 'go-it-aloners' in other realms of practice, in particular that of the party's internal life, even to the limited degree that the United Front/Eurocommunists felt necessary, would have involved doing battle with the 'go-it-aloners' which might have jeopardized change in the strategic sphere. Thus given the existence of currents within the party and, more importantly, given the nature of these currents, the development of different spheres of party practice—mobilization, alliance behaviour, internal life—was bound to be uneven.

That there were real political reasons for the development of contradictions between different spheres of practice, that this development was not simply due to mistakes, is clear from the actual history of *Union de la Gauche*. The margin of manoeuvre available to the United Front/Eurocommunists was so narrow and their position so precarious that on every occasion when a failure in their strategy seemed imminent, their leadership position was threatened, leading to remarkable zigs and zags in PCF behaviour. A good example of this process is found in the events around the Twenty-First Party Congress. When a series of by-elections in 1974 showed the PS beginning to threaten the PCF's own traditional electoral base, the 'go-it-aloners' took the offensive and managed to turn the leadership's original proposal for the Twenty-First Congress into a hard-line attack on the PS, resulting in a full year of virulent anti-Socialist polemicizing. Then, as the electoral period of 1976-8 approached, the balance shifted back dramatically. The great rush of Eurocommunism around the Twenty-Second Congress of 1976—distance from the USSR, the limited opening up of party life at the base, and the Twenty-Second Congress itself—were the response of the United Front/Eurocommunist current to the earlier signs of failure.[6]

In this general process of conflict and coalition between 'Unity' and 'go-it-alone' currents—always masked, of course, by the Communists' desire to present themselves as unanimous (a desire shared by both major currents) a third current, Left Eurocommunism, began to coalesce. Left Eurocommunism accepted the party's United Front strategy but was aware of the contradictions which existed between this strategic vision and the party's other practices. Its goal was to resolve these contradictions by modernizing the party's mobilizational and alliance behaviour and changing the party's internal life. Left Eurocommunism, often inspired by the PCI, posited the conditions of PCF strategic success in new ways of approaching the masses which would have encouraged them to participate in the definition and implementation of reform to change their lives. The Left Eurocommunists, in other words, took seriously the proposition of the Twenty-Second Congress that the central contradiction in French society was between advanced capitalism and democracy. In this view, the struggle for greater democracy—through workers' control, in part—was a struggle against monopoly capitalism and for socialism. If the 'go-it-alone' critique of the United Front/Eurocommunist perspective was that it was strategically wrong, the Left Eurocommunist position was that it was strategically correct, but that, for whatever reasons, the party had not been simultaneously given the means to carry out this strategy.

2. WHAT WAS TO BE DONE?

The defeat of March 1978 created a new situation for the PCF. The Right remained solidly in power. Faced with a deepening economic crisis, it was newly free to make French workers pay a high price for the economic changes which strategists for the French bourgeoisie felt necessary. *Union de la Gauche* and the Common Programme were both dead issues. Each major Left party could measure the extent of its failure and each was determined to rebuild its position. This new situation therefore obliged the PCF to change its line. But in what directions?

Abstract logic dictated that the party should have seized the occasion to begin to resolve all of the contradictions which had prevented success in 1978. But there was nothing abstract about the party's situation. At a moment when new approaches were called for, each current in the PCF moved forward to present different analyses of the failure and propose new solutions. Between the currents existed profound disagreement over what was logical and what was contradictory. Georges Marchais' injunction to the party to 'discuss' the situation after the election was an invitation for differences of opinion to appear in public, although, at the same time, the *Bureau Politique's* announcement that the Socialists were completely responsible for the defeat rather limited the prospects for debate. Changing the PCF's line at a moment when awareness of the contradictions the party faced was high and disagreement between currents ran deep promised to be a difficult and disheartening task.

The impossibility of communications with the Socialists, themselves faced with fundamental questions of how to proceed and engaged in their own inner party struggles, made some form of Communist 'going it alone' almost inevitable. However, 'going it alone' could have been undertaken in any number of ways. It was the specific mode of 'going it alone' upon which the PCF eventually decided which counted. The two key messages which came out of the Central Committee meeting at the end of April 1978 (the first since the election after more than a month of the prescribed 'discussion') resolved little. To begin with, the entire responsibility for the Left's failure was ascribed to the PS, which had 'turned to the Right'. Secondly, the PCF was henceforth to pursue the line of *union à la base*. The first message was not completely true. Many Communists recognized the PCF's share of the responsibility for the failure of the Left and the contradictory behaviour of the party. The second message was quite unclear. 'Unity from below' was a time-honoured PCF slogan, used often in the past when the party found itself isolated, as in the 'class against class' period, the 1939-41 years, and during the Cold War. It was thus recognizable to more experienced party members. But was it this old-style 'unity from below' which was meant this time, a 'unity' which consisted mainly in attacking social democrats and reinforcing inner party discipline? If so, it was a tactic and not a strategy. With *Union de la Gauche* at the end of its long road, what a confused party needed was a strategy more than a tactic, and this need was felt especially powerfully by the post-1968 generation of party militants who had known only *Union*. To many such militants 'unity from below' implied action unconnected with any vision of social change, a deeply troubling prospect.

In fact, the lack of strategic clarity in the call for 'unity from below' was not accidental. It followed from a profound lack of agreement between currents within the party and, even more importantly, within the leadership, about strategy, as we will presently see. Nonetheless, to many in the PCF, the leadership's proposal for a shift away from strategic clarity around *Union de la Gauche* to strategic confusion around 'unity from below' was deeply discomforting. The turn towards confusion was all the more troublesome because it occurred within the context of a major internal explosion of discontent about how the party worked, as well as its past activities. Thus a deeply divided leadership which could agree only on a confusing line was faced with the task of creating consensus around this line at a moment when the basic structures of the inner-party life, used to create consensus, were being fundamentally challenged.

What Strategy for the Future?

The United Front/Eurocommunist line had no clear future after March 1978. Left Eurocommunists, who had an alternative to this line which would have built on the 1978 failure without discarding the central policies of the older strategy, were too weak to prevail. Thus events ensured that the 'go-it-alone' current, coalesced in the party leadership around Roland Leroy, editor of *l'Humanité* and a member of the Secretariat of the party, was empowered to promote new political initiatives. Nevertheless, if the 'go-it-alone' current was in a position to suggest certain *tactics* for the post-electoral period, its primary ambition was to work a fundamental change in the PCF's *strategy*, one which amounted to a renunciation of Eurocommunism. On the level of strategy, however, no consensus was possible on a 'go-it-alone' perspective. The drama in all this, then, was that no current within the PCF was in a position to propose a strategy which could be accepted.

The short-term tactical aspects of the proposed 'go-it-alone' strategy were clear. The PCF should seek to prevent the Socialists from coming anywhere near the PCF's natural and traditional social base, while at the same time doing everything possible to deepen party support in this base. The target groups were workers, the poor, and the populations of regions especially hard hit by economic crisis. Working to appeal to such groups, the PCF could count on maximizing its own strengths, its ability to organize at the plant level, for example, and its credibility as a tribune for the poor and the economically threatened. These strengths were, simultaneously, the Socialists' greatest weaknesses. The PCF could generate and lead militant struggles against plant shutdowns, industrial restructuring, or the effects of the European Economic Community on southern farmers in ways which the PS, which lacked the resources, the skills and, for the most part, the will to do so, could not. Beyond this, such actions were to be accompanied by a constant and strident barrage of anti-Socialist propaganda designed to strip the PS of any and all Left credibility which it might have gained with the groups in question during the time of *Union de la Gauche*.[7]

The 'go-it-alone' current was not simply proffering short-term tactics, however. As a strategy, to 'go it alone' would imply a drastic change in PCF perspectives. The proposed line was based on the premise that the Socialists were irreparably class-collaborationist, that they could *never* be counted on to be loyal allies in any real process of change. The argument claimed further that, in the profound economic crisis faced not only in France but everywhere in Europe—a crisis which was destined to last indefinitely—social democracy had become the major strategic option of monopoly capitalism, the best way to enlist the co-operation of workers for anti-working-class policies. The principal conclusion which flowed from this analysis was that, as the crisis deepened, the PS would move ever more decisively to the Right, towards direct co-operation with the bourgeoisie. In the process, it would expose the hollowness of the progressive rhetoric which it had deployed in the seventies. In this context, if the PCF strengthened its position among workers and the poor, relentlessly denounced the Socialists, and maintained its radical purity, much of the social and electoral strength which had flowed to the Socialists during *Union de la Gauche* would abandon the PS and respond to the new appeals from the PCF. The 'go-it-alone' strategy, then, was based on a projection that French social democracy was headed for a disaster from which the PCF, if it followed an appropriate course, was bound to profit. The second major conclusion which followed from the 'go-it-alone' analysis was that the entire strategy of *Union de la Gauche* had been wrong, from beginning to end.

The short-term, tactical side of the 'go-it-alone' perspective was sufficiently plausible in the aftermath of March 1978 to provide a content for 'unity from below' which elicited support within the party beyond those who accepted the perspective as a full-blown strategy. By renouncing an immediate search for allies and the political restraint which that entailed, the PCF could concentrate its efforts on strengthening its position within those areas where it felt most comfortable and still had the best chance of success. They also effectively neutralized Eurocommunist strategic objectives. United Front/Eurocommunists and Left Eurocommunists could both see 'go-it-alone' tactics, as opposed to strategy, as useful for their own ends. The first current, looking to the moment when the balance of forces might shift in favour of the PCF so that United Frontism at the top could be renewed, could see some potential for re-balancing in 'unity from below'. Left Eurocommunists could approve the shift in PCF emphasis towards mobilizational activity at the base and away from simple electoralism. They could hope that, through their actions, the nature of this mobilization could become fully democratic and *autogestionnaire*.

Consensus on these 'go-it-alone' tactics was not total, however. To the degree to which 'unity from below' was not connected to a long-term perspective for broader social change, it discomfited numbers of Communists, accustomed to long years in which such perspectives had been clear. Some even wondered whether such tactics might not be counterproductive. If the PCF were unable to provide the masses with anything except local struggles without a foreseeable payoff in social change, might they not be further demobilized? Worse still, the Socialists would certainly be willing to provide a global view of change, however misleading it might be. Would not such a view be doubly enticing in the absence of any Communist counterpart? The most powerful, if difficult to weigh, opposition to this form of 'unity from below' came from important leaders of the Confédération Générale du Travail (CGT), the PCF's vital labour ally. The CGT was a mass trade union organization (staffed and run by tens of thousands of militants, many of whom were Communists) whose success depended, to an important extent, on its ability to appeal to workers on trade union grounds, regardless of political belief. The CGT had been badly burned in its mass appeal by its too-close identification with the PCF's position during the electoral period. This, plus the fact that the economic crisis also had a serious effect on its mobilizational capacities, made many of its leaders newly conscious of the need to establish greater CGT autonomy from the PCF. To the degree to which 'unity from below' meant the Communists would focus their efforts on attacking the Socialists, the danger was great that Communists acting as trade unionists within the CGT, would do the same thing and would further politicize the CGT, thus limiting its mass appeal.[8]

If the 'go-it-aloners' could create a coalition of support in the party on their tactics—even if this coalition had its limits—the longer-term strategy which they offered and tried to impose was powerfully divisive. To the degree to which it was sectarian and anti-pluralist, it threatened the very foundations of Eurocommunism, its strategic perspectives of peaceful change based on pluralistic alliance politics.[9] Because the 'go-it-alone' strategic perspective ultimately implied the denunciation of the United Front/Eurocommunist policies which the Marchais leadership and the party organization had carried on for a decade, with massive rank and file support, it was completely unacceptable to large numbers of Communists who believed in the United Front/Eurocommunist strategy. Left Eurcommunists saw themselves as the correctors of the flaws which had been allowed to develop in the PCF strategy in the decade, mainly of its top-down approach and its failure to devise new democratic and *autogestionnaire* mobilizing techniques. But their goal was a broadened and modified Eurocommunism. 'Going it alone' strategically was thus perceived as catastrophic to them as well.

Thus the PCF slipped into a confusing stalemate after March 1978. Old-style *Union de la Gauche* was at least temporarily unworkable. The post-electoral balance of currents within the party and its leadership gave more initiating power to advocates of the 'go-it-alone' perspective. But the proponents of such a perspective could gain acceptance only for their short-term tactics, and only for some of those. 'Unity from below' was defined in their terms, then, not because their strategy was acceptable but rather, because their tactical suggestions could create something of a consensus. On a strategic plane no consensus existed on 'going it alone'. Far from it. But no consensus existed on any other strategy either. In effect, as the PCF moved towards its Twenty-Third Congress it had no strategy, or rather, the different currents within the party each had their own, but with no one current able to impose its views on the whole party.

Organizational Contradictions and the Problem of Order

It was in this context of strategic conflict between different currents that problems in the inner life of the party exploded. When the mobilizational tension of the electoral period relaxed, Communists turned their attention naturally towards a search for explanations for the 1978 failure. Beginning immediately after the elections, the party, at all levels, scrutinized the past, the behaviour of the leadership and the internal life of the PCF in ways, and with a breadth of scope, which were entirely new in Communist history. No stones were left unturned and few opportunities were lost—including opportunities for public expression *outside* the party—to ask the most probing questions. The response of the leadership to the beginnings of debate rapidly turned the more discontented towards a thorough questioning of the party's internal life. Immediately after the election the *Bureau Politique* enjoined the party to a full discussion of what had happened, while at the same time itself giving schematic explanations of things—the most important being that the failure was the fault of the Socialists—which seemed to admit of no appeal. Moreover, if the party's official spokesmen often acknowledged that 'wide-ranging discussion' was taking place, they never acknowledged what was being discussed. *L'Humanité* did the same thing, which meant that the actual themes of the debate were never officially disseminated throughout the party. The characterization of the party's new openness at the rank and file level by a prominent *contestataire* as *le droit de râler* (the right to grouse without consequences) seemed rather appropriate.[10]

From the point of view of the Communists' need for new clarity, particularly about the party's own life, this explosion came at the appropriate moment. From the point of view of the leadership, concerned, at the critical moment of transition, with order, the timing could not have been worse. One of the principal responsibilities of the PCF's leadership has always been to ensure consensus within the party so that it could act in the world in a unified way. In the aftermath of March 1978 this duty was felt with great urgency. Historic failures in and of themselves carry the risk of disintegration for any party. Beyond this, the failure created a new situation calling for a changed line. Promoting consensus during a change of line would have been arduous. On top of all this, there was serious conflict, and not only among the leadership, about what this new line should and might be. The conflict was such that it created a balance of forces out of which no coherent new direction could emerge. In such a context, the development of a major internal crisis in the PCF was bound to intensify the leaders' fears of critics and disintegration. As if to fan such fears, the situation quickly led to unprecedented forms of rebellion. Prominent *contestataires* were so determined to press for change in the party that they flouted basic rules in the process. The flood of letters, petitions, articles and books which appeared outside the party's own forums (which, we have already noted, were almost completely closed to the protestors, even those who did first offer their contributions to party publications) in the 'bourgeois media' amounted to conscious efforts by rebels to circumvent normal patterns of party debate and create new channels of horizontal communication.[11]

It was not only the question of order which pushed PCF leaders towards restoring consensus in the party. The urgency of this task was reinforced by the play of currents within the leadership itself. The partisans of 'going it alone' were pushing Georges Marchais and his current on the defensive because of the failures of 1977-8 on issues of strategy. Crisis and dissent in the party would obviously become additional weapons against Marchais, and against the whole Eurocommunist approach, were they to spread too far. Thus the balance of currents as well as traditional responses and duties pushed the leadership to place its highest priority on the problem of discontent in the party. The resolution of the problem was not simple, however. The first tactic of the leadership was to identify and isolate the most dangerous protestors. Here the progress of Eurocommunization within the party, insufficient though it had been, made it impossible to label the *contestataires* as renegades and traitors and to expel them. In addition, rank and file Communists knew that the issues underlying the discontent were real and demanded that they be discussed. Thus, the most radical *contestataires* had to be isolated while the bulk of debate around the issues troubling ordinary Communists had to be directly into existing party channels in ways that would ultimately rebuild unity.

Identifying the milieu where the most troublesome protestors lived was not difficult. Only intellectuals possessed the will and the tools to carry discontent outside normal party channels, since their profession involved manipulating words and their institutional position gave them privileged access to the media. The first job for the leadership, then, was to isolate those intellectuals willing to break party rules to express their rebellious views from the rest of Communist intellectuals. This task involved, to begin with, giving the bulk of Communist intellectuals new reasons to express their views *within* the party and new issues about which to talk. The leadership counted on such expression to result in a moderation of positions. Perhaps the most significant internal step in this direction was taken by Georges Marchais very early after March 1978 when he announced that there would be no expulsions, no matter what. This meant that determined *contestataires* were deprived of a fundamental tactic, that of provoking the party leadership into the kind of retaliation which would have created martyrs.

The leadership's campaign to channel discontent into the party was pursued vigorously after the summer vacations of 1978—the leaders hoping, of course, that the long French vacations would themselves have a calming effect. Then, in the early fall, a number of new concessions were granted, some in party procedures, some on political questions. Pledges were made, for example, that the forthcoming Twenty-Third Congress would institute changes in party regulations so as to allow much more political discussion. The promise of regular open forums in *l'Humanité* and the other party press, made in the spring, was reiterated. Beyond this, the leadership moved to provide evidence that it was capable of confronting a number of issues of substance which the protestors had raised. For example, criticism had been rife about the high costs of the PCF's inability to confront its own past, in particular its historic acceptance of aspects of Soviet society and the Soviet party as a model for its own theory and actions. In September 1978, immediately prior to the most important Communist event of the new year, *La fête de l'Humanité*, the official party publisher released *L'URSS et nous*, a series of essays about the past and present of the Soviet Union.[12] *L'URSS et nous*, authored by five Communists, received the blessing of the *Bureau Politique* which urged all Communists to read and discuss its contents. The book documented the ghastly human costs of Stalinism and began to analyse Soviet social structure in a search for the causes of such aberrations, concluding with a strong condemnation of the persistent lack of democracy in the USSR. Since these questions had not been fully broached by the PCF previously, the book's appearance was greeted both inside and outside the party as a sign of progress. More important, party discussions of the book, as called for by the *BP,* clearly engaged Communist intellectuals.[13] On quite another issue, that of the PCF's historically inept approach to the proliferation of new, issue-oriented social movements, another party-sponsored book, *La Condition féminine,* engaged militants in a new reflection on the women's movement as well as a consideration of the party's treatment of women within its own ranks.[14]

The encouragement of debate—particularly among intellectuals —on issues as important as the USSR and the women's movement revealed the complexity of the leadership's tactics. *Vis à vis* the outbreak of protest within the party, both matters were diversions, in that they pulled militants' attention strongly away from the burning issues of the 1978 failure. The debate on the Soviet Union rapidly focused on 1956 and the PCF's error in not seizing the occasion of the Twentieth Congress of the CPSU to begin de-Stalinizing. This raised the possibility, of course, that Maurice Thorez, dead since 1964, would be blamed for 1978 because of what he had not done in 1956. On the other hand, the discussion about the USSR and women had their own positive dynamic. They were often the first party discussions by rank and file militants of these questions from critical points of view. Therefore, even if they did provide a diversion in the context of 1978, they also meant that in the future the PCF would be led to develop a more complex and subtle position on both the USSR and the women's movement. In addition, they allowed new areas of questioning to be officially opened within the party which could not easily be shut down or ignored in the future.

Later, in December, the leadership took the unprecedented step of inviting 400 selected Communist intellectuals, including a number of the most prominent *contestataires,* to a weekend encounter with the entire *Bureau Politique* to discuss the problems of intellectuals. It was quite unclear what the leadership intended to produce through this, except to give intellectuals some direct sense that the *BP* would listen to them and to give members of the *BP* their chance to tell the audience what the proper attitude of a Communist intellectual should be. Nevertheless, the meeting turned out to be much more tumultuous and frank than anyone had expected. *L'Humanité* faithfully published excerpts from the weekend, including a number of quite corrosive criticisms of the leadership made from the floor. Georges Marchais was visibly moved by the proceedings, to the point of promising, in an impromptu closing talk, that the PCF would undertake a profound overhaul of its perspective on the role of intellectuals in both society and the party.[15] The meeting of 400 was officially followed by a series of local encounters with intellectuals in party sections throughout the country.

Calls to understanding and real concessions were also accompanied by calls to order. The leadership's goal was not only to conciliate Communist intellectuals and reaffirm their place within the PCF (and therefore, discourage them from going outside to criticize) but also to re-establish limits on legitimate behaviour within the party. Thus, Paul Laurent, the *BP*'s most prominent 'liberal' and the one figure to whom protestors looked for support, published his own book about the PCF in the fall of 1978. *Le PCF comme il est* was full of discussion about the presence and extent of inner-party democracy. The book was adamant that the foundation of this democracy would only be democratic centralism, that the party's success depended on this rule, and that violations of this rule created 'tendencies' which would compromise the PCF's chances for success and survival. The message was clear: proprieties must be respected.

Urging respect for proprieties was not enough. The leadership wanted also to make sure that, once the more extreme *contestataires* were isolated, the party's own media of communication were free from contamination by *contestation* and gave no encouragement, even inadvertently, to unhappy Communists. Taking the party in hand meant that, in the fall and winter of 1978-9, the party's line, and *only* the party's line, was to be disseminated by the party press and throughout the PCF at all levels. In other words, the context of party debate was to be carefully limited, as necessary. There was obviously no problem with *l'Humanité*, controlled as it was by Roland Leroy, leader of the 'go-it-alone' current. In fact, *l'Humanité* was so well in hand that from reading it one would have had a very difficult time discovering that there was any discontent within the party at all. Such was not the case elsewhere, however. Thus when *La Nouvelle Critique,* the PCF's prestigious monthly for intellectuals, published the first of two instalments of observations on the party by *contestataires,* the leadership called in the editorial board, obliged them to stop publication of the second instalment, and threatened the very existence of the review if it did not change its ways.[16] *France Nouvelle,* the official weekly of the Central Committee which had, after the Twenty-Second Congress, become one of the better sources of intelligent Eurocommunist thought, was also dealt with. First of all, known *contestataires* on the editorial collective were excluded from the board.[17] Next, the contents of the magazine were subjected to ever more severe editorial control until *France Nouvelle* quickly lost all of its originality, becoming virtually indistinguishable from *l'Humanité* in its position. This process, in turn, led to the resignation of six members of the editorial collective, one by one.[18]

Controlling the PCF press more thoroughly was not the only

tactic deployed to shape and limit the context of debate within the party. Exemplary action was taken *vis-à-vis* party organizations themselves—the Paris Federation in particular—which had harboured more than their share of *contestation*. The *Fédé de Paris*, where 'liberalism' had been the work of Paul Laurent when he served as its First Secretary (before his promotion to the top party leadership), had become the most open and Eurocommunist of perhaps any of the PCF's Federations. Moreover, since Paris was also the centre of French intellectual life, it was not at all surprising to find that this Federation had a goodly share of *contestataires*. 'Working on' the *Fédé de Paris* to get it to solve its 'problems' with protestors was therefore a logical step for the leadership. Thus, in December the Central Committee raked the Paris Federation over the coals. In January the entire Paris Federal Secretariat was requested, by the *Bureau Politique*, to engage in a self-criticism about Paris' 'opportunism' in the past *vis-à-vis* the Socialists and its policies on intellectuals. Not only did the Secretariat refuse to do so but it also counter-attacked, accusing the *Bureau Politique* of erroneous appreciations of the experience of *Union de la Gauche* and the nature of the Socialist Party, plus blindness about the real problems which the party faced among new intermediary strata of the population.

The most public results of this move against Paris were the resignation of the Federal First Secretary, Henri Fiszbin, in January, followed by the resignation of almost all the rest of the Paris Secretariat at the April Conference of the Federation. But rather more important than these resignations were the effects of the threat to Paris on the behaviour of the whole Paris party organization, down to the level of sections and cells. Middle-level party officials knew that they would be held responsible if further troubles with *contestataires* broke out. They recognized that the *Fédé* itself was vulnerable to further sanctions if the future included more problems of protest. As a result, they themselves began to limit and channel debate at the base. Sometimes the methods used to do so were heavy-handed. More often, however, they were the more subtle approach of *permanents* in Paris disseminating what the French call *la bonne parole*. Party officials repeated over and over again, in their contacts with rank and file Communists, that things were not as bad as they seemed, that the party had made progress in recent times and that further progress was possible if militants struggled intelligently within the party to promote it. What Paris officials did, then, in response to attack from the top was to urge a tactical retreat on their Eurocommunist troops. Limits on inner party protest were presented as the best ways to survive into better days, when the good fight for Eurocommunism could be taken up again. For the most part, the message was well understood at the rank and file level.

The general tactics adopted by the party during this period led towards limiting debate and discontent as well. To begin with, the leadership followed the astute course of deluging the rank and file with different things to do and discuss, such that the central issues in the party's internal crisis were eclipsed by calls to day-to-day activity. Beyond this, the 'go-it-alone' approach adopted by the party after the elections stressed action towards workers, the poor and those most victimized by the crisis of French capitalism. Action *vis-à-vis* new middle strata was downplayed as a result. Such tactics, in themselves, stimulated strong responses of *ouvrierisme* in the PCF, reflex responses which were powerful among French Communists even in more ordinary circumstances. One major aspect of this *ouvrierisme* was, of course, anti-intellectualism. It has never been very hard for much of the PCF membership to see Communist intellectuals as potential agents of the bourgeoisie, redeemed only by their submission to the vanguard mission of the working class. This perspective, transformed into guilt, has always been present among Communist intellectuals as well. The party's year-long mobilization for the European elections in June 1979, illustrates this well. The PCF's position, strongly 'go it alone' and partly designed to attack the Socialists who were both quite European and tied international-ly to the German Social Democrats (to the PCF, the symbol of social democratic betrayal), was *ouvrieriste* and nationalist. The PCF opposed the expansion of the European Community to include Greece, Spain, and Portugal, while blaming 'Europe of the multi-nationals' and its French promoters and defenders for the 'decline of France'. Anyone (intellectuals in particular), who was sensitive to the different positions of the PCI and PCE and to any of the difficult realities of an already existing international division of labour was placed in an impossible situation. To the degree to which they voiced objections, they could be disqualified as anti-working-class and/or, in the context of the post-electoral difficulties, *contestataires*. As a result, they kept quiet, for the most part.

The so-called 'anti-Communist campaign', which the leadership discovered anew in the fall of 1978, had similar effects. The PCF's stress on this campaign was premised on the not altogether incorrect notion that in the aftermath of electoral defeat the bourgeoisie, and also the PS, had set their sights on a major reduction in Communist influence, with the destruction of the PCF as a longer-term goal.

According to the PCF, the media were the chosen instrument of this attack, which had as one of its central objects promotion of the belief that socialist change led automatically to *gulags* and that, in consequence, people would be wise to make the best of capitalism —all the fracas around the 'new philosophers' was cited as a prime example of this. One of the purposes of the stress on the 'anti-Communist campaign'—which later became the 'ideological war' in the project for the Twenty-Third Congress—was to create the atmosphere of a besieged fortress within the party. Whatever the accuracy of the leadership's analyses of the party's situation, mobilization to defeat the anti-Communist campaign created another powerful constraint on the expression of unorthodox views by Communists. More specifically, it created an automatic mechanism for the disqualification of anything *contestataires* said outside the party. Writing in *Le Monde,* publishing books on the PCF, appearing independently on television, being interviewed by the *Nouvel Observateur,* all became activities which demonstrated either the political naiveté or the treasonable intentions of any Communist who did such things.

By February 1979, when the PCF began the preparation of the Twenty-Third Congress, *contestation* had been roundly defeated. Intellectual *contestaires* still existed, to be sure, and still tried to make their voices heard *within* the party.[19] Indeed there was even some attempt to set up in Paris a regular public forum in which unorthodox views could be discussed, an experiment which revealed as much about the profound differences of opinion between protestors as anything else. What was important, however was that communications between *contestataires* and normal party life had been cut off. Serious discontent still existed within the PCF, with large numbers of rank and file Communists willing to speak their mind on any occasion. However, the bulk of discontent was directed inwards, through acceptable party channels. Moreover, an atmosphere of intimidation had been created which significantly moderated the thrust and intensity of this discontent. Few of the basic issues raised by such discontent had been dealt with, however, and in particular those about the way that the PCF worked internally. And, the process of controlling discontent had magnified old habits—which might in turn block serious confrontation with issues in the future. Complete consensus had not been restored either. For this however, the party leadership had an immense weapon in reserve—the preparation of the Twenty-Third Congress.

3. THE TWENTY-THIRD CONGRESS:
THE FUTURE BEGINS NOW?

The tri-annual Congress of the PCF is perhaps the most important single institution in the life of the party. The Congress, composed of delegates from the rank and file, is the official legislature for French Communist policy. The preparation of the Congress, in which past and future strategies of the party are elaborated, is the high point of the 'democracy' of democratic centralism. The Congress decides the PCF's line for the following three years. Its delegates elect the party's Central Committee, charged with overseeing the execution of the line between Congresses. The Central Committee, in turn, elects the *Bureau Politique* and the *Secretariat* of the party, the PCF's day-to-day leadership. Historically, PCF Congresses have had two major functions. First, they have had the manifest function of debate and deliberation on the party's past and future which the party's statutes have given them. Secondly, they have had the purpose of regenerating consensus within the PCF. Preparation of the Congress and the Congress itself have always had the goal of creating broad agreement within the party on the courses which it should follow, so that the PCF could face the world in the post-Congress period united.[20]

If the PCF's claim to hold democratic discussion prior to the Congress and its obvious desire to emerge from the Congress unanimous seem to conflict, it is because these two functions have, in fact, often been in opposition. Historically, the creation of unanimity around the leadership's policies has been more important than the consideration of policy alternatives for the Congress. The institutional key to this has always been the current leadership's power to stack the preparation of the Congress in favour of the policies which they desired. This power comes from two sources. First, the huge effort to prepare a Congress has always begun with the leadership's submission of a detailed and complete proposal to the rank and file of the policies which the Congress should adopt. This proposal then has provided the framework for pre-Congress discussion. In the history of the PCF this has meant that militants prepared Congresses on the basis of a line already decided upon by the leadership. There has never been any possibility, for example, of proposing and discussing alternative projects or of the leadership submitting a number of options to the party. As a result the task of the rank and file has been the cosmetic alteration and, ultimately, ratification of, a pre-existing line rather than open debate without *a prioris*. The quest for consensus has predominated over the desire for any consideration of policy alternatives. Beyond this, the leadership has always possessed a repertory of devices to ensure that the actual preparation of the Congress moves in the direction of the unanimous ratification of the project which they have proposed. At every stage, procedures for regulating debate, considering amendments, and electing representatives to the next level of preparation are organized by higher instances of the party.[21] The final result of these procedures and powers has not been that discussion and debate have been absent from Congresses and their preparation. Rather, it has been that the purpose of such discussion and debate has not been to make decisions. Instead, the preparation of Congresses has provided experience not unlike a vast inner-party school familiarizing Communists with the scope and characteristics of the party's new line in order to give them the facilities to deploy this line in the outside world after the Congress.

The primacy of solidarity over any real debate about policy alternatives in the history of the PCF's Congresses has not been accidental. Desire to balance the two functions in any equitable way disappeared in the Thorez era, when the practices of the Soviet Party were taken as a model. Perceptible change in the situation, perhaps more than in any other area, would be a tangible index of the PCF's real movement away from the legacies of Stalinism in its internal life. Thus, every Congress in recent times has been a test. The Twenty-Second Congress, for example, whose resolutions became the lynch-pin of PCF Eurocommunism, represented progress in the party's understanding of its environment but was prepared in the old ways. The Eurocommunist line came down from the leadership and the adoption of the new resolutions—the dictatorship of the proletariat was eliminated from party strategy by a virtually unanimous vote of the Congress—was engineered in the traditional fashion. The Twenty-Third Congress was an important event not only because of the complexity and confusion of its context, therefore, but also for what it might say about change in the PCF's internal life.

Alas, the Twenty-Third Congress could not stand aside from nor overcome the party's difficult position in 1978-9. The leadership's proposed Congress resolution, when it appeared in February 1979 to initiate the three months of Congress preparation, began with a title-slogan 'The future begins now'. Party militants who read the long text were entitled to ask to what future this referred. If it were a future of confusion, contradiction, and uncertainty, then the document's title was appropriate. Party policy was not supposed to reflect the chaos of reality, however, but to provide Communists with a clear line with which to make sense of the chaos. For the Twenty-Third Congress, the leadership's project fell short of this goal. It reflected, instead, the strategic and tactical bewilderment of the post-March 1978 period. Rather than setting out any clear perspective for the future, it *amalgamated* the positions of the currents existing within the party. While it did betray a certain bias, that of the 'go-it-alone' current, it did not foreclose other strategic possibilities. In short, it was a document designed to make peace among Communists in the present which would give those with future control over the party a number of options from which to choose.

The core policies which the document proposed were 'unity from below' and 'struggle'. The key to the future lay in mobilizing 'at the base', focusing on workers and white collar employees, the centre of the social alliance which, once constructed in the context of profound and ineluctible economic crisis, would flow outwards to incorporate new intermediary strata and thus shift the balance of power within the Left toward the PCF. 'Go-it-alone' strategic perspectives were evident also in the document's characterization of the PS as irretrievably class collaborationist *by nature*, incapable, unless forced by the class struggle, of doing anything but serve the bourgeoisie in its hour of need. The document also revealed that pro-Soviet elements within the PCF had gained new influence. The project, discussing recent history, the international balance of forces and recognizing that socialist countries still misunderstood that democracy was inseparable from socialism, nevertheless pronounced that 'the balance sheet is globally positive' for the socialist countries.[22]

The document would have looked like the product of a coalition between 'go-it-alone' strategists and keen defenders of the past attitudes towards the USSR if it had stopped there. And, had it done so, it would at least have had the virtue of some consistency. However, it went farther. The line pursued by the United Front /Eurocommunists in the seventies was not renounced at all; rather it was reaffirmed. Aside from the fact that the document underlined in several places that the Twenty-Third Congress followed the directions set out by the Twenty-Second, it was stated that *Union de la Gauche,* with certain changes based on analyses of the 1978 failure, was a future necessity, when and if 'unity from below' and 'struggles at the base' had sufficiently redressed the balance between the Communists and the Socialists. Moreover, it was not only the Marchais version of Eurocommunism which was reaffirmed. Left

Eurocommunists could find aspects of the project which supported their strategic position. 'Unity from below' was not only to be the old-style 'attack the Socialists and steal their base' formula. Instead, it was also to be *autogestionnaire.* Communists would seek out the problems of ordinary people and help them to organize democratically to solve these problems. Moreover, mass organizations and movements were to have their own lives, separate from and independent of that of the party. In this way, the PCF's goal was described as the creation of a society in which the division between those who direct and those who follow would be overcome. Indeed, a great deal of stress was placed on the notion that fundamental change would begin with diverse struggles for *autogestion* and for democracy, rather than be set in motion only by an electoral *grand soir* which would bring the Left to power.

In all this, then, almost everyone in the party could find things as well as bases for profound disagreement. What was lacking was a clear strategic perspective. In fact, this was because the party was unable to agree on any such perspective. The preparatory Congress document thus *did* reveal a significant change in the PCF. De-Stalinization, in the context of the failure of *Union de la Gauche,* had led to a strategic stalemate between the currents within the PCF which could not be overcome to produce a coherent Congress proposal. As a result, various coalitions between currents were formed, almost *ad hoc,* although the document seemed to give relative advantage to the 'go-it-alone' perspective (only in the tactical sense, however), to produce an incoherent document. Thus the Twenty-Third Congress would be unable to fulfil one of the historic functions of the PCF Congress, that of setting out a clear line for the party to follow into the near future. Because it offered something to almost everyone, it might, however, fulfil the other historic function, that of creating inner-party consensus.

The three months between the appearance of the leadership's document and the Congress itself in May provided the very strange spectacle of tens of thousands of Communists debating long and hard to achieve unity on a document whose contents were confusing in the extreme. Indeed, perhaps for this reason, there was more debate and discussion on the Congress proposal than most Communists could remember from the past. This happened partly because almost everyone, including most of those who were unhappy about March 1978 and its aftermath, knew that a demonstration of PCF unity to the outside world was important. The actual preparation of the Congress reflected this, even if it was carried on with little joy. At cell and section level, the degree of democracy in debate depended on the degree to which inner-party changes of the 1970s had already taken root. Where genuine openness had been institutionalized, genuinely open debate for the most part followed. In these cases, however, the structures of the document iself plus awareness on the part of militants of the balance of forces within the party led even severe critics of the party's recent past to *amend* the text rather than reject it. The text helped here. Its strategic balance, reflecting an evident conflict between perspectives within the leadership, gave almost everyone a position to defend *within* the document against other stances, *also* in the document. Amending the proposal meant approving it, of course. In many cases, probably the majority, approval was given because it was prompted from above, since the party organization had been fully mobilized to produce this result.[23]

It was at the next level of preparation, that of the federations of the PCF, that the leadership's desire to produce unanimity was most strongly visible. At the Paris Federal Conference, for example, the amount of institutional pressure brought to bear to produce approval of the leadership's project on a group of delegates who obviously favoured the project by an overwhelming majority to begin with was quite astonishing.[24] This is not to say that real debate and discussion were absent. If there was some genuinely contradictory and critical debate, however, the bulk of the discussion involved elucidating and analysing the Congress document rather than disagreeing with its basic choices. Even so, those presiding over the Conference encouraged an atmosphere of intimidation directed towards those in fundamental disagreement with aspects of the party's position. At the same time, all of the usual devices of contrived discussion, manipulated commissions for the consideration of amendments and prearranged nominations for positions as delegates to the Congress itself were deployed. In the judgement of observers, the same result of near unanimous approval (one vote against; four abstentions out of 580) would have been produced by free and open discussion. The anxiety of the Paris leadership seemed strangely out of place (and similar results occurred elsewhere) unless the difficulties and conflicts of the previous year were taken into account.

The Congress itself, five full days long, was a concert of unanimity, this time less contrived. It was a *grande messe, vieux style.* Speaker followed speaker to approve, illustrate, elaborate, or provide exegesis on the resolution. Out of the eighty or more

delegates who spoke to the Congress, only one made the slightest
critical remark about the proposal and his remarks, directed towards
the PCF's problems with intellectuals, were clearly within, and
perhaps prompted by, the leadership's own position on the question
(the two members of the *Bureau Politique* in charge of work with
intellectuals were both dropped from the *BP* at the Congress,
because of their inept performance). There were few signs at the
Congress of the huge explosion of protest which had occurred in the
party only months earlier. There were few signs either of the deep
malaise in large segments of the PCF about the lack of coherence in
the resolution produced by the leadership. Instead, the Congress
proceeded to make the leadership's text—and the stalemate between
currents in the party which it represented—into an historical
monument. The Congress document was passed, incoherence and
all, unanimously.

CONCLUSIONS

Did the strange spectacle of the PCF's Twenty-Third Congress
ratifying an incoherent policy proposal unanimously mean that
nothing had been resolved in the period since the 1978 elections?
Not quite! For after five full days of perfect ritual communion, an
immense surprise occurred in the last hour of the Congress. When
Gaston Plissonnier read the list of those elected to the *Bureau Politique*
and its Secretariat, the name of Roland Leroy was not included in
the Secretariat. In addition, several known supporters of the
Marchais United Front/Eurocommunist position had been promoted both to the *BP* and to the Secretariat. Roland Leroy, of course,
was the leader of the 'go-it-alone' current in the leadership. His
demotion meant at least a strategic, if not a tactical, defeat for the
'go-it-alone' group. Since no serious explanation of Leroy's 'defeat'
was given, one was obliged to resort to Kremlinological methods to
piece together what had happend. In fact, Leroy had pushed his
post-election advantage in the leadership too far and in ways which
had upset the delicate balance of forces within the party, thus
creating a coalition of forces against him, which led to his dramatic
downfall. In particular, as the Congress approached, Leroy and the
'go-it-alone' forces had tried to organize a basic repudiation of the
entire *Union de la Gauche*/Common Programme experience.[25] This
presented the rest of the PCF with the possibility that the drive
towards Eurocommunism, the stewardship of Marchais (and company), and the all-important Twenty-Second Congress would all
be disavowed. Despite the ways in which the preparation for the

Congress had been structured from the top to prevent any outbreak of *contestation* and to produce acceptance of the document, the last few weeks of inner-party discussion (and especially the section and federal conferences) revealed a substantial amount of rank and file resistance to any such drastic disavowal. Officials sent from higher levels to follow these instances of the Congress preparation could not help but notice this opposition to a complete and unequivocal disavowal of *Union de la Gauche* and repudiation of the Twenty-Second Congress. The sentiments of many militants, then, were added to the realities of the external world, to block the full implications of a 'go-it-alone' strategy.

Ultimately, then, the Twenty-Third Congress was a victory for Eurocommunism. Marchais' opening and closing speeches to the Congress affirmed this. In the first, the Secretary-General made a special point of strongly reaffirming the PCF's commitment to Eurocommunism, defining it as a democratic and pluralist vision of transition to socialism. In the second, he re-emphasized that the Twenty-Third Congress was to be interpreted as the continuation of the work of the Twenty-Second. In practical terms, it was not clear what the victory of 'Eurocommunism' implied, however. Permission was granted to the leadership to move back towards *Union de la Gauche* when circumstances looked propitious. However, the immediate tasks of rebalancing forces within the Left would have to absorb quite a bit of Communist effort before such circumstances could exist. *Union de la Gauche* was in the PCF's future, then, but probably not before the Presidential elections of 1981.

While the positive aspects of the reaffirmation of Eurocommunism at the Twenty-Third Congress are most important to underline, the negative side should not be overlooked. The defeat of the 'go-it-alone' strategic offensive had occurred not in open debate on issues of principle, but behind the closed doors of the leadership. The party in general had been apprised neither of the dimensions of conflict among its leaders—in which the future of the party was at stake—nor of the reasons why the conflict had concluded with the defeat of one of its major protagonists. Here one saw evidence of some change in the PCF, yet insufficient change, which created new problems. Decision-making in the PCF had once been completely centralized around the Secretary-General. Collective leadership had replaced this in recent years and this was an important step. Yet, collective leadership, given the existence of currents within the party, created conflict within the leadership. The doctrines of collective responsibility and secrecy observed at the top of the party meant, however, that this conflict was carried on without its nature being communicated to rank and file Communists. There are diverse reasons, good and bad, why debate on different strategic and tactical options has not been extended to the party as a whole—as it has, to a degree, within the PCI. Such debate might generate 'factions' within the party. It might also undermine the PCF's cherished self- and public image of unanimity. It might, finally, sap the party's ability to act coherently in the outside world. On the other hand, forces within the leadership effectively represent currents which really exist, and which have, in different forms, always existed, within the party. Thorezian-Stalinist autocratic centralism simply pretended that the reality of the party was otherwise. It is no longer possible to pretend this. But what now exists is an *ad hoc* system of representation of currents in the leadership covered up by a facade of unanimity. The disadvantages of the system are obvious. Ordinary Communists do not truly participate in the discussions which decide PCF policy. Rather, it is leaders who carry on this discussion in their place, but without revealing its contours and content. In the process, a mythological picture of unity in the party is perpetuated which, in itself, limits the scope of discussion and debate at the base as well as making it very complicated to cope with any instances of conflict which do break out.

The Twenty-Third Congress of the PCF was important, then, more for what it revealed about the party's problems than for solutions which it provided to them. It showed a party internally divided between different strategic currents. The advance of Eurocommunism had clearly been threatened by the 'go-it-alone' current and if the Congress blocked this threat, it did the blocking in a mysterious way which allowed few prognoses for Eurocommunism's future. Basic problems in the party's inner-life remained unresolved. Indeed, the frenetic rush earlier to isolate the *contestataires* and to produce unamimity at the Congress itself may well have been steps *away* from a resolution. The party leadership made new pledges to confront the PCF's past—most notably promising to produce a new official history of the PCF, thereby admitting by implication that existing histories were inadequate. But, by deciding that the 'balance sheet' of Socialist countries was positive, the Congress risked reinforcing some of the more powerful negative reflexes created by this past. The conception of 'unity from below' expressed in terms of democracy and *autogestion* was a promising innovation in the discussion of PCF mobilization behaviour, but there existed little evidence that the party as whole knew how to put this into practice. The sectarian characterization of the Socialists as inevitable class collaborationists would certainly not make PCF alliance behaviour any more subtle in the future either. The 'future' which 'begins now' at the Twenty-Third Congress is, therefore, an uncertain one for the PCF.

NOTES

1. Here the list of such things is long. Contradictory Central Committee discussion around the signature of the Common Programme in 1972 was hidden from the party until 1975. Only then did ordinary Communists and others learn about the extent of conflict within the party leadership about the signature. In 1974 the rapid shift from harmony with the Socialists to a year-long and quite virulent polemic against them was decreed from above in mysterious ways. The party's shift on defence policy in 1977, which led to a complete reversal of the PCF's positions on the French nuclear deterrent from opposition to support, was never discussed by the party as a whole. The summer 1977 hardening of negotiating positions in the *actualisation* talks with the Socialists, undoubtedly connected to a shift in the balance between currents in the leadership, has never been explained. We could go on, but the point is obvious.

2. For further discussion of this see Geroge Ross, 'The New Popular Front in France', in *The Socialist Register 1977* and George Ross, 'Crisis in Eurocommunism, The French Case', in *The Socialist Register 1978.*

3. The term *current* is used ably, although in a somewhat different sense from the way we use it, in Gerard Molina and Yves Vargas, *Dialogue à l'interieur du parti communiste* (Paris: Maspero, 1978). In a more recent quasi-official book published by the PCF's publishing house, Jean Burles also uses the term. See J. Burles, *Le parti communiste dans la société française* (Paris: Editions Sociales, 1979).

4. The great *affaires* in the PCF's history were, in fact, the settling of accounts between the party leadership and the representatives of currents who refused to accept the leadership's definitions of PCF strategy. Barbe-Célor in the late 1920s was the first. The major post-war *affaires* were those which led to the elimination of Charles Tillon and André Marty in the early 1950s (because of their nationalism), and the banishing of Marcel Servin, Laurent Casanova and a host of lesser figures in 1961 (because of their disagreement with Thorez over the nature of Gaullism and the strategies which ought to be followed to deal with Gaullism). The last, if lesser, *affaire*, was the expulsion of Roger Garaudy in 1969-70 because of Garaudy's positions on new middle strata and intellectuals.

5. In the months after mid 1975 the PCF denounced the Societ Union's lack of democracy and its actions on human rights, took new steps to make the PCF a mass, as opposed to a *cadre* party, and abolished the

party's committment to a dictatorship of the proletariat at the Twenty-Second Congress. It also joined the Italians, Spanish and Yugoslavs in opposing Soviet hegemonism at the Conference of European Communist Parties in East Berlin in 1976.

We have stressed the importance of leaders in making inchoate feelings into coherent positions. In this process of Eurocommunization after 1975 it is clear that the role of Jean Kanapa, Georges Marchais's 'brain' and *eminence grise,* was absolutely central. Kanapa, the PCF's international affairs specialist in the mid 1970s, shifted the PCF's positions on the Soviet Union and promoted new contacts with the PCI. Kanapa was also the chairman and chief energizer of the Central Committee work group which prepared the resolution for the Twenty-Second Congress, hence the promoter of the abandonment of the dictatorship of the proletariat. His death in September 1978 was an important blow to the dynamics of the United Front/Eurocommunists. Georges Marchais, essentially a politician oriented to day-to-day action, lost his major connection to theory and longer-term analyses. One can never be sure of the exact importance of individuals in shaping organizations, but the absence of Jean Kanapa was certainly of great significance in the PCF's difficulties after his death.

6. There were other notable instances of conflict between currents causing shifts in PCF policy. It is more than likely, for example, that the PCF's hardened position in the negotiations with the PS over updating the Common Programme in the summer of 1977 followed from a shift in the balance of currents at leadership level.

7. The party developed a unique tactic for discrediting the PS in this period, its stress on the Socialists' alleged 'double language'. Essentially this tactic, directed mainly towards PCF militants, accused the Socialists of lying about their real politics—right wing—when the Socialists said anything with a left tinge, and accused the Socialists of telling the truth—right wing—when the Socialists did talk like social democrats. Such 'heads I win, tails you lose' manicheanism was redolent of the bad old days of the 'class against class' period of the late twenties.

8. The history of the CGT in this period is another story altogether, and a fascinating one at that. The CGT reacted to the 1978 defeat by taking a pronounced turn towards new openness and new independence from the PCF. Its Fortieth Congress in Grenoble in November, 1978 was almost certainly the most democratic and innovative Congress in modern CGT history. It is clear that a number of important CGT leaders, including some Communists, believed that such a new course was, in itself, necessary to ensure the CGT's future. It may also be that the CGT was being prompted in such directions to counterweigh the predominance of 'go-it-alone' perspectives in the party as a weapon on the side of the United Front/Eurocommunists. Certain evidence about the behavior of Georges Seguy, CGT Secretary-General, indicates that he was profoundly opposed to the turn in the *Bureau Politique* of the party, of which he was an important

member towards 'going it alone'. The CGT is always more comfortable, for reasons of mass appeal, when the party is open to other political forces, least so when it is isolated.

9. The degree to which most of the PCF was attached symbolically to the positions of the Twenty-Second Congress—the high point of PCF Eurocommunism—was evident from the fact that even the most ferocious advocates of 'going it alone' were obliged to present themselves as continuing in the line of the Twenty-Second Congress, even when this was not true.

10. The *'droit de râler'* notion comes from Molina and Vargas, *op.cit.* See also their very interesting contribution in H. Weber and O. Duhamel, *Changer le PCF* (Paris: PUF, 1979).

11. On this see Ross, *Socialist Register 1978, op.cit.,* pp. 179 ff., and footnotes.

12. A. Adler *et al, L'URSS et Nous* (Paris: Editions Sociales, 1978).

13. Debate on *L'URSS et Nous* in the party was not calm. The book attacked some long-cherished rank and file illusions about Socialist societies which numbers of Communists were not eager to relinquish. Indeed, by December or so the book had created a considerable backlash in the party, perhaps contributing to the inclusion in the proposal for the Twenty-Third Congress of the section which concluded with the 'globally positive balance sheet' for Socialist countries. It is certain that the debate led to the coalescence of a pro-Soviet sub-current in the leadership, around the powerful Gaston Plissonnier who, in turn, probably played a major role in the demotion of Roland Leroy which we discuss in the conclusions to the present essay.

14. See Yann Viens, *et al, La condition féminine* (Paris: Editions Sociales, 1978).

15. For accounts of this meeting see *l'Humanité,* 11 December 1978, pp. 3-9.

16. See *La Nouvelle Critique,* November and December 1979. This latter issue contains a painful explanation by the editors of why they acceded to the leadership's pressure. The articles whose publication was blocked were published, in part, by *Nouvel Observateur* in December.

17. Jean Rony, an eminent *contestataire* who would not give in, and also a member of the *France Nouvelle* board, simply ceased to be invited to board meetings. For a poignant discussion of the *France Nouvelle* affair see Yvon Quiles, another ex-editor, in *Maintenant,* No. 1., 5 March 1979.

18. At about the same time there was a purge of personnel at *Editions Sociales,* the party publishing house, connected in part to a financial crisis but also with the presence of rebels among the directors of *ES.*

19. Books from PCF dissidents flowed from French presses with incredible rapidity. Both *Les Editions du Seuil* and *François Maspero* established full series of such books. In the Seuil series, all published in 1979, see Raymond Jean, *La singularité d'être communiste,* Jacques Brière (ex-*France Nouvelle*), *Vive la crise!'* Gerard Belloin (also ex-*France Nouvelle*), *Nos rêves, camarades,* Antoine Spire, (ex-*Editions Sociales*), *Profession*

Permanent. In the Maspero collection, all 1979, see F. Bouillot and J. M. Devésa, *Un parti peut en cacher un autre,* Christine Buci-Glucksmann *et al, L'Ouverture d'une discussion,* Etienne Balibar, Guy Bois, G. Labica, *Ouvrons la fenêtre, camarades!* See also Hélène Parmelin, *Libérez les communistes!* (Paris: Stock, 1979). Jean Rony's *30 ans du parti* (Paris: C. Bourgois, 1978) is also noteworthy. *Contestataires* also wrote regularly in *Maintenant* in the spring of 1979. Dissident journals such as *Luttes et Débates* (Paris) and *Positions* (from the Bordeaux PCF student group) were also influential. Perhaps the most interesting book of all from this period on the PCF is Weber and Duhamel, *Changer le PCF, Op.cit.* The pieces in this book by Molina and Vargas and Labica are excellent, while the articles by Christine Buci-Glucksmann and Jean Rony are perhaps the best discussions of the Left Eurocommunist position to be found anywhere.

20. 'Preparing the Congress' means a long and complex series of activities. First the party leadership publishes its proposal for a Congress Resolution. Next this proposal is debated and amended at cell level, and the cell elects delegates to represent its positions at the Section Conference. During the three month pre-Congress period in 1979 cells were enjoined to meet weekly to discuss different aspects of the proposal. The next step, the Section Conference, repeats the same actions in a concentrated period of two days, while electing its new leadership and delegates to Federation Conference at the same time. The Federation Conference deliberates again on the proposal for two or three days and elects delegates to the Congress. Congress itself sits for almost a week before voting the final resolution.

21. Every preparatory stage for the Congress above that of the cell (and more often than not at the cell level as well) is overseen by a figure (or figures) from the higher leadership, who often colludes with the chair to supervise the momentum of discussion. Amendments to the proposal are considered, first of all, by small committees appointed by the leadership of the instance in question (Section, Federation, Congress) who are empowered to recommend the acceptance of some and the refusal of others. Again, more often than not this means that amendments are considered which provide editorial or other change in accordance with leaderships' desires, and not in accordance with the desire for open debate. Candidacies for positions of delegates to the next higher instances (Section to Federation, Federation to Congress) are considered in similar Committees which propose a list of nominees only as long as necessary to fill the number of posts and clearly in accordance with that the leadership desires. Such committees also use a number of other criteria, such as social origins, for deciding on officers and delegates, criteria which can be used to manipulate nominations. In 1979, over and above all of this, PCF leaderships at all levels were enjoined to follow certain quite specific criteria of appointment designed to filter out possible *contestataires.* In all of this it is extremely difficult for any obvious unorthodoxy to reach the floor of the Congress itself.

22. The apparition of this *bilan globalement positif* in the Congress proposal probably was due to change in the international environment (in particular the 'human rights' campaign of the Carter administration and the Sino-Vietnamese war), to the inner-party backlash against *L'URSS et Nous* which we have already discussed, and to the new ability of pro Soviet members of the leadership to bargain their support for other policies in exchange for retrenchment on the question of existing Socialist countries, given conflict between currents in the party.

23. Numbers of cells, and a few isolated sections, actually rejected the proposal. But even on these levels, where discontent was most powerful, the proposal was usually approved overwhelmingly.

24. The presence of such a favourable body of delegates was not due to chance, of course. Delegates had been carefully filtered at Section Level in most sections to weed out possible opponents of the proposal. Thus only a very small number of people actually reflected the degree of discontent persisting at the base in their Conference speeches.

25. In the last three weeks or so before the Congress a new and powerful theme was introduced from above into the Congress preparation. This was that the Common Programme had, from the beginning, created a 'demobilizing logic'. There was some attempt on the part of the United Front/Eurocommunists to balance this by discussion of the 'positive aspects' of the Common Programme experience. But it was clear that the debate was being prodded from quarters in the party who believed that this experience had no 'positive aspects' and that it ought to be repudiated outright.

THE POLITICAL TRANSITION IN SPAIN:
AN INTERPRETATION*

Julio Rodriguez Aramberri

1

It may appear to be an impossible task to account for what has happened in Spain between 1975 and 1979; what was expected to happen at the beginning of that period has not occurred. The turn that events have taken is well known. In the spring of 1979, after elections to both the Constitutional Assembly and the legislature, and municipal elections, the government of the country remains in the hands of those who have exercised power for the last forty years. And yet there is one important difference: in those four years, the dictatorship has given way to a democratic State, and those who lead that State now enjoy the same legitimacy as those of any other Western European country. There are, of course, any number of objections that can be raised to that assertion—not least among them the fact that the first President of a democratic government was one of the last Ministers in Franco's regime; nevertheless, that transition has been realized in Spain.

Until now, there have been almost no attempts to interpret the new situation. The usual description, offered by both right and left wings in parliament—is that now at last, after 150 years of political agitation, all social forces have reached responsible agreement in producing a democratic constitution of national concord. This, they say, will guarantee a free and peaceful future, in which the

* This article only seeks to offer a perspective on the process as a whole: it is not a substitute for the detailed historical task that has still to be undertaken. Even in the general field of concern that it does cover, there are a number of questions (the problems of nationalities in the Spanish State; the concrete situation of the different social forces; terrorist activities, etc.) that have not even been posed. This essay is no more than an attempt to find the logic of the situation in Spain as a whole, together with some reflections on the problems that arise from it for anyone who attempts to approach the facts in the light of a Marxist method.

172

opportunity to govern will be open to anyone who can command sufficient popular support. This image of an as yet unknown future, however, does not explain how such an agreement came to be possible nor what social and political mechanisms produced it. Leaving aside the illusion of the stages of economic growth à la Rostow, and the chimerical theories of industrial society—neither of which enjoy very much favour any longer in this period of crisis—a Marxist critique must begin by explaining one fundamental question; how is it that a process of class struggle that most observers regarded as deeply menacing on the eve of Franco's death, should in the intervening period have been so attenuated?

On both right and left, the louder voices have concurred in interpreting the facts on what we might call a neo-Machiavellian basis. The common slogan is 'Nothing has changed'—though it takes on different nuances according to the political position of the user. For some groups of the extreme left, it means that we are still living under a dictatorship whose appearance alone has changed. It is true, of course, that there have been only minimal changes in the State apparatus; yet whatever yardstick of democracy one uses, there is no sense in which the Spanish State in 1979 is a dictatorship. There is a free opposition, a parliament, elections, civil liberties, etc.—all those elements that underlie a democratic regime.

Others[1] distinguish between the Franco regime and the present one by pointing to what they call the 'broadening of the political class', or governing elite, to include representatives of the left-wing parties. Such a view both ignores the form in which class domination is exercised, and leaves the specific character of the changes that have taken place unclear. Why, after all, did such a change not take place five or ten years earlier, given such social and psychological assumptions; was the ambition of the leaders of the left-wing parties and their aspiration to join the oligarchy not as real then as now?

Among those Marxists who have rejected simplistic explanations, the results have been equally unremarkable. The best-known attempt to offer an explanation, in fact, was made by N. Poulantzas[2] —and as such it merits some detailed attention. His analysis, an attempt to apply to a concrete case some of the categories developed in his *Social Classes in Contemporary Capitalism*, takes as its starting point the political crises in some States of southern Europe from 1974 onwards; these crises are situated in the context of the changing international balance of forces in the capitalist world. During the sixties, this change generated in these countries a process of *dependent industrialization*[3], whose impact was considerable, especially on the ruling classes; for its result was the division between the old comprador bourgeoisie and the fractions that Poulantzas calls the *internal bourgeoisie*[4]. Although monopoly capital has a strong presence in both, the first represents above all the agrarian and financial interests, while the second consists in its majority of industrial fractions. On the international level, the first is linked to US support, while the second is orientated towards the Common Market.

These fractions also confront one another on the political terrain, for the comprador bourgeoisie favours the continuation of military dictatorship in those countries, the internal bourgeoisie advocates a process of liberalization that will enable it to adapt the political machine to its own needs. The changes in Portugal and Greece between 1974 and 1975, and the changes that Poulantzas envisaged in Spain at the time he wrote his book, would be the result of the displacement of hegemony within the ruling classes towards the sector of the internal bourgeoisie—together with the creation of a new political framework. As far as the dominated classes were concerned, this change in the political centre of gravity would have important consequences for them, insofar as the internal bourgeoisie would be their ally in the transition to a democratic regime.[5]

This is not the place for a detailed analysis of the general hypothesis, rendered less relevant in any case by the passing of time. Yet it is worthwhile underlining some of its limitations. First, on the methodological level, Poulantzas suffers from an excessive desire, despite his insistence on the relative autonomy of different levels, to find an economic correlation for all transformations in the political superstructure. Undoubtedly, the economic changes that took place during the sixties in the countries of Southern Europe provide the backcloth for the events of the seventies; but to my mind they do so, above all, to the extent that they affect the global relations between classes rather than the transformations that occur from time to time within the ruling classes. By emphasizing the second aspect, Poulantzas exaggerates the internal divisions within the ruling classes while leaving aside one factor that is absolutely necessary for that analysis—namely, the relations between the dominated classes and the political organizations that represent them. Thus the fundamental role in events played by the Socialist and Communist parties is relegated to a secondary place.[6]

A second question concerns the existence or otherwise of this economic division within the ruling classes. Of course there are different tendencies; but these differences are not in my view (at least the Spanish case) structural and economic so much as divergences over the political decisions to be taken and their foreseeable consequences. Poulantzas's demarcation between the old and the internal bourgeoisie and their concomitant financial/agrarian, industrial fractions with their different orientations towards the USA or the EEC are artificial in the case of Spain and do not correspond to reality.[7] It certainly does not enable us to understand the move of banking capital towards the Union of the Democratic Centre (UCD)—which in Poulantzas's terms would represent the internal bourgeoisie—not the corresponding distancing from Alianza Popular (which would seem more in accord with those financial interests); nor would it explan why the vast majority of the Spanish bourgeoisie *as a whole* feels itself to be represented by the UCD.

The third and final critique to be levelled at Poulantzas is that he sows illusions about the possibility of an alliance between the internal bourgeoisie and the dominated classes. Certainly there was in Spain an increasing tendency among a large part of the bourgeoisie to favour the democratic reform of the dictatorship. It was very careful, however, to set out clearly the limits of change and to emphasize that it alone would determine the rate and direction of such change, thus ensuring that the mass movement would not go beyond those boundaries. As we shall see, these limits were quickly accepted by the major parties of the left; an alliance would have been practically impossible on any other terms.

We have thus set out the basic theses that underpin the present essay. In the context both of the international economic crisis and the social transformations that were taking place in the 1960s, there had occurred in Spain a change in the global relation of forces between the two major classes, marked by an increasing paralysis in the Francoist State which favoured the mass movement. A political crisis was germinating which threatened to become a crisis of bourgeois domination unless it could be contained. If that bourgeoisie, on the other hand, was to retain power, then it must urgently find a new democratic legitimacy. Such a transformation could not occur on its sole initiative; it would have to be *the result of an agreement with the left.* That was the key issue.

Such an agreement could only occur within a democratic State—but not any democracy. It would have a strong right-wing orientation as a result of the limitations on the process laid down by the bourgeoisie, and be designed to ensure that it would recover the political initiative. These limitations were three, all concerned with the maintenance of the State apparatus and its continuing control by the bourgeoisie. The first was the acceptance of the monarchic form of the State as a guarantee of institutional continuity. The second laid down the necessity that Spain should maintain its territorial unity—though the concrete form that it would take would have different bases than those laid down by the oppressive Francoist State. Finally, the reins of power would be kept in reliable hands during the process of transition; for the bourgeoisie did not propose to accept, except under extreme pressure, the formation of a provisional government to oversee the transition. Within these limitations, it was prepared to open negotiations with the forces of the left on many other aspects of the future organization of a democratic regime. The way in which those limitations came to be defined and, let it be said, the ease with which they were accepted by the left, give the transition to democracy in Spain a special character.

2

The death of Franco (on 20 November 1975) found both major classes of Spanish society unprepared. It was neither unexpected, nor had there been any lack of attempts to create alternative organizations[8]; yet neither the right, nor the mass movement—in which the Spanish Communist Party (PCE) and other left organizations played a central role—had either a political programme or the organization necessary to ensure an outcome in their favour to the crisis that occurred in the wake of Franco's death.

The vast majority of the bourgeoisie had remained loyal to the Franco regime; despite its inability to respond to the political crisis of the beginning of the seventies with anything other than further repression[9], there was no internal rupture. There were, and increasingly clearly, differences of opinion over tactics; but the bourgeoisie as a whole remained united until the death of the General, and made no attempt to find a political alternative.

This should not be interpreted to mean that the right is absolutely incapable of evolving. The liberalizing, neo-democratic, reformist current was gaining influence, and argued the need for substantial political change. The *bunker,* the sector of the intransigents, was losing influence to the reformists; so already by that time it would be wrong to imagine that the only solution that they would be able to find would be at a 'continuism' along the lines of Caetano in neighbouring Portugal.

Within the bourgeoisie, there were only tiny sectors who had fought against the dictatorship[10]. It is true that there had been a certain flowering of bourgeois and petit-bourgeois parties with democratic pretensions since the sixties; but all of them were prepared to wait for a change in the political framework which would allow them to occupy the centre of the stage. On the other hand, this bourgeois opposition combined a lack of energy with an enormous distrust of the mass movement and the Marxist left, though slightly modified no doubt in the case of the Socialists. With the two examples of Greece and Portugal before them, the bourgeois opposition knew that they were incapable of producing anything like the first, and feared more than anything a repetition of the second. That placed it in a mid-way position between the reformists of the regime and the left, without enabling it to play an independent political role.[11]

The left, however, also lacked a clear political project or a unitary organization capable of imposing one. It enjoyed considerable strength, as a result of a forceful mass movement which exercised considerable political pressure. Yet that movement too was very contradictory in its composition and its aims; it embraced working-class and popular struggles, the national question and general democratic demands.

The struggles of the working class, and later progressively of white collar workers, revolved fundamentally around the maintenance of living standards and the improvement of working conditions. The illegal status of all organization and all resistance under the dictatorship, however, tended to turn them very quickly into struggles against repression. The inevitable police intervention brought demands for freedom for detainees, the right to strike, the disbanding of the police, etc., which almost immediately endowed any economic struggle with a political character. A similar thing occurred at the organizational level; without trade union or negotiating rights, the workers organized themselves into representative commissions and strike committees, closely linked to the rank and file through mass meetings, with the result that their struggles became increasingly radical.[12]

Another aspect of the mass movement were the actions that took place around the national question. For years, Franco's policy had been to persecute any autonomist expression, be it political or cultural; yet these demands had become increasingly insistent as the years passed[13], and had built a strong organizational base.

Lastly, the mass movement developed around slogans of a general, political kind, at the head of which was the demand for a total amnesty for political prisoners and exiles, and a demand for democratic freedoms. In this area too, the movement had grown from partial actions and a fundamentally student character to mass actions which made it possible to draw together all the different sectoral struggles.

In the 1970s, the mass movement developed an enormous strength, and realized actions which put the dictatorship in an insoluble dilemma—how to repress or to make concessions without reinforcing the movement still further? This was the sign for the great majority of the bourgeoisie to start arguing the need for political change. A solution had to be found to a political crisis which could, under its own impetus, develop into a crisis of domination.

And despite all its problems, such a solution was available. The political domination of the bourgeoisie had now to be situated in a new, democratic framework. A democratic regime would be able to find solutions for many problems that were intractable under the dictatorship. Above all, it would normalize production, limit workers' actions to their 'natural' economic level and would provide the employers with a real spokesman in their dealings with the unions. A measure of self-government for the nationalities and regions of the State would allay the danger of a breakdown in national unity, a danger that was clearly present in the very wide demand for self-determination that the whole of the left was putting forward at the time. Lastly, a democratic regime—or the promise of one—would de-activate the general actions, and allow the often antagonistic interests represented within the mass movement to express their differences freely. Democracy appeared to be the best way of holding back the movement and at the same time to restrain the uncontrolled opposition that a maintenance at all costs of the Francoist State could generate.

These limits coincided, furthermore, with the vision put forward within the mass movement by its political representatives. Since 1956, the PCE's whole policy of *national reconciliation* had been directed towards the creation of a democratic State like those in the rest of Europe. There had been different forms of political action argued to achieve these ends[14]; yet the goal was constant. The position of the Socialists was not very different. As the inheritors and defenders of the Republican tradition, they saw in the formation of a bourgeois-democratic regime the best means to reinforce their political position and to initiate the social reforms that would make it possible to advance towards the achievement of their maximum

programme. Finally, despite their intricate internal disputes concerning the true party of the proletariat, the Maoist organizations
were equally unable to envisage the building of their Popular
Republic on any other economic base but capitalism. If the
differences regarding possible alliances, the rate of change or
concrete tactics were enormous within the left, there was no such
divergence over the ultimate objective. Save for a few hundred
Trotskyists, the next phase of the Spanish political process was seen
by all to involve the formation of a bourgeois-democratic State.

Thus, at least in theory, the foundations were laid for an
agreement between the great social forces; but those foundations
were as ambiguous as they were broad. There are many forms of
articulation of political democracy; and, even within a single
framework, the extension of democratic freedoms varies according
to the global relations between the classes. Thus it is not a question
of criticizing the democratic road in the name of a socialism which,
as we have seen, hardly anybody believed possible; the problem is
that the democratic process in Spain has been carried forward in
such a way that the possibility that the present democratic
framework will permit a resolute struggle for socialism is very
remote indeed.

The issue may be clearer if we follow the distinction made by
some writers on constitutional law, between a granted democracy,
an agreed democracy, and a revolutionary democracy. For all its
formalism, this distinction shows the solution to the problems of
transition in Spain to have been the second—a pact between the
major forces of right and left within the framework of limitations
imposed by the former—as we have already shown. The history of
these years is a history of confluence at that intermediate level,
avoiding both a granting of democracy (from above) and a political
revolution that would have involved the formation of a provisional
government under pressure from the mass movement. Each phase of
the 'Spanish political miracle' has centred on the attempt to reach
such an agreement.

3

The first phase is characterized by the non-viability of a granted
democracy, as demonstrated in the complex events which are briefly
described below.

The first path chosen by the Spanish bourgeoisie, although
uncertain of its results, led to a granted political reform—designed,

defined and tightly controlled by the existing power. The forces of the opposition would be given neither a voice nor a role to play. This solution was attempted by the Arias government of December 1975 to July 1976.

The idea, as it was expounded by Fraga Iribarne, one of its main exponents, was to form a regime similar to that of West Germany, with a strong executive and the exclusion of the PCE and other left organizations from political life. The initiative would be in the hands of the government and the Cortes; once the reform was drafted, the 'permitted' forces would be invited to participate; thus the reform extended no further than the democratic opposition and the socialists. Yet at no time were the time scale or the conditions of the reform made clear.

As far as the opposition and the mass movement were concerned, it was a totally unacceptable proposal, and the response was not long in coming. Between December 1975 and February 1976, Spain was in the grip of an almost total general strike[15] whose demands were both economic and political (including demands for the resignation of certain ministers, for democratic rights, etc.), and which showed both the power and the determination of the movement. The general strike, led with great caution by the PCE especially, was the clearest sign that the plans of the government could not work. So that government found itself facing the same dilemma as the last Francoist governments—to repress or to integrate. The events of Vitoria and Montejurra[16] showed clearly that they were not capable of the first; at the same time, the government lacked the initiative to carry through the kind of reforms that would be acceptable to the opposition.

Thus far from dividing it, the prospect of a democracy granted from above had only succeeded in uniting the opposition both organizationally and in common programmes. At the beginning of 1976, in Paris, Professor Ruiz Gimenez argued that 'democracy must come quickly if we are to avoid civil war'; his view clearly summed up the feelings of the democratic opposition and significant sectors of the bourgeoisie who remained within the regime, yet felt increasing desperation at the government's lack of initiative'[17] Neither Ruiz Gimenez nor anyone else in the circles in which he moved actually believed in the possibility of civil war—but his dramatic tone did give a clear message; that a different road to that proposed by the government would now have to be found in order to pre-empt and limit the effects of the political crisis to come. That explains why, from then on, the bourgeois opposition showed itself better disposed to an effective approach to the left.

The consequence of the general strike and the events of Vitoria was the formation of a broad opposition front, Democratic Co-ordination (CD), at the end of March 1976. CD brought together the ex-members of the Democratic Junta and the Platform for Democratic Convergence—that is liberal and social-democratic sectors—independent personalities, Left Christian Democracy (Ruiz-Gimenez), the Carlist Party, almost the whole of the left (PSP, PSOE, PCE, MCE, ORT and PTE) as well as the two major underground trade union organizations, the UGT and the Workers Commissions (CC.OO). It was presented as as short-term agreement, to last until there was a democratic break with the regime and a constitutional government was formed. Such a break would come with the achievement of a set of minimum conditions: constitutional process, amnesty, freedom of organization and the granting of political rights and freedoms to the nationalities and regions of the Spanish State. The programme was close to that of the more moderate sectors and included no demands that would be incompatible with the maintenance of a capitalist system.

In formulating its understanding of how such a break would come about, CD talked about the need to mobilize the popular masses and form a provisional government. At no point, however, did this lead to any kind of united or co-ordinated effort at mobilization; on the contrary, in insisting that any such action required unanimous agreement, the initiative was left in the hands of the moderate groups and parties—organizations that would never have been able to set such activity in motion (even if they had wanted to) because they had never had the slightest contact with the mass movement. As far as the provisional government was concerned, it was never clear what its relation to mass activity would be. For CD's ambiguous nature was a sign of its intention to open negotiations with the government and the powers that be in order to avoid the danger of the break taking the form of a political revolution, as it had in Portugal.[18]

It is not surprising, then, that in the months that followed, the democratic break should have been attended with all sorts of modifying adjectives, the most popular of which were *agreed* or *negotiated break*. Between the granted reforms that had already proved not to be viable, and political revolution, the opposition as a whole, bourgeois and left, were opening the way to a negotiated solution.

A decisive factor here was the attitude of the PCE. For it held the key to the mass movement, and was in a position to determine its extent and its terms of activity. If the PCE leaned towards negotation in exchange for its legalization, the road to compromise was open; the PCE understood this perfectly, and showed itself disposed to agreement. At the end of June 1976, the Executive Committee of the PCE issued a statement in which it reiterated the need to abandon a politics of 'all or nothing' and supported the notion of 'an agreed democratic break' within the limits proposed by the CD. The statement ended in a way which unmistakeably pointed to a conditional recognition of the Monarchy.[19]

During the period of transition, there was a frequently stated view that the defence of a Republican regime was no more than an overnight conversion to the current legitimacy. A modern State, went the argument, could be equally democratic whether it was a Republic or a Monarchy. If that was the case, then the PCE's policy would have been entirely reasonable; but the real problem was a very different one. The King was the visible head of a State apparatus that the right wished to maintain intact at all costs. To pose the question of a Republic was not merely to take an outmoded position, but to argue for the democratization of the State apparatus itself. In its whispered conditional recognition of the monarchy, the PCE was abandoning that demand; and everyone saw this clearly.

In May 1976, the options of the regime's reformists and the opposition came increasingly close. The CD's statement on the reform plans presented by the Arias government[20] showed that, although these were unacceptable, others would not be, and that it (CD) was prepared for a 'negotiated break'. Finally, it affirmed that the future provisional government could be the object of negotiation with those sectors of the existing power prepared to recognize democratic freedoms; which gave the eixsting government the initiative as far as defining the limits of reform was concerned. At the same time, CD suspended its call for mass mobilization and repeated its old minimum conditions for negotiations. The statement coincided in almost every particular with the proposals presented by J. M. de Areilza, at the time Foreign Minister, in the search for a national agreement.

The issues were thus clear and both sides had shown their willingness to seek agreement. Its concrete form had yet to be decided; inevitably, that task would fall to a new government.

4

In the eleven months between July 1976 and June 1977 (elections to the Constitutional Assembly) the pact found concrete form. It was not an easy manoeuvre, but with the formation of the Suarez government the right regained the initiative they had lost after the general strike at the beginning of 1976. In exchange, free elections were promised; the task of preparing and winning them fell to the Suarez government.

Adolfo Suarez was almost unknown when he was given this mission; a protégé of Carrero Blanco, under whose Ministry (of Information) he had been Director of Spanish Television (TVE), he became Minister of the (Francoist) Movement under Arias. He had made no change in its structure, nor was he identified with any political option other than that of saving the interests of his class. He is a type of politician that frequently emerges from the Spanish bourgeoisie at times of crisis, whose distinctive feature is neither the formulation of ambitious policies nor any great ability as a statesman, but the immediate defence of those interests and a prodigious capacity for manoeuvre and negotiation.

The negotiations would have to take place on two levels at once; on the one hand, the left would have to be convinced of the need for the reforms offered and their authenticity. And this required some immediate decisions in the political sphere. On the other hand, the right as a whole would require proof that the negotiations would be undertaken with firmness and without abandoning any of its fundamental conditions. For many representatives of the right, change was both necessary and dangerous, for nearly all of them had taken part in repression and/or corruption—the two great pillars of the dictatorship. That is why they demanded that the process of transition take place little by little and always at the initiative of the government.

Suarez had to take this very seriously. The issue of amnesty, for example, is instructive in this respect. As we know, amnesty was the most consistent demand through every action of the mass movement. In the end, amnesty was achieved in the form and within the limits set out by the government, that is through staged and arbitrary measures designed to ensure that they were never seen as the result of popular action. The first amnesty (July 1976) was to recognize this constraint by extending its clauses only to those who had neither participated in nor were accomplices of crimes of violence. The second decree, on the eve of the elections (March 1977), did include them; but the government reserved to itself the final decision on the release of those whose offences were considered the most serious. A total amnesty would come only with the constitution of the new democratic Cortes (parliament) in October 1977, and even then there were exceptions to it which were accepted by the left, the most important of which was the exclusion of members of the Military Democratic Union (UMD)[21]. In every case, amnesty was the result of a government initiative.

Having promised elections and made its first moves in the matter of amnesty, the government would now set out to seek the explicit consensus of the different fractions of the bourgeoisie and the basic institutions of the State apparatus—fundamentally the army.

Little is known, other than unreliable rumours, about events within the military or the attitudes of its commanders during this period. The military bureaucracy, highly-disciplined, has allowed few leaks and the important decisions have been taken in the utmost secrecy. In any event, their effect has been an acceptance of political reform, apparently contradicting the image of an army disposed at any time to launch a *coup d'état*, an image frequently presented by the PCE and other left organizations. There are few real reasons to confirm this hypothesis, despite the obsessive way in which it has been repeated. To say this is neither to glorify the army nor to fall into the mythology of professionalism. In Spain as elsewhere, the army is the backbone of bourgeois domination, and especially during and since the Civil War, has exercised its repressive functions without scruple. Yet even an officer corps as carefully selected on the basis of its loyalty to authority and its opposition to democracy and socialism, as closed in upon itself and marginal to civil society as the Francoist army, is not totally impervious to either social pressures or the political decisions adopted by the ruling class. It was these hard political realities that pushed and continue to push the majority of the army towards the view that negotiated reform is the only realistic alternative, despite the strong reservations it may have internally about democracy. In terms of the arguments put forward in this essay, then, it is clear that the attitude of the army reflected the same global *political project*.

The project and the attitude could of course change, if repression appeared as the only alternative. But at the time we are describing, reform was the basic option. Thus the army and the bourgeoisie were prepared to accept a wider basis of negotiation if the left, through mobilizing the mass movement in order to strengthen its negotiating position, refused to bow without reply to the conditions imposed by the right. The illusion of an imminent *coup*, far from describing adequately the real relations of forces at the time, in fact served to justify the timorous policies of the left.[22] It is in fact very likely that, far from fomenting a *coup*, responsible mass mobilization would have broadened the field of democracy. On the other hand, the failure to demand the purging of those sectors who were in favour of a *coup*, thus allowing them to move with total impunity up to the present, is one of the most disturbing elements when one looks ahead to future social conflicts. It is still more disturbing that the left, in order to ingratiate itself with the supposedly constitutionalist sectors of the army, demands that it be given still more fire-power—conveniently forgetting how those professional capacities will be used when the occasion arises. At all events, in the autumn of 1976, after a series of meetings, the military gave the government the green light to proceed with its plans for political reform. The changes and reforms in the military that followed[23] thus consolidated this way forward; the obstacle represented by the Francoist Cortes, where the most extreme right elements were over-represented and might thus not vote in favour of the abolition of the dictatorship, was thus overcome. This once again testified to the unanimity achieved by the different sectors of the bourgeoisie. The Cortes approved the government's draft proposal for political reform, and it was subsequently confirmed by the national referendum of 15 December 1976. Thus the negotiations for political change—if there were any at all—would be conducted on a basis determined by the right, and the opposition would have to accept them in their totality.

Within the opposition, the winds of change were certainly not blowing strong. At the end of the summer, the opposition appeared to reach its organizational peak with the constitution of the Platform of Democratic Organizations (POD), which brought together CD and similar formations among the different nationalities and regions. The POD's programme, however, was the most minimalist yet. Behind the obligatory but consistently unrealized call for 'peaceful popular mobilizations' and the still ritual formula of 'democratic break', the statement was silent on the formation of a provisional government and accepted the continuing existence of the Suarez government. In fact, 'the meeting of united organizations expresses its willingness to negotiate with the existing powers of the State, among them the government, believing it to be essential that the negotiations should take place in a public and unitary way on the part of the opposition'.

In the months that followed, as government plans became clearer, even the minimum conditions for negotiation began to disappear. The opposition, while maintaining a lukewarm abstentionism before the referendum which was designed to sanction government plans, finally formed a Negotiating Commission jointly with the tiny groups that were still not included in the CD or the POD, which would meet with the government and begin a series of still ill-defined negotiations. This was the famous Commission of Nine[24], which presented itself as the voice of the whole opposition and whose representation included organizations from the liberals to the Maoists; the latter—irony of ironies—represented by none other than Santiago Carrillo, general secretary of the PCE.

Now the opposition was going to the Moncloa Palace to negotiate what for years had been regarded as the prior conditions for any negotiation (amnesty, legalization of all political parties and trade union organizations, etc.). The acceptance of the limits set by the right could not have been clearer. The public character of the negotiations, which the opposition had always promised, was never ensured; and the negotiations went no further than approval of the electoral law[25] and the exploration of government intentions. This, then, was the outcome of the initial demands of the various organizations united within the opposition.

This attitude of negotiation and even of determined collaboration was further reinforced by the events of the so-called *semana negra* (black week) in Madrid.[26] For the left's conclusion from those events was that the government must be given further room for manoeuvre, while it should itself make no demands of its own. This attitude has been constant in the face of all terrorist actions ever since, actions which have occurred with suspicious regularity on the eve of important events or whenever the left dare to exhibit a minimum, but determined opposition to the government. So the government had the initiative; all it had to do now was to adopt a series of measures that would ensure that future elections would be held, and above all that the political parties would be given legal status. Here the thorny question was the legalization of the PCE, but after a series of evasive measures, the government finally decided to face up to it.[27] And it could not be said that, in doing so, it faced any insurmountable resistance.

Since then, the PCE has presented its legalization as a victory; it was that, but not for the reasons usually given. For the PCE argues that its legalization was a result of its good sense, its sensitivity and its realism; that it was the subjective triumph of an able leadership which managed astutely to overcome the various obstacles placed in its way. To accept this would be to justify the enormous concessions that the PCE had to make.[28] If we take as our starting point a very different evaluation of the relations of forces between the classes, of the impossibility of effecting a democratic change in Spain without the legal presence of the PCE, then these concessions, far from being a subtle manoeuvre, appear rather as a contribution to forging a State in which elements which will always represent a real danger to the consolidation of democracy and the possible socialist future, will be left intact.

In the second place, the very legalization of the PCE shows how unreal was the threat of a *coup* to which we have already referred. If there was any occasion when the army could have risen or imposed its veto, it was when the PCE was legalized. Yet the army—though not without tensions—ended by accepting the decision and did not stage a *coup*. So it does not represent a victory for the intelligence or respectablity of the party, but a 'necessary' consequence of the global political options of the bourgeoisie, which the army finally understood and accepted.

The legalization of the PCE, however, still left outside the legal framework the other organizations to its left as well as many others of a radical nationalist character—and above all, it let the government put itself forward as the intermediary. The stage was now set for the next stage—the elections. Certain prior measures were still necessary, however. First, the government moved to broaden the base of the amnesty which has already been mentioned;[29] immediately afterwards, it embarked on the dissolution of the National Movement. It is important to bear in mind the way in which this was done, for the issue did not exclusively concern the right. The funds of the Movement largely consisted of goods taken from the parties of the left and the trade unions after their defeat in the Civil War. The logical demand would have been that this wealth should be returned to its legitimate owners, who would have need of it in the coming elections.[30] Yet the left, save for some protests, made no move in this direction; in fact it accepted that the personnel of the Movement should be integrated into the Civil Administration of the State—which certainly would not weaken it.[31]

One question remained—and it was a decisive one; the political organization of the right. Up to this time, it seemed to have found itself in an impasse. Leaving aside the more extremist groups, only two alternatives existed, and neither of them seemed adequate to the task. On the one hand, the only important organization was Alianza Popular, a coalition of various Francoist sectors who continued to argue for greater control of the political process and whose solutions tended to coincide with those that had already proved impracticable under the Arias government.[32] An electoral victory by Alianza Popular, would necessarily result in the reproduction of the same crises and tensions that had characterized that government's last months. For the more far-sighted sectors of the bourgeoisie, this option led nowhere.

Elsewhere on the right, political and organizational confusion were rife, the result of the considerable weakness of the democratic bourgeoisie. The Spanish people in those days were witness to a proliferation of dozens of unknown sets of initials that emerged in the attempt to ensure a political future for eleventh hour democrats and professional careerists.

As ever, the solution to the dilemma was to come from government. In the weeks prior to the beginning of the electoral campaign there began what the mass media called 'the disembarkation of the old Francoists', set in motion from within the State under the personal direction of President Suarez. Thrusting aside the representatives of the small groups and their awkward attempts at organization, the Union of the Democratic Centre (UCD) was formed; it was a union of power rather than a party, drawing together the different wings of old and new bourgeois opposition and the reformist sector of the dictatorship, now legitimated as a result of 'having made possible the transition to democracy'. UCD thus became *the* party of the great majority of the bourgeoisie for the present, gathering its most important currents and personalities. It reinforced in Spain a tendency already known in the majority of advanced capitalist countries, to form a single political representation of the right, closely tied to the State apparatus, and a reflection of capitalist concentration on the one hand, and the incapacity and lack of political alternatives among the small and middle bourgeoisie on the other. Their different sectors accepted the mediation of a single leadership, disputed the benefits of the State among themselves and put their faith in a State machine which was the fundamental means of ensuring the electoral victories that were indispensable to its continuity as a party. With the formation of the UCD, everything was ready for the elections.

The electoral campaign was to bring little that was new. Despite events in Euzkadi,[33] it developed in a way that showed all parties to be prepared to respect the compromises agreed upon. With the exception of some groups on the far left, the rousing slogans of previous years were either silenced or radically altered. Nobody called the monarchy into question or called for the purging of the State; the demand for self-determination for nationalities[34] now became a call for autonomous statutes. A deaf ear was turned to allegations of Francoist corruption; worse still, the left again accepted the fallacy that, at root, the campaign was determined by the option of dictatorship or democracy, and concentrated its fire on Alianza Popular, presenting UCD and President Suarez as sincere democrats prepared to fight for the democratic consolidation of the country.

Nonetheless, the election results were more complex than the campaign or the events prior to it might have led one to expect. Despite its control of the State apparatus and the mass media (the very powerful TV in particular)[35], UCD gained scarcely more than 30 per cent of the votes and did not obtain a majority in the Congress of Deputies, despite the advantages it had gained through the electoral law negotiated with the opposition. In relative terms, this represented a defeat for its policies and a sign of the desire for change among the majority of Spanish society. So even in the climate of demobilization imposed upon itself by the left, the vote reflected an undeniable desire to break with Francoism. Alianza Popular suffered a spectacular defeat for the same reason; and that is something to be borne in mind when we come later to weigh the question whether the Spanish political process could have proceeded in any other way. The rest of these votes went in Cataluña and Euzkadi to the bourgeois nationalist parties.

The left as a whole received 45 per cent of the votes, though the percentage was considerably higher in the industrialized areas. In Cataluña, Socialists and Communists surpassed the 50 per cent mark, while levante, Andalucia and Madrid emerged as clear centres of left-wing support. The largest section of left voters gave their support to the Spanish Socialist Workers Party (PSOE) which unexpectedly became the second largest party in the country in terms of votes and parliamentary representation. The PCE achieved less than 10 per cent of the vote, with its support almost non-existent in places like Castille and Galicia, traditionally right-wing regions, but also in Euzkadi. The extreme left was literally swept off the board.

So the electoral results again gave the impression of a balanced relation of forces between the classes. The conclusion drawn from that by both right and left was that the politics of agreement should continue.

5

The eighteen months between the elections to the Constituent

Assembly and the promulgation of the constitution were also marked by an agreement between right and left whose net result would be to benefit the former in terms of the relations of forces. The two fundamental instances were the signing of the Moncloa Pact of October 1977[36] and the elaboration of the constitution throughout 1978.

An economic-social agreement, with all its political repercussions, was an imperative for the right. The Spanish capitalist economy, which had made such spectacular advances through the sixties, found itself by 1973 in a crisis caused as much by factors in the international situation as by specific local features. The very political instability of the previous two years had clouded the picture. Since 1973, the rate of profit had declined considerably, while the politico-economic struggles of those years ensured the growing share of the national income represented by wages. There were various symptoms of the crisis; above all an excess productive capacity which obliged firms to reduce their production, and even in many cases to close down, which raised the unemployment levels. It is difficult to calculate the numbers of unemployed (partly because there is no single agency empowered to measure them, partly because the statistical methods used are unsatisfactory, and because government deliberately sets out to reduce the official figures) but it is no exaggeration that there were between 800,000 and one million people out of work in Spain by the end of 1977. In the same year, inflation rose by 27 per cent, and there were times (the June-August period) when the consumer price index rose by 44.8 per cent. Spain's international position was also deteriorating sharply, as its balance of payments deficit reached five billion dollars. Private investment was holding back and the four years since the start of the crisis had seen a negative growth in investment by the private sector. Finally, the fact that the centre of the stage was occupied by political events whose resolution was a prior condition for any attempt to solve the problems added a temporary obstacle which severely aggravated the situation.

The Moncloa Agreements were the first serious measure taken to confront the situation; though there was nothing new in their content. They were simply a plan to stabilize the capitalist economy with a view to future takeoff. The measures were classical; to keep inflation down to 10 per cent in 1978 through a wage ceiling and the devaluation of the currency in order to increase the international competitiveness of spanish goods. It involved accepting a very high unemployment level with no corresponding gain except unemployment benefits which still do not cover the whole working population.

The major difference was that this stabilization plan was the result of negotiations with all the political forces represented in parliament, and thus with the representatives of the wage earners too. These latter defended their acceptance of the conditions on the basis that they were getting something in return, the famous 'compensations' based on some promises in the field of education (the creation of 700,000 new school places) and of control of the most obvious centres of corruption (the Social Security) and/or political manipulation (creation of a Control Commission at the Radio and Television system, RTVE).

The left was not very demanding. One of the most striking things is the total absence of any reference to the return of their goods and funds to the free trade union organizations. Like the Movement itself, the vertical (Francoist) unions had impounded the funds of the pre-Civil-War trade union organizations and added to them through the contribution that every Spanish worker was obliged to pay as a result of his obligatory membership of those unions. These funds, which were vital for the development of a free trade union movement, and had often been demanded by the trade union organizations, were not even mentioned during the negotiations and remain in government hands to this day. On the other hand, the decision to sign the Agreements and the moderation of the left in general were justified by reference to the need to consolidate democracy because, if that were not done, the danger of a *coup* would again arise.

Unlike other political processes which still remain open to change, the Moncloa Agreements have the advantage that they can already be judged and conclusions reached about them. The balance sheet, a year after their signing, is clear. The Agreements achieved the objectives of putting capitalism back on its feet, as the right proposed; for the left, they brought no benefit at all. Inflation fell considerably in 1978, to a little more than 16 per cent; exports grew as a result of devaluation, the currency reserves increased, tourism expanded and the remissions from Spaniards overseas reached new levels. There were, and are, areas of concern, like the low level of private investment, and the unknown factor of the behaviour of the international economy. But at the time the Moncloa Agreements served to moderate workers' demands through the mediation of their political parties and trade union organizations, and persuaded them to accept the existing levels of unemployment. In its first year, democracy yielded considerable profits to the bourgeoisie,[37] confirming again that it was in their own terms preferable to the pre-existing situation or any return to dictatorship.

The compensations granted to the left, despite their modesty, remained unpaid. Far from putting the workers in a better position, the Agreements marked a low point in the movement and helped to create a climate of social and political apathy that still persists. From then on the liquidation of the mass movement, which was already in the air before the elections, has now become a reality. What mass initiatives do take place will be the result of specific problems of one of the nationalities (Euzkadi particularly) rather than of any agreement to carry forward any generalized workers struggle.

The other major field of agreement between right and left concerned the elaboration of the constitution. Both in the way in which it was carried out and in its content, the constitution would crown a transition to democracy that was to the benefit of the right alone.

As far as its method of elaboration was concerned, UCD's principal concern was to prevent public discussion of the constitution; in this it was supported by the left which made no protest nor took any action against it. In fact, open discussion would immediately bring out the fact that democracy can include many different ways of organizing political institutions and freedoms, and that it was in the interests of the right to create the instruments most useful to them. On the other hand, in a public discussion, the left would have to take decisions. Up till now, the acceptance of each and every condition imposed by the right had been justified, as we have seen, in terms of the necessity to ensure free progress towards the elections. Once the electoral strength of the left had been demonstrated, however, there was no longer any need to continue in a subordinate position. Yet the secret meetings and the unpublished topics for discussion were quickly accepted and the issue was resolved behind closed doors.[38]

The same occurred with the meetings of the Constitutional Commission whose task was to give concrete form to the text of the proposals. After a few meetings where the left's alternatives were systematically defeated, left and right agreed to keep back from parliament the real nature of their discussions. The opinions and speeches that were delivered had clearly been agreed beforehand, so that the sought-after parliament became no more than a backcloth against which unfolded a drama that was of no interest to anyone.

The left, having abandoned any politics based on the mobilization of the masses—an aspect of democracy at least as important as parliament—was condemned to listen impotently to empty rhetoric. The paradox was that it was precisely the left, which saw no other way but the parliamentary way, that was incapable of using parliament to put forward its own alternatives or, at the very least, its potential for opposition.

Thus the constitutional discussions came to an end, and the new constitution was approved and promulgated on 29 December 1978, in the face of a general indifference and a high proportion of abstentions that in places like Euzkadi reached 50 per cent of the electoral roll.

What can be said about the Constitution? Perhaps the best thing one can say about it is that it is a text that serves admirably the purpose of those who drew it up; it fulfils almost all the aims that the right had set out at the beginning of the period we have been considering. That is the reality behind the declarations that it is a Constitution for every Spaniard, the only political text of concord in Spanish constitutional history, the framework that will allow everyone to participate in the tasks of government if they have the necessary support, etc. Both in what it says and what it leaves unsaid, the text of the constitution both creates a body of democratic institutions and ensures that they cannot be used to initiate a transition to socialism. This is nothing new in bourgeois constitutions—it is their very nature; but in the Spanish case considerable precautions have been taken. By 'constitutionalizing' the Francoist State apparatus, and explicitly recognizing the situation of the various powers that be, the 1978 Constitution lays down a very restricted framework for democratic rights and institutions, and they will become even more restricted as long as the relations of forces remain favourable to the right. Throughout the period of transition, and up to now, terrorist actions have been made the excuse to bring about a real reduction of democratic freedoms and the concentration of special powers in the hands of the executive. Let us consider some of these aspects further.

The key article of the Constitution is Article 38, which explicitly lays down a market economy. Thus there is within it a sharp prohibition on any eventual collectivization of the means of production. It is true, of course, that the left today is very confused as to what it means by socialism, and that neither nationalization nor central planning are sufficient guarantees of its realization. Yet nor is this establishment of a market economy in a text that commits the armed forces to its defence (article 8) anything other than a constitutional call for a *coup d'état* should any left-wing government threaten to carry the country towards socialism. In the light of this provision, the references to planning (article 38), the social function of the right to private property (article 33, 2) and of course the right to work of all Spaniards (article 35,1) are mere words, which will have to yield should they ever enter into conflict with the sacrosanct principle of the market economy.

Without in the least denying the importance of the existence of a democratic regime or the influence that it will have on the development of the workers' movement, it is clear that so long as the key principle of a market economy persists, the political rights of the citizen will always yield to bourgeois demands whenever a conflict arises.

But in the second place, the very implementation of the institutions and principles of democracy ensure a very restricted democracy. It is clear that, as far as functioning institutions are concerned, the Spanish text seriously limits the powers of the legislature and is less far-reaching than the Italian constitution of 1947, to take a neighbouring example. Furthermore, and most significantly, each and every demand of the conservative social forces is included in the constitution. Above all, it defines Spain as a parliamentary monarchy. It gives the armed forces a blank cheque in the defence of the institutional order. Finally, while separating Church and State, it recognizes the latter's influence in the areas of education and the family and this will have a negative effect on the school system, and on such issues as divorce and abortion.

The constitution also says much in what it omits; throughout the text and especially where conflicts are involved, it refers on more than fifty occasions to future laws that will be promulgated to develop the constitution. In fact, the effective regulation of democratic rights and freedoms has yet to be developed, and it not clear at this point what limits will be placed upon them. In any event, however many and broad future dispositions may be, the fact is that the police, the judges and the administration empowered to watch over them and set the limits in practice are the same ones that participated for years in the repressive policies of Franco.

6

To recapitaliate: the process of political transition towards a democratic State in Spain was made possible by an agreement between the majority political representatives of the two great social classes; this agreement has been shaped, in its limitations and its rate of progress, by the conditions imposed by the right. All this took place in an international framework which favoured and assumed precisely this kind of transition, and has contributed to it as far as possible.

For anyone who believes that the Marxist method is the best way to approach social and political processes, this poses a number of questions that are difficult to articulate, let alone to resolve. The first and obvious question is, could it have been otherwise? I believe we can say that it could; nothing was pre-determined. It is the relations of forces between the classes, and the conscious decisions taken by the different actors that have shaped the final outcome. If the left had behaved differently, the position of the Spanish bourgeoisie today might well be much less comfortable. It is the vacillations and the limits placed upon the process by Socialists and Communists, above all, that have been the determining factor in the present situation.

This requires further comment, and a further question: for what might the developments have been that we have argued were possible? To put it another way, did there exist in Spain a pre-revolutionary situation which would have made it possible to envisage a socialist revolution as its outcome? Here the answer is no. Despite the strength of the mass movement, despite its militancy and the new forms of organization that it had developed, we have already shown that none of its demands were incompatible with the maintenance of a capitalist regime. Further, the strategy of those organizations which were hegemonic within that movement specifically discounted such a possibility. To speak of a socialist revolution in Spain in the classical sense of an insurrectionary seizure of power and the general creation of workers' soviets, was mere rhetoric.

What then is left? The whole issue revolves around the ambivalent meaning of democracy. What we have argued is that, for a number of reasons, the two major forces of the left allowed the right to recover the political initiative, and thus allowed the transition to occur within very narrow limits as far as both freedom and the future march towards socialism are concerned. The major criticism to be made of these forces is that they did not offer radically democratic policies which could have weakened the right-wing alternative; they too easily accepted the continuing existence of institutions and mechanisms which not only would not help to deepen or consolidate democracy, but which could in a different set of circumstances become its worst enemy. The refusal to take up the struggle to weaken and to clean up the State apparatus was the fundamental error of both Socialists and Communists. Their other mistake was to identify democracy and parliament, and consciously to abandon the use of the other equally democratic means—mass pressure and the autonomous organization of social movements; in fact they held back whenever they were able any attempts at direct democracy which they did not control. Finally, the refusal of both to consider an alternative united policy was another element that contributed decisively to the recovery of the political initiative by the right.

Socialist and Communists both have their own version of events. For the Socialists, it was impossible to go any further forward because of the internal limitations of the movement itself, which was never broad or combative enough to impose substantial political change. Even if that were the case, the truth is that the Socialists made very little effort to change that situation;[39] they preferred to channel their activity into seeking an agreement first, and negotiating later, presenting themselves as 'alternative candidates for power' at such time as the right and the UCD should go into decline and there was a need for changes. Albeit with gritted teeth, the Socialists accepted all the terms of the social consensus and made no effort to present firm and decisive opposition even on their favoured parliamentary ground.

The Communist school of thought starts from different premises: the limits on the process of transition were not so much internal to the mass movement, as external. The argument repeated *ad nauseam* is that if the process overflowed those strictly defined limits, the response would have been a *coup d'état*. We have shown to what extent such an argument is a rationalization. In fact the difficulties in carrying out a *coup* were not so much technical problems as the constraints imposed by the options that the bourgeoisie as a whole had at its disposal. The right needed the democratic agreement at any cost; it sought to achieve it under the best possible conditions and there is nothing to suggest that it would not have had to negotiate further had it found itself face to face with a determined opposition. Yet that is what the PCE never put to the test. Every condition put forward was accepted without question. And here a distinction must be made; while both major forces of the left must take responsibility for the present situation, the PCE is more responsible because its possibilities were greater. For during the period of transition, the PCE was the single decisive factor within the mass movement. If the concrete objectives of a radical democracy (the purging of the State apparatus, recuperation of trade union funds, amnesty, etc.) had been supported by a resolute policy of mass mobilization, the agreement would have taken on a shape far more favourable to the left. The PCE, however, obsessed by the image of national collaboration in France and Italy between 1944 and 1947, preferred to accept the minimalist parliamentary road and thus allow the right to recover the initiative.

So the other face of the transition in Spain stems precisely from the fact that, persuaded by more or less plausible arguments, the left failed to pose its own alternative. It is not that it failed to offer a socialist project; that requires much further clarification as to what such a project should have been and how it could be realized. For beyond that, the left seemed to have no political solutions of its own *even to the problems of the present democratic phase.* This has often led it to renounce its role as opposition and become a political subordinate of right-wing governments. The result is the creation of the illusion that the class struggle has disappeared from the political sphere. Right and left seem to have the same objectives, and even propose to achieve them with the same or very similar methods. The left alternative is largely discounted, and the fact that the same situation has occurred elsewhere (in Italy and Portugal, for example) only confirms the fact that the European left is caught in one of the gravest crises in its history, which requires it to reappraise its strategy and its tactics.

Translated by Mike Gonzalez

NOTES

1. A reading of Jose Vidal Beneyto's book *Del franquismo a una democracia de clase* (Ed. Akal, Madrid, 1977) yields a similar conclusion, as in a more subtle way does his article 'Le revers de la médaille' in the special number of *Pouvoirs* (no. 8, 1979) devoted to the political transition in Spain.
2. N. Poulantzas: *La crisis de las dictaduras:* (Siglo XXI, Madrid, 1976).
3. *ibid.,* pp. 15, 21.
4. *ibid.,* pp. 45 ff.
5. *ibid.* pp. 61-7.
6. Poulantzas in fact refuses to take this factor into account: 'I will not attempt to analyse it, for it alone would merit a whole book. In fact, on the one side it involves the *objective co-ordinates,* both global and specific to that country, and on the other the strategy of the organizations of the left and in particular of the Communist parties that have been the spearhead of the struggles against the dictatorships'

(ibid. p. 100). But to refuse to consider this decisive factor of the process is to refuse to understand it, and in fact suggests that the central question in that process has been the divisions within the bourgeoisie.

7. A reading of one of the most recent and best documented books on the question—Juan Muñoz, Santiago Roldán & Angel Serrano's *La internacionalización del capital en España* (Edicusa, Madrid, 1978)—yields nothing to confirm Poulantzas's dichotomy.

8. In July 1974, fundamentally under the leadership of the PCE and including the socialists of the PSP and some independent personalities, the Junta Democratica was formed in order to achieve a democratic break through a National Democratic Action. The Junta was regarded with suspicion precisely because the Communists were at its heart. In June 1975, an alternative organization—the Plataforma de Convergencia Democratica—was formed, principally by the socialists of PSOE and the Democratic Left of Dr Ruiz-Gimenez. Other left groups later joined it.

9. In August 1975, as a result of new armed actions by the ETA and the FRAP (an organization with a Maoist orientation which then favoured a *people's war*), the government approved the Anti-Terrorist Decree-Law which gave considerable powers to the police, suspended the right of *habeas corpus* and the protection of the home, etc., and demanded urgent trials to deal with cases of terrorism, which were left to the jurisdiction of the military. The application of this Decree led to the five death sentences (three on ETA members, and two members of FRAP) with which General Franco ended a life of repression.

10. A rather exaggerated account of these sectors and (involuntarily) of its immense limitations can be found in J. Tusell *La oposición democrática al franquismo (1939-62)* (Ed. Planeta, Barcelona, 1977).

11. In fact, although the electoral fate of these sectors has since been uneven, the democratic opposition was the vehicle of moderation and responsibility within all the combined organizations of the opposition and a fundamental channel of communication between the major organizations of the left and the reformists within the regime.

12. On this subject, still to be analysed in depth, see the best contribution to date: J.M.Maravall, *Dictatorship and Political Dissent* (Maravall, Tavistock, 1978), and by the same author, 'Remarques sur le mouvement ouvrier dans la transition à la démocratie en Espagne' in the edition of *Pouvoirs* quoted above.

13. The most spectacular case is that of ETA in the Basque Country which, from a heterogeneous theoretical base (orthodox nationalism; the assumption of a Third-Worldist ideology of national liberation; references to a Basque socialism, etc.) posed the necessity for a move towards armed struggle, from the late sixties onwards. Despite a succession of schisms culminating in a split into two wings (military ETA and politico-military ETA) ETA has continued to argue for the armed road, and carried out the most spectacular acts of direct, minority violence ever known in Spain.

14. Basically, the differences between the PCE leadership and F. Claudin and J. Semprun (Federico Sanchez), which led to the latter's expulsion in 1964, were not concerned with the necessity of this strategy of reconciliation but with the rate of advance and the subjectivism of the Communist Party leadership. For it was argued that the leadership had failed to see how economic development had given the Franco regime more room for manoeuvre and that the drive towards democracy in Spain could not occur simply as a result of communist initiatives like the Peaceful General Strike which had so signally failed. See, on the question, F. Claudin, *Documentos de una divergencia comunista* (Ed. El Viejo Topo, Barcelona, 1978) and J. Semprun *Autobiografía de Federico Sánchez* (Planeta, Barcelona, 1977).

15. On the January strike and its political repercussions, see M. P. Izquierdo *De la huelga general a las elecciones generales* (Ed. de la Torre, Madrid, 1977). As examples of the position of the leadership of the Workers' Commissions at the time, see the articles by N. Sartorius in *Triunfo*.

16. In Vitoria, at the beginning of March 1976, after a long and bitter strike, the police opened fire on a workers assembly, leaving three dead and many wounded. In May 1976, in Montejurra, the ultra-right fraction of the Carlist party, with the full knowledge of the Civil Guard, the Governor of Navarra and the Home Ministry, occupied the mountain top that was the traditional scene of a Carlist celebration and fired on the crowd below, killing two and leaving more than twenty wounded.

17. At the beginning of May 1976, the American magazine *Newsweek* published an interview with the King in which he asserted, among other things, that Arias had been 'an unmitigated failure'. The interviewer (A. de Borchgrave) commented that 'what concerns the King most is that Arias's policies are polarizing Spanish political life, turning both right and left against the government'. The declarations were denied by the Ministry of Information and Tourism, but never by the King's Press Officer.

18. Throughout Spain organizations began to be formed in imitation of CD, with different components and similar programmes, albeit with different emphases, and usually more concrete in their references to the question of self-determination of nationalities (e.g., the Galician Taboa, the Catalan Consell, the Valencia Taula, etc.)

19. In May 1976, one of the best-known Communist leaders—Ramon Tamames—explained the economic criteria which should guide an eventual provisional government, a CD government, in which in any case the PCE would probably assume Ministerial responsibilities. For Tamames, the basic concern of that government must be to keep the confidence of the employers. From this he drew the conclusion that it would have to renounce any structural transformation or nationalization plans; should seek help from the IMF and the EEC; should decree an amnesty for tax evaders; and assist small and medium business, etc. With such a programme, there was little danger that a Communist spectre would haunt Spain.

20. In May too, Arias announced a confused series of reforms intended to inject into the old organic democracy of Franco a moderately parliamentary system. He also offered, subject to government approval, the legalization of political asociations (he still refused to call them parties) provided the Communists remained beyond the pale. The Francoist Cortes was then to provide one of the finest exhibitions of absurdity in their attempts to draft a text that excluded the Communists without naming them.

21. The Military Democratic Union (UMD) is the only clandestine democratic organization, as far as is known, ever to have functioned within the army. Although it claimed at its high point to have embraced hundreds of officers, the repression of its members involved only a dozen or so, all of lower rank; since then, nothing more has been heard of such activities.

22. Santiago Carrillo's theses on the military, developed in several places and particulary in 'Eurocommunism and the State (Lawrence and Wishart, 1977) maintain that, in general, there is in the advanced capitalist countries a division within the army between the traditional sectors with an authoritarian mentality, and the professionals, better qualified technically and advocates of an efficient, modern army, at the service of the nation and its democratic institutions. It is precisely this latter section that, in Spain, has opposed the maintenance of Francoism and supported the democratic transition. As far as the left is concerned, the best way to bring about a convergence with this sector would be to support a rationalist policy to increase the professional capacity and technical efficiency of the army.

     Carrillo's theses reveal a wrong analysis of the army in general and the Spanish army in particular. This is not the place to analyse it in detail. But as far as the first is concerned, it is sufficient to point out that until 11 September 1973, General Pinochet was one of the foremost exponents of this professional and democratic view. In terms of this theory, his behaviour since then is a mystery. In the Spanish case, the passive attitude of the army in the face of the end of the dictatorship was the product of a set of circumstances determined by the general interests of the class which the army, as an institution, serves; there is nothing to suggest that in a different situation in the future a Pinochet could not emerge from the most professional and efficient sectors.

23. The most spectacular change of personnel was the appointment of General Gutiérrez Mellado to the Ministry of Defence, who still remains responsible for military policy. At the end of 1976, the General initiated a series of reforms designed to separate the army from active political intervention and to give it a more professional image.

24. The Commission of Nine was formed practically at the same time as the opposition proposed abstention in the referendum on political reform, and its overwhelming majority were members of bourgeois parties. Further, Carrillo's presence at the negotiations, which the

government still found unacceptable, was avoided through a subtle piece of manipulation. The opposition representatives would attend the negotiations with the government in sub-commissions of four, which would avoid embarrassment for President Suarez, as Carrillo was not a member of any of them.

25. For the Congress of Deputies, the opposition accepted the system of proportional representation according to the D'Hont rules. Yet as the province was the electoral unit, the rules favoured (as would be seen in the subsequent elections) the over representation of conservative, rural Spain as compared with urban, industrial sectors. This gave enormous primacy to the majority parties and penalized those with fewer votes. Unless the left can present a united front at elections, which still seems a remote possibility, the electoral law will ensure that there is no socialist majority in parliament.

26. Between Sunday 23 January and Friday the 28th, the following events took place: on the 23rd, a student taking part in a pro-amnesty demonstration was murdered by a group of ultra-rightists: on the 24th a student was killed in a police charge; on the same day an ultra-right-wing group killed five people in the office of a group of lawyers working for the Workers' Commissions; on the 27th GRAPO (a terrorist organization claiming extreme left ideological positions) killed three policemen, and two more on the 28th. That same week, for the first and only time, the newspaper *El Pais* published an editorial calling for the formation of government that included the opposition.

27. The PCE was legalized on Easter Saturday, 9 April, 1976, when most of its political leaders were on holiday. During the first few days of the following week, there was serious agitation by the right, from Alianza Popular to the extreme right, and several meetings of important army personnel. The crisis, however, went no further than the resignation of the Minister of the Navy, Admiral Pita da Veiga.

28. In a *Note* from the Army Ministry to all officers, dated 16 April 1976, it was stated that the Army High Council, in response to the legalization of the PCE, had decided to inform them that this act 'has provoked a general revulsion in the army. Nevertheless, considering the national interest to be of a higher order, it is prepared to recognize the realities in a disciplined way. *(Cambio 16,* 25 April 1976). It added that the Council 'unanimously considers it an unavoidable obligation to defend the unity of the Nation, the Flag, the integrity of the institutions of the Monarchy and the good name of the Armed Forces'. These conditions were immediately accepted by the PCE whose Central Committee met and agreed to accept the Monarchy and renounce the (republican) tricolour flag.

29. The new amnesty measures gave the government the right to decide to grant amnesty and allowed it to exile those under sentence of death, which it did in subsequent weeks.

30. The Movement had several thousand functionaries, recruited from the most right-wing elements, and many of whom were armed. But above all it had at its disposal an important chain of mass media (thirty-five

newspapers, various magazines, a news agency and a chain of radio transmitters).

31. Perhaps one of the most grotesque features of the new democratic phase is to see the old functionaries of the Movement's Women's Section charged by the present Ministry of Culture with directing the various centres of social assistance, one of whose functions is to set in motion a timid programme of birth control. For years the Women's Section had argued that the woman's place was in the home and that families should be as large as possible—that no limits should be set on the number of children God chose to send parents.

32. In fact Alianza Popular considered it necessary to reduce the number of concessions to the left, of which they considered the government to have made far too many; since the legalization of the PCE could not now be retracted, at least a regime of law and strict order should be imposed. On the other hand, AP still had many supporters within the State apparatus, and a good part of its voting support came from the old Francoist bureaucracy.

33. Just a month before the elections, the celebration in Euzkadi of a pro-amnesty week was met with increasing police repression which left a toll of dead and wounded. In response, there was on Monday 16 May a general strike in all four provinces of the Basque country in which more than 500,000 workers took part.

34. We are not defending this slogan here; personally I believe that question of nationalities has to be posed in much greater depth than has been done by the parties of the left; in the Spanish case, indeed, they have discussed the issue in a totally irresponsible, if not openly demagogic way. Concretely, on the question of self-determination, the left has for years fallen back on the most exaggerated interpretations of its significance, often coinciding with the most radical nationalism, only at the moment of truth to accept meekly the weak measures for self-government or autonomy that the central power was prepared to concede.

35. The extremely important role of television in Spanish politics in recent years is revealed in statistics published in the magazine *La Calle* which showed that 79.4 per cent of those interviewed assiduously watched TV at least once a day. Given that the circulation of Spanish newspaper, at the same time, is very small (there are very few that sell more than 200,000 copies daily) and that more than half the population does not read even one book a year, it will be seen how important the question of TV becomes.

36. On the Moncloa Agreements, the most detailed analysis appeared in the journal *Argumentos* no. 18 (December 1978). While the majority of left-wing commentators attributes to them an exclusively economic character, Professor Fuentes Quintana, then Minister of the Economy and principal architect of the Agreements, points out that what is really important about them is their political rather than their economic effects (p. 51).

37. The share of wages in national income fell in 1977-8 for the first time

for many years.

38. After an extraordinary series of events, the draft of the text of the constitutional proposal was published in the magazine *Cuadernos para el diálogo*, in the face of indignation from the left's contributors to the proposal, who bemoaned the breaking of the gentleman's agreement to keep silence, which they had all faithfully kept to.

39. On the politics of the left in general, and of the PSOE in particular, the article by L. Paramio and J. M. Reverte merits special mention; its very title is a programme—'Sin imaginación y sin principios' (With neither imagination nor principles) in *Zona Abierta* no. 18.

THE FAILURE OF
AMERICAN SOCIALISM RECONSIDERED*

Jerome Karabel

Of all the questions that have bemused observers of political life in America, perhaps none has been as perplexing as that of why the United States, alone among the advanced industrial countries, never developed a truly mass-based socialist movement. Foreigners, in particular, have long been struck by the almost universal antipathy of Americans toward socialist ideas. Writing of the America of the 1830s, Tocqueville astutely observed that in 'no other country of the world is the love of property keener or more alert than in the United States, and nowhere else does the majority display less inclination toward doctrines which in any way threaten the way property is owned'. This attitude, Tocqueville argued, was uniquely suited to a society in which most of its members possessed property. Yet more than half a century later—and long after the formation of a massive wage-earning class—Engels, in a letter to Sorge, observed that the pervasive attachment to private property witnessed by Tocqueville persisted among American workers: 'It is remarkable,' he wrote, 'how firmly rooted are bourgeois prejudices even in the working class in such a young country.' Perhaps, suggested an exasperated Engels, the dogged resistance to socialist ideas among American proletarians reflected a pronounced theoretical backwardness: 'The Anglo-Saxon race—these damned Schleswig-Holsteiners, as Marx always called them—is slow-witted anyhow.'

Theoretical backwardness was, to be sure, in no short supply in the brashly self-confident America of the Gilded Age, but as Engels himself well understood, socialism failed to take root in the American working class for reasons more substantial than the crude pragmatism of the national culture. The United States, Engels noted, was the quintessential bourgeois society, free of feudal remnants, but free also of a 'permanent and hereditary proletariat'.

*A shorter version of this essay appeared in *The New York Review of Books* on February 8, 1979.

As such, it was a society lacking in class consciousness: the worker, seemingly surrounded on every side by opportunities to become an independent man, directed his energies toward rising *from* his class rather than *with* it. Indeed, in 1892, a year prior to the publication of Frederick Jackson Turner's famous essay on 'The Significance of the Frontier in American History', Engels put forward a thesis arguing that the existence of 'free land' promoted a 'speculative mania' among native-born workers which diverted them from the class struggle and the formation of a labour party.

With the closing of the frontier, however, the stage would be set for the growth of class consciousness in the indigenous American working class. This, combined with the inexorable spread of wage labour into segments of the population that had previously been self-employed, would, Engels thought, be sufficient to stimulate the development of a mass socialist movement. And once this movement gained momentum, the absence of pre-bourgeois barriers and the 'corresponding colossal energy of development' would enable it to advance 'with an energy and impetuousness compared with which we in Europe shall be mere children'.

For a time, Engels' vision of an increasingly powerful American socialist movement seemed amply confirmed by events. The Socialist Party of America, founded in 1901 with 10,000 members, had, by 1912, grown to 118,000. More impressively still, it had elected some 1200 public officials throughout the nation, including the mayors of such cities as Milwaukee, Schenectady, Berkeley, and Flint. As the movement pressed forward, a vibrant socialist press spread the party gospel across the land in over 300 periodicals. The *Appeal to Reason,* a weekly journal published in Kansas, was the most popular of the socialist publications, reaching an extraordinary circulation of 761,747 in 1913.

Yet one should not exaggerate the height of the socialist wave, even at its crest. In 1912, the high point of Socialist Party strength, Eugene Debs, by far the Party's most popular leader, received a bare 6 per cent of the popular vote. To put this figure in perspective, it suffices to note that George Wallace's third-party presidential candidacy in 1968 received more than 13 per cent of the vote, and that even James B. Weaver, the lacklustre candidate of the Populist Party in 1892, did considerably better than Debs. After 1912, though Socialist Party strength did not decline nearly as precipitously as has been suggested by some, there can be no denying that the optimism that had infused the Party in its first dozen years waned with the reforms of the first Wilson administration. Despite a brief upsurge during the First World War, particularly among immigrants opposed to American participation in the conflict, the Socialist Party of 1919, wracked by bitter internal disputes and staggering under the weight of massive state repression, found itself shattered almost beyond recognition.[1]

The Communist Party of America was soon to take the place of the Socialist Party as the dominant force on the left, but it was never to gain the degree of popular support once enjoyed by the party of Debs. Not even the Great Depression, which struck the United States with an extraordinary ferocity, was sufficient to give birth to a mass-based radical movement, either of the Communist or the Social Democratic variety. The American working class, it seemed, was immune to the appeal of socialism even under the most auspicious conditions. But why?

*

One of the boldest attempts ever to address this question is Werner Sombart's *Why Is There No Socialism in the United States?* First published in German in 1905 as a series of articles in the *Archiv für Sozialwissenschaft und Sozialpolitik* (where Max Weber had just recently published *The Proortestant Ethic and the Spirit of Capitalism*), it was initially hailed by the American Socialist Party, and an abbreviated version of the introduction and first section appeared in the theoretical journal, the *International Socialist Review*. American Socialist leaders were, however, offended upon reading the second section of the work, for in it Sombart argued that the economic success of American capitalism had made the average worker into a 'sober, calculating businessman without ideals'. The *International Socialist Review* thereupon ceased further translation and, indeed, in 1907 published a bitterly hostile review of Sombart which had appeared in *Vorwärts*, the newspaper of the German Social Democratic Party.[2]

Only now fully translated into English, *Why Is There No Socialism?* sets out to explain how socialism, supposedly a necessary reaction to capitalist development, could be so weak in the very nation where capitalism was most advanced. Sombart's manner of posing this question, which assumes that politics is a direct outgrowth of developments in society's economic substructure, betrays his considerable debt to the evolutionary, and at times mechanistic, Marxism then fashionable in academic socialist circles.[3] His answer, however, reveals a keen and original intelligence unwilling to remain within the bounds of orthodoxy.

The conservatism of the American worker could be traced, Sombart suggested, to his unique political, social, and economic position. Politically, what was most distinctive about the United States was the extraordinary power of the doctrine of 'popular sovereignty'. This doctrine, though laden with elements of myth, ultimately derived its strength from the real power of workers to vote, to remove unpopular officials from public office, and to get themselves elected to positions of influence in the two major political parties and even in the state itself. Socially, the American worker found himself in a society in which daily relations between people of different classes were uniquely egalitarian. Further, his chances to rise from his class were considerably greater than those of workers in Europe, in part because of America's more democratic character, in part because of the special opportunities provided by free land in the West. Though Sombart did not, contrary to the impression conveyed by some of his interpreters, consider mobility to be the keystone of his argument, he did believe that a 'confrontational mentality would most certainly have developed in America ... if escape from the orbit of the capitalist economy, or at least from the restricted confines of wage labour, had not stood open to so many groups of workers'.

In the end, however, Sombart, himself deeply influenced by the vulgar materialism that then dominated the German left, looked to economic factors to explain the antipathy of American workers to socialism. Indeed, by far the longest section of *Why Is There No Socialism?* is devoted to establishing a proposition that, even then, was hardly in need of documentation: that the average American worker enjoyed an immensely higher absolute standard of living than his German counterpart. In the United States, Sombart wrote in an oft-quoted phrase, 'all socialist utopias came to nothing on roast beef and apple pie'.

During the three-quarters of a century that has intervened since Sombart's essay first appeared, it has exerted a profound influence, at times unacknowledged, on those who have kept alive the perennial debate about American 'exceptionalism'. In retrospect, what is perhaps most remarkable about Sombart's contribution is how central the factors he enumerated—affluence, mobility, the frontier, universal suffrage, the two-party monopoly, and the democratic tenor of daily life—have remained in contemporary discussions of the question.[4] Sombart's essay, worthy of assessment in its own right as one of the most powerful analyses ever written about the sources of American socialism's enduring weakness, also merits careful examination for what it can reveal about the limits of conventional explanations. For if recent advances in historical research have permitted the debate about American exceptionalism to inch forward in some respects, the general explanations offered continue to bear a striking, and in some ways a disconcerting, resemblance to Sombart's own.

*

In pointing to the sheer affluence of the American working man as the main obstacle to the development of socialism in the United States, Sombart was hardly alone. Even Engels, whose materialism was generally more nuanced than Sombart's, once wrote: 'The native American working man's standard of living is considerably higher than that of the British, and that alone suffices to place him in the rear for some time.' The assumption underlying this perspective—that the spread of material affluence inexorably undermines the appeal of socialism—is an engagingly straightforward one, but it is much too crude to account for the complex historical relationship between affluence and radicalism. Under some circumstances, as in the increasingly prosperous Germany of the late nineteenth century and in France in 1968, affluence may in fact be accompanied by an upsurge in socialist activity. And within the working class itself socialism often finds its greatest support among the most favoured sectors of the proletariat: craftsmen and other skilled workers.

In the specific case of the United States, there are perhaps even more compelling reasons to reject the affluence thesis, at least in the unrefined form presented by Sombart. For from the perspective of a worker accustomed to a certain standard of living, the absolute level of wages may be less important than the rate at which they increase over time. And here, contrary to what analysts of both left and right have assumed to be the case, the evidence suggests that real working-class wages rose *less* rapidly in the United States in the crucial 1860-1913 period than in Sweden, Germany, France, and the United Kingdom—all of which spawned major socialist movements.[5] Further, the American economy during the years between the Civil War and the First World War was perhaps even more subject to violent cycles of boom and bust than the economies of other capitalist nations. During the not infrequent years of depression, hundreds of thousands of American workers were forced into the ranks of the unemployed, and millions of others faced real declines in their standard of living. Throughout the period, substantial segments of the working class tottered precariously at the margins of subsistence. For them, as for the countless other Americans who led grim, poverty-stricken lives, the image of the United States as a land of affluence must have seemed a sordid myth.

Yet to observe that life was not all 'roast beef and apple pie' for American wage earners is not to deny that the standard of living enjoyed by the average American worker compared very favourably with that of the typical proletarian in even the most advanced European countries. Nor is it to deny that America's relative wealth exerted a significant influence on the trajectory of working-class politics. But it is to deny that affluence undermined working-class radicalism in America in the simple manner suggested by Sombart and other celebrators of American 'abundance'. For if the sheer wealth of American society militated against the emergence of a mass-based socialist movement, it did so less through the *embourgeoisement* of the proletariat as a whole than through facilitating the development of a special relationship between capital and strategic sectors of the working class.

*

When Sombart visited the United States in 1904, he was struck, as had been Tocqueville before him, by the informal and egalitarian tone of daily life in America. In the United States, wrote Sombart, the 'bowing and scraping before the "upper classes", which produces such an unpleasant impression in Europe, is completely unknown'. On the contrary, the American worker 'carries his head high, walks with a lissom stride, and is as open and cheerful in his expression as any member of the middle class'. While in Europe the carriage and countenance of the proletarian marked him as a member of a class apart, in America, Sombart suggested, the impression conveyed by the worker made it veritably impossible to distinguish him from members of the middle class.

If Sombart's rather hyperbolic portrait of the social position of the American worker at the turn of the century betrayed a woeful lack of familiarity with the subtleties of American class relations, it nonetheless managed to capture an elemental, if often neglected truth—that there really *was* something different about the texture of daily life in the United States. The evidence for this was everywhere: in the lesser visibility of class differences in speech, manner and dress; in the free and easy interchange between individuals of sharply differing circumstances; in the widespread refusal of Americans to become personal servants; in the preference of even the rich for labour over leisure; and in the respectability accorded to virtually any kind of honest work.

This absence in America of a sense of 'rank'—a sense that, as Bryce once put it, some men are made of porcelain and others of earthenware—does not, to be sure, substantively alter the system of class domination; on the contrary, it may, by according to even the most common labourer a modicum of dignity and respect, help sustain it. A certain egalitarianism in personal relations, though hardly to be confused with an egalitarian distribution of wealth and power, can prove surprisingly effective in softening the intensity of class conflict.[6]

A quintessentially capitalist society, the United States, Sombart suggested, accorded status not on the basis of who one was, but rather what one did. Born bourgeois, the United States was a society without feudal residues and free, accordingly, of those pre-capitalist groupings—the aristocracy, the peasantry, and the artisanry—whose presence gave European societies a pervasive sense of class consciousness. Whatever other resources a nascent socialist movement in America might possess, the ability to tap a deep reservoir of popular class consciousness was not among them.

Nor could an emergent American socialist movement draw strength from another vital carry-over from feudalism—a powerful artisan tradition whose origins could be traced to the guilds of the late Middle Ages. This tradition, which showed a remarkable degree of persistence into the era of industrial capitalism, provided the early European working-class movement with both a leadership and a mass base.[7] Heirs to the corporatist legacy of feudalism and to a system of production in which the workers controlled the labour process, artisans could envision, albeit perhaps only in a fragmentary way, an alternative social order in which workers would be their own masters and production would be for use rather than profit. More critically still, their capacity to translate their visceral opposition to the encroachments of industrial capitalism into solidarity action was immensely enhanced by a deeply ingrained sense of mutual trust and group distinctiveness that came to them almost as a matter of birthright. The absence in the United States of an analogous group of traditional artisans meant that the early American working class confronted the introduction of the factory system without the distinctive set of pre-capitalist values and the extraordinary capacity for organized political action that such a stratum would have provided.

But if America was, as Sombart insisted, free of the residues of pre-capitalist classes found in greater or lesser degrees in the post-feudal nations of Europe, what kind of society, then, *was* the United States? To a greater extent than any nation before and perhaps since, white America in the early nineteenth century was a society of independent producers—a society consisting overwhelmingly of farmers, shopkeepers, and craftsmen who owned the property they worked. There were, to be sure, vast disparities of wealth in the America of Tocqueville, but these were softened by a wide distribution of property which extended to perhaps four-fifths of the free men who worked.[8] Especially in the freewheeling early years of the Republic, the widespread availability of free land and the absence of sharp class lines made the opportunity to acquire property seem well within the grasp of all who had the industry to work for it. Thus when Abraham Lincoln, in an address to Congress, praised the 'just, and generous, and prosperous system' in which the 'prudent, penniless beginner in the world, labours for a while ... then labours on his own account for another while, and at length hires another new beginner to help him', he was espousing not the values of an emergent industrial capitalism, but rather the conventional wisdom of a society of small property owners.

*

But was the self-made man, whose reputed existence did so much to justify the vast inequalities of turn-of-the-century America, anything more than mere myth? On this question Sombart was cautious, for he was well aware that 'the Carnegies and those parroting them' wished 'to lull the "boorish rabble" to sleep by telling them miraculous stories about themselves or others who began as newsboys and finished as multi-millionaires'. Yet despite his scepticism about the rags-to-riches stories then so common in America, Sombart insisted that the 'prospects of moving out of his class were undoubtedly greater for the worker in America than for his counterpart in old Europe'. This thesis—that the political quiescence of the American worker was intimately related to his uniquely high chances of rising from his class—is perhaps the most famous single argument in *Why Is There No Socialism?*, but it is also one of the least well documented. Fortunately, however, the recent appearance of a spate of painstaking quantitative studies permits us to examine Sombart's oft-cited contention in light of new evidence.

If a single result stands out from the growing body of historical research on social mobility, it is that relatively few individuals moved very far, either upwards or downwards, in the supposedly open American class structure. Short-range mobility—for example, from skilled worker to clerk or shopkeeper—has, to be sure, been fairly common in the United States, and at least three in ten sons of blue collar workers seem to have obtained white collar status in the past century. Long-range mobility, however, has been much less frequent; in Boston, for example, no more than one youth in ten born into a working-class home ever succeeded in becoming a professional or a substantial businessman.

Was there, then, nothing at all to the Horatio Alger stories of boys of modest origins rising to the very top—stories read, according to one estimate, by perhaps fifty million Americans.[9] About one point, there can be little doubt: members of the business elite have, in America, historically been recruited overwhelmingly from the scions of the upper and upper-middle class. Yet before relegating the notion of the self-made man to the dustbin of history, one must acknowledge the small, but not insignificant, number of men who began as workers and managed to make themselves into large-scale businessmen.[10] Especially in a culture in which the virtues of the self-made man were ceaselessly celebrated by politicians, journalists, schoolteachers, and clergymen alike, the existence of even a few such spectacular cases may have been sufficient to sustain the national cult of individual success.

Sombart's mobility thesis, however, consisted of something more than the argument that a small number of workers rose to the top in the United States; it asserted, in addition, that escape from the confines of wage labour was more common among American workers than their European counterparts. Perhaps because this formulation conformed so closely to the common-sense wisdom of the laymen, sociologists have long found it fashionable to deflate the notion, arguing instead that mobility rates have been roughly similar in the United States and Europe.[11] Yet this new orthodoxy has itself been challenged in recent years by the findings of several meticulously documented studies in social history. The sons of nineteenth-century workers in Boston and Poughkeepsie, it seems, had appreciably greater chances of obtaining non-manual jobs than their confreres in Bochum (a middle-sized German town in the Ruhr) and Marseille.[12] While one should be careful not to make too much of the findings of such a small number of studies, they do provide support for Sombart's argument that the American wage earner had comparatively high chances of escaping from his class.

Perhaps even more damaging to working-class solidarity than widespread vertical mobility and the Horatio Alger ideology it helped to sustain, however, was the oft-noted American penchant for moving from place to place. For if vertical mobility undermined the working class's capacity to engage in collective struggle indirectly by legitimating the ideology of individual self-advancement, geographical mobility did so directly, by destroying the bonds of mutuality and trust that make collective working-class action possible.

In communities in which the population is constantly changing, it is difficult for people to get to know one another, much less to develop the intimate friendships that form the sinews of class solidarity. Yet such communities have been typical not just of the mobile suburban America of the post-First-World-War era, but also of the America of the past. Indeed, if the figures of a dozen studies are to be believed, they provide an astonishing portrait of American rootlessness; throughout the past century and a half, no more than 40 to 60 per cent of the population residing in a given community at a specific point in time could be found there a mere decade later.[13]

The extraordinary willingness of Americans to uproot themselves cannot be understood apart from the allure of a rich and unexplored continent. If in other countries the itinerant wage earner was commonly viewed as a victim of class exploitation, in the United States he became transformed into a symbol of individual initiative and resourcefulness. The worker on the move was, according to national mythology, the worker on the make.

In such an ideological atmosphere, Sombart observed astutely, even those workers who did not move could derive a certain serenity from the feeling that they, too, *could* move and, in so doing, escape from their class. Their main route of escape, Sombart wrote, echoing but never explicitly citing the 'frontier thesis' made famous by Frederick Jackson Turner, was to the vast expanses of unsettled land in the West. For Sombart, it was well-nigh impossible to exaggerate the significance of 'free land'—its existence, he suggested, enabled 'many men with sound limits and no capital ... to turn themselves into independent farmers' and was, accordingly, 'the principal reason for the characteristic peaceable mood of the American worker'.

Though not without appeal, Sombart's argument that the open lands of the West served as a 'safety valve' for discontented workers faces a simple problem: very few industrial wage earners ever, in fact, became independent farmers or, for that matter, farmers of any sort. Migration between 1860 and 1900 was not primarily, as Sombart had implied, from East to West, but from the farm to the city. Indeed, for every industrial labourer who moved to the land, as many as twenty farmers may have moved to town. If a safety valve existed at all during this period, it was perhaps to be found less on the frontier than in the rapidly growing cities which absorbed the surplus population of politically volatile rural areas.[14]

Yet the frontier may have undermined the appeal of socialism in more subtle ways. By absorbing large numbers of Eastern farmers and immigrants who might otherwise have flooded the labour markets of the large cities, the unsettled lands of the West indirectly supported the maintenance of relatively high wage levels in the industrial working class. Further, the frontier, through the apparent plenitude of the opportunities it offered, lent crucial support to the cherished American belief that the way for those at the bottom to improve their condition was through individual mobility rather than collective struggle. And finally, the frontier was instrumental in the formation and maintenance of the national ethos of ceaseless movement from place to place—an ethos that, by encouraging transience among industrial wage earners, must have rendered them less able to mobilize themselves for political and social action and therefore more subject to the control of the community's more stable and affluent members.[15]

*

Transience among Americans, however, was limited neither to the adventurous who sought their fortune on the frontier nor to those more conventional souls who migrated from farm to city. Indeed, many of the millions of immigrants who swarmed into the United States in the late nineteenth and early twentieth centuries did so with the intention of ultimately returning to the familiar villages and towns of the Old Country. Arriving en masse in the United States at precisely the moment of greatest potential conflict between labour and capital, these itinerant immigrants helped give American society its distinctive character. For in the United States, alone among the advanced countries, the actual work of industrialization was to a considerable extent carried out by wage earners who were not indigenous.[16]

Strangely enough, Sombart, otherwise so sensitive to those aspects of life in the United States that undermined working-class solidarity, had almost nothing to say about the massive immigrant presence in the American working class and its role in fragmenting the proletariat into a bewildering array of mutually suspicious nationality groups. This insensitivity to the immigrant experience—undoubtedly the most serious oversight in Sombart's search for the sources of socialist weakness in the United Stages—led him also to ignore a fundamental feature of American working-class life: the pervasive tendency among foreign-born workers to view their status in America as temporary. Yet this sense of transience, especially widespread among workers in such key industries as mining and steel, was to profoundly affect the political trajectory of American labour.

Contrary to national mythology, most immigrants did not come to the United States with visions of freedom and democracy foremost in their minds. Instead, the majority embarked on a voyage to a distant and alien land for a much more prosaic reason—they simply could not make a living in their native countries. Apolitical peasants whose position as property-holders was endangered by the disintegration of the traditional agrarian life of Eastern and Southern Europe, they came to America for one reason: to make money. If all went well, they reasoned, their earnings in the United States would enable them to return to the lands of their birth with sufficient funds to purchase a piece of land. As one Slavic steelworker put it: 'A good job, save money, work all time, go home, sleep, no spend'.[17] Most of such workers went to America alone, many of them fully expecting that they would rejoin their families in Europe within a few short years.

Many immigrants to America thus viewed their status in the New World as a temporary one. And, to an astonishing degree, it was. Between 1907 and 1911, for every 100 Italians who were arriving in the United States, there were 73 who were returning to Italy. For Southern and Eastern Europeans as a whole, between 1908 and 1910 (a bad, a middling, and a prosperous year), 44 departed from the United States for every 100 who arrived.[18] And these figures, if anything, *underestimate* the extent of feelings of transience among immigrants, for they do not include those countless individuals who hoped to return to the Old Country but somehow never managed to do so.

Patterns of immigrant movement back and forth across the Atlantic showed a striking correspondence with the fluctuations of the business cycle. As immigration peaked during periods of boom, so it plummeted during the not infrequent years of bust, when veritable throngs of immigrants boarded ships bound for their native lands. Nor surprisingly, those immigrants who were least successful in the United States seem to have been the most likely to return to Europe.[19] If, as Frederick Jackson Turner had suggested, a 'safety valve' did indeed exist for the discontented American worker, it was apparently to be found less on the frontier than in tired old Europe.

Yet immigrants to America, though possessing the very real and not infrequently exercised option of returning to their native countries, were nonetheless capable of engaging in militant struggles in their adopted land. Such struggles were especially likely to take place when reductions in their wages or layoffs threatened to undermine their chances of realizing the goal that lured many of them to the United States in the first place—to accumulate enough money to purchase a parcel of land in their home country. Over such bread and butter issues as these, tightly bound ethnic communities time and again exhibited an extraordinary solidarity. Immigrant struggles—in McKees Rock, in Paterson, in Lawrence —were among the most bitter in American labour history. Yet the militancy shown by immigrants during prolonged and frequently violent class struggles generally did not reflect a commitment to socialism. For immigrants, with the exception of a small minority who brought with them from Europe a strong history of political radicalism, showed no greater capacity than native workers to translate their economic grievances at the work place into a broad political movement for fundamental social change.[20]

If class consciousness—as the more subtle of the Marxist historians have insisted—grows not only out of common experiences of exploitation at the point of production but also out of common experiences of association in the community, then its relative weakness among immigrant workers is quite explicable.[21] For while immigrants, often clustered together in tightly-knit ethnic neighbourhoods, had no shortage of common communal experiences, these experinces tended to reinforce not class but ethnic identity. From the local tavern to the lodge to the neighbourhood church, ethnic segregation in daily life outside of the work place was the rule rather than the exception. And marriage, at least within the first generation, was almost always within the ethnic group.[22] Under these circumstances, it is little wonder that a feeling of ethnic identity was more deeply ingrained among immigrant workers than a sense of class consciousness.

The political system, too, served to accentuate ethnic consciousness and to deflect any stirrings of class solidarity. For by its very
structure, the highly decentralized American state elevated to great
importance politics at the level of the local community—the very
level where ethnic divisions were most salient. Within the ethnic
community, an extensive network of local affiliates of powerful
urban political machines inducted immigrant workers into the
American way of life. For many of them, their first and primary
contact with the political system was via the neighbourhood ward
boss. Often of the same ethnic group, he would provide them—
in return for loyal support of the machine—with jobs, housing,
relief, and, when necessary, help in court. These benefits, while
real, advanced the short-term, individual interests of immigrant
workers at the expense of their long-term collective interests. Yet
in New York and elsewhere, many of the immigrant workers were
so well integrated into the local machines by the turn of the
century as to make socialist organizing among them virtually
impossible.

For most immigrants to America, life in the United States,
however brutal and degrading it might have been, was better than
life in the Old Country. Especially for those who remained in
America long enough to settle down, slow but steady progress was
commonplace. In the steel industry, for example, the constant
arrival of new waves of workers provided wide opportunities for
those immigrant labourers who stayed in the mills to move into
better paid semi-skilled and unskilled jobs. Upward movement
among the children of immigrants was even more common, though
their position in America's class structure remained far beneath that
of the offspring of the native born. Compared to their own parents,
however, the children of immigrants were notably successful in
moving into non-manual jobs, not only as clerks and shopkeepers,
but also, in exceptional but much publicized cases, as managers and
professionals.

Yet for most immigrants, and for their children as well, life
remained confined to manual labour, often of the most onerous and
unremunerative variety. If many of them guarded a feeling that
something was fundamentally wrong with a society that possessed so
much but gave them so little, few were willing to run the risks of
embracing socialist ideologies in a nation evidently so hostile to any
form of radicalism. To be 'American', the hard-pressed and
vulnerable immigrant knew, meant to renounce all beliefs that in
any way threatened the regime of private property. Life in America

was hard enough for a 'Hunky' or a 'Dago'; one did not need to make it harder by being a 'Red' in addition.

Those immigrants who, despite these conditions, nonetheless adhered to traditional notions of worker solidarity found their commitment sorely tested by the attitude of their American brethren. To many working men born in the United States, the immigrant labourer, especially the Eastern and Southern European, was an alien and inferior being. Indeed, in the eyes of his old-stock counterpart, the immigrant worker was not even a 'white man'.[23] An unwelcome intruder who supposedly endangered jobs and depressed wage levels,[24] the strange-tongued foreigner, with his peculiar customs, was separated from the native worker by a cultural chasm. 'Here I am with these Hunkies,' complained an old-time steelworker whose friends had left the plant. 'They don't seem like men to me hardly. They can't talk United States. You tell them something, and they just look and say "Me no fustay, me no fustay", that's all you can get out of 'em.'[25]

Employers were quick to capitalize on the deep antipathies that existed among workers of varying cultural and ethnic origins. One preferred tactic was to hire workers of several different, and preferably antagonistic, nationalities to work in the same plant. There, management characteristically reserved skilled positions for native-born workers or 'old' immigrants and relegated 'new' immigrants to the ranks of the semi-skilled and unskilled. Ethnic lines thus coincided with skill lines, thereby adding a sharp cultural edge to already existing cleavages of economic interest between craft workers and common labourers.

The split between relatively privileged native-born and 'old' immigrant workers, on the one hand, and overworked and underpaid 'new' immigrant workers, on the other, had fateful consequences for the working-class movement. For it permitted the formation of a native-born and old-stock working-class aristocracy which, aided and abetted by the state and by segments of the capitalist class, was able to exert a controlling influence over the whole of organized labour. This control—exemplified by the almost uninterrupted tenure of the brilliant and pugnacious Samuel Gompers as president of the American Federation of Labor from 1886 until his death in 1924—was bitterly contested by socialists. Indeed, as late as the American Federation of Labor convention of 1894, a plank calling for the 'collective ownership of the means of production and distribution' was only narrowly defeated. Yet by 1901, the year in which the Socialist Party was founded, the

American Federation of Labor had decisively rejected the idea of an independent working-class party and had adopted in its place a philosophy of securing immediate bread and butter gains for the worker within the framework of the market economy.[26] Organized labour, in other countries the very foundation of socialist strength, thus became in the United States a powerful ally of the existing capitalist order.

*

While Sombart neglected the extraordinary ethnic heterogeneity of the American working class, he lavished considerable attention on what he considered to be its distinctive political position. For him, this distinctiveness resided in the very extensiveness of American democracy, with universal suffrage and the popular election of the great majority of important public officials. To an extent unknown in Europe, the ideology of popular sovereignty—the belief that the people, and the people alone, actually govern—reigned supreme among American wage earners. If adherence to such an idealistic doctrine betrayed a certain naïvete among supposedly hard-headed American workers, it also testified to their genuine capacity to secure remarkable concrete results: the removal of unpopular judges and police chiefs, the election of professed pro-worker candidates to crucial state and local offices, and, above all, the granting to wage earners of an astonishing number of patronage jobs. The 'strong aversion of the American worker to Socialist tendencies', Sombart suggested, was 'explained in part' by this unusual relationship to the state.

Yet for all his insights into the peculiarities of the political position of the American worker, Sombart somehow managed to miss the essential point: in the United States, alone among industrial nations, the lower classes were incorporated into the institutions of parliamentary democracy *prior* to the Industrial Revolution and the emergence of a modern proletariat. As Selig Perlman pointed out in his neglected classic, *The Theory of the Labor Movement*, socialist movements in Europe derived their initial strength more from the struggle for elementary political rights than from the battle for economic advancement.[27] In America, however, the free gift of the ballot and the extension to workers of the basic rights of citizenship preceded the birth of the labour movement. Possessing the same political rights as members of other classes, American workers were denied the very experience of exclusion that might have brought them together as a class. As Karl Kautsky, bemoaning the difficulties faced by his Socialist comrades in America, put the matter in 1904: 'Just as the struggle for truth is much higher than the untroubled possession of a truth earlier discovered, so the struggle for freedom is very much superior to the effortless possession of a freedom that others have won before.'[28]

By the time American workers faced the full brutality of industrial capitalism, a long heritage of faith in the existing political system, if not the prevailing order, had already established itself in the labour movement. This faith, while based in part on certain formal democratic rights enjoyed by the white working class— among them universal suffrage, equality before the law, and basic civil liberties—was also rooted in the real power of workers to use the political system to advance their interests. At the community level, as Alan Dawley has shown in an illuminating study of the Industrial Revolution in nineteenth-century Lynn, this power could be used to remove strike-breaking police chiefs via the election of pro-labour mayors.[29] The elevation of 'friends of the working man' to the highest position of honour in the community did not, to be sure, pose a threat to the rule of private capital, but it did give workers a strong feeling of power. If Dawley goes a bit far in insisting that in the eyes of the working men, 'the government was but the executive committee of the people', there can be no denying that the great majority of early industrial workers viewed what was then the world's only political democracy with something approaching reverence.

Another vital source of the widespread legitimacy enjoyed by the existing political order was the unusually open and inclusive character of the two major American political parties. Democrats and Republicans alike, Sombart observed, recruited numerous party activists from the ranks of the working class. Party leadership, too, had a strong popular cast, and the choice of former wage earners, often of immigrant extraction, as candidates for high office offered vivid evidence of the system's openness. To an extent unknown in Europe, at least during the early stages of the Industrial Revolution, promising working-class leaders would be co-opted into the system through the powerful allure of elective or appointive office. This capacity to absorb talent from the working classes has been cited by labour historian David Montgomery as 'perhaps the most effective deterrent to the maturing of a revolutionary class-consciousness among the nation's workers during the turbulent social conflicts of the late nineteenth century'.[30]

A deep-seated adherence to the institutions of political democracy thus developed in the early American working class—an adherence based in part on ideological commitment, in part on the provision of tangible benefits. When, in the late nineteenth century, the struggle between labour and capital had become an unmistakable feature of the economic landscape, a substantial proportion of the working class had already developed deep loyalties to one or the other of the two major parties. Thus, by the time that the Socialist Party of America was founded in 1901, a powerful institutional framework —its cornerstones a reformist labour movement and a highly sophisticated, but self-consciously non-ideological modern party system—had arisen to incorporate into the existing order the farmers and immigrants then streaming into the nation's factories. Once this institutional framework was in place, it was, as the Socialists were soon to learn, remarkably difficult to dislodge.

The absence of a set of institutions capable of introducing new entrants to the ranks of wage labour to collectivist viewpoints proved particularly damaging to the prospects for socialism in the United States, for the American working class was, perhaps more than any other, constantly infused with waves of non-working-class elements: native-born farmers, Southern blacks, and European peasants. Those forces that did shape the political consciousness of the American working class—organized labour, the two major parties, and, above all, the dense cultural life of the working-class neighbourhood—encouraged the growth not of class consciousness, but of a narrow interest-group mentality. In America, the same individual could, as a worker, wage bitter economic struggle against his capitalist employer while, as a neighbourhood resident, follow the conservative leadership of the local ethnic elite.

In the split between the worker as labourer and the worker as community resident may lie the solution to one of the great riddles of American history: why a working class so evidently capable of extraordinary militancy in its struggles at the point of production, was apparently incapable of translating this tradition of economic militancy into a broader demand for fundamental political change. For in America linkage to the political system had, since the abolition of property requirements for suffrage during the era of Jacksonian democracy, been rooted not in work, but in the community. If, by the late nineteenth century, the conflict between capital and labour had become starkly visible at the point of production, the same could not be said for daily life in the community. Yet it was at the level of community, where bonds of ethnic solidarity were typically stronger than the ties of social class, that the Socialists, if they were to succeed, had to carry out the difficult task of party organization.[31]

*

The failure of the Socialist Party to establish roots in working-class communities during the early part of this century and its inability to survive the repression unleashed upon it in the years during and immediately after the First World War have left an enduring legacy of defeat from which the left has never really recovered. Even the Great Depression, seemingly the ideal economic setting for the emergence of a socialist movement, could not, despite the tireless organizing efforts of radicals of various persuasions, shake the commitment of the great majority of Americans to the two-party system and the capitalist order of which it was a crucial component. And the New Left, whatever its other accomplishments, failed miserably in its awkward attempts to establish links with a working class which, though restive itself, was deeply suspicious of the privileged young people who dominated the movements of the 1960s.

The consequences of this legacy of defeat are with us still. Perhaps the most dramatic is the growing unwillingness of the populace to participate in a political system that offers them no genuine choice; in the 1976 presidential election, despite much talk about a massive turnout, a mere 53 per cent of those eligible to vote even bothered to show up at the polls. The absence of a vibrant socialist movement is also responsible, at least in part, for the persistence, on a scale unknown in Europe, of appalling public squalor amidst immense private wealth. The United States, one suspects, is the only advanced industrial society in which even the middle class lives in constant fear that a relatively brief stay in the hospital may lead to financial ruin; the feeble American Welfare State, now the object of a concerted attack from the right, remains by far the least developed of the advanced capitalist societies.

Writing in 1905, Sombart described the particular form of capitalism then existing in America as the most exploitative in the world. If in the seventy-three years that have since intervened, this has not fundamentally changed, perhaps it is because the type of mass socialist movement which elsewhere has challenged and substantially circumscribed the power of private capital has, in America, still to be constructed.

NOTES

1. For an incisive analysis of the specific factors that led to the disintegration of the Socialist Party, see James Weinstein, *The Decline of Socialism in America* (New York, Vintage, 1969).

2. The review was accompanied by a footnote from A.M. Simons, the editor of the *International Socialist Review*, noting that the journal had printed the 'valuable statistical portions' of Sombart's study, but had stopped further publication when it came to 'the nonsense on the conditions of American workers'. Simons's ire had been aroused by Sombart's claim, in the preface to the 1906 book edition of *Warum gibt es in den Vereinigten Staaten keinen Sozialismus?*, that American Socialist leaders had endorsed the correctness of his interpretation and that *International Socialist Review*, in reproducing sections of his work, had expressed agreement with his viewpoint.

3. Himself a former Social Democrat who, at the time of his visit to the United States (1904) retained a certain sympathy for socialist ideals, Sombart wished to address a question of urgent interest to radicals everywhere—whether the trajectory of capitalist development was likely to lead the worker toward or away from socialism. Of his later relationship to National Socialism, the book jacket says simply that 'his political orientation became progressively more reactionary as he grew older'. Yet as C.T. Husbands notes in his scholarly and provocative introduction to the volume, 'it is only with considerable good nature that one can refrain from calling him a Nazi during the last years of his life'. As anyone who has read Sombart's *Deutscher Sozialismus*, written in German in 1934 and translated into English as *A New Social Philosophy* in 1937, can testify, even this is something of an understatement. For it was in the foreword to this volume that Sombart, noting that he had refrained from commenting directly on the politics of the current government, insisted that that was not because he was 'indifferent or unfriendly to the Hitler government; not in the least'.

   In the text of *A New Social Philosophy*, Sombart betrays a chilling anti-Semitism. Reflecting upon the so-called 'Jewish question', he writes: 'In order to free ourselves from the Jewish spirit—said to be the chief task of the German people and, above all, of Socialism—it is not enough to exclude all Jews, not even enough to cultivate an anti-Jewish temper.' Arthur Mitzman, author of the most detailed treatment of Sombart's life and work now available in English, has suggested that his later fascism was already foreshadowed in his analysis of the First World War as a conflict between *Heldenvölker* (hero nations, notably Germany) and *Handlervölker* (trading nations, historically exemplified by the Jews but best represented in the twentieth century by England). For a fascinating discussion of Sombart's complex, and in many ways contradictory, personality, see Mitzman's *Sociology and Estrangement: Three Sociologists of Imperial Germany* (New York: Knopf, 1973).

4. A representative collection of recent contributions to the debate about American exceptionalism is contained in the stimulating volume edited by John H. M. Laslett and Seymour Martin Lipset, *Failure of a Dream? Essays in the History of American Socialism* (Garden City, New York; Doubleday, 1974). See also Seymour Martin Lipset, 'Why No Socialism in the United States?', in Seweryn Bialer and Sophia Sluzar (eds.), *Sources of Contemporary Radicalism* (Boulder, Colorado: Westview Press, 1977), pp. 31-149, 346-63 for a comprehensive treatment of the topic which includes an excellent bibliography.

5. E. H. Phelps Brown with Sheila V. Hopkins, 'The Course of Wage-Rates in Five Countries, 1860-1939', *Oxford Economic Papers* (June 1950), p. 236.

6. Bryce, commenting upon the America of the late nineteenth century, understood this very well: 'though the troubles that have arisen between capital and labour may not soon pass away', he wrote in 1888, 'the sense of human equality, the absence of offensive privileges distinguishing class from class, will make those troubles less severe than in Europe, where they are complicated by ... arrogance on the one side and envy on the other'.

7. On the persistence into the late nineteenth century of the corporatist traditions and institutions of the pre-industrial European working class, see the study of William H. Sewell, Jr., 'Social Change and the Rise of Working-Class Politics in Nineteenth-Century Marseille', *Past and Present* (November 1974), pp. 75-109. For a general treatment of artisans in late-eighteenth-century England and France, see Gwynn A. Williams, *Artisans and Sans-Culottes: Popular Movements in France and Britain during the French Revolution* (London: Edward Arnold, 1968).

8. For detailed evidence on the massive inequalities of pre-Civil-War America, see Edward Pessen, 'The Egalitarian Myth and the American Social Reality: Wealth, Mobility and Equality in the "Era of the Common Man"', *American Historical Review* (October 1971), pp. 989-1034. The figure on the proportion of the white working population that owned property in the time of Tocqueville is from C. Wright Mills, *White Collar* (New York: Oxford, 1951), p. 7.

9. R. Richard Wohl, 'The "Rags to Riches Story": An Episode in Secular Idealism', in Reinhard Bendix and Seymour Martin Lipset (eds.), *Class, Status, and Power* (New York: Free Press, 1966), pp. 501-6.

10. Evidence on the social origins of the American business elite, as well as an interesting case study of manufacturers in nineteenth-century Patterson, is contained in Herbert Gutman's 'The Reality of the Rags-to-Riches "Myth"' in his collection of essays, *Work, Culture, and Society in Industrializing America* (New York: Vintage, 1977), pp. 211-33.

11. The classical statement of this argument is presented in Seymour Martin Lipset and Reinhard Bendix, *Social Mobility in Industrial Society* (Berkeley: University of California, 1959).

12. The precise figures are Boston—41 per cent; Poughkeepsie—26 per

cent; Marseille—11 per cent; Bochum—12 per cent. These figures are derived from Stephen Thernstrom, *The Other Bostonians: Poverty and Progress in the American Metropolis, 1880-1970* (Cambridge: Harvard, 1973); William Sewell, Jr., 'Social Mobility in a Nineteenth-Century European City: Some Findings and Implications', *Journal of Interdisciplinary History* (Autumn 1976), pp. 217-33; David Crew, 'Definitions of Modernity: Social Mobility in a German Town, 1880-1901', in Peter N. Stearns and Daniel J. Walkowitz (eds.) *Workers in the Industrial Revolution* (New Brunswick, New Jersey: Transaction, 1974), pp. 297-332. For a lively general discussion of rates of mobility in Europe and America, see the debate between Thernstrom and Lipset in Laslett and Lipset, *Failure of a Dream?*, pp. 502-52.

13. Thernstrom, *The Other Bostonians,* pp. 221-32. In 1880 London, in contrast, 63 per cent of the residents were native to the city. See Gutman, *Work, Culture, and Society,* p. 40.

14. Fred A. Shannon, 'A Post Mortem on the Labor Safety Valve Theory', *Agricultural History* (1945), pp. 31-37. On the debate over the frontier thesis, see Ray Allen (ed.) *The Frontier Thesis: Valid Interpretation of American History?* (New York: Holt, Rinehart, and Winston, 1966) and Richard Hofstadter and Seymour Lipset (eds.), *Turner and the Sociology of the Frontier* (New York: Basic, 1968).

15. Thernstrom, *The Other Bostonians,* pp. 231-2.

16. The sheer magnitude of the immigrant presence in American life was most deeply felt in the great industrial cities. In 1880, between 78 and 87 per cent of the residents of San Francisco (78), St. Louis (78), Cleveland (80), New York (80), Detroit (84), Milwaukee (84), and Chicago (87) were immigrants or children of immigrants. In 1880 London, on the other hand, 94 per cent of the inhabitants were from England and Wales. Gutman, *Work, Culture, and Society,* p. 40.

17. Quoted in David Brody, *Steelworkers in America: The Nonunion Era* (New York: Harper and Row, 1969), p. 100.

18. Thomas Kessner, *The Golden Door: Italian and Jewish Immigrant Mobility in New York City 1880-1915* (New York: Oxford University Press, 1977), p. 28; Brody, *Steelworkers in America,* p. 106. Overall, between 1820 and 1924, approximately 30 per cent of those immigrating to the United States returned to their home countries, with the proportion of returnees increasing substantially during later periods. For a general discussion of patterns of intercontinential migration, see Gerald Rosenblum, *Immigrant Workers: Their Impact on American Labor Radicalism* (New York: Basic Books, 1973), pp. 45-53.

19. Kessner, *The Golden Door,* p. 29.

20. Socialist tendencies among immigrants were perhaps most pronounced among workers of German and East European Jewish backgrounds. Both groups, it is worth noting, had considerable experience in Europe as urban wage earners, and both exhibited strikingly low rates of repatriation.

21. Among those Marxist scholars who have been in the forefront of those insisting on the importance of cultural as well as work experiences in

the formation of class consciousness have been Herbert Gutman, E.P. Thompson, *The Making of the English Working Class* (London: Victor Gollancz, 1963); and John Alt, 'Beyond Class: The Decline of Industrial Labor and Leisure', *Telos* (Summer 1976), pp. 55-80.

22. Evidence on ethnic intermarriage among first-generation immigrants is available in Julius Drachsler, 'Intermarriage in New York City: A Statistical Study of the Amalgamation of European Peoples', in *Studies in History, Economics and Public Law* (New York: Columbia, 1921); Ruby Jo Reeves Kennedy, 'Single or Triple Melting-Pot? Intermarriage in New Haven, 1870-1950', *American Journal of Sociology* (July 1952), pp. 56-9; Bessie Bloom Wessel, *An Ethnic Survey of Woonsocket, Rhode Island* (Chicago: University of Chicago, 1931).

23. The tendency of native-born American workers, as well as foreign-born Northern European workers, to call themselves 'white men' as a means of distinguishing themselves from Southern and Eastern Europeans is noted by John Higham in his superb study of American nativism, *Strangers in the Land* (New Brunswick, New Jersey: Rutgers, 1955). In general, the American working class at the turn of the century was split not just into natives and foreign born, but also 'old' and 'new' immigrants. Revealingly, the former were often referred to as 'English-speaking men', although they included Dutchmen, Germans, and Scandinavians. The 'new' immigrants—principally Italians, Slavs, Hungarians, and Jews—were thus seen not only as foreign and non-English speaking, but also as racially distinct. See Issac Hourwich, *Immigration and Labor* (New York: B.W. Huebsch, 1922).

24. Contrary to what native wage earners believed, the arrival of masses of immigrant labourers actually improved their position, propelling many of them upward into the ranks of skilled and supervisory workers. Indeed, it was only because Eastern and Southern European immigrants were available in large numbers to fill the least desirable jobs that it was possible for native-born workers to be elevated into a relatively aristocratic position. For documentation of this point, see Hourwich, *Immigration and Labor*, pp. 148-76 and Thernstrom, *The Other Bostonians*, pp. 111-44.

25. Quoted in David Brody, *Steelworkers in America*, p. 119.

26. Faced from its inception with the opposition of the American Federation of Labor to an independent working-class party, the Socialist Party adopted a strategy of 'boring from within'. The results of this strategy were not impressive, for despite substantial strength within the American Federation of Labor—at times between 1901 and 1912 it controlled as many as one-third of the delegates to the national convention—the Socialist Party was unable to move the organization in the direction of either industrial unionism or independent political action. William M. Dicks's *Labor and Socialism in America: The Gompers Era* (Port Washington, New York: Kennikat Press, 1972) provides a useful account of the complex relations that existed between the American Federation of Labor and the Socialist Party and John

H.M .Laslett's *Labor and the Left* (New York: Basic, 1970) contains some interesting material of socialist influence in several major industries.

27. Selig Perlman, *A Theory of the Labor Movement* (New York: Augustus M. Kelley, 1928), pp. 167-8.

28. Quoted in R. Lawrence Moore, *European Socialists and the American Promised Land* (New York: Oxford, 1970), p. 110. Lenin, too, shared Kautsky's belief that the problems of socialists in America derived from the separation of the struggles for political and economic democracy effected by the early granting to the working class of elementary political rights. If socialism was a feeble force in American life, Lenin wrote in 1907, this was because it faced 'the most firmly established democratic system, which confronts the proletariat with purely socialist tasks'.

29. Alan Dawley, *Class and Community: The Industrial Revolution in Lynn* (Cambridge: Harvard University, 1976). Herbert Gutman, in a careful study of a number of small industrial communities, also found that workers in late-nineteenth-century America often wielded considerable political power. This power, Gutman suggests, reflected not only the numerical strength of the working class, but also the substantial sympathy that its plight aroused among middle-and-upper-middle-class elements hostile to industrial, as opposed to traditional, business enterprise. Herbert Gutman, 'The Worker's Search for Power: Labor in the Guilded Age', in H. Wayne Morgan (ed.), *The Gilded Age: A Reappraisal* (Syracuse: Syracuse University Press, 1963), pp. 38-68.

30. David Montgomery, *Beyond Equality: Labor and the Radical Republicans 1862-1872* (New York: Vintage, 1972), p. 215.

31. For a provocative discussion of the split between the immigrant worker as labouring ethnic at the point of production and cultural ethnic in the community, see Ira Katznelson, 'The Patterning of Class in the United States: An Approach to American Exceptionalism', presented at the 1976 Annual Meeting of the American Political Science Association, Chicago.

THE CONTRADICTIONS
OF SOCIALIST ECONOMIES:
A MARXIST INTERPRETATION

Domenico Mario Nuti

1. *Premise*

Public ownership of the means of production (in its forms of state, co-operative and local ownership) and macro-economic planning are the fundamental features of socialist economies of Marxist-Leninist inspiration. The known variants of this type of economy differ mainly in the extent and mix of public ownership, the degree of central control and its extension beyond the macro-economic sphere, the actual techniques of management and planning. These economies differ from both 'associationist' (or 'self-management') socialism of Yugoslavian type where there is no planning, and social democracy of Scandinavian type where private ownership and enterprise continue to dominate.

The large body of economic literature on socialist economies is devoted almost entirely to the practicability and efficiency of resource allocation in various models of socialism with different degrees of centralization, to the development of planning techniques for the co-ordination of economic life and a discussion of their merits relatively to the automatism of markets, and to an analysis of the economic implications of alternative decisional rules and incentive schemes in the management of public ownership. Thus the socialist economy has been investigated primarily as a kind of *capitalism without capitalists.* This is true even of Marxian economists such as Oskar Lange and Maurice Dobb, whose theoretical contributions—important as they are—are confined to these areas of inquiry, mostly in response to the challenge of bourgeois economists such as Hayek and Mises.[1] Paradoxically, with very few notable exceptions, the Marxian approach to modes of production has been seldom applied to socialist economies of Marxist-Leninist inspiration, and the development of a political economy of socialism has been delayed, slow and fragmentary. This paper is intended as a contribution to this underdeveloped area of Marxian economics.

228

2. Marxian Method and Socialist Economies

Marxian political economy, based on dialectical materialism, seeks the laws regulating the emergence, development and transformation of an economic system in the existence of 'contradictions' in the system and in the adaptation process generated by the resolution of those contradictions. Man's activities of production and accumulation modify nature leading to the development of *productive forces* (which stand for the endowment of natural and man-made resources and the state of technical knowledge); this development eventually leads to the emergence of contradictions between the productive potential of society and the prevailing *productive relations* (i.e., the rules about ownership, the organization of labour in production, the distribution, consumption and accumulation of the social product). Productive forces and productive relations define a *mode of production* (such as slavery, feudalism, capitalism, socialism, communism; 'economic system' is an imperfect synonym because it lacks the primacy attributed by Marx to production in economic life, and the reference to the state of productive forces). Productive relations, which are the *economic basis* of any social formation, are modified by the resolution of these contradictions. This, in turn, generates further contradictions between the economic basis and the *superstructure* of society, i.e., those social relations other than production relations as well as the expressions of social consciousness which are indispensable to the very existence of a given mode of production. The interaction between productive forces, productive relations (the economic basis) and superstructure, which is best seen as a simultaneous process rather than one of direct and sequential causation, determines the *laws of motion* of any society.[2]

'Contradiction' in this context is best understood as incompatibility increasing over time, as disequilibrium, or unstable equilibrium, of economic magnitudes and institutions, which brings about a process of adaptation and change towards a better correspondence of productive forces, productive relations and superstructure.[3]

This deceivingly simple and powerful apparatus has been used extensively and fruitfully by Marx and other political economists for the analysis of the capitalist mode of production and of precapitalistic economic formations. Its application has led to important insights into the hidden exploitative nature of capitalism, the role of competition and the process of industrial and financial concentration, the problem of effective demand (Rosa Luxemburg,

Kalecki), the political cycle (Kalecki), the role of class conflict in economic growth (Goodwin) and in the explanation of inflation (Rowthorn), the analysis of imperialism (from Lenin to Baran-Sweezy). The same cannot be said for the analysis of the socialist mode of production. It is true that many economic historians—deliberately or involuntarily, and whether or not they would accept the Marxian label—have taken into account some of the questions raised by the Marxian approach in their study of Soviet economic history, emphasizing for instance the low initial level of development of the Soviet economy, or the connection between Soviet accumulation policy and the development of institutions in the inter-war period. But political economists have only rarely applied the Marxian method to the socialist economy; indeed many have denied its applicability to the socialist economy altogether.

Bukharin and Rosa Luxemburg, for instance, believed that the end of capitalism would mark the end of political economy as a science; with 'the transition to a planned mode of production consciously organized by the entire working force of society' no longer would there be a science of the laws of development of the economy (Luxemburg, 1954), but presumably only a body of planning techniques of a kind described by Lange as 'praxeology' (Lange, 1959; this, as the science of human rational choice, is simply part of mainstream economics).

Soviet and, later, East-European official texts have more explicitly claimed the correspondence of production relations and productive forces under socialism, i.e., the end of conflicts and dialectical contradictions. New economic laws are claimed to emerge under socialism, such as the 'law of the increasingly complete satisfaction of the growing material and cultural requirements of the people through the continuous development and perfection of social production', the 'law of planned proportionate development'; these vague propositions are simply a wishful restatement of the fact that the socialist economy is planned. The 'law of value', in the sense of market discipline, is recognized as operating at least in the sphere of consumption goods; this simply acknowledges that central planning is not all-embracing. The most significant statement in the official texts is the so-called 'law of the faster growth of the production of the means of production relatively to the production of means of consumption'; this is an accurate statement of the accumulation policies actually followed in the Soviet Union and Eastern Europe to date—with sporadic and short-lived exceptions—but the policy has no necessary foundation outside the case of a closed economy which is either trying to accelerate its growth or/and is facing a rising capital intensity of production. To regard this as a law of socialism is simply an attempt to legitimize the accumulation policy actually pursued.[4] These pseudo-laws clearly have nothing to do with the Marxian 'laws of motion' of society. They are just part of the official ideology, i.e., are a component of the socialist 'superstructure'.

In East-European literature in the sixties a rather crude version of the Marxian approach was put forward, to explain the proposed and partly implemented reform of the Soviet-type centralized model prevailing in the area. Measures of decentralization, it was argued, were made necessary by the transition from *extensive* economic development with abundant labour and natural resources to *intensive* development with scarcity of labour and resources. This theory is in line with Soviet-type orthodox political economy of socialism, in that a discrepancy between the level of development of productive forces and the prevailing productive relations is regarded as soluble without conflicts, antagonisms or dialectical oppositions. As we shall see later on in this paper (section 6) the transition was important, but *in itself* is not an explanation of institutional change and economic performance in Eastern Europe from the mid sixties to date. Nor can the drive for reform be associated with a smooth, conflict-free transition between models: suffice to mention the Poznan events in 1956, the abrupt end of the Hungarian experiment in 1956 and of the Czech experiment in 1968, the Baltic events of 1970, and so on.

The fact that the actual development of socialist countries did not conform to the picture of conflict-free and harmonious societies hopefully expected by early socialist writers and—with much less justification—portrayed by official texts and simple theories of transition, has led a number of critics claiming to work in the Marxian tradition to fill this analytical vacuum. These Marx-inspired critics, who do not construct a Marxian political economy of socialism, follow three basic lines:

1) An orthodox Trotskyist line (exemplified by Trotsky, 1937; Mandel, 1968 Vol. II, 1974) which, broadly speaking, regards the Soviet Union as a 'bureaucratically deformed workers' state' (an expression actually attributed to Lenin) and Soviet-type economies as 'transitional societies' conditioned by the low level of socio-economic development reached at the time of transition between capitalism and socialism, subject to their own 'laws' different from those of either capitalism or socialism, exhibiting a basic contradiction between economic planning and the permanence of commodity

production in the sphere of consumption goods, in other words a contradiction due to the coexistence of market and plan (this contradiction is stated but not analysed in any detail). Soviet society is regarded as ruled by a bureaucracy (i.e., a social layer comprising all those who exercise management and leadership functions in any sector of social life); this is not regarded as a *class,* because it does not appropriate the surplus though it decides its allocation; but there is a conflict between 'the potential optimization of growth and the use of resources deriving from planning and socialization, and the indifference of the new ruling bureaucracy to such optimization' (Mandel, 1974, p. 17). The development of a transitional society into a fully socialist one requires: the growth of productive forces, workers' self-management, political democracy, the withering away of commodity relations, a permanent (cultural) revolution in daily life, and the international development of revolution (Mandel, 1974).

2) The line of International Socialism (exemplified by Cliff, 1964; Harman, 1975); it shares with the Trotskyist line the notion of the degenerated revolution and the internationalist imperative, but goes further in its critique of Soviet-type societies by arguing that the bureaucracy is a new *ruling class* with a specific class interest in securing and maintaining a privileged standard of living and also in capital accumulation for the expansion of military power or even for its own sake. Unlike the Trotskyists, this view considers 'control' over the means of production to be as good as 'ownership' for the definition of a class; Soviet-type societies (including Maoist China and North Korea) are defined as 'bureaucratic state-capitalist' societies, consequently requiring an anti-bureaucratic working-class revolution, which can only be successful on an international scale.

3) The Maoist line (exemplified by Bettelheim-Sweezy, 1971, Bettelheim, 1974) has much in common with the previous view in that it regards Soviet-type societies as 'state capitalist', ruled by a 'state bourgeoisie' whose purpose is domination at home and imperialism abroad; but it differs significantly in its more positive assessment of Stalinism, in its positive assessment of the Maoist experience as the proof that the transformation of productive forces is not a precondition for the transformation of social relations; it is more analytical, for instance, it identifies 'economism' as the cardinal error pervading the Soviet experience, and it discusses the difference between nationalization and socialization; it is also characterized by a very critical assessment of the economic reforms which have taken place in Eastern Europe in the mid sixties,

regarded as evidence of the capitalist trend of these state-capitalist societies. The difference between the Maoist and the IS position is not one of nuances; for instance, the IS condemns Soviet intervention on the ground that although Czechoslovakia was at the time taking the capitalist road, the Soviet Union had no business to intervene as it has been taking exactly the same road back to capitalism (See Bettelheim-Sweezy, 1971).

The trouble with these three lines is not so much the tenuous and debatable nature of their connection with Marx—which in itself is not very important—*but that they are unconvincing and positively misleading interpretations of the experience of realized socialism.* A detailed analysis of these lines is beyond the scope of this paper, but apart from their own mutual inconsistencies there is already a considerable literature which very effectively criticizes them.[5] For instance, it has been stressed that 'control' over the means of production exercised by the bureaucracy does not include self-appropriation of the product nor right of disposal of those means, and that privileged access to consumption is not by itself sufficient to define a class (Lane, 1977, 1978; Lane-O'Dell, 1978; Miliband, 1975); that although the Soviet-type state is run *for* the workers and *in their name* rather than *by* them and is therefore not a class*less* society, it is not a society with *class conflict* but a one-class society confronting the state (Lane, 1977); that indeed Soviet workers exhibit the features of a class deeply 'incorporated' into the Soviet system (Lane, 1978); that Soviet-type planning has nothing in common with capitalist attempts at macro-economic management because of the capitalist failure to control investment, and that Soviet-type markets differ from capitalist markets not only in scope (not fully extending to production goods) but also in the sectoral immobility of Soviet-type enterprises (Nuti, 1978); and so on.[6] Of course there are fragments of these three approaches which are not only correct but also useful for the construction of a political economy of 'realized' socialism, and indeed will be embodied in my own attempt at presenting a Marxist version of such a political economy. For instance, Mandel's treatment of the historical conditioning and therefore the relativity of the Soviet model; the IS emphasis on the unrestrained accumulation drive of Soviet type economies and the ensuing cyclical patterns; the Maoist distinction between nationalization and socialization of the means of production. But it must be stressed that this is about all that can be rescued from these approaches; that the acceptance of these points does not imply acceptance of any of these approaches, and indeed these same points are made by a number of people totally unconnected with these approaches; and that ultimately the weakness of these approaches is that while they amount to an indictment of the Soviet-type model and a revolutionary strategy, whatever the merits of their case *they do not provide a theory of the functioning and of the development of these societies.*

The best, most coherent and comprehensive attempt at constructing a Marxian political economy of socialism is represented by the work of the Polish economist Wlodzimierz Brus (1964, 1973, 1975). Influenced by the Polish experience of the mid fifties, Brus developed a classification of socialist economies depending on the degree of centralization of current production decisions at the level of enterprises and sectors, discussed the relative merits of the centralized and the decentralized model as well as their suitability to different levels of development and to different purposes, and raised the question of Marx-type conflicts within the socialist economy (the emergence of groups, the weakening of incentives, the monopolistic bias due to industrial concentration, the possibility of market disequilibria in the sphere of consumption goods, the deterioration of labour discipline and instability of the labour force, the danger of bureaucratization—these are all phenomena conflicting with the socialization of the means of production and the progressive role of economic planning; Brus 1963, especially Ch. 1). Brus analysed in greater detail some of these conflicts in a collection of essays (1973) discussing among other things the socialization of the means of production as a *process* rather than a single act; the political premises and implications of economic decentralization, in particular the role of institutions of workers' self-government; the impact of central planning on innovation; the political and not purely technical nature of macro-economic decisions, and the technical limits to political choice; the informational advantages of political democracy. He clearly stated that 'Socialism does not put an end to socio-economic contradictions' (Brus, 1973, p. 82) and claimed that 'under socialism, economic and political factors are inseparable' (p. 89). His latest book (1975) brings together all these strands following a declared Marxian methodology, broadening the analysis to include Yugoslav self-management, an analysis of the specific East-European conditions which conflicted with the implant of the Stalinist model, and a discussion of the political and economic aspects of recent economic reform in Eastern Europe. He concludes, in spite of misgivings, that 'there exist economic laws determining the necessity of real socialization of the means of production and thus setting the direction for the further evolution of socialism in relation to the form which it has taken in the USSR and the people's democracies'; this, in turn, means 'the necessity of political democratization' (Brus, 1975, p. 207).

The East-German writer Rudolf Bahro must also be included—at least partially—within the scope of a Marxist attempt at constructing a political economy of socialism (Bahro, 1977, 1978). In fact Bahro sails dangerously close to the Trotskyist-IS positions outlined and criticized above; he also devotes no more than half a page to the recent economic reform (regarded as no more than part of a cat-and-mouse game between two components of the bureaucracy, namely central bureaucrats and managers) and devotes a great deal of space instead to a picture of socialist society which at least for the rest of this century must be regarded as utopian. But he provides very perceptive insights on the connection between the Soviet model of 'despotic industrialization' and of the Marxian Asiatic mode of production; the characterization of the 'proto-socialist' Soviet system, implying an embryonic stage of socialism; the connection between state repression and underdevelopment; the implications of the prevailing division of labour and the existence of a 'surplus of human expertise'; the role of the party as a 'double bureaucracy', and the 'insuperable contradiction between the social task of the party and its political and organizational form of existence as a political organization' (Bahro, 1978, p. 246). Bahro's class analysis of Soviet-type societies leads him to rule out the possibility and indeed the desirability of a pluralistic (i.e., multi-party) political system, but he expects those societies to evolve following a process of renewal and democratization of the communist party (Part Three, Ch. 12).

In the belief that the socialist economies of Eastern Europe present Marxian-type contradictions and are subject to laws of motion deriving from their attempted resolution a Marxian model is developed here of the interaction between capital accumulation, economic decentralization and political liberalization. This model is based on and tries to explain the experience of the Soviet Union and East-European economies in the post-war period, and leads to conditional predictions about their possible development paths. In order to put the model in a historical perspective, and to review and consolidate the elements of a Marxian political economy of socialism, the model is preceded by a discussion of the main features of various stages of socialist development (war communism 1918-21; New Economic Policy 1921-8; centralized socialism 1928-65; other East-European economies, and the economic reforms), their preconditions, achievements and problems. The inadequacy of the cruder 'transition' theory of economic reforms is also discussed.

Naturally, given the broad area reviewed and the limits of the format of this paper, I will have to be selective in the choice of themes and of evidence, and sometimes more assertive than I could wish. The justification is that this is meant as a contribution to political economy, not to economic history; and before I am accused of reductionism' or of 'determinism', I wish to stress that I am aware that political and social phenomena have a life of their own quite independently of the underlying economic forces, and that I do not believe in either the exclusiveness or the uniqueness of the impact of economic factors. Nevertheless, I am convinced that many political and economic features of East-European countries (including their least likeable features) are neither the consequences of the personality of leaders nor necessary and immutable characteristics of socialism.

3. *War Communism (1918-21)*

It is widely believed that according to Marxist doctrine the proletariat could seize power and gain control over the means of production only in the most advanced capitalist countries; what Marx actually postulated is that the establishment of socialism would require a level of capitalist development sufficient for the creation of an industrial proletariat, and of some degree of class consciousness and organization; after that the possibility of overthrowing the capitalist system would depend on the development of class struggle; the breakdown of capitalism would therefore occur in the weakest link of the system.[7]. It is worth recalling the 'level of development of productive forces' in Russia at the time of the Bolshevik take-over, characterized by the following features:

1) Despite the progress made in the late nineteenth century, with industrial growth at an average annual rate of 5.8 per cent over the period 1885-1913 and an industrial working class estimated at 2.5 million in 1913 (over three times the size of the industrial working class in 1861-70), Russia was still extremely backward: 80 per cent of its population consisted of illiterate or semi-literate peasants and its industrial large-scale output was only 6.9 per cent of American gross industrial output, and Russian per capita production in 1913 was only 4.8 per cent of American (Lane, 1978).

2) Not only was the industrial sector small, its structure was incapable of sustaining rapid self-supporting development: in 1913 nearly half of total industrial employment was in textiles, with only 15 per cent of industrial employment in the metal industry and 8.8 per cent in mining (Lane, 1978).

3) Agriculture was similarly underdeveloped: in terms of calories produced per male agricultural worker Russia ranked last but one among European countries in 1860 (doing better than Italy) and by 1910 had only suceeded in moving one up the list, overtaking Spain (Nove, 1969).

4) Population was growing fast, and labour was abundant;

5) On the contrary, capital was short, and in 1913 about one-third of the capital of private companies was foreign owned (Nove, 1969).

6) Russia's trade relations were typical of an underdeveloped country dependent on the industrialized West; over half of total Russian exports were accounted for by cereals and other foodstuffs; a third of all imports were made up of manufactured goods and raw materials, and semi-manufactured goods accounted for nearly a half. Trade dependence on the West and especially on German supplies (accounting for half of Russian imports) was such that 'in the First World War Russia continued to import certain commodities from Germany (mainly chemicals, metals and machinery), explicitly exempting these from the general prohibition of trade with enemy countries' (Dobb, 1966, p. 37).

7) The war effort and war destructions, aggravated by transportation difficulties, had led to grave scarcities and deficits of fuel, materials and food.

Pre-revolutionary 'production relations' in Russia were a mixture of capitalist, feudal and pre-feudal elements: the modern capitalist formation (industrial bourgeoisie and wage-labourers) concentrated in a few towns; the feudal formation only partly liquidated since the 1861 emancipation of serfs; the 'Asiatic'[8] formation represented by the Tsarist autocracy, its bureaucracy and the Orthodox state church, and most of the peasantry.

The model of socialism established by Soviet rule in these conditions is that of War Communism. It was characterized by the rapid expansion of State ownership and economic control over economic activity; the 'militarization' of labour; the obligatory delivery and requisition of the agricultural surplus; the organization of the entire economy effectively by centralized barter on a vast scale; the demonetization of the economy, first *de facto* because of hyper-inflation, then *de jure* at least within the state sector; the progressive payment of wage in kind according to a 'class ration'; the abolition of internal private trade; the establishment of consumers' co-operatives with compulsory membership; the provision of an increasing range of services free of charge; the direct allocation of inputs according to a system of priorities (See Carr,

1952, Ch. 17; Dobb, 1966; Szamuely 1974). War communism lasted from early 1918 to the beginning of 1921, when the Xth Congress established the New Economic Policy (NEP), characterized by the restoration of private production and trade, the re-establishment of ordinary monetary flows and the stabilization of the currency, the introduction of the principles of cost accounting and autonomy in state firms.

War Communism has been neglected as a model of 'realized socialism'. It is mostly regarded as a set of emergency measures, similar to wartime mobilization and centralization in capitalist countries—an interpretation encouraged by Soviet official sources suggesting that NEP was what Soviet leaders wanted to establish from the beginning, had they not been prevented by invasion and civil war[9]. On the contrary, László Szamuely points out that, whatever the impact of war necessity on actual choice, War Communism as 'a centralized subsistence economy, managed by instructions, based on egalitarian principles' was the image and operational concept of a socialist economy in the writing of Kautsky, Hilferding; Bukharin, in its most developed form (1920); Preobrazhensky, Strumilin; many of the direct partici- pants in state administration; Trotsky of course, and Lenin him- self (Szamuely, 1974); not only before War Communism, but all the time while it was taking shape. It was only after the event, after it became apparent that the system could not survive the economic and political pressures it had generated, that it came to be regarded as a 'deviation from the normal course', 'a temporary measure' which 'was not nor could be a policy that corresponded to the economic tasks of the proletariat' (Lenin).

War Communism came to an end (not without opposition, and recriminations about the 'retreat' this represented) because of economic difficulties (the multiplication of priorities; the disruption of supplies; difficulties with grain procurements, just to name a few) and political pressures (strikes, absenteeism, opposition in the factories, the Kronstadt rebellion, etc.). Basically, War Communism delivered survival, but could not deliver reconstruction, nor (at that time and in that form) industrialization; it was destroyed by its own contradictions. But it remains an important landmark in the development of socialism 1) because it was the first model of realized socialism (though admittedly in far from ideal conditions); 2) because—as we shall see—it provided a guideline for the Stalinist model of another brand of War Communism, the war against

underdevelopment; 3) because it generated some of the economic
and political problems of the Stalinist model.

4. *The New Economic Policy (1921-28)*

The first measure of the New Economic Policy was the replacement of compulsory deliveries of agricultural surplus by a tax in
kind, leaving peasants free to trade any remainder over and above
the tax and their own requirements. This was supposed to save the
smychka, i.e., the alliance between workers and peasants, and
improve food supplies. 'The development launched by the reform in
the spring of 1921 soon exceeded the original targets. The emergence
of local trade led to the development of a wide internal market; the
logic of modern economy rapidly burst the primitive framework of
barter and demanded modern money and credit relations. The
Soviet State recognized its importance in time and, already in the
summer of 1921, it took the first steps to normalize monetary and
credit turnover. (One of the most important ones was the creation-
—as a matter of fact, the reopening—of the State Bank in early
October 1921). Also the blood circulation of industry was resumed,
state enterprises began to rely on market possibilities in their
purchases and product sales'—this is how Szamuely succinctly
summarizes the process of transition to the NEP. Denationaliza-
tions, leasings (often to former owners), freedom to organize small
scale private enterprises (not exceeding ten to twenty workers in
theory, much greater in practice) followed. The state budget was
balanced, the currency was stabilized and made convertible,
concessions were granted to foreign capital, foreign trade increased.
The economy recovered. (See Dobb, 1966; Nove, 1969; Carr, 1952,
1954, 1958.)

The superstructure rapidly adjusted to this new economic basis.
Economic liberalization brought about complete political centralization. Fearing the danger of a capitalist threat to the new order, all
political parties other than the Bolsheviks were finally banned and,
at the same Xth Congress that introduced NEP, Lenin's proposal
that organized groups or faction within the party itself should be
banned was approved and immediately acted upon. Deutscher
comments that this was not yet strictly a ban on inner-party
opposition; dissenters were still encouraged to express dissent in the
party newspaper and discussions, and leaders of all shades of
opposition were elected to the new CC; but Lenin 'insisted that
opposition should remain diffuse and that the dissenters should not
form themselves into solid leagues. He submitted a resolution, one

clause of which (kept secret) empowered the Central Committee to expel offenders, no matter how high their standing in the party (Deutscher, 1954, p. 519). 'The arrangement under which opposition was permitted provided it remained dispersed could work as long as members of the party disagrees over secondary or transient issues. But when the differences were serious and prolonged it was inevitable that members of the same mind should band together' (Deutscher, *ibidem*).

A further adjustment in the superstructure is a 'theoretical revision' (Szamuely, 1974, Ch. 4). Already in the autumn of 1921 Lenin formulated the three basic principles of management on which the New Economic Policy was founded: 1) personal incentive, 2) economic accounting (*khozraschot*) and 3) the utilization of commodity and money relations in the construction of socialism. At the XIth Congress in March 1922 Lenin 'called competition with private capital on the domestic and the international market "the pivot of the New Economic Policy", "the quintessence of the Party's policy"; he held it to be a "crucial test", "the last and decisive battle" on which the fate of socialism depended' (Szamuely, *ibidem*, pp. 77-8). It appears from Lenin's writings that not only did he accept the idea that state enterprises should conduct a market economy, but even looked at this as a possible way of implementing a central state plan. Szamuely argues that Lenin had arrived, or was on the way to arrive, at the idea of a system of socialist planned economy using methods of market economy and relying on material incentives (Szamuely, 1974, p. 79).

This interpretation of Lenin's vision may or may not be correct. The fact is that the mode of production represented by the NEP—basically a mixed economy of a kind which today would certainly obtain the blessing of the IMF—delivered reconstruction, but was unable to do more than that; indeed it soon generated its own contradictions. Let us review the state of development of productive forces and its prospects under NEP in the late twenties:

1) the reconstruction of the economy was completed at some point between 1926 and 1928, according to the yardstick used;

2) growth had been based mostly on the reactivation of existing capacity and the reabsorption of available factory labour; but gross investment in the mid twenties was not greatly in excess of depreciation (Nove, 1969)

3) 'Socialism in one country'—not as the slogan that Trotsky called 'a reactionary, narrow dream', and Sartre 'an ideological

monstrosity' (Sartre, 1977), but as a fact of life, given the failure of European revolutions—precluded any extensive use of foreign capital either in the form of loans or direct investment in order to finance capital accumulation;

4) given the coexistence of a private and a socialized sector, the problem was not only that of obtaining capital accumulation, but also that of generating capital accumulation *within the socialized sector* (Preobrazhensky's 'primitive socialist accumulation'); this could be done in the circumstances either by expropriating the peasants (directly, or manipulating the terms of trade between private agriculture and socialized industry) or the Nepmen, thereby undermining the foundations of NEP, or by compressing the living standards of workers in the socialized sector; alternatively, accumulation would have had to proceed at a slow pace;

5) unemployment arose and fluctuated during the NEP; it reached 1.24 million at the beginning of 1924, fell to 950,000 in the next year, but began rising again to reach a figure of 1.6 million in 1929 (Nove, 1969, p. 115; there were only 8.5 million 'workers and employees' in 1924). A slow pace of accumulation would have caused the permanence, if not the increase, of labour unemployment, which presumably would have destroyed any pretence at even a semblance of socialism;

6) profiteering Nepmen were thriving;

7) the tax in kind having been replaced with a money tax, agricultural procurements had to go through the market; the deterioration of agriculture's terms of trade had led to supply difficulties (the 'scissor crisis' of 1925); the same difficulties were arising at the end of the twenties; the contradiction generated by NEP boiled down to the dilemma between *either* the use of price incentives to obtain a higher marketed surplus, which would have led to the further development of a *kulak* class and the abandonment of the idea of using agriculture to finance primitive socialist accumulation; *or* the acceptance of low levels of agricultural production and marketed surplus;

8) finally, 'socialism in one country' also meant limited prospects for international trade; the Soviet Union had already accumulated a considerable amount of short-term international debt, the servicing cost of which was mounting; the amount of traditional agricultural exports available for export was falling in volume; terms of trade were deteriorating (Dohan, 1976).

It should be clear that there was a contradiction between the maintenance of the NEP mixed economy and the simultaneous achievement of economic growth, growth of the socialized sector, and minimum standards of socialist distribution.

The growing tension between productive forces and productive relations manifested itself, among other things, under the guise of intense discussion around two major themes: the accumulation strategy, and the nature of economic planning (Erlich, 1960; Spulber, 1964; Carr-Davies, 1974; Dobb, 1960, 1965). The theoreticians of the right wing, like Shanin, Bazarov and Bukharin, advocated simultaneous agricultural and industrial growth with heavy industry following the development of agriculture and light industry. Shanin, for instance, maintained the necessity of a sequence of development in which priority would be given in turn to agriculture, then to light industry following the demand expansion from the agricultural sector, and then to heavy industry only after the growth of these sectors had brought about a sufficient expansion in the demand for capital goods. The left opposition, represented mainly by Preobrazhensky, maintained instead that the lead in the process of industrialization should be taken by heavy industry and that the demand for capital goods would be generated in the very process of the expansion of heavy industry (see the collection of contemporary contributions in Spulber, 1964; also, Preobrazhensky, 1965). The argument of the left is well presented and formalized by Feldman who developed Marx's schemes of expanded reproduction into a mathematical model of acceleration of growth, analysing the growth and accumulation potential of a closed economy with a small heavy industry and plentiful labour provided priority was given to investment in the machine tool industry (translated in Spulber, 1964; Feldman's model was improved by Domar, 1956).

In the discussion on planning two schools emerged, which soon became to be known respectively as the 'genetic' and the 'teleological' (or purposeful) approaches to economic planning. The genetic school, with Groman, Bazarov, Kondratieff, viewed planning as an extrapolation of past trends, conditioned by many objective constraints including the capacity levels in the pre-war period; they regarded the plan as a forecast, and attached importance to balanced growth. The teleological school, represented for instance by Strumilin, on the contrary stressed the wide extent of the planner's discretion in shaping the future, especially in the long run and at the cost of accumulation; they regarded planning as a deliberate act of change, an act of war even, to change the structure of the economy, and were prepared to accept unbalanced growth in order to implement such change (Carr-Davies, 1974; Spulber, 1964). Meanwhile in the Soviet economy there were a number of plans, but no overall consolidated macro-economic planning; though there was 'exercise of government control over economic processes', and techniques were being developed for improving the government's grip on the basic proportions in the economy (material and financial balances, control figures, planning procedures, and so on; see Carr-Davies, 1974).

5. Centralised Socialism in the USSR (1928-1965)

The contradictions of the NEP and the hesitations about accumulation and planning were resolved by Stalin in the manner that is well known. The 'productive relations', indeed the entire social formation of the NEP, had to give way. The new social formation that took shape in the years 1928-32 was very different; it was characterized by:

1) the establishment of five-year planning as well as shorter operational plans, of great ambition and encompassing the entire economy, for the accelerated industrialization of the country by means of massive capital accumulation. Hunter analyses the 1929 'optimal' version of the first Five Year Plan and by means of input-output analysis shows that it was not feasible, as the growth of gross and net outputs were not mutually consistent; he drafts alternative expansion paths and shows that it would have taken at least eight years to reach the targets of the plan (Hunter, 1973). But then we must remember that sophisticated techniques for the evaluation of plan variants were not yet available; that over-ambitious targets followed from the decision to industrialize fast ('To slacken the pace of industrialization would mean to lag behind and those who lag behind are beaten. We do not want to be beaten. No, we do not want to ... We are fifty or a hundred years behind the advanced countries. We must make good this lag in ten years. Either we do so or they crush us'; thus spoke Stalin in 1931, quoted by Deutscher, 1961, p. 328); that planning was seen as an act of mobilization of physical and personal resources, according to the teleological approach. To talk of 'disappearance of planning in the plan' (Lewin, 1973) because of ambitious and unrealistic targets seriously underestimates the degree of central steering and control. It is true however that the massive accumulation effort and the teleological approach caused three main features of Soviet planning: the tightness, or tautness of the plans; the ensuing establishment of a set of priorities for key products (the 'leading links') which happen

to represent bottlenecks; the emphasis on physical magnitudes and the very minor role assigned to prices.

2) the forced collectivization of agriculture. The operation had a huge human cost, which cannot be ignored in its economic evaluation. However there has been a tendency recently to cast doubts on the effectiveness of collectivization even leaving aside the human cost, mostly on two grounds. The first is reliance on Chayanov's work on the peasant economy (1966; Lewin, 1968), stressing the development potential of traditional agriculture. However, Chayanov's analysis of the unresponsiveness of peasant agriculture to external stimuli and his expectation of a slow pace of spontaneous collectivization weaken or possibly reverse the assessment of that potential. The second reason for reconsidering the effectiveness of collectivization is the fresh empirical evidence on the measurement of agricultural 'surplus' provided by Barsov (1969, reviewed by Millar, 1974); it turns out that—far from exacting a 'tribute' from the peasants by means of unequal exchange, as Stalin intended—collectivization neither worsened the terms of trade between agriculture and industry, nor made a positive contribution to the finance of primitive socialist accumulation. The fact that peasants were less badly done by—in economic terms—than was previously thought, however, does not mean that collectivization was generally ineffective from the viewpoint of industrialization. As Ellman rightly points out, collectivized agriculture provided a greatly increased supply of wage goods (which, we might add, would have probably required terms of trade even more favourable to agriculture in the absence of collectivization, i.e., a greater drain on investable resources); it provided industry with a large addition to its labour force, unthinkable without collectivization due to the falling living conditions in the towns; it provided substantial exports; contributed to import substitution (by increasing output of cotton and tea) and it was transformed into a residual sector which absorbed shocks such as bad harvests (Ellman, 1975, pp. 858-9). Besides, it has been pointed out recently that meteorological conditions in the 1928-32 period were 'particularly catastrophic' (Cooper-Davies-Wheatcroft, 1977), which turns previous assessments of collectivization into underestimates. These arguments are not, *per se*, an economic justification of forced collectivization; they simply weaken the case for spontaneous collectivization, and stress its contribution to industrialization.

3) the setting up of a sectoral structure of economic government, with the reorganization of the Supreme Council of the National

Economy (better known as *Vesenkha*) into three industrial People's Commissariats or Ministries—the first step in a process of increasing specilization of Commissariats according to industries which continued until 1953. The ministerial sectoral structure, with chief-departments (*glavki*) reappearing with responsibilities for functional aspects such as finance, supplies, investment, will remain the backbone of central planning until 1957, with the central planning commission (*Gosplan*) with basically advisory rather than executive functions. Of course the number of Ministries and their subdivisions, the relative scope of republican and all-union Ministries, the specific tasks of Gosplan (for instance, the relative scope of short versus long-run planning) altered over time, and other organs of co-ordination or specific competence emerged and disappeared, but the basic structure of the centralization of supply and sales remained fundamentally unchanged until the 1957 reform in the Soviet Union.

4) the reinforcement of central control by means of the financial monitoring of plan implementation, the so-called 'control by the rouble'. In 1930-32 the state bank assumed a new role, not only as a central bank, but as a bank having the monopoly of short-term lending, a monopoly enforced with the prohibition of direct financing of firms by suppliers and customers. The basic principles of operation of money and credit are those of providing the payment flows corresponding to the planned physical flows, and the separation of financial flows into two separate circuits, one of cash for the payments of wages and the purchase of consumption goods, the other of bank money consisting of book entries in the bank accounts of enterprises for purchases and deliveries of goods between themselves.

5) the confirmation of the principle of economic accounting (or *khozraschot*), i.e., the covering of costs by receipts and the making of the planned profit (or planned loss),[10] any additional profit being syphoned off into the state budget by a turnover tax (practically a tax by difference, indistinguishable from profit), investment funds and most of the working capital being obtained free of charge from the state budget (subject to the observance of official rules concerning the choice of techniques). The retention of profit by enterprises was governed by, and did not govern, the rate of accumulation.

6) prices or price-fixing criteria were decided centrally; production goods were available to enterprise at those prices via direct allocation in conformity with planned tasks; consumption goods were available to consumers at those prices subject to availability; if

consumer prices were not market-clearing prices, either goods piled up in excess inventories or shortages (queueing, waiting lists, black markets) developed. The price level of consumer goods rose dramatically from the inception of the first Five Year Plan to the early fifties, partly because of wage drift, partly because of planned pressure on real consumption to finance capital accumulation, partly because of under-fulfilment of plans for consumption goods which ranked low in the system of priorities.

7) one-man management (*edionachalie*), terminating—theoretically at the end of the twenties, in practice much later—the 'triangle' made by the union, the party cell and the manager. The director and other managerial officers had not only a salary but also a system of progressive bonuses for the fulfilment and over-fulfilment of various indicators of performance, mostly expressed in physical units, in terms of gross output, except for the use of constant (rather than actual current) prices for the aggregation of heterogeneous products of the same enterprise.

8) the transformation of trade unions from organs for the promotion of workers' class interest to production-minded institutions, with a narrow role in welfare and social insurance, and totally subservient to the government wishes;

9) the rejection of egalitarian principles (*uravnilovka*) in the structure of wages and other material rewards, (given above all the scarcity of skilled labour), as well as in privileged access to consumption goods for selected categories, and the widespread use of piece-rate payment systems. There were also non-material incentives relying on 'socialist emulation', shock workers, and other initiatives for the mobilization of labour and working effort.

10) finally, the systematic undertaking of capital accumulation on an increasing scale, with priority to industry rather than agriculture, heavy rather than light industry, the sectors producing production goods rather than consumption goods. This feature of the new social formation—which we could call centralized socialism—is put at the bottom of the list here in order to allow a convenient digression on its rationale, because the system's high propensity to accumulate—indeed, I will argue later on, its *excessively* high propensity to accumulate—is an important factor in the analysis of the contradictions of the system and the modality of its transformation.

' "Accumulate! Accumulate!": the maxim that Marx had associated with capitalism, became the maxim of those who claimed to be his followers' (Hicks, 1966, p. 264). In the Soviet Union the rapid increase in investment began in 1928, and continued up to

1936 with only one year of relaxation in 1933. Abram Bergson's calculations of the share of accumulation in national income (including services) at current prices came to 23 per cent in 1928, 21 per cent in 1937, 23 per cent in 1950 and 24 per cent in 1955. After the war, in Eastern Europe and the USSR the share of accumulation in the net national material product was for so long—with the exception of East Germany and Czechoslovakia—within small margins of 25 per cent, that United Nations sources refer to 'the pragmatic rule ... that about a quarter of (material) national income should ideally be allocated to accumulation' as the guiding principle of investment policy in these countries (UN-ECE, 1967, Ch. 7, p. 7) The drive to intense capital accumulation concentrated in heavy industry was the direct consequence of the decision to accelerate economic growth in the specific Soviet conditions: a closed economy, abundant labour, availability of materials, scarcity of capital, small productive capacity in the sectors producing capital goods. But the new system set in motion forces which at various levels in the economy transformed this particular policy into a general tendency. This also led, whenever options were open and considered, to the choice of a particularly intensive version of this accumulation policy; while at the stage of implementation priority was systematically given to the fulfilment and over-fulfilment of investment plans at the expense of consumption.

This high propensity to accumulate is regarded by some critics of the Soviet economy as a connotation of the class interest of the bureaucracy. Harman, for instance, argues that ' ... the bureaucrats ... control the means of production, which they attempt to expand at a faster speed than their rivals internationally. This they can only do by holding back workers' living standards, by acting as a bitter opposition to working-class interests, both domestically and internationally' (1974, pp. 18-19). Kuron and Modzelewski similarly argue that 'the material power of the bureaucracy, the scope of its authority over production, its international position (very important for a class organized as a group identifying itself with the state) all this depends on the size of national capital. Consequently, the bureaucracy wants to increase capital, to enlarge the producing apparatus, to accumulate' (1968, p. 17); 'Production for consumption is from its [the bureaucracy's] class point of view, a necessary evil, whereas production for production is its goal' (1968, p. 18).

Yet there is no *a priori* reason to suppose that the accumulation drive of the socialist mode of production must be due to the interest of a particular class or pressure group. It is perfectly conceivable for the central decision makers (meaning anybody who is in a position to affect the rate of accumulation in the economy) to act individually and out of altruistic concern, without benefiting in any way either individually or as a group, and yet generate more accumulation than the population as a whole would have wished if given a choice. The point is that the central decision makers in the socialist society considered 1) are likely to have a longer time horizon than the rest of the population; 2) are concerned with the survival of the system and with reaching a level of affluence consistent with the transition to full communism; 3) are not constrained—in the Soviet version of 'democratic centralism'—by the need to present alternatives to the population and seek its consent for the pursuit of an accumulation policy. This is sufficient to generate an accumulation bias.

It is difficult to establish whether the same kind of accumulation bias is present at the micro-level, i.e., at the level of state enterprises. In this system enterprise managers are directed from above, but they have power of initiative, they participate in rounds of bargaining with the centre and the Ministry for the definition of their technical-financial plan, and they have considerable discretion about which of the many directions and rules to break; they can also modify to their advantage the information flow in their communications with the centre. Their structure of rewards is not entirely dissimilar to that of the managers of corporations in capitalist economies. They receive a salary, an important bonus for fulfilment and over-fulfilment of output plans, subject to a minimum profit constraint; their status and prestige in the community depends also on the size of the enterprise they direct, and their prospects for a higher salary (and possibly for career advancement) are also related to growth and therefore accumulation in their enterprise. Unlike their capitalist counterparts, they have no discretion about the reinvestment of their profit—at least in theory, though in practice higher than planned profits makes it easier to undertake more investment than planned; on the other hand, they pay no interest on their funds (except on a fraction of their working capital), do not have to worry about gearing ratios, debt/service ratios, the stock market evaluation of their shares, take-over bids due to excessive growth, or bankrupcy, all the things which constrain the accumulation drive of capitalist managers. State enterprises under centralized socialism cannot move outside their sector of operation, but their managers can probably enlist local support for expansionary projects.

In conclusion, it seems plausible that, even if managers of state enterprises could not exercise and initiate a bias in favour of accumulation—which they very well might—there seems to be no apparent reason why they should oppose the high propensity to accumulate of the central organs. In these conditions the priority to accumulation, especially in heavy industry, turns a particular policy which is plausible under special conditions into a general and glorified norm of conduct, and an integral part of the 'superstructure' of the Soviet-type system (Nuti, 1978). This is a fundamental difference between economic systems. Capitalism has a tendency to chronic under-investment, as witnessed by the 15 million unemployed today in the Western world, frustrating democratic institutions because private ownership and free enterprise take capital accumulation away from parliamentary and government control. Socialism creates the preconditions for a public control over accumulation, given public ownership and macro-economic planning, but economic and political centralization equally take accumulation away from public control; thereby generating chronic over-investment even—as we shall see—in conditions of full employment of labour.

The 'superstructure' of the Soviet model of centralized socialism under Stalin's rule was also made of other, sinister and unpalatable, features: namely, Stalin's terror and repression. Roy Medvedev sees Stalin's despotism as being primarily the product of Stalin's personality and will, apparently fearing that the consideration of historical trends might lead to a denial of Stalin's responsibility (Medvedev, 1971, and the editor's introduction). There is no reason, however, why one should not pass on Stalin whatever moral judgement one sees fit and yet put at least some of his actions in a historical perspective.

First, there is a connection between some of Stalin's policies and the experience of War Communism. Deutscher writes: 'There was hardly a single plank in Trotsky's programme of 1920-1 which Stalin did not use during the industrial revolution of the thirties. He introduced conscription and direction of labour; he insisted that the trade unions should adopt a "productionist" policy instead of defending the consumer interest of the workers; he deprived the trade unions of the last vestige of autonomy and transformed them into tools of the state. He set himself up as the protector of the managerial groups, on whom he bestowed privileges of which Trotsky had not even dreamt. He ordered "socialist emulations" in the factories and mines; and did so in words unceremoniously and literally taken from Trotsky. He put into effect his own ruthless version of "Soviet Taylorism" which Trotsky had advocated. And finally he passed from Trotsky's intellectual and historical arguments ambiguously justifying forced labour to its mass application' (Deutscher, 1954, p. 515). Then there were the implications of the gradual decline of the party's internal life, from the ban on factions to the monopoly of the Stalinist faction, to the personal rule of the faction's chief (Deutscher, 1967, p. 31-33). Brus argues that the centralized 'étatist' model of socialism *'étatises the party too'*, the most direct manifestation of this being the mutual interpenetration of the party apparatus and the state apparatus of repression; hence Brus concludes that 'the étatist model of socialism does not meet the criteria of socialization of the means of production' (Brus, 1975, pp. 54-7). Bahro relates Stalinism to the pressure of the technical superiority of imperialist countries and their policy of military intervention and encirclement, the constant external threat creating 'the specific fortress neurosis in which friend and foe could no longer be distinguished'; and also, ultimately, to the combination of the Russian semi-Asiatic past and the formidable task of industrialization, generating 'industrial despotism' (Bahro, 1978, Ch. 3).

The social formation which emerged in the Soviet Union at the turn of the thirties achieved an impressive economic performance. The actual measurement of Soviet economic growth has been the object of lengthy discussions, but, even if we disregard official indexes, we find that independent Western computations indicate a threefold increase in industrial production from 1928 to 1937 (of which a twofold increase was from 1932 to 1937) with a further increase of about two and a half from 1937 to 1955 (Bergson, 1961; Nutter, 1962; Treml-Hardt, 1972). Such speed of industrial development was accompanied by unprecedented urbanization; the rise of active population of both sexes; the achievement of high standards of education. Soviet 'real' household consumption per capita, however, actually *declined* between 1928 and 1940 (at a rate of 0.6 per cent per year), grew at a modest rate in the forties (1.9 per cent) and did not start rising significantly until the fifties (6.7 per cent per year in 1950-55); (Bergson, 1961). Victory in war and survival in a hostile environment were also no small—though difficult to quantify—achievements.

These achievements, however, were accompanied by a mounting range of problems, deeply rooted in the production relations of the centralized socialist formation examined above. These problems were partly the same kind of problems that had arisen during the period of War Communism (see above) but other problems developed as the permanence of centralized planning over time led to learned patterns of behaviour—among the participants in the planning and production process—and the cumulative build-up of drawbacks, holding back the further economic progress of the system. The first official recognition of these problems is contained in Bulganin's Report to the CC of the CPSU in July 1955. Bulganin lists:

1) the autarkic tendencies of the sectoral Ministerial system, trying to secure supplies by a costly vertical integration;

2) the delay with which enterprises received their plans;

3) the failure to secure regular supplies, producing structural under-utilization of plant;

4) the neglect of the quality of products, and of the introduction of new products, due to the purely quantitative methods of planning and of assessment of performance;

5) the systematic mismatching of production assortment and the structure of demand—especially in the field of consumption goods—because of selective over- and under-fulfilments by enterprises;

6) the 'petty tutelage' exercised by Ministries and party committees over managers, which, reducing their power, also discouraged initiative;

7) the cyclical nature of production, with the concentration of output towards the end of the plan period (*shturmovchina*);

8) the emergence of regional unbalances. To alleviate these problems, Bulganin suggested in his report three main remedies: the introduction of greater material incentives; greater autonomy for the enterprise director, and greater use of foreign technology. There were also other problems, which were reported in the press and increasingly debated by economists and engineers:

9) gross distortions in the use of inputs or in the quality of output due to the physical indicators used, and to the 'cult of gross output' (*kult vala*);

10) the concealment of reserves of productive capacity by managers desiring to be in a position to fulfil the plan comfortably; managerial restraint in over-fulfilling, for fear of the centre systematically upping planned targets over the best past performance; managerial attempt at negotiating lower output targets and greater input assignments (of both working and fixed capital) than technically necessary.

Basically, the model of centralized socialism that had proved suitable to Soviet conditions at the turn of the thirties and to the objectives of the thirties and forties, was becoming inadequate to the Soviet economy in the fifties, centralized socialism had delivered —at a cost—industrialization, victory in war and reconstruction, but was becoming increasingly inadequate to manage what we could loosely term 'economic maturity'. Yet the Soviet centralized model was transplanted, without any adaptation, to the other East-European countries that started on the road to to socialism after the last war.

6. *The Other Socialist Economies of Eastern Europe; Economic Reforms*

Some of the conditions of Eastern European countries were similar to those of the Soviet Union and conformed to the Soviet-type model: 1) their economies were relatively underdeveloped, agricultural and labour-abundant, with the exception of the Bohemian region in Czechoslovakia, the Silesian region in Poland, and East Germany (which however was less developed than West Germany); 2) with the exception of Czechoslovakia, they had not had much experience of parliamentary democracy and had been ruled by either foreign or domestic dictatorships in the inter-war period; 3) they were facing the tasks of reconstruction after the war; 4) they also operated in a hostile international environment, socialism in ten countries being not significantly different from socialism in one country (as demonstrated among others by the cases of Spain, Vietnam, Chile, etc.).

But these countries also had specific conditions which did not conform to the Soviet mode of production, nor with its Stalinist superstructure. Brus lists some of these different conditions: 1) the generally higher level of economic development and social diversity in the People's Democracies, with respect to that of Russia in 1917, which not only made the drawbacks experienced in the Soviet Union more immediately felt, but also made the positive results of the model more weakly perceived by the population and less politically effective; 2) a higher degree of development of democratic institutions, in short of 'the level of civilization in relations between people', as well as a stronger cultural and economic link with the West; this made the purely educational function of Soviet ideology less effective, indeed caused a greater perception 'of the disparity between slogans and reality'; 3) the weakness of the internal roots of the socialist revolution, that made socialism an imported product imposed from outside (with the exception of Czechoslovakia, where the Communist Party won nearly 40 per cent of the total vote in the free elections of 1946, and of Yugoslavia where the transition to socialism enjoyed the support of internal forces; internal support was also generated everywhere by agrarian reforms); 4) 'the factual domination of the Soviet Union over the People's Democracies, multiplied in some cases—particularly Poland—by factors of a historical and psychological nature, made it difficult to use nationalistic ideology as an instrument for political attraction of the masses', although the German question provided some nationalistic backing for the leading role of the Soviet Union (Brus, 1975, Ch. 2, section 2).

The transplant of a uniform and ready-made model of socialism had two other adverse effects. First, there was 'no return to the system of soviets of Lenin's time, which also facilitated their adaptation since it permitted them to be formally linked with the traditional institutions (parliament, direct elections, universal franchise, etc.)' (Brus, 1975, p. 60); in other words, the genetic inheritance which might have permitted the quicker development of a socialist 'mutant' more suitable to East European conditions was effectively lost. Second, the Soviet discouragement of the development of socialist mutations hindered the very evolution of the socialist mode of production. In fact, as Bahro incisively puts it, backing his statement with Marxian material, 'in the evolution of species we find that the most advanced form at time t never originates from the form furthest developed at time $t-1$. It is always a branch that is not yet too highly specialized, and with too restricted a structure, a still "unformed" branch, that reaches the next highest level' (Bahro, p. 64). In other words, even if we regard the Soviet centralized model as the peak of socialism at the end of the last war, we should expect the further development of socialism to take the form of the emergence and development of a side branch, rather than the further perfecting of the Soviet model. In the event, the only new 'mutant' of European socialism was Yugoslav self-management of 'associationist socialism'; the description and assessment of that model goes beyond the scope of this paper, but the presence of strong syndicalistic and capitalistic elements in that system make it an unlikely candidate for the progress of the socialist model.[11]

The progressive unsuitability of the Soviet centralized model of socialism to Soviet conditions at the turn of the fifties, let alone to East-European conditions after reconstruction, roughly at the same time, led to the emergence and the exacerbation, everywhere in the area, of the drawbacks of the system already discussed in the previous section. Pressure for economic and political change mounted. Evidence of this can be found in the official endorsement of criticisms of the functioning of the system; the East German events of 1953; the Poznan events of 1956; the Hungarian events of 1956; the accumulation of above norm inventories of consumption goods nearing saturation (cameras, watches, bicycles, low quality textiles, etc.); the slowing down of the pace of economic development at the turn of the sixties, at a time of acceleration of growth in Western economies; the recurrence of economic fluctuations in the increments (and sometimes even the levels) of income, consumption and accumulation (Ellman, 1973). The situation was worsened by the progressive reduction of reserves of labour and natural resources around 1960, which is probably responsible for the deterioration and unsteadiness of growth.

These pressures for change, and especially the advisability of a 'change of gear' due to the transition from extensive to intensive stages of development, were rationalized in East-European literature under the guise of a theory of socialist evolution reminiscent of Marxian political economy. The Soviet-type centralized model of socialism—it was argued—was best suited to economies experiencing extensive economic development due to the use of increasing amounts of labour and investment in conditions of ample reserves of labour and raw materials; now that those reserves were being exhausted the East-European economies were switching to intensive development depending primarily on productivity increases, and the new emphasis on efficiency and technical progress required a change of the socialist model in the direction of decisional decentralization with a greater scope for enterprise autonomy and market relations[12]. The very distinction between extensive and intensive factors of development—in the sense used in this context of a distinction between the relative contribution of various inputs increases and of technical progress—is purely conceptual and presents formidable theoretical and empirical problems[13]. Nevertheless, the distinction between economies with or without natural and labour reserves, and the transition from one condition to the other, must be an important factor explaining and promoting change, especially within the Marxian tradition attaching so much importance to the necessary correspondence between the development of productive forces and of productive relations. In spite of its wide and uncritical acceptance in the West,[14] however, a theory of socialist evolution stating the transition from a system for extensive development to one for intensive development is too crude and simple. Why was the lack of correspondence, or even contradiction, between centralized socialism and economic maturity not resolved by a simple gradual change of the socialist model, towards forms of decentralization?

The actual progress of economic reform in East-European countries and the Soviet Union does not follow any such simple pattern of change. In the mid fifties, i.e., before labour and natural resources scarcities were felt, a reform movement appeared and receded not only in Hungary (where it was forcibly truncated) but also in Poland (1956-8). In the Soviet Union Bulganin's 1955 suggestions remained a dead letter, and in 1957 measures for regional decentralization were adopted instead, with the institution of regional economic councils (the *sovnarkhozy*) which reproduced and indeed enhanced at the regional level all the problems of the centralized Soviet system, substituting localism (*mestnichestvo*) and regional autarky for the autarky of the abolished Ministries; that reform was—as Nove puts its— 'not a step forward, but a step sideways'. (Nove-Nuti, 1972). Towards the mid sixties a new wave of reforms would seem, at first sight, to make a clean sweep of the old economic system. In 1965 in the Soviet Union, for instance, after ample discussions the regional economic councils are abolished and old-fashioned sectoral Ministries take their place; the enterprise however is given greater autonomy and discretion, actual revenue and profitability are used to measure the performance of enterprises, and material incentives linked to those measurements are paid to managers and workers. Managers are empowered with the reinvestment of some of their profits; they have access to credit at an interest rate instead of getting investment funds free of charge from the state budget; in general, a greater 'market discipline' is envisaged, to replace the structure of central planning. Yet a couple of years later the reform stops short of the promised measures of decentralization and begins to recede, so much so as to be called 'the reform that never was'. Other countries present a similar experience (perhaps with the exception of Hungary, at least until recently). Everywhere we still find excess demand due to persistent accumulation pressure, sectoral immobility of enterprises, central control of inter-industry transactions and deliveries (Ellman, 1977, Nuti, 1978). New phenomena appear, such as the attempt to solve centrally planning problems by the application of mathematical methods, the increased reliance on the import of foreign technology, the emergence and development of large corporations in industry (everywhere in Eastern Europe from the turn of the seventies) accompanied by increasing industrial concentration (Nuti, 1977). This process is associated with conflicts and confrontations ranging from international incidents to food riots.

Obviously there is no simple, monotonic relationship between the level of development and economic or political decentralization, applicable to the post-war evolution of the socialist economies of Eastern Europe. In the rest of this paper a more complex picture of the interaction between these factors is attempted, in order to comprehend and unify the phenomena described above. Starting from a number of observations a model is constructed, and its possible behaviour over time is investigated.

7. A Marxist Model

The following observations about the relationship between capital accumulation, economic and political decentralization are central to our discussion of the current contradictions of the socialist economies and the pattern of their possible resolution.

1) No economic decentralization was contemplated, or even discussed, until after Stalin's death (1953) and the political liberalization represented by the denunciation of Stalin and the mooting of destalinization at the XXth Congress. In Yugoslavia, decentralization began before 1953, but was preceded by other forms of political liberalization.

2) The only country where economic decentralization was allowed to develop in the fifties (apart from Yugoslavia) was Poland, and this was not only preceded by political liberalization, with the advent of Gomulka to power in the autumn of 1956, but was also followed by further political decentralization (such as, for instance, the spontaneous emergence of workers' councils at factory level, outspokenness in political and economic discussion, etc.). In Hungary, where economic conditions were very similar to those of Poland, the crushing of the experiment of political decentralization marked the end of any prospective economic reform for a decade. Even the Soviet regional decentralization of 1957 was followed by political changes such as Krushchev's division of the party between industrial and agricultural sections—which can be considered as a form of political decentralization, or at least of political diffusion. In Czechoslovakia in 1958 this link between reform and political developments, reinforcing each other, is also confirmed.

3) The destalinization process and the limited measures of democratization in Eastern European countries led to a short-lived consumption boom in the second half of the fifties. In Poland Gomulka's fall in December 1970 was followed by an acceleration of consumption;

4) the Polish decentralization of 1956 was made possible by the acceleration of consumption growth, which alleviated some of the previous accumulation pressure (resulting in the actual fall of real consumption per capita in the early fifties); the decentralization came to an end at a time—and, I would argue, because—of reintensification of the accumulation effort. In the Soviet Union, conversely, Bulganin's endorsement of material incentives and greater autonomy for enterprises, followed in 1955 by a decree on the rights of enterprise directors, and in the Plenum of December 1956 by Peruvkin's proposals for economic decentralization, were abandoned in the investment crisis which endangered the sixth Five Year Plan by the end of its first year. The same relationship between lack of success or end of reform and the intensification of the accumulation effort can be observed for the East-European reforms of the mid fifties, as well as for the recent recentralization in Poland after the institutional changes of 1974.

This pattern of events, which cannot be explained by a crude Marx-inspired view of the connection between development level and centralization, can be explained by—and provides empirical evidence for—a model of dialectical interaction between capital accumulation, economic decentralization and political liberalization. The model consists of the following generalizations:

1) economic decentralization is both preceded and followed by political liberalization;[15]

2) the model of centralized socialism and its 'superstructure' lead to a strong bias in favour of capital accumulation (see above, section 5);

3) intensive capital accumulation with the passing of time and because of its own success in raising income and consumption reveals to an increasing extent the drawbacks of the centralized model (listed in section 5 above), among other reasons because of the increasing complexity of the structure of the economy and technological advance, and because of the greater unpredictability of consumer behaviour at higher levels of consumption per capita;

4) economic decentralization, however, can only be successful if introduced in the absence of excess demand, i.e., in the absence of the economic strain generated by intensive and accelerated accumulation (unless the pressure is eased by external factors, such as massive foreign aid, or the relaxation of the defence effort, or a substantial improvement in the terms of trade, or a sudden, unexpected and substantial technological advance; conversely, any adverse trend in these factors militates against the feasibility and success of decentralization);

5) the bias in favour of capital accumulation exhibited by the centralised socialist model can be eliminated only by a measure of political democratization, reinstating the social and political control of the wider population over the level and direction of capital accumulation. Such control. is a fundamental prerequisite of the genuine *socialization of the means of* production; it is not guaranteed by the mere presence, next to the party, of organized sectional interest groups no matter how vocal, nor even by the 'incorporation' of the working class into the socialist state, The sheer failure of the centralized model to deliver the economic goods is not sufficient to generate economic decentralization; on the contrary, the central authorities are likely to react to a deterioration of economic performance with the tightening up of both economic and political centralisation.

We can now formulate conjectures about Marxian 'laws of motion' of the model of centralized socialism. Two development paths can be envisaged. The first is a *virtuous circle* leading to the smooth progress of both economic forces and productive relations envisaged by the official Soviet-type texts of the political economy of socialism. The second is a *vicious circle* leading to a pattern of economic and institutional cycles of a kind which is closer to the actual experience of the Soviet Union and the East-European countries, which may last for an indefinite period until it gathers the impetus to transform itself into a virtuous circle, because of an endogenous modification of the parameters or a change in external factors such as those mentioned above. In theory this vicious circle could end with the collapse of the system; I would rule this out not through optimism but because of the positive if slow adaptability of the socialist mode of production observable in the transition from War Communism to NEP, from NEP to the centralized model, to forms of regional and functional decentralization, the existence of the Yugoslav model, the development of the Chinese model; besides, the capitalist mode of production seems long past its prime and is ridden with its own conflicts and contradictions, so that it does not represent a credible alternative.

The first course, of harmonious development, would have to start with an autonomous initiative of political democratization (such as that promised by the 1956 destalinization, or the Prague Spring in 1968). As long as the leading and dominant position of the Soviet Union lasts, this political democratization will have to originate from the Soviet Union. Bahro appears confident of good prospects for such a democratization, because of the failure of the monolithic

party structure to conform with the interests of potential development, and because of the capacity for change displayed by the
Czech Communist Party in the mid sixties. Brus stresses the sheer
informational advantages of a democratization process, which
appear indispensable for the rational conduct of economic affairs
(Brus, 1975, Ch. 4). Whatever the strength of these arguments, an
important role must be assigned to external factors, political and
economic: neither the oil crisis, nor the right-wing exploitation of
Czech democratization in 1968, nor the selective right-wing endorsement of Soviet and East-European dissenters while ignoring both
left-wing dissent in those countries and macroscopic forms of
repression in capitalist countries, nor a Western-Chinese *rapproche-
ment*, are likely to favour such a process of political democratization.

Suppose such a process could start and gather momentum
without regressing to forms of bourgeois liberalism (a class-based
multi-party system, for instance, would be a regressive step in
countries which have nationalized the entirety of the means of
production; see Bahro, 1978, Ch. 12). Genuine social control could
then be reinstated over the level of direction of accumulation and
development; a deceleration of the accumulation effort would be
likely to follow, creating the economic conditions for the successful
introduction of measures of economic decentralization. These
measures would be required by objective conditions and would be
tailored to those conditions by general participation in their
shaping. In turn, economic decentralization would be likely to lead
to further democratization (ranging from a greater participation of
workers in management to better protection of consumers and other
sectional interests in the community). The danger would arise of
excessive strides towards decentralization, regressing to forms of
capitalism or of syndicalism. During the Prague Spring, for
instance, there were proposals for the re-establishment of free trade
and currency convertibility, the immediate exposure to the penetration of foreign capital, the deliberate creation of unemployment to
make the economy more flexible, as well as the revamping of
inegalitarian middle-class interests; these proposals appear to have
enjoyed the support of members of the government. On the other
hand, the transplantation of the Yugoslav-type market economy
and syndicalistic self-management would effectively destroy any
chance of social control over the macro-economics of employment,
accumulation and growth, landing the system in the same problems
and contradictions of the Yugoslav and the capitalist economy:
chronic under-investment, inflation, personal and regional inequalities,

unemployment, and so on. If a course could be steered, clear of these dangers and involutions into capitalism or back into centralized socialism, any further progress would have to come to grips with an entirely different range of problems, such as the very foundations of the division of labour in society, discussed by Marx and Engels in their characterization of 'full communism' or a change in the structure of needs. This is uncharted territory, and to address ourselves to these problems is not only premature and futile, but also counterproductive and damaging because it alters the focus and distorts the perspective in which current problems are analysed.

The other development path, which is what we actually witness in the experience of the socialist countries of Eastern Europe, is a familiar economic and institutional cycle, locking the same factors analysed above into a vicious circle. The cycle starts with measures of economic decentralization, motivated by a deterioration of economic performance due to the drawbacks of the centralized system, and made possible by a minimum of relaxation of central political control. Political democratization (in the sense of reinstatement of genuine social control over macro-economic trends) does not go far enough, or quickly enough, to overcome the built-in accumulation bias of the old system. As a consequence, the economy remains in a state of strain and pressure on resources which does not give the economic decentralization measures a chance to operate in a congenial environment; inflation and economic anarchy are likely to result. Even if decentralization worked, it would not have a significant impact on the living standards of the population, and therefore would not be perceived as a progressive evolution; the opposition of those sections of the population which are at least temporarily adversely affected by the reform (such as the traditionally-minded enterprise-managers, the workers displaced by economic reform—as in the widely-known Schechino case in the Soviet Union,—the groups which improve their position absolutely but worsen it in relative terms) prevails over the mild support (or indifference) of those who enjoy the small, and thinly spread, benefits of the reform. The decentralization process comes to an end; disappointment with the results leads to a tightening up of central control, both economic and political; accumulation continues its course, regenerating, possibly to a greater extent, the already known drawbacks of the old system. The economic and political cycle starts again.

In this cycle the transition from 'extensive' to 'intensive' growth (discussed in the previous section) plays an important role in *triggering* off the process of change, when accumulation policies which may have been plausible—at least in principle—with the reserves of labour and natural resources are continued without the same justification after those reserves are no longer available. Thus the transition may explain the *timing* of the reform movement, but its role in explaining the actual development and success of the reform movement can only be limited, as it is just one piece of the puzzle we have tried to piece together. The continued importance of the new stage of development reached by East-European socialist countries is due to the failure of accumulation policy to adjust itself to the new conditions.

In fact, labour availability has become strained in all East-European countries (except Albania) in the first half of the seventies. The natural growth rate of the population has been falling; the outflow of agricultural labour has decelerated in absolute terms; the participation of the female population of working age has virtually the same rate as that of men; the re-employment of retired people has been stimulated, but this can only be a limited source of additional labour; possibilities of employing foreign labour remain extremely limited. Labour shortages are reported in many branches, most frequently in construction; regional and sectoral shortages are present even in countries with relatively abundant labour (UN-ECE, 1977). Another constraint is given by the supply of material inputs (raw materials, fuel and power, agricultural production) and recent developments in world markets have highlighted the increasing strains. These countries have been relatively protected from the worst effects of the oil crisis, due to the Soviet Union being a net oil exporter and to the availability of coal, the Soviet supply of oil to other East-European countries on long-term contracts and at a price gradually rising but lagging behind the international price of oil (especially on the spot market); the relative insulation of East-European countries from the inflationary impact of the price rise of oil and materials. But these countries have suffered from the oil crisis indirectly through the impact of the world recession on their foreign trade; also, future prospects for reserves and technology are not promising, as the exploitation of new resources (such as in Siberia) require both new technology and huge investment costs. Hence the shift from the accelerated development of heavy industry to a more balanced growth that includes formerly neglected sectors such as agriculture and consumer goods industries, and new industries as chemicals.

In the seventies growth performance has been reasonably good, in spite of the declining pace (growth of net material growth has averaged 7.4 per cent in 1966-70 and 6.2 per cent in 1971-5, and is planned at an average 5.3 per cent in the 1976-80 plans in the whole of Eastern Europe and the Soviet Union). But growth is being 'bought' at increasing additional costs in terms of investment, and there are manifest signs of strain, such as the mounting foreign indebtedness of East-European countries, and the increasing inflationary pressure on consumption (Nuti, 1978). Yet there is no sign of a change of gear in accumulation policy in the current Five Year Plans, and gross investment ratios (as a percentage of national product) are actually increasing throughout the area (in the Soviet Union from 27 per cent in 1966-70 to 29.9 per cent in 1970-71 and 29.5-30.1 per cent in the current Five Year Plan; higher shares and increases are recorded in the rest of the area). Socialist demand for growth seems to be rigid with respect to the price of growth in terms of forsaken current consumption.

Is capital accumulation in the socialist economies of Eastern Europe excessive? Two arguments can be used to substantiate a positive answer. The first is Kalecki's postulate of socialist accumulation policy, that the planning authorities should only be willing to 'buy'—as it were—additional points of percentage growth of income at an increasingly smaller sacrifice in terms of the additional percentage of current income that has to be withdrawn from consumption and accumulated. By the standard of this postulate, socialist · accumulation has been excessive at least during the seventies, because a lower growth has been 'bought', as we have seen, at a higher total cost in terms of accumulation shares. In spite of the apparent plausibility of the postulate, Kalecki's argument has no necessity; in more familiar terms, it amounts to saying that the share of a consumer's expenditure on a given good should be a decreasing function of the price of that good, and we know from consumer theory that the validity of this proposition depends on the actual preferences of the consumer. In the same way, the validity of the Kalecki postulate is not universal but depends on the actual preferences of the socialist leadership between current and future consumption. But there is another angle to Kalecki's theory of socialist accumulation that considerably strengthens his case; namely, it is very plausible to assume that a 'socialist planner' should not be willing to raise the share of accumulation in national income if this leads to higher *income* but not to higher *permanently maintainable consumption*, the positive impact of growth on consumption levels being more than offset by the negative impact of a higher rate of accumulation. If this milder restriction on the time preferences of the 'social planner' is accepted, then there is indirect evidence that accumulation in the socialist economies is 'excessive' in Kalecki's sense: the sacrifices of the population will only pay off in the long run if and when the accumulation policy is reversed.

The other argument for regarding socialist accumulation in Eastern Europe as 'excessive' is not deductive but empirical, and rests on the observation of very broad margins of unutilized capital equipment in many industries. This 'petrification of capital' (Staniszkis, 1979) is not due to lack of effective demand, as in capitalist countries, but to structural problems: namely, capital being immobilized in the wrong sector, or in the wrong technical form, or simply unused because of difficulties in the supply of materials and components. This can be the consequence of the unsuitability of the planning apparatus to the level of development; it raises the costs of growth and undermines the case for further accumulation unaccompanied by an attempt to remove those structural problems.

On the basis of these two arguments, we can say that there is at least a presumption that accumulation is excessive in Eastern Europe. Since accumulation rates are high and rising, something else has to give way. In the repetition of the political cycle described above, the pressure of accumulation and its low productivity are the mainspring of further economic and institutional changes. In particular, three important aspects of East-European development fall neatly into place within this framework of analysis, though here they can only be mentioned in passing:

1) the diffusion and increasing reliance on mathematical methods in economic planning, regarded as a possible substitute for economic decentralization, replacing the informational role of markets with automatic data processing (Lange, 1967, Ellman, 1973). Apart from being still a poor substitute for economic decentralization, limited as it is to specific problems and areas in its effectiveness, the diffusion of mathematical methods does not promote or replace political democratization and cannot, in itself, alleviate the contradictions of the socialist economies.

2) the increasing trade dependence on the West in the importation of modern and advanced machinery to narrow the technological gap. The existence and permanence of a technological gap is well documented (Amann-Cooper-Davies, 1977). The introduction of more advanced Western technology raises the productivity of investment and allows the system to absorb more accumulation than would be possible with local technology. For Poland, for instance, it

has been calculated that an increase in machinery imports from the West by about 10 per cent of all the machinery investment leads to a 1 per cent acceleration in the growth of industrial labour productivity (Gomulka, 1977); other East-European countries record an even higher contribution of capital imports from the West to productivity. But this cannot be a permanent source of productivity growth and a vehicle for high accumulation, for two reasons: first, the continuation of the policy depends on the ability of East-European countries to raise significantly their exports to the West of non-primary products, or their already heavy indebtedness, both prospects being difficult to envisage; second, the gradual reduction of the technological gap would reduce and eventually eliminate this source of productivity and justification of high accumulation;

3) the emergence and development of large corporations throughout Eastern Europe, usually corresponding to the horizontal integration of a production sector, sometimes vertically integrated, or locally integrated especially in the agro-industrial sectors. Thus we have the *VVB* and *Kombinate* in the GDR; *Wielkie Organizacje Gospodarcze, Kombinaty* and *Zjednoczenia* in Poland; the *Centrala* in Rumania; the *Obyedinienie* and the *Firma* in the USSR, and so on. This is a fresh compromise with centralization; it represents what elsewhere I called 'depolarization', namely delegation of powers from both the centre and the enterprises to an intermediate level (Nuti, 1979). It derives not so much from the economies of scale associated with industrial concentration, but from the necessity to ensure at the same time some delegation of tasks from the centre to lower levels, and the co-ordination of sectoral decisions and intersectoral transactions. The growth of the large corporation does not, however, solve the problems of the centralized model, because it makes the wider participation of workers in economic decision-making more difficult, and because it aggravates the accumulation bias of the system (given the growth-mindedness and the greater autonomy of large corporations). It is therefore not surprising that the trend towards the greater autonomy of large corporations is being being reversed (for instance in Poland) with a partial restoration of central control.

Thus the repetition of the political and economic cycle does not follow mechanically the same course. Beside the major contradictions described above, and the very noticeable institutional developments they generate (like the three trends just mentioned), there are subsidiary contradictions which superimpose their effects on the broader pattern of the cycle. Three such subsidiary contradictions spring immediately to mind:

1) that between the technological level of agriculture and its institutional organization. In fact the traditional neglect of investment in agriculture, following not in principle but in practice from the logic of accumulation and priority to industry and heavy industry in the original Soviet conditions, exacerbates the pressure on natural resources and has another important side-effect. Namely, under-capitalized agriculture does not lend itself to state farming using wage labour, peasant farming being a preferable institutional arrangement from the viewpoint of productivity of resources when production methods are backward. Rejecting both peasant farming and investment in agriculture has led to low productivity levels, trade dependence in the provision of food for the population and animal feed. This is responsible both for the poor provision of foodstuffs (meat, for instance) and for the conflict between imports of food and imports of machinery. In the last Five Year Plan the need for modernizing agriculture has been recognized in the USSR and elsewhere, but there is the danger that the old pattern of priorities might reassert itself;

2) the contradiction between profit and plan. For a given stock of natural and man-made resources and a given technology (i.e., in Marxian parlance, for a given level of development of productive forces), and a given real wage, the amount of total profit, or surplus, generated in the entire economy could be taken at best as an indication of the economic efficiency of the *entire* economic system[17]. The distribution of profit among enterprises operating in the economy, however, will not necessarily reflect the economic efficiency or the 'good work' of individual units. Profit is an ambiguous signal. It may indicate that workers and managers in the enterprise have above average abilities and/or work harder than average, in which case there is no reason why the product of that enterprise should be produced in larger quantities, though there may be a justification for rewarding the workers and managers of that enterprise. Or it may indicate that the production of that sector is not keeping pace with demand, and needs expanding faster, in which case there seems to be no case for rewarding the workers and managers of that enterprise. Or it may indicate that something has gone wrong elsewhere in the economy (for instance, some of the enterprise's inputs have been overproduced or underpriced, or the overall level of demand has got out of hand), in which case there is no case for either expanding the enterprise's product faster or for rewarding enterprise members. A similar argument can be made for losses. Profit at the enterprise level will be the simultaneous result of

all these forces and is therefore a poor foundation for decentralizing decisions in an economy which is still centrally co-ordinated by a visible hand. For profit to be used as an indicator of performance, a source of bonuses and of investment self-finance, as it has been envisaged at various stages in the East-European economic reforms, the scope of enterprise autonomy should be extended to the point of dismantling not only the centralized system of supply—which is still partially extant everywhere—but also the limits to intersectoral mobility in the operation of enterprises, and the constraints of investment planning itself. This antithesis between profit and plan is not one that can be solved by the search for an 'optimum' mix between the two elements of economic co-ordination; any mix being an arbitrary and unsatisfactory compromise;

3) finally, there is a contradiction between workers sharing in the distribution of bonuses geared to the performance of their enterprise, (or being damaged by a poor performance, for instance in their prospects of career and employment, as has been often the case during the economic experiments conducted in the implementation of reform), and their total lack of participation in decision-making at the enterprise level. Responsibility without power has never been a good formula for the effectiveness of a system of penalties and rewards. If, on the other hand, workers' participation in decision making was broad and effective, they would effectively turn into 'entrepreneurs', as in the Yugoslav system, with the ensuing dangers of anarcho-syndicalism.

A further source of variation in the political and economic cycle experienced by the socialist economies is the sheer quantitative change in the scale of phenomena, which sooner or later may induce qualitative change in the development process.

All these are reasons for the extremely varied morphology of the pattern of economic and political change in the socialist economies, which defies simple generalizations and predictions. They are reasons, for instance, why one should regard with some scepticism the extrapolations of fashionable econometric models of the socialist economies, no matter how detailed and refined (indeed especially if very detailed and refined), at least until the socialist economy has reached a degree of institutional stability comparable to that of the capitalist economy. On the other hand, it is precisely the variety and complexity of the socialist economies and of the continuous and often drastic changes they undertake, that makes it an interesting and worthwhile subject to study, and makes indispensable the application to those economies of the Marxian method of political economy.

NOTES

1. See, for instance, Hayek (1935), Lange (1937), Dobb (1969).
2. The classic Marxian statement of the theory of 'modes of production' is in his 'Introduction to the Critique of Political Economy' (1904, Appendix) and is developed in the *Grundrisse* as well as in other writings by Marx and Engels. See also Antonio Labriola (1896) and Oskar Lange (1959, Ch. 1).
3. Lucio Colletti argues that Marxists 'have never entertained clear ideas on this subject [of dialectical contradiction].' He distinguishes between 'real opposition' (or 'contrariety' of incompatible opposites, which is an opposition without contradiction; it does not violate the principles of identity and non-contradiction and hence is compatible with formal logic and with scientific analysis) and 'dialectical contradiction' (as opposition which is contradictory and gives rise to a dialectical opposition incompatible with scientific analysis (1975). In this paper 'contradiction' is used in the sense of Colletti's 'real opposition'; Colletti's claim that for Marx the contradictions of capitalism are not 'real oppositions' but 'dialectical contradictions in the full sense of the word' rests only on flimsy references to Marx's crisis theory and is not at all substantiated; the confusion seems to be entirely of Colletti's making.
4. 'Under socialism, the character of the interplay of the productive forces and productive relations is altered. Production relations are brought into line with the level and character of today's productive forces ... ' (Kozlov, 1977 p. 87). See also D. M. Nuti, 1973. The applicability of the law of value and of the law of faster growth of the production of means of production have been debated at various stages in Soviet and East-European countries as a way of airing changing views about the scope and role of markets and about accumulation policy, in particular in the early sixties. Priority to means of production came under serious criticism in Poland under the influence of the Kalecki school (Kalecki, 1969); Polish texts on the political economy of socialism stress the relativity of this priority principle (see Nuti, 1973) which however is still a basic *tenet* of Soviet texts (See Kozlov, 1977). A refreshing exception among Eastern European texts is Brus (1967), a Polish text now out of circulation in which 'the fundamental task of the political economy of socialism is to uncover economic conflicts and indicate the general direction of their solution', the orthodox 'laws' are criticized and alternative models of organization of the socialist economy are related to the specific economic conditions which make them viable (See Nuti, *cit.*).
5. For a general criticism of Marxist-inspired criticisms of Soviet-type societies see Lane, 1977, 1978; for specific criticism of the International Socialist position see Purdya, 1978; for a critique of the Maoist approach see Miliband, 1975.

6. Many of these arguments apply also to the view that Soviet society partakes so much of the features of industrial societies in general as to be assimilated to these societies for analytical purposes. (See Giddens, 1973).

7. 'Marx himself even toyed with the idea that in Russia it might be possible for capitalist development to be largely, if not entirely, by-passed, and the transition to socialism occur on the heels of a purely bourgeois-democratic revolution which had the peasantry as its main driving force' (Dobb, 1967).

8. In Marx's approach to pre-capitalist economic formations the Asiatic mode of production, or oriental despotism, is characterized by autocracy and centralization of economic power in the hands of the state (with state ownership of the land) the *raison d'être* of which is the undertaking of public works on a vast scale, especially in agriculture. (Marx, 1964). Marx refers to a specific Slavonic version of this mode of production, based on direct communal property (*Ibidem,* p. 97; see also Marx's letter to Vera Zasulich, 8 March 1881, *Ibidem,* pp. 142-5). For a good discussion of the 'Asiatic' features of Russian society and their impact on subsequent developments under Socialism see Bahro, 1978, Ch. 3, 'From Agricultural to Industrial Despotism'.

9. 'The principles of the New Economic Policy had been worked out by Lenin still in the spring of 1918, but their implementation was interrupted by intervention. Only after three years was it possible for the Soviet power to proclaim this policy again, and to put it consistently into practice' (Politicheskaya ekonomiya, Uchebnik, Moscow 1954, pp. 330-1, quoted by Szamuely, 1974, p. 74). The latest Soviet handbook of political economy of socialism devotes seven lines in all to War Communism, dismissed as 'being only necessitated by war and dislocation' (Kozlov, 1977, p. 37).

10. See, for instance, Timofiejuk (1968): ' ... socialist economies are switching from extensive growth (based mostly on increases of employment and investment) to the intensive stage of growth (based mostly on labour productivity and the effectiveness of investment). This transition demands fundamental changes in the methods of planning administration and the management of the national economy' (p. 124-5).

11. The Chinese model is an equally questionable model for advanced industrial countries. Also, recent changes in the Chinese economy suggest that the Maoist model may have been a short cut to the Soviet model rather than a genuine alternative.

12. In the 1959 official Soviet textbook of Political Economy *Khozraschot* was defined as 'a method of planned operation of socialist enterprises which requires the carrying out of state determined tasks with the maximum economy of resources, the covering of money expenditure of enterprises by their own money revenues, the ensuring of profitability of enterprises'.

13. An illusion of scientific precision has been provided by aggregate econometric analysis, of a kind which has been discredited and is

going out of fashion in the West. Thus Nachtigal (1967), for instance, claims that in Czechoslovakia in the decade 1951-60 productivity growth contributed over one-third of total income growth, whereas in the years 1961-4 productivity made a *negative* contribution equal to -133.2 *per cent* of total income growth while the increase in material-intensity of production (which in the decade 1951-60 had passed from small positive to small but increasing negative contributions to growth) in the years 1961-4 made a further negative contribution equal to -87.5 per cent of total income growth; 'extensive sources', i.e., factor increases are alleged to have contributed from 55 to 85 per cent of total income growth in various periods of the fifties, and 320.7 per cent (sic) of total income growth in the years 1961-4. This is a pseudo-exact and mystifying way of simply saying that in the early sixties income growth declined (indeed became negative in 1963) in spite of the continued accumulation effort; this throws no light on the causes of the decline because any quantitative assessment of relative weight of growth factors depends crucially on perfectly arbitrary assumptions about substitutability in production and/or about the speed and nature of technological change. This has not prevented Western observers from undertaking similar exercises allegedly providing the increasing weight of 'extensive sources of growth' in the Soviet Union and Eastern Europe during the fifties and early sixties (see for instance Boretsky, 1966), leading to predictions of declining growth performance (such as Weitzman, 1970, and Desai, 1976), for the Soviet economy). Under alternative assumptions, and by means of more sophisticated econometrics, Gomulka (1976, 1977a) reaches different and less pessimistic conclusions. For an excellent survey of 'sovietological econometrics' see Gomulka (1977b).

14. See for instance Wilcynski (1972) whose book on socialist economic development and reforms bears the subtitle 'From Extensive to Intensive Growth under Central Planning in the USSR, Eastern Europe and Yugoslavia'.

15. The political centralization that followed the launching of NEP seems an exception (see above, section 4). This was probably due to external threat, rather than to internal developments; also, the ban on factions was not actually exercised until later. The qualification that, *beyond a certain point,* the progress of economic decentralization *can* bring about political centralization to offset involutionary dangers does not alter significantly the *nature* of the argument, though it causes a greater instability of the system.

16. This limit to the advisability of further accumulation corresponds to what is known in conventional economic literature as the 'golden rule' of accumulation, stating that in a steady state the level of permanently maintainable consumption per head is maximized when the economic system grows at a rate equal to the profit rate. In general, this has very limited implications because a higher growth rate than the 'golden rule' suggests would reduce consumption in the medium run but could raise it later on over and above what it would have been without

additional accumulation and growth. In the case of a socialist economy, however, the transfer of consumption from present to future generations beyond the permanently maintainable level of consumption is rather hard to justify. Hence the 'golden rule' can be interpreted as a limit to accumulation.

17. This proposition implies a rather long list of assumptions, ranging from the absence of external effects to the acceptability of the price system for the evaluation of profits; the proposition is put forward for the sake of argument, to emphasize the distinction between the macro- and micro-economic significance of a profit indicator.

REFERENCES

Amann R., Cooper J., Davies R. W., *The Technological Level of Soviet Industry*, Yale University Press, New Haven and London, 1977.

Bahro, R., 'The Alternative in Eastern Europe', *New Left Review*, November-December 1977, no. 106.

Bahro, R., *The Alternative in Eastern Europe*, New Left Books, London, 1978, originally published as *Die Alternative: zur Kritik des realexistierenden Sozialismus*, Europaische Verlagsanstalt, 1977.

Baran, P. A., Sweezy, P. M., *Monopoly Capital*, Monthly Review Press, New York and London, 1966.

Barsov, A. A., 'Sel'skoe khoziaiastvo i istochniki sotsialisticheskogo nakopleniia v gody pervoi piatiletki (1928-1933)', *Istoriia SSSR*, 1968, no. 3.

Barsov, A. A., *Balans stoimostnykh obmenov mezhdu gorodom i derevnei*, Moscow, 1969.

Bergson, A., *The Real National Income of Soviet Russia Since 1928*, Cambridge, Mass., 1961.

Bettelheim, C., *Les luttes de classe en URSS, 1917-1923,*, Maspéro-Seuil, 1974.

Bettelheim, C., Sweezy P. M., *On the Transition to Socialism*, 2nd edition, 1971.

Boretsky, M., 'Comparative Progress in Technology, Productivity and Economic Efficiency: USSR versus USA'; in: US Congress, 1966.

Brus, W., *Ogolne problemy funkcjonowania gospodarki socjalistycznej*, PWE, Warsaw 1964, translated into English under the title: *The Market in a Socialist Economy*, Routledge and Kegan Paul, London, 1972.

Brus, W., (Ed.), *Ekonomia Polityczna Socjalizmu*, 3rd edition, Warsaw, 1967.

Brus, W., *The Economics and Politics of Socialism – Collected Essays*, with a foreword by Maurice Dobb, Routledge and Kegan Paul, London, 1973.

Brus, W., *Socialist Ownership and Political Systems*, Routledge and Kegan Paul, London, 1975.

Carr, E. H., *The Bolshevik Revolution, 1917-23*, Vol. 2, Macmillan, 1952; Vol. 3, Macmillan, 1953, London.

Carr, E. H. *The Interregnum 1923-24*, Macmillan, London, 1954.

Carr, E. H., *Socialism in One Country, 1924-26*, Vol. 1, Macmillan, 1958, Vol. 2, Macmillan, 1959, London.

Carr, E.H., R.W. Davies, *Foundations of a Planned Economy, 1926-29,* Macmillan, London, 1969.

Chayanov, *The Theory of Peasant Economy,* English translation, 1966, originally published in 1926.

Cliff, T., *Russia—A Marxist Analysis,* IS books, 1964, reprinted as *State Capitalism in Russia,* Pluto Press, 1974.

Colletti, L., 'Marxism and the Dialectic', *New Left Review,* no. 93, September-October 1975.

Cooper J. M., Davies R. W., Wheatcroft S. G., 'Contradictions in Soviet Industrialisation', *mimeo,* Centre for Russian and East European Studies, Birmingham, 1977.

Desai, P., 'The Production Function and Technical Change in Postwar Soviet Industry: a Reexamination', *American Economic Review,* Vol. 66, no. 3, 1976.

Deutscher, I., *The Prophet Armed, Trotsky: 1879-1921,* Oxford University Press, 1954.

Deutscher, I., *Stalin,* London, 1961.

Deutscher, I., *The Unfinished Revolution,* London, 1967.

Deutscher, I., *Russia after Stalin* (with a new introduction by M. Liebman), London, 1969.

Dobb, M. H., *An Essay on Economic Growth and Planning,* Routledge, London, 1960.

Dobb, M. H., 'The Discussions of the Twenties on Planning and Economic Growth', *Soviet Studies,* October 1965.

Dobb, M. H., *Soviet Economic Development Since 1917,* London, 1966.

Dobb, M. H., 'The Discussions of the 1920s about Building Socialism', *Annali dell'Istituto Giangiacomo Feltrinelli,* Milan, 1967.

Dobb, M. H., *Welfare Economics and the Economics of Socialism: Towards a Commonsense Critique,* Cambridge University Press, London, 1969.

Dohan, M. R., 'The Economic Origins of Soviet Autarky, 1927/8-1934', *Slavic Review,* Vol. 35, no. 4, December 1976.

Domar, E. D., *Essays in the theory of economic growth,* New York, 1957.

Ellman, M., Planning problems in the USSR: the contribution of mathematical economics to their solution , 1960-71, London, Cambridge University Press, 1973.

Ellman, M., 'Did the Agricultural Surplus Provide the Resources for the Increase in Investment in the USSR during the First Five Year Plan?' *Economic Journal,* December 1975.

Ellman, M., 'Seven Theses on Kosyginism', *De Economist,* no. 1, 1977.

Erlich, A., *The Soviet Industrialisation Debate, 1924-28,* Cambridge, Mass., 1960.

Fallenbuchl, Z. M., (Ed.) *Economic Development in the Soviet Union and Eastern Europe,* Praeger, 1976.

Giddens, A., *The Class Structure of the Advanced Societies,* Hutchinson, London, 1973.

Gomulka, S., 'Soviet Postwar Industrial Growth, Capital-Labour Substitution, and Technical Change: a Reexamination', in Fallenbuchl (Ed.), 1976.

Gomulka, S., 'Slowdown in Soviet Industrial Growth 1947-1975 Reconsidered', *European Economic Review*, 10, no. 1, 1977a.

Gomulka, S., 'Notes on the New Sovietological Econometrics' (mimeo.), Whitehall/Academics Conference, LSE, December 1977b.

Gomulka, S., 'Growth and the Import of Technology: Poland 1971-80', *Cambridge Journal of Economics*, March 1978.

Goodwin, R., 'A Growth Cycle', in Feinstein, C. (Ed.), *Capitalism, Socialism and Economic Growth, Essays in Honour of M. H. Dobb,* Cambridge University Press, London, 1967.

Harman, C., *Bureaucracy and Revolution in Eastern Europe,* Pluto Press, 1975.

Hayek, F. A. (Ed.), *Collectivistic Economic Planning,* London, Routledge, 1935.

Hicks, J., Growth and Anti-Growth, *Oxford Economic Papers,* November 1966.

Hunter, H., 'The Overambitious First Soviet Five Year Plan', *Slavic Review* no. 2, June 1973, Vol. 32.

Kalecki, M., 'Political Aspects of Full Employment', *Political Quarterly,* 1943.

Kalecki, M., *Introduction to the Theory of Growth in a Socialist Economy,* Blackwell, London, 1969.

Kozlov, G. A., (Ed.), *Political Economy: Socialism,* Progress Pulishers, Moscow, 1977.

Kuron, J., Modzelewski, K., *An Open Letter to the Party,* London, 1968.

Labriola, A., *Del materialismo storico, dilucidazioni preliminari,* E. Loescher, Rome, 1896.

Lane, D., *The Socialist Industrial State—Towards a Political Sociology of State Socialism,* Allen and Unwin, London, 1976.

Lane, D. S., 'Marxist Class Conflict Analyses of State Socialist Society', in Scase, 1977.

Lane, D. S., *Politics and Society in the USSR,* 2nd edition, Martin Robertson, London, 1978.

Lane, D. S., O'Dell, F., *The Soviet Industrial Worker—Social Class, Education and Control,* Martin Robertson, London, 1978.

Lange, O., 'On the Economic Theory of Socialism', *Review of Economic Studies,* 1937.

Lange, O., *Political Economy,* Vol. 1, PWN-Pergamon Press, Warsaw-London 1963, originally published in Polish in 1959.

Lange, O., 'The Computer and the Market', in Feinstein, C., *Capitalism, Socialism and Economic Growth: Essays in Honour of M. H. Dobb,* Cambridge University Press, London, 1967.

Lewin, M., 'The Disappearance of Planning in the Plan', *Slavic Review,* Vol. 32, no. 2, June 1973.

Luxemburg, Rosa, *What is Economics?;* Pioneer Publishers, New York, 1954.

Mandel, E., *Marxist Economic Theory,* Merlin Press, 1968.

Mandel, E., 'Ten Theses on the Social and Economic Laws Governing the Society Transitional between Capitalism and Socialism, *Critique,* no. 3, Autumn 1974.

Marx, K., 'Introduction to the Critique of Political Economy', an Appendix to *A Contribution to the Critique of Political Economy,* Kerr & Co., 1904.

Marx, K., *Grundrisse: Foundations of the Critique of Politcal Economy* (rough draft), Penguin, 1973.

Miliband, R., 'Bettelheim and Soviet Experience', *New Left Review*, no.. 91, May-June 1975.

Millar, J. R., 'Mass Collectivisation and the Contribution of Soviet Agriculture to the First Five Year Plan', *Slavic Review*, Vol. 33, no. 4, December 1974.

Nachtigal, V., 'Extensity and Efficiency of Economic Growth in Czechoslovakia', *Czechoslovak Economic Papers*, Prague, no. 9, 1967.

Nove, A., *An Economic History of the USSR*, Penguin, 1969.

Nove, A., Nuti, D. M., *Socialist Economics*, Penguin, 1972.

Nuti, D. M., 'The Political Economy of Socialism—Orthodoxy and Change in Polish Texts', *Soviet Studies*, October 1973, Vol. XXV, no. 2.

Nuti, D. M., 'Large Corporations and the Reform of Polish Industry', *Jahrbuch der Wirtschaft Osteuropas*, Vol. 7, Munich, 1977.

Nuti, D. M., 'Investment, Interest and Degree of Centralisation in Maurice Dobb's Theory of the Socialist Economy', *Cambridge Journal of Economics*, no. 2, 1978.

Nutter, G. W., Bornstein I., Kaufman, A., *Growth of Industrial Production in the Soviet Union*, Princeton, 1962.

Preobazhensky, E., *The New Economics*, with an introduction by A. Nove, Oxford 1965.

Purdy, D., *The Soviet Union: State Capitalist or Socialist? A Marxian Critique of the International Socialists*, the Communist Party, London, 1978.

Rowthorn, R. E., 'A Conflict Theory of Inflation', *Cambridge Journal of Economics*, no. 2, 1977.

Sartre, J. P., 'Socialism in One Country', *New Left Review*, no. 100, November 1976-January 1977.

Scase, R., (Ed.), *Industrial Society: Class Cleavage and Control*, Allen and Unwin, London, 1977.

Spulber, N., (Ed.), *Foundations of Soviet Strategy for Economic Growth; Selected Soviet Essays, 1924-30*, Bloomington, 1964.

Staniszkis, J., 'On Some Contradictions of Socialist Society: the Case of Poland', *Soviet Studies*, Vo.. XXXI, no. 2, April 1979.

Szamuely, Làszlò, *First Models of the Socialist Economic Systems—Principles and Theories*, Académiai Kiadò, Budapest, 1974.

Timofiejuk, I., *Mierniki wzrostu gospodarczego*, PWE, Warsaw, 1968.

Treml, V. G., Hardt, J. P., (Eds.), *Soviet Economic Statistics*, Durham, North Carolina, 1972.

Trotsky, L., *The Revolution Betrayed*, 1937.

United Nations-ECE, *Economic Survey of Europe 1965*, Part II, Geneva, 1967.

United Nations-ECE, *Economic Survey of Europe in 1976*, Part II, Geneva, 1976.

US Congress, Joint Economic Committee, *New Directions in the Soviet Economy*, Washington GPO, 1966.

Weitzman, M., 'Soviet Postwar Economic Growth and Capital-Labour Substitution', *American Economic Review*, Vol. 60, no. 4, 1970.

Wilcznski, J., *Socialist Economic Development and Reforms*, London, 1972.

A COMMENTARY ON
RUDOLF BAHRO'S ALTERNATIVE

Ralph Miliband

At the time this is written (July 1979), Rudolf Bahro is still in prison in the German Democratic Republic, purging an eight-year sentence for 'treason' which he received in June 1978. His real crime was that he, a functionary of the East German state and party apparatus and a party member since 1952 (he was then seventeen), wrote a book which was published in West Germany in 1977 and which is deeply critical of the 'actually existing socialism' he has served in different capacities and in different spheres for more than two decades. His imprisonment and his sentence have provoked a campaign of protest in a number of countries, notably West Germany but also France, Britain and Italy. This is all to the good, and, must go on until Bahro is released; and what is done on his behalf is also helpful to other 'dissidents' in East Germany who suffer pressure and persecution.

However, it would be no service to Bahro if the fact that he is a 'cause', and a very good cause, were to inhibit critical consideration of his book. It is an important work, which well deserved the award of the Isaac Deutscher Memorial Prize for 1978. Its English title, *The Alternative in Eastern Europe,* (New Left Books, 1978) may suggest a more restricted compass than is warranted. It does mainly deal with Eastern Europe and Soviet-type regimes: but many of the problems with which it is concerned are of a more general character and are directly relevant to basic issues of socialist theory and practice, and notably to the general issue of the distribution and control of power under socialism. Whole-hearted support for Bahro is obviously compatible with a stringent appraisal of his book.

A preliminary point about it is that Bahro proceeds from the premise that there does exist a desirable *socialist* alternative to 'actually existing socialism'. Unlike so many 'dissidents' in and from Eastern Europe and the USSR, whose bitter experiences have led them to reject socialism altogether and often to turn into fierce reactionaires and apostles of the Cold War, Bahro remains in this book the uncompromising advocate of a socialist vision of the future, and above all concerned to explore how the obstacles to its realization may be overcome. So much is he concerned with a socialist future that much which he says about it has occasionally been dismissed as 'utopian' even by Marxists and other sympathetic readers. But if by 'utopian' is meant constructs which belong to the realm of fantasy, Bahro is not guilty of the charge: he may well underestimate the difficulty of achieving many of the objectives he believes to be central to the socialist project. But that is something else. It is only if one believes that *any* socialist vision is utopian that Bahro qualifies/for the label: but that is more of a comment on those who apply the label than on Bahro. In many respects, he is if anything rather 'anti-utopian' and very hard-headed, even possibly too much so.

Bahro beings with a fundamental postulate, namely that socialism, in so far as it entails what he calls the 'overcoming of subalternity' and the free association of equal citizens, is incompatible with economic backwardness and the requirements of industrialization. He goes very far in suggesting that the incompatibility is absolute. In the Russian case, he notes, it was inevitable that backwardness should 'levy an institutional tribute on the Bolsheviks' (p. 90). Indeed, 'the more one tries to think through the stations of Soviet history ... the harder it becomes to draw a limit short of even the most fearsome excesses, and to say that what falls on the other line was absolutely avoidable' (p. 90).

This is an 'economic determinism' pushed to extremes. There is obviously no way of disproving that all that happened in Stalinist Russia, including the 'most fearsome excesses', was inevitable. But the claim is nevertheless unreasonable, in that it leaves no room whatever for any element of contingency, whereas such an element must be presumed always to exist. In this context, this makes an enormous difference. Bahro writes that 'it was not only on account of the constant threats to it, but rather because of the positive tasks' of driving the masses into an industrialization which they could not immediately desire, that the Soviet Union had to have a single, iron, "Petrine" leadership' (p. 116); but also that 'if a more gifted man than Stalin had managed to adapt himself to this aim, then the *ideological* resources that the old party tradition already possessed would have stretched somewhat further, and the most extreme expressions of the terror would have been avoided. Russia would have been spared the Caesarian madness, but hardly more' (*ibid.*). But 'hardly more' is not an adequate description of the difference which another outcome to the struggles of the twenties could have made.

The point is not purely historical. Bahro writes that 'the peoples of the backward countries' require not only revolution, but also 'a strong state, often one that is in many respects despotic, in order really to overcome the inherited inertia' (p. 58). But the 'inherited inertia' is in any case being overcome, not least because of the fierce pace of super-exploitation to which many 'backward countries' are being subjected by multi-national capitalist enterprise; and a 'strong state' can mean different things, and may be strong in different ways and in different degrees. It is surely dangerous not to make distinctions here and to underestimate what 'more or less' can mean in practice.

On the other hand, Bahro is right to point to the exceedingly unpleasant fact that countries whose people 'are just in the process of organizing themselves for industrialization' do need a strong state; and he is very probably and unfortunately right in also saying that 'their state can be nothing other than bureaucratic' (pp. 128-9). It was often said, until not very long ago, that the Chinese had conclusively disproved the latter point in their own process of 'organizing themselves for industrialization': recent convulsions, 'revelations' and about-turns confirm that such claims were exaggerated or spurious. Still, the point holds that 'bureaucracy' has many different facets and degrees, and that some forms of it are less stifling and arbitrary than others.

In any case, it is not with countries in the early stages of industrialization that Bahro is concerned, but with societies that have made the big industrial leap under the auspices of 'actually existing socialism' or where it at any rate prevails—countries such as the USSR, the German Democratic Republic and Czechoslovakia. His starting-point in regard to all of them is that they are in a state of deep and structural crisis:

> It has gripped all countries of the Soviet bloc, affecting all areas of life, and it is ultimately based on the contradiction recognized by all Marxists, between the modern productive forces and relations of production that have become a hindrance to them, coming to a head. The abolition of private property in the means of production has in no way meant their immediate transformation into the property of the people. Rather, the whole society stands property-less against its state machine. [pp. 10-11.]

'Relations of production' here stands for a political order

dominated by a state/party apparatus which was monopolized all power and which is stifling the vitality of the social and economic order as well as the political one. As he also notes somewhere else,

the oligarchy at the top of the pyramid decides the goals for which the surplus product should be used, and subjects the *entire* reproduction process of economic, social and cultural life to its regulation. As in the case of all earlier systems of domination, the steady reproduction of its own monopoly, and when possible its expanded reproduction, goes into the overall calculation of social development and has to be paid for by the masses. [p. 241. Italics in text].

The contradiction, for Bahro, squarely resides in the political realm, which stifles the 'surplus consciousness' generated by industrial development: whatever was impossible at the beginning of the industrializing process because of the retarded state of the productive forces and society in general, has now become possible because of economic development, and is being repressed by a rigid, self-regarding and bureaucratic state/party apparatus. Bahro also clearly places the *source* of power in the political realm. It is not economic power which produces or determines political power, but the other way round: it is their location in the state/party apparatus which makes it possible for leaders to exercise economic and ideological as well as political control. It is also this location which ensures the economic privileges of the dominant groups ('exploitation in our system is a *political* phenomenon, a phenomenon of distribution of political power' (p. 97); and the more favourable the location, the greater the privileges.

The privileges with which Bahro is most concerned are not the obvious material ones, but those that have to do with the exercise of power, and from which the others derive. Again and again, it is to the concentration of power at one end and its trophy at the other than he returns:

Do the working masses of the 'socialist' countries '[he asks]' have even the least positive influence on the decisions that bear on their material fate, and ultimately therefore on their overall fate? On decisions as to the proportions between accumulation and consumption, between production for war and for peace, between building of homes and building of monuments, between expenditure on education and expenditure on the propagandist self-portrayal of the power structure, between the costs of liberating women from domestic slavery and the cost of security for those 'in charge of society'? Of course not. [pp. 151-2]

It is this 'division of labour' between rulers and ruled which is for Bahro the cancer of 'actually existing socialism': 'we must thank Edward Gierek', he also writes, 'for the forthright way in which he summed up the problem of our societies after the Polish December (1970) crisis, with the slogan: "You work well, and we will govern well" (p. 176). This is what Bahro rejects; and that rejection is at the core of his vision of a socialist alternative to 'actually existing socialism'. For he believes that the pain and suffering of the process of industrialization have at last produced the conditions in which it is possible for the people to take an ever-larger share in the determination of all aspects of their own lives. His first premise is that the 'overcoming of subalternity' is possible and is one of the great defining elements of the socialist project. What he wants and believes possible is at least the beginning of a 'cultural revolution' that would break down a functional fetishism which condemns most people to permanently fixed and subordinate tasks, and which effectively robs them of self-determination: the first condition of this 'cultural revolution' is the 'de-bureaucratization and genuine social-ization of the activity of management, the participation of all individuals in disposal over the reproduction process'; its second condition 'bears on the elevation of the collective worker to the level of the given principles of science and technique of the time, which are at work in the production process' (p. 276). But the 'cultural revolution' of which Bahro speaks reaches out much further even than this and encompasses all aspects of existence.

The most difficult questions concerning Bahro's work do not lie in his reaffirmation of socialist ideals, but rather in his views of the ways in which progress is to be made in realizing them in the countries with which he is mainly concerned.

The first such question has to do with the social class or stratum which is to initiate and lead the movement for change. On this, Bahro is honestly and resolutely forthright:

New and higher cultures [he writes] are never created without the masses, without an essential change in their condition of life, nor without their initiative, at a definite stage of maturity of the ongoing crisis. But in no known historical case did the first creative impulse in ideas and organization proceed from the masses; the trade unions do not anticipate any new civilization. [p. 149.]

This is somewhat different way of advancing a proposition similar to the Leninist view of what could be expected from the working class, and what could not; and which largely determined the kind of party which Lenin and the Bolsheviks brought into being. In so far as the working class cannot by its own efforts be the agent of its own emancipation, the vanguard party must assume a major historical role; and the less advanced and prepared the working class, the greater must be the role of the party. This being the case, frantic efforts must then be made to obscure and deny the gap that separates class and party, which leads to illusionism and myth-making. Bahro rejects this: but he also rejects, as I have noted, the notion that all that is required is to place back the emphasis on the working class and to declare it to be the subject of its own and society's emancipation. Those upon whom he relies to constitute the leading element, in social terms, of the movement for change are the people who exercise managerial and 'intellectual' functions in the societies of 'actually existing socialism' and who form the middle and higher echelons of the 'collective worker'. The initiative for fundamental change, he writes, 'can only proceed from those elements who are most bound up with the developmental functions and tendencies of the forces and relations of production'; and he believes that it is the 'intellectualized strata of the collective worker' who will 'for the time being inevitably set the tone' of a transformed socialist society (pp. 328-9).

Of course, Bahro knows perfectly well that there are many people in this stratum who are themselves 'reactionary and bureaucratized' and are part of the privileged and parasitical order that has to be changed. But he also believes that there are many others who are well aware of the need for change, and for an end to 'the permanent tutelage of society by the state' and to 'the permanent treatment of people (individuals and collectives) as infantile subjects of education' (p. 313). He derives this belief from different sources: from the Czech Spring of 1968, which showed that many of the people whom he has in mind were prepared for change, and were prepared to take great risks to see it brought about; from a 'structural' analysis, which leads him to think that, more and more, 'the Soviet scientists, technicians and economists will come up more obstinately than ever, and ever more frequently, too, against the fundamental incompatibility between the old superstructure and the new productive forces'

(p. 335); and it is difficult to believe that he does not draw from his own experience as well in thinking that there are many people in the stratum to which he himself belonged who want change in progressive directions:

> Those ideologists of all kinds [he writes] who are pressed into the roles of party and state officials, from social scientist through to journalists, from artists to their censors, from the strategists of natural science to teachers of history—these are all continuously demeaned, both directly and indirectly, by proscriptions, by the reprimands and the praises of the arrogant politbureaucrats (the petty ones still more than the great ones). In order to follow the norms and rituals of official 'intellectual life', they must mostly learn to present the public image of pathetic cretins. [p. 324.]

The changes which are inscribed on the agenda of the countries of 'actually existing socialism', and which nothing can remove from their agenda, will tell whether Bahro's expectations are realistic or not. But his hopes must not be misunderstood: he neither underestimates the role of the working class in the process of change; nor does he seek to present scientists, technicians, managers and 'intellectuals' as the new 'universal class' in place of the working class. On the contrary, he is concerned to stress both the importance of the 'intellectual' stratum *and* the limited nature of its demands, from the socialist perspective that Bahro holds. Although he attaches importance to demands for 'liberalization' and the exercise of democratic freedoms, this, he also says, does not reach deep enough and touch the heart of the matter, the heart of the matter being for him a society in which a structured, functionally sanctioned system of authority relations prevails and must be overcome.

I think that Bahro rather underestimates the significance and reach of democratic demands in the societies of 'actually existing socialism'—or for that matter anywhere else: now as always, the battle for democratic freedoms everywhere is not simply a prelude to the battle for socialism, but an intrinsic part of it; and he is unduly dismissive of what he calls a 'superficial and impatient radicalism' which erupted in Czechoslovakia in 1968 alongside the Action Programme of the Czech Communist Party 'and which ultimately served the purpose of securing the uninhibited and uncontrolled development of these privileged forces [i.e., 'intellectuals, economists and technicians'—*R. M.*] on the TV screen, in culture, in the state apparatus and in the leading positions of economic management' (p. 307).

Whether appropriate to the Czech Spring or not, Bahro's suspicion (or qualified suspicion) is consistent with the argument that runs like a thread throughout his book, namely that socialism does not mean the replacement of one oligarchy by another, but the dissolution of oligarchy: the 'tendency' to which he objects in the Czech Spring is that which was leading, as he sees it, to the 'appropriation of political power on the basis of "competence", i.e., of the effective socio-economic status that its representatives had acquired in the two decades since 1948' (p. 308). What Bahro has in mind is perhaps best expressed in the following quotation:

> Political revolution or reformation only has meaning if it improves the conditions for the technical and at the same time cultural revolution that liberates people step by step from the chains of the traditional division of labour and the state, and ensures them the preconditions for the free development of all, right down to the primary cells of society [p. 182.]

It is an obvious exaggeration to say that political revolution or reformation *only* has meaning if it achieves the purposes which Bahro stipulates; but it is nevertheless salutary, not least for an 'intellectual' stratum engaged in more or less acceptably creative work, to be reminded that, in socialist terms, the notion of democracy has to go far beyond political arrangements if it is to erode effectively and ultimately dissolve the 'subalternity' in which others parts of the 'collective worker' are permanently located. In this respect, Gahro speaks in the most authentic socialist voice and cannot be faulted.

But if neither the 'working class' nor the 'intellectual' stratum can be expected to represent the 'universal' interest, how then is that interest to be expressed, and by whom?

It is here that Bahro is least convincing and that his perspectives are most clouded. He does not believe that ruling Communist parties, as they now function, can serve as agencies of socialist emancipation. On the contrary, 'the party leadership is working not to overcome this late class society of ours, but rather to consolidate and perpetuate it, and would like to confine social and economic progress to their necessary limits' (p. 242). In fact, the state and the Party in these systems are the main constitutive elements of a single apparatus of power and domination, each reinforcing the other.

On the other hand, he categorically rejects party pluralism as an 'anachronistic piece of thoughtlessness, which completely misconstrues the concrete historical material in our countries' (p. 350). Parties, he seems to believe, must represent distinct and antagonistic social classes and elements. In so far as such classes and social elements do not exist in the countries of 'actually existing socialism', except for the 'class' conflict between the people and the party/state apparatus, there is no basis for a plurality of parties.

This is unconvincing. The notion that independent political groupings and parties can only have a meaningful existence if they are based on clearly defined classes is much too simple and reductionist, in stipulating that political activity can only be significant as a reflection of 'pure' class representation; and that the alternative 'political fragmentation of the workers' movement is only a phenomenon of groups of intellectuals, with their claims to power and their rivalries' (p. 350). The experience of capitalist societies shows the matter to be much more complex than this; and Bahro provides no good reason for thinking that it is simpler in post-capitalist societies—unless it is forced into simplicity, by a system which he rejects.

This is not to say that a plurality of parties is a sufficient condition for the achievement of socialist democracy; and it may even be the case that it is not a necessary condition for radical changes to occur in the countries of 'actually existing socialism'. To fasten on such plurality as paramount or critical may well be unduly rigid: much would depend on the alternative. For Bahro, the alternative consists in a new form of party or political organism, a League of Communists, to which he devotes considerable attention and which is inspired by Gramsci's concept of the party as a 'collective intellectual'.

The League of Communists is intended to give expression to all the 'emancipatory interests' in society and to 'inspire the system of social forces and organizations in the name of a constructive but substantially transforming counter-force, which puts the state hierarchy in its proper place ... this means a division of social power, the installation of a progressive dialectic between state and social forces, and not just temporarily as within the party process itself, but rather for the whole duration of the transition. The result will be a situation of dual supremacy, in which the statist side gradually becomes less dominant' (p. 361).

The absolutely key question here is the relationship of the party or league to the state. Bahro wants his League of Communists to stand outside the state apparatus, so that there may be a possibility of 'bringing contradiction into the government apparatus' (p. 370).

Communists, he also says, 'must organize the social forces in such a way that these confront the apparatus on a massive scale as autonomous powers, and can force it into progressive compromises' (p. 371). Again, he makes the point that the League will have different tendencies and fractions (which is interesting in relation to the discussion of party pluralism); but he then immediately adds that the existence of tendencies and fractions in the League of Communists 'naturally presupposes that the state and administration are not directly dependent on the League and its internal debates' (p. 366).

But this separation of the party or league from the state raises more questions than it solves: for it leaves *the state* in a position of *independent power,* which is precisely what needs to be overcome. Bahro is eloquent and convincing in outlining the role of the League, namely 'the unification, coordination and direction of intellectual and moral efforts for elaborating a strategy and tactics of cultural revolution' (p. 376), on the basis of inner-party democracy and equality; and it might be argued that the very fact that it was possible for such an organization to come into being would mean that the problem of the control of the state was already much less acute: a state that would enable a League of Communists, such as Bahro has in mind, to operate freely would be a different state from any that we know in the countries of 'actually existing socialism'. There is something to this argument (which is not incidentally Bahro's argument), but not enough. For it would still be essential—and it will remain essential for any foreseeable future—to find ways and means of controlling the state in its policies and actions. The trouble with Bahro's League of Communists is that there is no obvious mechanism whereby it would be able to constrain the state apparatus and compel it to enter into the 'progressive compromises' of which he speaks, let alone impose new policy directions upon it.

The independence of the state in relation to society is the greatest of all political problems in Soviet-type regimes. This is as true for China as for the USSR and for Vietnam as for Cuba or Hungary: policy is made at a level which leaves out the people altogether, and the more important the decisions, the less say do the people have. Not only are such decisions not subject to determination by the people: they are not even subject to genuine discussion and debate in society. It is symptomatic of a general state of affairs in these regimes not only that the people of Vietnam should have had no say in that country's invasion of Cambodia, or the people of China in that country's invasion of Vietnam, but that there should have been no debate on these acts of state policy. Genuine debate, with effects on the outcome, is not part of the political culture of the countries of 'actually existing socialism'. Capitalist democracy hardly shines in this respect either: but its political practice is much superior to that of Soviet-type regimes. So long as this remains the case, socialists everywhere will be in great trouble.

Bahro wants to remedy this state of affairs; but the means he proposes are not adequate to the purpose. However, I do not wish to conclude this commentary on a negative note. Bahro may not answer the questions he poses: but he does pose them, with great courage and honesty, in the name of a humanism without sentimentality which embodies the values and aspirations that makes socialism the hope of mankind. In an epoch like the present, so ravaged by cynicism, doubt, disillusionment and despair, his voice reaches out from his jail and speaks of better days to come, or rather of better days to be made, East and West.

MASS COMMUNICATIONS
AND 'INFORMATION TECHNOLOGY'

Frank Webster and Kevin Robins

Eighteen hundred thirty-four, the year of Büchner's
Hessian Courier
Charles Babbage, obsessive-compulsive, Fellow
of the Royal Society, founder of operations
analysis
conceived the punch card.
H.M. Enzensberger 'C.B. 1792-1871'

1

This article aims to provide an overview of recent developments in
mass communications made possible by the micro-electronics 'revolution'. It sets out to assess the impact of these new technologies
on social relations—or, more correctly, to analyse the technologies *as*
social relations. Thereby it intends to treat them as forms assumed
by the capital relation as it seeks to impose itself ever more firmly
and extensively on social life.

It is today possible to discern a process of convergence and
integration of once disparate technologies. At one level, hitherto
independent products are merging into systems within particular
sectors of society. Word processors, telecommunications equipment
and computers are becoming key elements of integrated systems in
the business sector. And video cassettes and discs, television games,
home computers and viewdata services form key components of
systems in the home. At a more general level even these systems are
merging into what may be seen as an over-arching communications
industry which incorporates, most importantly, computing and
various forms of telecommunications. This is identified, but not
conceptualized, by the recently coined term 'information technology'. In consequence, corporations once unchallenged within their
own sphere are being thrown into confrontation with each other.
Although this process is still embryonic the impact is already being
felt, most notably with the introduction of word processors. It is

clear that this impact will increase, not just on employment, but on all social relations, permeating many aspects of everyday life.

However, it is necessary to begin with some brief theoretical observations. Because assessments of technological innovation all too easily result in futuristic utopian—or dystopian—scenarios, we feel it essential that analysis of such developments be conceptually informed by more adequate principles than we have yet found within the theoretical framework of current Marxist cultural and media research. Such work is particularly restrictive when trying to understand mass communications phenomena which are only in their emergent phases. Indeed, it is our contention that recent developments in 'information technology' are calling into question many aspects of this research. A re-examination of theoretical positions is required, especially a rethinking of the interrelations between social and economic forms and theory and (historical) reality.

The history of Marxist cultural and media theory is inextricably linked with the history of the base/superstructure metaphor. This metaphor, universally criticized in its cruder and mechanistic incarnations, has nevertheless proved singularly irrepressible. Such a conceptualization is indeed part of everyday consciousness: it does indicate the spontaneous perceptions of members of society. It is an element of commonsensical modes of thought which make it difficult to think the interpenetration of different aspects of society in any other way. This phenomenon, which has discernable historical origins, has been accepted by and theoretically refurbished by that school of thought which now exercises 'hegemony' over Marxist cultural studies. This movement gravitates around the early texts of Althusser and draws upon particular concepts ('determination in the last instance', 'overdetermination', etc.) to pose anew the relation of base and superstructure (now called the 'economic' and 'ideological' levels).

The base/superstructure metaphor, in any of its guises, reflects the way in which society *appears* as fragmented and divided, in which culture *appears* as external to the economic infrastructure, thereby reproducing the surface appearances of society.

On the one hand, the effect on media studies has been to isolate from the social totality the 'level' of ideology or culture. Specialists in cultural analysis are able to examine this as the sphere in which social relations are produced and reproduced, the sphere in which ideology is effective, and in which hegemony is secured. On the other hand, this 'culturalism' is complemented by recent analyses which examine the economic infrastructure of mass media. This work concedes the study of social relations to the 'culturalists', contenting itself with the description of ownership and control of the media, the business and economic aspects, which are now devoid of all social relations.

'Economism' and 'culturalism' complement—and moreover necessitate—each other, reflecting just how insidious is the permeation of that strained metaphor into both everyday consciousness and theoretical elaborations. This permeation is effective—or rather subversive—for negative rather than positive reasons. That is, because it precludes an understanding of the social whole and of the central importance of Marx's concept of the relations of production. Unable to respond to 'the relations of production in their totality' (Marx), the metaphor becomes reified, and the attempt to permutate the possible relations between base and superstructure assumes priority. 'That is to say, the analytic categories ... have, almost unnoticed, become substantive descriptions, which then take habitual priority over the *whole social process* to which, as analytic categories, they are attempting to speak'.[1]

The dynamics of social production are obscured by those concepts which are currently used to theorize the 'superstructure', notably by 'ideology' and 'culture'. Called upon to explain more than they are capable of, these concepts have become transfixed, ossified and ahistorical. They no longer illuminate reality, but rather use the reality itself to substantiate the validity of the concepts. It is precisely such deductivism that has resulted in the relation between theory and historical reality being obscured.[2]

It is essential that we overcome such fixities of concept, for concepts are social constructions; having no claim to exist as definitive entities in their own rights, but serving rather as heuristic instruments for research, they are shaped by their existence in the real historical world. Historical reality is likely to subvert our concepts, demanding in consequence that we constantly reassess, debate and reshape them in order to respond to emerging phenomena. For these reasons it is essential to pose the question of history within theory itself.

Our work on 'information technology' focuses upon emerging phenomena, upon new technologies and industrial configurations, and the social relations they embody. 'Information technology' is decidely not a new recruit to the 'Ideological State Apparatuses' just as it is not a desocialized entity belonging to some autonomous economic or technological realm. Rather it is a new phase of capital accumulation, situated in a particular historical time, which expresses both the social and economic moments of the relations of production.

Potentially, 'information technology' provides the basis for an upsurge in productivity,[3] but also—and necessarily—for the re-composition of social relations. This will occur through new forms of production, new forms of the labour process, but also through new patterns of consumption resulting from new capital and consumer goods. Satellite communications, video and cable television and information banks will create changes in leisure and work patterns, in processes of human interaction and communications, in aspects of centralization and decentralization, in sensibility and consciousness.

Processes of convergence in communications have already been noted by mass media researchers. Most noteworthy is the work of Armand Mattelart and Herbert Schiller. The latter has boldly observed that 'the mass media, advertising, public relations, market surveys, public opinion polling, and even the school system are inseparable components of a communications apparatus fashioned to accommodate a privatized production and consumption economy'.[4] In a complementary manner, Mattelart has described the integration of the electronics, telecommunications, mass media, space and defence industries,[5] showing how culture can no longer (if it ever could) be treated as an autonomous sphere since the border-lines between political, economic, military and cultural affairs are weakening.[6] These indices of convergence, when combined with the technological integration taking place within these sectors, point towards an unprecedented concentration of powers.

Both Schiller and Mattlelart focus primarily on the relation between advanced capitalist communications organizations and the Third World. It is on this international scale, in what has been termed 'cultural imperialism', that the significance of recent developments is perhaps most perceptible. Mattelart himself views these trends as indicators of 'the contours of the ideological offensive by the dominant classes in this stage of international capital accumulation'.[7]

Today the significance is becoming more clear on the domestic scene. Especially important to the future of advanced capitalist societies are the telecommunications and data processing industries from which have developed so much of the new 'information technology'. The sphere of information processing, storage and distribution has been assigned a priority role in assuring the dominance of, particularly, American corporations. The likes of GE, IBM, ITT, Xerox, ATT&T, Exxon and RCA have massively invested in the production (and use) of the new technologies. US interests are pursued by Japanese and Western European organizations. These powerful forces present a formidable, perhaps even overwhelming, obstacle to any alternative strategies for change. 'The fusion of economic strength and information control or image-making, public opinion formation or call it what you will, is the new quintessence of power, international and domestic'.[8]

An emphasis on information has gained currency in wide circles. There is much talk nowadays of the 'Information Age', the 'information Revolution'. In recent months, following the 'discovery' of micro-electronics, there has been a new boom in futurology. Once it was grasped that the 'chip' is a device whose function is to hold and act upon information, that these integrated circuits are cheap and capable of application in a whole battery of specific 'information technologies', then forecasts about a new era flourished.

The discussions, predictably, are not posed, in Schiller's terms, as a question of power, but instead are seen as the rise of a new information-based service economy or a future 'wired society' which will provide information on tap. Extravagant claims are made that 'information technology' provides the basis for another industrial revolution, a panacea which will solve political, ecological and Third World industrialization problems.

The academic underpinning for such positions is provided by the tenets of 'post-industrial' theorists, the most significant of whom is Daniel Bell, which suggest that we are living in a 'knowledge society'.[9] Bell's claim, first offered almost a decade ago, that 'if capital and labour are the major structural features of industrial society, information and knowledge are those of the post-industrial society',[10] has been given renewed vigour and edge by developments in 'information technology'.

Misguided by his conservative optimism, Bell ignores the fact that information is now treated as a commodity in the way capital handles the motor car or any other saleable product. At the same time, he seems unaware that 'information technology', used in its present form, while it may extend the quantity of 'knowledge' in circulation, provides no necessarily qualitative improvement, but rather leads to the mechanization of 'knowledge'. It routinizes and downgrades much mental labour. Nevertheless, despite the inadequacies of Bell, his provocative theses have provided a guiding light for many enthusiasts of the future 'Information Age'.

For James Martin, the ideologue of the 'wired society', 'Man will have the opportunity to once again become civilized in a "post-industrial" society.'[11] In this 'satellite age democracy' it will be possible to 'build a world without pollution, without massive destruction of nature's beauty, without human drudgery'.[12] Martha Williams claims that it is now feasible 'to couple information research with high technology to help us to utilize the world's information resources to solve the pressing problems of science and society'.[13] For John McHale we are on the verge of post-industrial society, one based on technologies of a 'Third Industrial Revolution', which are relatively 'non-resource depletive, extremely economical in their energy uses and have correspondingly low impacts on the environment'. In this society there will also exist 'the possibilities of widening participation in decisions and policies through more direct citizen interaction via information systems'.[14]

All this, of course, is based upon a rather naive estimation of 'information technology'—indeed of technology *tout court*. It is reminiscent of the belief in the efficacy of the 'technological fix' so popular in the sixties. On the premise that 'the collection and exchange of information underlies all that we do, and the structures and functions of industrial societies depend absolutely on its prompt and ample supply'[15] it is possible to see quantitative increases in the provision of 'information technology' as a solution to the world's problems. However, such a vision simply overlooks the reality that information is inseparably connected to the distribution of social, economic and political power.

If we may reject the claims made for a post-industrial 'knowledge society' we must nevertheless still seriously examine the issue of information. Bell correctly emphasizes that information today is a strategic resource, that 'post-industrial society is organized around knowledge, for the purpose of social control and the directing of innovation and change'.[16] Irrespective of his misinterpretations, Bell has identified an important phenomenon. His emphasis on the transforming power of the service sector, the number of 'knowledge workers', expenditure on research and development, etc.,[17] is mistaken. Against this, we would argue that the significance of information lies in directions other than those delineated by Daniel Bell, that what is central is the increasing subsumption of know-ledge/information under the capital relation, which is facili-tated by the new electronic means of storage and distribution. This represents an extension of the separation of mental and manual labour to society as a whole; it is a question of the *form* being assumed by information as an aspect of the social relations of power.

That information will become an overriding social and political issue is clear from a recent Conservative Party draft policy document which declares that 'Britain needs to profit from information just as one and two centuries ago we created wealth from the agricultural and industrial revolutions'.[18] It continues:

> The battle lines are already being drawn for the struggle to control information in Britain. Government administration, worker collectives, corporations, police and security forces, and foreign corporations and Governments all seek to preserve their own privacy while finding out as much as possible about every one else. Information is the commanding height of tomorrow's economy.

2

We argue, in the following, that apparently disparate technologies —teletext, viewdata, electronic mail, data banks, word processors or cable television—must actually be considered as components of an extensive communications network, as yet only in the early stages of its formation, which is being brought about by the process of integration and convergence referred to above. By its advocates this has been called the 'wired society', a term which obscures and neutralizes the social and economic logic of what is a new phase of accumulation, entailing new forms of production and consumption, and a new role for communications in the organization and definition of social relations. This phase will develop through the struggles between IBM, AT&T, Xerox, etc., to define the contours of the new communications system, thereby to control it; and it will develop through struggles between these corporations and those producers and consumers who will have to come to terms with these new technologies. The outcome of these struggles can scarcely be predicted. But they will be intense, for at stake is the establishment of what Daniel Bell appropriately calls an 'infra-structure'.

The Director of the Japan Computer Usage Development Centre has outlined the growth of 'information technology' in four stages. A period of innovatory and pure research with space and defence applications (1945-70) was followed by a second, 'management-based stage' (1955-80) in which government and private enterprise seek to rationalize management. In the third, 'society-based stage', the objectives are to develop the social usages of 'information technology' (e.g., telemedicine, computer-aided learning) (1970-90). Finally, the 'individual-based stage' (1980-2000), sees the installation of home terminals and thereby private applications of the technology.[19] In this article we consider the second and fourth stages, business systems and home systems, as being central. For the purposes of analysis we discuss them separately, beginning with business systems, which have, for obvious reasons, taken off first, laying the infrastructure within which home systems—and indeed the mass media—will be recomposed as parts of a more extensive (mass) communications and information network. It must be borne in mind, of course, that the technological and chronological precedence of business systems is by no means absolute, that home and business systems increasingly influence one another, as they, increasingly, seem to be fusing into a single network.

It is also important to stress two further points both of which we lack the space to develop here.[20] First, it must be emphasized that these new technologies have a history. Secondly, these origins are integrally related to the history of micro-electronics, which is the enabling technology for recent developments.[21]

Business Systems

This section begins by looking at some of the central business services and products being developed. The discussion will be followed by a survey of the struggles being waged by rival corporations to develop and gain acceptance for their own information systems.

Business services will primarily consist of computer/communication systems which use a range of telecommunications equipment (cable, satellite, microwave, etc.) and a range of computer time and equipment sharing techniques in order to provide services to customers relating to information, data processing and, of increasing importance, text handling. In the words of a Department of Industry report,

> the running of even a moderately industrialized economy requires the collection, storing, retrieving, processing and generally moving around of a great variety of information, numerical or otherwise, often in large volumes and often very quickly. The computer makes the first four of these activities possible on a scale which was unthinkable a generation ago ... The telecommunications system makes the transportation of information possible on the scale required ...[22]

Among such services offered by 'information utilities' are time-shared remote computing, computer-aided learning, message delivery, information retrieval from remote data bases, and funds transfers.[23]

The Automated Office

Central to the economic development of 'information technology' is the office, which, it is projected, will evolve on the basis of new developments in micro-electronics towards the 'paperless' or 'automated' office. The rationale for automation of the office lies in the attempt to increase productivity in this sector which is characterized by high labour-intensity in handling huge volumes of information. This 'economic' goal is inseparable from the 'social' question of control over work and the labour process in offices. That this is a strategic market, and potentially a lucrative one, is made clear by the prominence of such corporations as Philips, 3M, Burroughs, Eastman Kodak, Exxon[24], IBM and Xerox—with the latter two having already fully developed strategies for the 'office of the future'. In Britain GEC has recently acquired the American office equipment manufacturer, A. B. Dick, and the NEB has now formed Nexos Office Systems in order to attack the integrated office system market.

At present the main component and cornerstone of office automation is the word processor (WP), by which is meant electronic equipment for the preparation, editing, storage and retrieval of text. WP equipment exists in various degrees of complexity, the simplest being merely an electric typewriter with a magnetic storage device (e.g., the IBM 'selectric' typewriter), which allows the operator to correct, add, delete and modify information electronically without erasing it. This is, and will remain for some time, the most prevalent form of WP precisely because it bestows greater 'efficiency' upon secretarial and typing work.

More complex WP systems are computer-based, being either 'stand alone' (mini-computer) devices or connected to in-house or remote mainframe computers. The more sophisticated machines have a visual display unit (VDU) for text entry and editing, increased memory capacity, a micro-processor unit for more elaborate editing facilities, and a high speed printer for producing hard copies.[25] It is only when WPs have access to large memories and when they have communications capabilities that their full potential is realized; they become then the basis for electronic memos and files, and for an alternative inter-office message system (i.e., electronic mail). When WPs are linked to each other and to computers by means of a telecommunications system they become true communicating word processors (CWPs).[26] They cease to be elaborate typewriters and become computer terminals within a complete office automation system.[27]

As yet CWPs have not been developed systematically, and even in the United States less than 10 per cent of WPs have communicating facilities. However, it is evident that the evolution of text processing systems into communication networks is only a matter of time. Many PTTs are exploring an advanced text-communication service, named Teletex, which is designed to supersede telex and integrate with developments in CWPs. Already West Germany and Sweden are planning CWP (or Teletex) networks under PTT auspices.[28] And the CCITT, the international standards organization for telephony and telegraphy, is attempting to establish standards for a Teletex system that will allow the message and data facilities of CWPs to operate over public data networks.[29]

Electronic Mail

CWPs clearly provide one strong basis for an electronic mail service (EMS), but the term in fact refers to a much broader range of electronic message communications. The most common at present is facsimile transmission, which, along with enhanced telex, forms an intermediate step towards true electronic mail, i.e., computer to computer communications. The British Post Office is now planning to lease facsimile machines, whilst the French government has made a much more positive commitment to facsimile. The US Postal Service is negotiating with several European PTTs over the possibility of introducing an international facsimile service called Intelpost, whilst within the United States it is planning a more advanced service, Electronic Computer-Originated Mail (ECOM), in which 'letters' are electronically generated and transmitted to a destination post office, where they are converted to hard copy and delivered.[30]

True EMSs—those which operate an end to end electronic service—have their origin in message dialogues between experienced users of data communications networks such as the Arpanet system. Such systems, which remain internal to one particular network, have, however, also been made available by Tymshare, with its On Tyme message-switching service, and by the Telenet data network with a similar service. It is the establishment of data networks that in fact offers an infrastructure for EMSs, and the Post Office's decision to go ahead with its public packet-switched data service (PSS) is a step in the direction of computer mail. The logical extension comes when this is the infrastructure not only for CWPs, but also for Prestel terminals, in which case electronic mail can be directed straight to the home.

As yet EMSs are in their embryonic stages, though it has been estimated that computer mail should be cost competitive with postage by the mid 1980s. A report by Communications Studies and Planning, and Mackintosh Consultants, claims that annual EMS sales will rise from $180 million in 1978 to $1100 million in 1987 in Europe, and during the same period in the United States from $350 million to $1400 million.

Electronic Funds Transfers

(EFT) refers to the electronic implementation of financial transactions, or, as James Martin puts it, 'EFT recognises that money is merely a form of information.'[31] Martin goes on to delineate four types of EFT, 'representing successive steps towards an EFT society'. The first involves transfers of money between banks, and is by far the most common. Examples of this are the Bank Wire II network in the United States, which transmits funds transfer messages, miscellaneous reimbursement messages and administrative messages, and, on the international level, the SWIFT network.[32] The latter leases private communication lines to offer high speed transmission of money, messages and bank statements between banks in North America and Western Europe. One obvious advantage of such systems, beyond the reduction of paper work, is that they speed up the circulation of money, such 'high velocity money' making it possible to utilize capital that would otherwise be idle.[33]

Martin's second type of EFT refers to transfers between the computers of other corporations and bank computers, whilst the third describes banking terminals for cash dispensing. The fourth type, least developed but potentially of greatest significance, is the electronic point of sale (POS) terminal, which would allow customers in shops and restaurants to directly debit their accounts in payment for goods.[34] A logical consequence of this would be the use of domestic Prestel terminals for the same purpose.

Data Banks, remotely accessed via telecommunications links, are now becoming major elements within communications networks. The first commercial applications were those providing rapidly changing information of value to business, such as rail and airline reservation systems and stock market quotation services. Through initiatives by governments and large corporations, applications are extending inexorably to such specialized forms of information as credit reports, market research information, legal and medical files, health and demographic information, police records, etc.[35]

It is at this corporate level that one can see the power invested in the organization of and access to information—for this information, important because of the commercial and political uses to which it may be put, is treated as proprietary and sold only to those with large resources, i.e., business, governments and scientific establishments.[36] The inaccessibility of such information has created what is becoming a major political issue. The readiness of large corporations to violate 'data privacy' and their ability to convey information across national borders[37] led Sweden, for example, to pass a Data Act (1973) to control the export of data files. This example has been followed by eighteen more countries. Such electronically conveyed information is, of course, extremely difficult to monitor.

A second kind of data bank is that which 'helps a scientist, technician, administrator, librarian, information specialist or other intermediary locate information rapidly and precisely ... '[38], namely that which stores bibliographical and scientific-technical academic information. It is this kind of system that has been used to generate the ideology of free and unbounded access to information for all scholars. The 'on-line information revolution' began in the United States in the early seventies, reaching Britain in 1976 when American systems were relayed via international networks such as Telenet and Tymnet. Most of the world's fifteen or so major on-line retrieval services are in fact situated in the US, the pre-eminent ones being Lockheed Information Systems and Systems Development Corporation (SDC).[39]

In view of the European dependence on American telecommunications, computers and data bases (with about 100 available on the major systems) the Council of Ministers of the Commission of the European communities initiated in 1975 an action plan to establish a data transmission network providing access to databanks within the EEC. The packet-switched data network, now called Euronet, and the array of data banks, designated DIANE, are due to commence operations in late 1979, providing what has been called 'a common market in the field of scientific, technical, economic, legal and social information'.[40]

The two kinds of data bank referred to so far are aimed at the commercial and government markets, but there is a third kind, the data bank accessed to a domestic viewdata terminal (see below) which is oriented towards the private consumer. Such a system will offer less sensitive information, being primarily concerned with forms of electronic publishing and with advertising and sales functions. Such is the disparity between Departments I and II of the economy.

The services we have described—and those to be discussed in the following section—are transmitted through various telecommunication channels, most notably telephone cables, co-axial cables, microwave radio, communication satellite channels and optical fibres. These channels could coexist and reinforce one another, but are in fact becoming the vehicles in a struggle between the giant electronics corporations for control of the 'information infrastructure'. It is the American experience that shows most dramatically the way in which the communications aspect has come to the fore in the struggle to capitalize on 'information technology'. Competition has become acute in the 1970s with the arrival of new kinds of common carrier in competition with the telephone companies (i.e., mainly AT&T). In August 1969, the US Federal Communications Commission (FCC) allowed Microwave Communications Inc. (MCI) to set up a public microwave system between St Louis and Chicago, a system which soon extended nationwide. And the now defunct Datran was also permitted to develop a microwave data communications system. In 1972 the FCC initiated its 'open skies' policy, authorizing common carriers to construct and operate satellite systems for domestic telecommunications. At present there are five satellite carriers: the American Satellite Corporation, RCA Americom, SBS, Comsat General, and Western Union.

In the United States, James Martin distinguishes five different kinds of organization providing data networks.

1. Established Telephone Administrations—an example being AT&T's Dataphone Digital Service (DDS), which was developed as a result of competitive innovations by specialized common carriers;
2. Specialized Common Carriers (e.g., MCI, Datran, the satellite companies);
3. Value-Added Common Carriers (VACCs), which add computers to existing links in order to enhance the services which can be offered to end users (e.g., Telenet, Tymnet, Graphnet);
4. Private corporations;
5. Service corporations (e.g., SWIFT).[42]

Since the importance of the last two has already been made clear we shall here concentrate on the first three types, where the battle to establish a public data network architecture is being waged.

This struggle took off in 1968 when the regulatory climate began to favour competition and thereby to open up the question of whether data communications would operate through the telephone network or through a separate infrastructure. During this period there has been a continuous erosion of AT&T's monopoly position over the phone system, initiated by the 1968 Carterfone decision which permitted the connection of terminal equipment to AT&T's lines.[43] Also of significance were the above mentioned decisions to allow specialized common carriers to compete with the phone company.

The major protagonists in the data communications war are AT&T and IBM, with Xerox, ITT and the VACCs playing important supporting roles. Standing at the frontier where telecommunications and data processing meet, IBM and AT&T are now preparing to invade each other's hitherto sacrosanct territory and defend their own. AT&T is trying to enter the data processing business, and to keep all but carriers out of the telecommunications field, whilst IBM feels the need to ensure that its products have a communications link on which to operate and thereby guarantee the viability of its planned 'office of the future'.[44]

AT&T launched a major assault in July 1978 when it announced a projected Advanced Communications Service (ACS), still in the planning stage, but intended to provide for a shared data communications network, the interfacing of incompatible terminals and computers, various data communications' facilities, and overall maintenance and management of the network. This would create a national communications facility on the same scale and model as the phone service, giving also the possibility of text transmission, electronic mail and electronic office functions. Through its system, which uses relatively standard techniques and aims at a large marketplace, AT&T is seeking to take network protocols and architecture out of the hands of computer vendors and put them into the telecommunications network.[45]

The major obstacle in AT&T's way is that as a common carrier it is precluded by law from providing data processing services. AT&T is arguing that its system does not qualify as data processing because the substantive content of messages is unchanged. But clearly AT&T—forced into a defensive position within its own telecommunications sphere and involved in massive anti-trust legislation—is taking the offensive. As IBM's Lewis Branscomb has observed, ACS 'moves far down the path toward the offering of data processing services by a monopoly carrier'.[46] In so doing it is clearly on a collision course with IBM. A recent commentator has noted that ACS 'marks the long-awaited declaration of commercial war between IBM and Bell ... IBM recognizes the challenge and sees itself as able to respond across the board—in computing, in telecommunications, and in office automation'.[47]

IBM's response has been to enter the satellite communication market through the formation of Satellite Business Systems (SBS) which it jointly owns with Comsat General and Aetna Casualty and Surety Co. Facing competition in its traditional market, IBM is eager to get into new businesses and aims through SBS to provide a communications service for the few hundred large US corporations and government departments with high data transmission rates and dedicated satellites. SBS is due to be launched in the 1980s and will offer such services as teleconferencing, inter-computer communications and high-speed facsimile transmission. The major obstacle for SBS is, however, the same as for ACS—legislation.[48]

In November 1978 Xerox launched its challenge when it disclosed plans for a data communications network, to be available in the early 1980s, which would use leased satellite capacity combined with local microwave radio links. The service, named Xten,[49] will provide document distribution, data communications and teleconferencing facilities. This system, which represents a diversification away from Xerox's traditional business and a move towards the 'office of the future', is aimed, like ACS, at a broad market, but will operate with high speed transmission like SBS.

Finally, it is important to keep in mind the challenge from the VACCs, such as Tymnet and Telenet, which provide enhanced services through the existing telephone network. Significantly, Telenet has recently been merged with General Telephone and Electronics Corp. (GTE) in order to strengthen its hand in the oncoming struggle with ACS, SBS and Xten.

The example of the United States provides, then, an indication of the real struggles and upheavals, only now beginning to take shape, which underpin the convergence of computers and telecommunications. In Britain developments have been more muted, largely due to the monopoly position and legislative powers of 'the most important single business in Britain'[50], the Post Office. There is, however, a strong lobby aimed at relaxing the Post Office monopoly, notably from the Conservative Party which wants to permit 'the establishment of "value added services" on lines leased from the Post

Office by private companies'—such services would include facsimile, teleconferencing and message collection and distribution.[50] What is certain, though, is that in Britain and the US the development of electronic business systems is on the agenda, and that this develop- ment will be structured and guided by corporate rather than democratic processes. It is in this context of the ongoing convergence of telecommunications and computers that we must now look at domestic systems.

Domestic Information Systems

The invasion of the consumer electronics field by 'in- formation technology' is still at an early and tentative stage. How- ever, just as computing and telecommunications are converging with various types of office equipment to form business systems, so too are they converging with domestic electronics equip- ment to create 'home entertainment systems' which will in- corporate television, video equipment, home computers, television games, teletext and viewdata. As yet these two types of system are distinct, but it is seemingly inevitable that they will tend increas- ingly to integrate, with the manufacture of consumer systems being one division within an integral 'intelligent' electronics (i.e., compu- ter/communications) industry. The extent to which this happens rests on the outcome of the impending struggles between existing consumer electronics companies, particularly television manu- facturers and other sectors of the electronics industry which are seeking to penetrate the lucrative consumer markets—notably computer, (micro-)electronics components and telecommunications interests.

Just as the pivot for the electronic office will be the (communicat- ing) word processor, so that for the 'electronic home' will be the television set, enhanced to become a 'video entertainment centre' and, eventually, a form of computer terminal. The whole strategy for bringing 'information technology' into the home is premised on the fact that television sets are already installed in most households. It has been estimated that 97 per cent of British homes have televisions, that there are some 24 million sets currently installed, of which two-thirds are colour, and that there will be about 80 per cent colour television penetration by the early 1980s.[51] Because even the market for colour sets is approaching saturation, and because sales have been in decline since 1975, television manufacturers have been trying to find ways to enhance television sets. As the first generation of colour sets, bought in the early seventies, comes up for replacement, customers are now being offered additional features such as teletext and remote control.

But is is not just the television manufacturing industry that is aiming to amplify the capabilities of the television set. Micro-electronics component manufacturers see television as the basis for developments that will supersede the pocket calculator and digital watch markets—video games and teletext decoders being obvious applications for 'chip' technology. The Post Office is aiming to extend its telecommunications services by using the television console as a computer terminal. Teletext services provide the foundation for using television as a channel for 'electronic publishing'. It has been said that 'in its forty year history, the role of the domestic television receiver has not changed at all. Its sole function is to show programmes distributed from a central point for mass consumption ... essentially television is as it was when the BBC first started broadcasting from Alexandra Palace.'[52] The development of viewdata, video equipment and new cable television services is bringing this phase in the history of television to a close.

In our view the key element for initiating a new phase will be the viewdata service, transforming the TV set into a computer terminal linked to a very extensive data network, and becoming increasingly the centre around which other new products and services will cohere. Important in this context is the fact that it is viewdata that will form a bridge between business and domestic information systems. We have already suggested that electronic message services, EFT and data banks find their domestic extension with the viewdata terminal. The implications of this are that the 'viewdata terminal of the future will not be an adapted television set but an "all-purpose" computer terminal linked to the user's own network for word processing and the like, and possibly also to international data networks'.[53]

Of the other products that we discuss, personal computers will absorb video games, and then probably enter into competition with viewdata systems, which will be seeking to fulfil a similar function. The extent to which they will compete—or even become integrated—remains uncertain. Cable television is significant in so far as particular developments in the United States, where telephone companies are legally barred from providing data processing services, show that cable may well provide an alternative transmission channel to telephone wires for a viewdata service. Finally, we see video equipment as augmenting the traditional role of television as an entertainment medium, but also, through the dense information storage capacity of the video disc, developing into an alternative medium for the dissemination of information. The extent to which all these new products coexist or compete with each other rests on many variables. We can be sure, though, that television is being restructured as an aspect of 'information technology'. As a Philips representative has commented: 'We're on the edge of an information explosion which is going to give a big boost to the electronics industry, because audio and TV will have to become part of the home information system.'[54] Such systems aim to provide a range of information and entertainment services that will intensify media consumption.

Viewdata and Teletext

There are three major channels for dissemination of electronic information. The first is the use of wide-band cables, such as is used by cable television services, and we discuss this below. A second method is that of narrow-band broadcasting, usually called teletext, in which graphic and textual information is inserted into the spare lines of broadcast television signals. An early version of this was the RCA Home Facsimile System, developed in the mid 1960s, which broadcast data in a television signal for hard-copy reproduction by an electrostatic printer associated with a TV receiver. More recently the BBC and IBA have introduced full teletext services, called Ceefax and Oracle respectively, which transmit digitally encoded information to be picked up by a special decoder in the television set, stored in an electronic memory, and generated as words and symbols on the screen. The success of establishing teletext as a full public service rests on the early agreement between the BBC and the IBA to unify teletext standards, and upon the willingness of set manufacturers to develop silicon chip decoders. Although in early 1978 there were only 8000 teletext sets in operation, it is estimated that by 1985 7 million households will receive the teletext service.[55] Further success will depend upon such innovations as a printer for copying teletext pages, and the development of 'telesoftware', by which is meant the capability to broadcast computer programmes to a receiver modified to function as a domestic computer.[56]

Teletext, however, does have limitations, the most important of which are that the number of 'pages' of information that it can broadcast is restricted and that it is only a 'one-way' service with no facility for interaction with the information bank. Such limitations do not apply to the third kind of channel for data dissemination, the narrow-band cable system, known as videotex or viewdata, which uses the telephone cable network to allow an interactive service. Besides allowing a more sophisticated use of a central data bank, viewdata also permits such extra 'active' functions as message transmission and EFT services. As such it threatens to make teletext redundant.[57]

The first and best know viewdata system is that pioneered by the British Post Office and now registered as Prestel. It was inaugurated as an experimental system in September 1975, and opened as a public service in London in March 1979. The Post Office has now spent £17 million on development, and plans to spend another £18 million over the next two years. Prestel, which was designed to be compatible with teletext protocols, is intended to be cheap, standardized and easy to operate.[58] Information for Prestel's data bank is supplied by independent 'information producers', ranging from educational institutions to retail companies, and from news media to charity organizations, for whom the Post Office acts as a common carrier. Unlike teletext, there is no technical limit to the amount of data Prestel can handle, and even at this early stage its present 163 competing suppliers of information are providing 122,000 'pages'.[59]

As yet Prestel has not taken off in any big way, with sets still costing £1200, and there are only an estimated 1000 viewdata sets installed. Mackintosh consultants calculate that there will be about 300,000 installations by 1985, but stress that viewdata is a product for the 1990s rather than the 1980s.[60] The main objective for the Post Office at present is to gain international acceptance for Prestel, both by selling it abroad—which it has done in Germany, Holland, Hong Kong and Switzerland—and by having it accepted as the international standard for viewdata equipment. Already other countries are developing similar systems, notably Canada, France, West Germany, Japan and Sweden. The French system, Antiope, represents a particular threat to Prestel, in that it combines teletext and viewdata into one system and could also integrate easily with business systems such as CWPs and the data bases to be linked by Euronet.[61]

The flexibility and potential of viewdata is illustrated by the variety of services it will provide. The major function is to provide information (topical, reference, professional, commercial, etc.) which, because Prestel is interactive, can be tailored to the particular needs of individual users. Secondly, viewdata is a message communication medium. Although at present the message service is rudimentary, it could provide the basis for an electronic mail service between subscribers. Thirdly, it can provide the basis for domestic

EFT services, allowing users to make purchases of goods sold through viewdata networks. A fourth possibility is that the viewdata computers could be used for providing a calculations service—although the development of 'telesoftware' is a more likely prospect. A UK firm called CAP has produced a form of computer software that can be transmitted down telephone lines and stored in suitably adapted Prestel receivers. This endows the Prestel terminal with 'intelligence', turning it into a personal computer.[62]

Although Prestel was originally aimed at the general public it would seem that its emphasis has now shifted to the commercial environment. It would seem that its business applications will lead increasingly to its incorporation into business information networks. Recently the Post Office waived the rule that only TV receivers could link with Prestel; in consequence firms other than television manufacturers can make equipment for the viewdata system. Now electronics firms are also manufacturing private viewdata systems specifically for the business market—Philips has already produced a system, and Pye, STC and GEC are working on such equipment. It seems probable that computing and telecommunications interests will see viewdata as a profitable field for investment, and that initially the business market will be the target for exploitation.

Video Games and Personal Computers

The progress of video games reflects the rapid changes in micro-electronics technology in the 1970s. The first consumer video games were marketed (by Magnavox) in the United States in 1972. By 1975 the development of special purpose integrated circuits made possible the incorporation of several games into one package. We have now reached the third generation of games, which are based on micro-processors (i.e., very small computers), and can be programmed to play many different games by inserting 'software' packages. The success of video games is illustrated by the rise in UK sales from 95,000 in 1976 to 625,000 units in 1978, with programmable games taking a growing market share.[63]

What is most important in the context of this article is the fact that the upmarket video game is becoming indistinguishable from the personal computer. Commodore's PET home computer, for example, is based on a micro-processor similar to that used in Fairchild's video games unit. Personal computers, first marketed in March 1975, represent the replacement market not only for electronic games but also for pocket calculators. Launched initially as enhanced video games, the personal computer will be aimed not only at the domestic market, but increasingly at the business and professional sector. In 1978 250,000 were sold and this figure is expected to rise to 500,000 in 1979. Given such an expanding market it is not surprising that companies like Hewlett-Packard, Sharp, Siemens, Texas Instruments and Toshiba are establishing their positions, whilst General Electric, IBM and RCA have plans to enter the field.[64]

In the attempt to bring 'information technology' into the home, personal computers present a serious rival to viewdata systems (particularly in America). Developments are under way to link them to television screens and to provide them with communications facilities. The FCC, indeed, intends to encourage the use of personal computer networks for electronic mail services. As viewdata systems and personal computer networks come to look increasingly alike,[65] we can be sure that there will be a long period of conflict in which each will attempt to assert its supremacy in the single long-term market for which both are competing.

Cable Television

James Martin has said that 'few media have a greater potential for changing the culture of a society than the co-axial cables being laid into homes by the cable television companies'.[66] Since the early 1950s, when cable television was first developed in areas with poor broadcast reception, ambitious claims have often been made for its potential. Here we are restricted to looking at cable television only in so far as it converges with developments in 'information technology'. What is so important about the co-axial cables used in wired television is their enormous information-carrying capacity. This permits not only many extra programme channels (currently up to thirty with more to become available with improvements introduced by optical fibre cables), but also additional services such as telephone and viewphone facilities, meter reading, electronic mail delivery, fire detection alarms, and access to computers.[67] The nature of the cable, as opposed to broadcasting, also allows it to operate in both directions, and thus to provide an interactive service. It is such versatility that gives cable an undisputed long term potential, and, moreover, makes it a rival to viewdata.

This applies particularly to the United States, which has some 4000 cable systems reaching over 13 million homes. Since 1968, when regulatory restrictions on cable TV began to be lifted, there have been indicatons that some of cable's potential, including a viewdata service, may well be fulfilled. This would, of course, be in the hands of the large conglomerates now controlling cable systems. The most developed example, which also highlights the corporate aspect of cable, is the Warner Communications' QUBE system located in Columbus, Ohio. This system provides thirty channels: ten television stations, ten pay-TV channels and ten 'community channels' providing local programmes and text information. The subscriber is provided with a hand-held control unit with which he is able to select programmes for which he pays at differential rates. His request is processed by one of four computers, which also prepares a monthly bill. QUBE also allows viewers to 'talk back' to the studio by pushing buttons on their control units—in this way they can vote on programmes or make bids in televised auctions. In addition to this pseudo-participation, Warners are planning to add such facilities as fire and burglar alarms linked from subscribers' houses to the central computers.[68]

What such a system could become is foreshadowed in the Osaka suburb of Higashi-Ikoma, where a cable system using fibre optic cables has a camera and microphone installed in subscribers' homes to permit 'true' two-way television. This project is in fact a test-bed for the 'wired city', and is actively supported by such companies as Matsushita, Fujitsu, Toshiba, and by the Ministry of International Trade and Industry. Additional services, for instance electronic text transfers, will be added by the 1990s.[69] Another project, begun as early as 1972 at Tama, a satellite town of Tokyo, uses co-axial cables to offer subscribers reception of video programmes, computer-aided learning, data retrieval, seat reservation, tele-metering, facsimile and other services.[70]

Video

Cable and video are the most recent entertainment media, and as such, will be components in the evolving domestic information/entertainment systems. Although they may come to coexist, they are in many ways rivals in the attempt to bypass broadcasting and supply commercial entertainment to television owners. Video may well have the edge in that its means of dissemination is especially simple and requires no expensive infrastructure. This is both the strength and weakness of video. Lacking any need for a foundation on a telecommunications network (though utilizable within one) it is operable without massive capital investment. At the same time, precisely because it does not possess this telecommunications element probably limits its long-term role in an area where the latter is a critical prerequisite for the integration which will allow the production of comprehensive systems for the home.

Despite this, video is currently taking off rapidly. Video tape/cassette recorders are at present being extensively marketed as a logical complement to the television. These extensions of traditional TV are limited in what they offer. They allow chiefly the manipulation of viewers' time along with the opportunity to purchase pre-packaged video materials (e.g., golf tuition, soft pornography).[71] As such, they are of less significance than the more versatile video disc.

Throughout the 1970s there have been attempts to develop and market a videodisc. Except for the unsuccessful Telefunken-Decca (TelDec) disc launched prematurely in 1975, the first commercially viable disc first went on sale in Atlanta, Georgia in December 1978. This Philips MCA disc may well come into fierce competition with any of the forty or so discs now being developed world-wide.[72] Because these videodiscs all have different systems and standards, and are therefore incompatible with each other, a race is now on to establish a product that will become the industry standard. That the stakes are high[73] is testified by the presence in the field of such major corporations as Philips, RCA, Sony, Thomson-CSF, JVC and Mitsubishi.

There are several important points to be made about the videodisc. The first is that is is a significant new entertainment medium. It will be a cheap complement to the LP record: currently a disc version of *Jaws* costs as little as £7. The second, and more important, point is that the disc is also an instrument for publishing and information storage. The Philips optical-laser videodisc is able to provide a freeze-frame facility with, at present, the capacity for 54,000 still frames. This means that it could develop as an electronic book. The production of cheap throwaway discs could make it an electronic form of journalism and advertising.[74] Moreover, this dense information storage capacity makes the disc a very promising information medium. IBM and Xerox, for example, are reported to be working on videodisc systems, probably for the purpose of storing commercial and industrial data.[75] Already the US Department of Defence is making use of the Philips/MCA disc for purposes of information collection.[76]

The videodisc is thus more than an entertainment medium. Potentially it is a new communications medium. As such it stands alongside viewdata, personal computers and cable television as one of the new media which are competing in the race to produce domestic information/entertainment systems. While it may lack the long-term potential of other technologies which draw more on telecommunications and computing facilities the videodisc is a powerful medium. The prospect of its eventual integration into home information systems, wherein it will serve as a video library, is real.

3

> Machinery is accomplishing in the world what man has failed to do by preaching, propaganda, or the written word.
>
> Henry Ford

This article has deliberately taken a broad and sweeping perspective in order to point to the convergence and integration of what might otherwise be taken for disparate products. It has tried to interpret the significance of developments in 'information technology' in a way that is opposed to the idealism of futurists and post-industrialists who seem oblivious to the real relations of power underpinning their 'information age'. We can agree with these thinkers that information is becoming an increasingly important phenomenon: but there will be no society *based* on information. Analyses which suggest such a scenario do so only by overlooking the practical social contexts from and in which information is produced and situated.

On the other hand, it is our belief that these newly emerging phenomena cannot be adequately thought out if it is assumed that they can be pigeon-holed in different 'levels' of the 'social formation'. Are business information systems a part of the 'economic' level, while domestic systems belong to some 'ideological' (or 'cultural') sphere? What in the past has been called base and superstructure are now tightly interwoven, an organic unity. To define, *a priori*, 'culture' and 'economy' as external to each other, to assume the structural autonomy of culture, is to close one's theory to a reality that is subverting it.

Recent developments in 'information technology' need to be historicized, that is, put into social and historical context. What is especially important is that, although they have a complex pre-history, it is now, in the period of crisis and recession of the 1970s, that they are really beginning to take shape. In our view this is primarily because 'information technology', and more generally the micro-electronics technology on which it is based, represents a possible solution to the present crisis. Potentially 'information technology' could provide a foundation for a new cycle of production, a new phase of accumulation. Moreover, it is by theorizing 'information technology' in relation to this process of accumulation that one is able to situate it in a substantive context. Thereby it becomes an integral component of a real social process which is the history of capital, rather than being related to some abstraction called the 'economic' or 'capitalism'.

'Information technology' will play a central role in generating a new cycle of capital and consumer goods. But this process cannot be taken to be merely an 'economic' activity. Accumulation is a 'real life process' which expresses all social relations (those of both work and of leisure). It is that 'organic set of social relations whose evolution is the condition for perpetuating the wage relation'.[77] It embraces the labour process (ways of working, structures of authority, etc.). the kinds of consumption it requires (in recent years most obviously in the form of mass consumption), and the social relations and lifestyles that support it. Aglietta has stressed that Fordism—the phase of accumulation now in crisis—cannot be regarded as merely a technical form of the labour process, but it is in fact 'an articulation between process of production and mode of consumption'.[78] This is of course to take up the insights of Gramsci on *Americanism and Fordism*. Gramsci recognized that accumulation is a total social process, arguing that if Fordism is to be established, then 'a long process is needed ... during which a change must take place in social conditions and in the way of life and habits of individuals'.[79] The history of accumulation is not an economic record, but the history of a whole series of social changes.

It is not by chance that we mention here the name of Henry Ford. For the phase of accumulation that is presently taking shape will supersede, yet extend and elaborate, that initiated by Fordism. That is, against those post-industrialists who argue that 'information technology' marks the end of a certain kind of society, we see it as actually a continuation of capitalist organization. In particular it extends and refines the Fordist variant. Central to this continuity with Fordism is the question of machinery, by which is meant 'the historical reshaping of the traditional, inherited means of labour into a form adequate to capital'.[80] Machinery, especially since the days of Fordism and increasingly today, is the means of mediating the social relations of production.

As we have said, technology which adopts micro-electronic devices will provide a major contribution to a new phase of accumulation. The reason for this is that it is a 'heartland' technology which will give 'leverage' to almost all industrial sectors.[81] A central part in any attempt to restructure production will be played by 'information technology'. The latter is axiomatic for many reasons. One factor is that it constitutes a massive potential market for suppliers of 'information technology', recent estimates predicting as much as a 30 per cent annual growth in sales for particular products.[82] Also very important will be the ability of 'information technology' to introduce mechanization into areas that have not previously been characterized by automation. Technological 'efficiency' introduced into offices, libraries, government and administration will necessarily incur similar sorts of reorganization, deskilling, routinization, rationalization, and alienation that have become a feature of productive industries such as manufacturing.

Above all, perhaps, the integration of computers and telecommunications at the heart of 'information technology' will extend and intensify the already advanced separation of mental and manual labour. If Taylor attempted the 'deliberate gathering in on the part of those on the management's side of all the great mass of traditional knowledge which in the past has been in the heads of the workmen ... '[83]; and if Henry Ford refined this principle by investing machinery, rather than managers, with this knowledge; then we may say of 'information technology' that it will carry this principle to new sectors of industry and administration. And we can even go further, to suggest that potentially 'information technology' is tending towards the imposition of a similar principle beyond the limits of the factory and office and on to the scale of society as a whole. That is, we can perhaps say that we are moving towards a situation in which 'general social knowledge' is being absorbed into the machinery of 'information technology'. As we witness the enroachment of the control culture, government information and private data banks on to an increasingly observed public we are perhaps experiencing a shift to 'rationalized' practices far beyond the workplace.

We have shown that 'information technology' will also develop in the domestic sector. Products originating as enhancements of the television will provide a new generation of electronics consumer durables, facilitating an extension and intensification of media consumption. Inevitably these products will provide electronic channels into the home for advertising, consumer information, electronic selling and electronic publishing. On this basis the speed and efficiency with which commodities and capital circulate will be increased. And so too will domestic information/entertainment systems extend that 'mobile privatization' that, for Raymond Williams, characterizes the present broadcasting media. The roseate picture of the consumer participating in politics, education, etc., from the comfort of his living room ought not deflect us from the fact that this 'interaction' will take place in a context which forms part of a growing privatization of life. Moreover, this process itself must be gauged against the increasing centralization of information ushered in by the organizations and interests which are developing and exploiting 'information technologies'.

Domestic and business information systems will tend to converge. It is clear that such convergence will develop under the dominance of business systems, which will assimilate consumer systems (e.g., Prestel) and extend their own networks (e.g., EFT, electronic mail) in so far as it is to their advantage. This convergence will do little to break down the separation of, on the one hand, increasingly centralized private and governemt data networks handling 'sensitive' and 'valuable' police, military, or business information, and, on the other hand, publicly accessible networks which handle commercial and comparatively less important information.

Finally, it is worth emphasizing that the success of 'information technology' as a resolution for the current crisis is not assured. It will depend on a number of factors, not least capital's ability to co-ordinate the possibilities for developing productivity and strengthening control over social relations. IBM for one acknowledges that the successful implementation of this technology is not guaranteed. They not only have to contend with fierce competitors, but also—and in the long term much more problematical—with an unpredictable public which can be awkward in matters of social control.

Recognizing this, IBM have started offering history lessons. Anticipating and addressing suspicions and fears felt about the introduction of 'information technology' a recent advertisement tells us that 'Between the years 1811 and 1816, a band of textile workers had just the answer to the threat of technology. They literally threw spanners in the works.' We are told that 'the action of the Luddites carries a very instructive lesson' as regards recent technological innovation.

Such a public relations campaign undermines opposition (and potential opposition) by asserting that the choice is a stark one between an unconstructive dismissal of invention or acceptance of 'progress'. Defining this 'progress' IBM distorts both past and present: the vista becomes one of neutral technology, inevitable advance, harmony ... In short, no choice at all. A first step in opposition is to lay bare the real interests which are disguised by the rhetorics of 'progress'. Our article, we hope, has added to the analyses which probe the rationales behind the introduction of 'information technology'. Much more difficult will be the transition from theoretical accounts to practical encounters with the new technologies in everyday situations.

NOTES

1. R. Williams, *Marxism and Literature*. OUP, 1977, p. 80-81. (our emphasis).
2. It is to Raymond Williams and E. P. Thompson especially that we are indebted for historicizing Marxist concepts, providing a basis for by-passing sterile debates which merely polish and refine abstract concepts.
3. See I. Barron and R. Curnow, *The Future with Microelectronics*, Frances Pinter, 1979, p. 39-42.
4. H. I. Schiller, 'Authentic National Development versus the Free Flow of Information and the New Communications Technology' in *Communications Technology and Social Policy*, [G. Gerbner et al (eds.)] New York, Wiley-Interscience, 1973, p. 475.
5. A. Mattelart, *Multinationalinales et systèms de communication*, Paris, Anthropos, 1976.
6. A. Mattelart, 'Cultural Imperialism in the Multinationals' Age,' *Instant Research on Peace and Violence*, 6, 4, 1976, p. 160.
7. Mattelart, *Multinationales* ... p. 2; 'the strategy that the dominant classes have adopted to thwart popular movements', A. Mattelart. 'Les appareils idéologiques de L' "Etat multinational" ', *Politique Aujourd-'hui*, January-February, 1975, p. 65.
8. H. I. Schiller, *Mass Media and American Empire*, New York, Augustus M. Kelley, 1969, p. 1 cf. H. I. Schiller. 'Computer Systems: Power for Whom and for What?' *Journal of Communication*, 28, 4, Autumn, 1978.
9. 'the new role ascribed to knowledge is the culminating and convergent point of all post-industrial theorists', K. Kumar, *Prophecy and Progress: The Sociology of Industrial and Post-Industrial Society*. Allen Lane, 1978, p. 221.
10. D. Bell, 'The Coming of Post-Industrial Society; *Dialogue*, 11, 2, 1978, p. 4. Daniel Bell has updated his thesis to take account of new technologies. See: 'Teletext and Technology', *Encounter*, (XLVIII), June 1977, p. 9-29. 'Communications Technology—for better or for worse?', *Harvard Business Review*, May-June 1979, p. 20-42.
11. J. Martin, *Future Developments in Telecommunications*, Prentice-Hall, 2nd edition, 1977, p. 17.
12. J. Martin, *The Wired Society*, Prentice-Hall, 1978, p. 6.
13. M. Williams, 'On-Line Retrieval—Today and Tomorrow; *Proceedings of 1st International On-Line Information Meeting*, London, 13-15 December 1977, Oxford and New York, Learned Information, 1978, p. 1.

14. J. McHale, *The Changing Information Environment*, Elek, 1976, p. 21, 38.
15. M. Laver, *Computers, Communications and Society*, OUP, 1975, p. 1.
16. D. Bell, *The Coming of Post-Industrial Society*, New York, Basic Books, 1973, p. 20.
17. For a critique of Bell on these grounds see K. Kumar, 1978, *op. cit.,* esp. p. 219-30.
18. Conservative Party, *Proposals for a Conservative Information Technology Policy*, Provisional Draft Report, mimeo, 1979, p. 6.
19. Y. Masuda, 'A New Development Stage of the Information Revolution', *Applications of Computer & Telecommunications Systems*, Paris, OECD, 1975.
20. We cover these issues and areas with the necessarily detailed historical reconstruction in a forthcoming book *The Social Meanings of Information Technology*.
21. See E. Braun and S. MacDonald, *Revolution in Miniature*, 1978, CUP, 1978. The micro-electronic device is aptly seen by C. Freeman as a 'heartland' technology—i.e., as a technology in the manner of steam power and the electric engine. See his paper *Government Policies for Industrial Innovation*, The Ninth J. D. Bernal Lecture, 1978, p. 12.
22. *Report of the National Committee on Computer Networks*, Dep. of Industry, London, 1978, p. 1.
23. I. de Sola Pool. International aspects of computer communications. *Telecommunications Policy*, December 1976, p. 33.
24. On the significance of the entry of oil concerns like Exxon, Sun and Gulf into office automation see L. McCartney, 'Exxon: Another Computer Giant?' *Datamation*, July 1978; and Exxon's new tactics for diversification. *Financial Times*, 22 May, 1979.
25. See *Office Technology: The Trade Union Response*, APEX, March 1979.
26. A. D. Wohl, 'Communicating Word Processors', *Datamation*, March, 1978; D. J. W. Jones, 'Towards the Paperless Office', *Post Office Telecommunications Journal*, Spring, 1977; A. E. Cawkell, *'The Paperless Office'*, Institute for Scientific Information, Uxbridge, 1979.
27. 'An office information system is a network of interactive computer terminals which functions as a medium for textual and other information, and which actively applies computer power to help the user process, communicate, and manage that information.' R. C. Harkness, 'Office Information Systems,' *Telecommunications Policy*, June 1978, p. 92.
28. 'Post Office Thinks about Electronic Letterboxes', *New Scientist*, 7 December 1978, p. 770.
29. On Teletex see R. Clark, 'Videotex—an Overview of Electronic Information Services,' *Computer Communications*, April 1979, p. 52-3; J. Soulsby, 'Electronic Mail', *Computer Communications*, February 1979, p. 13.
30. 'Fight over Electronic Mail', *Datamation*, December, 1978. On EMSs more generally see J. Soulsby *art. cit.;* R. R. Panko, 'The Outlook for Computer Mail', *Telecommunications Policy*, June 1977.
31. J. Martin, *Future Developments ... op. cit.,* p. 240.

32. E. Meyers, 'EFT: Momentum Gathers; *Datamation,* October 1978.

33. See S. Rose, 'More Bang for the Buck: The Magic of Electronic Banking', *Fortune,* May 1977.

34. See, for example, Barron and Curnow, 1979, *op.cit.,* p. 154-9.

35. See *Computers and Telecommunications,* Paris, OECD, 1973, p. 67.

36. C. Martin, 'Computer Systems: Prospects for a Public Information Network', *Journal of Communication,* Autumn, 1978, p. 173.

37. See *Report of the Committee on Data Protection,* Cmnd 7341, HMSO, 1978; J. Eger, 'Transborder Data Flow', *Datamation,* 15 November 1978.

38. C.A. Cuarda, 'Commercially Funded On-line Retrieval Services —Past, Present and Future' *Aslib proceedings,* January 1978, p. 2.

39. See C. A. Cuarda, *op.cit.* p. 7-8; D. Magrill, 'Information at the Touch of a Button', *New Scientist,* 12 January 1978.

40. W. Huber, 'Recent Developments within Euronet', *Computer Communications,* April, 1978, p. 79; see also M. White, 'Why Europe is caught in the data net', *New Scientist,* 1 February 1979; P. Williams, 'Access to Information in Europe', *Computer Communications,* December 1978.

41. W. White and M. Holmes, 'The Future of Commercial Satellite Telecommunications', *Datamation,* July 1978.

42. J. Martin, *Future Developments ... op.cit* p. 162-3.

43. P. Gibson, 'Ma Bell Faces Life', *Forbes,* 1 November 1977; J. M. Eger, 'Consumer Needs and the Telecommunications Monopoly sought by AT&T', *Computers and People,* January 1978.

44. H. Anderson, 'IBM versus Bell in Telecommunications', *Datamation,* May 1977.

45. On ACS see R. Rinder, 'ACS is Coming', *Datamation,* December 1978; W. D. Gardner, 'Bell's ACS Network', *Datamation,* June 1978; P. Hirsch. Ma Bell Drops the First Shoe. *Datamation,* August 1978.

46. Branscomb on ACS. *Datamation,* October 1978, p. 55.

47. D. Butler, 'IBM in Europe', *Datamation,* October 1978, p. 108.

48. V. McLellan, SBS Partnership may be Doomed', *Datamation,* January 1979.

49. On Xten see 'Xerox Plans Nationwide Data Transmission', *Financial Times,* 17 November 1978; P. Hirsch, 'Xten from Xerox', *Datamation,* December 1978.

50. *Proposals for a Conservative Information Technology Policy,* mimeo, 1979, p. 41.

51. On television installations see *Social Trends 9,* HMSO, 1979; *B.R.E M.A. Annual Reports;* 'Tune into Cash-rich TV Rental Shares', *Investors Chronicle,* 26 May 1978; 'TV Rental', *Investors Chronicle,* 19 January 1979.

52. A. Burkitt, 'Teletext Arrives on the Screen', *New Scientist,* 27 May 1976, p. 459.

53. Post Office Engineering Union, *The Modernisation of Telecommunications,* June 1979, p. 54.

54. Quoted in C. Barron, 'Format Fears at Philips', *Management Today,* August 1978, p. 101.

55. *Teletext and Viewdata.* Mackintosh Publications, 1977, p. 83.

56. TV Software Could be Hard on Prestel', *New Scientist*, 2 November 1978, p. 361.

57. To some extent the services are compatible at present and they may be able to coexist. Teletext has one major advantage in that its service is free to those owning a television and decoder.

58. E. Williams, 'Strengths and Weaknesses of Prestel', *Computer Communications*, 2, 2, April 1979.

59. 'Viewdata: Whose System Wins?', *Economist*, 12 May 1979, p. 115.

60. *Teletext and Viewdata*, Mackintosh Publications, 1977.

61. *Economist*, 12 May 1979, p. 116; R. Clark, 'Videotex—an Overview of Electronic Information Services', *Computer Communications*, 2, 2, April 1979, p. 52-3; B. Marti. Videotex Developments in France, *ibid.*

62. On the applications of viewdata see S. Fedida, 'Viewdata', *Electronics and Power*, June 1977; M. Tyler, 'Videotex Prestel and Teletext', *Telecommunications Policy*, March 1979; P. Marsh, 'Prestel Impressions', *New Scientist*, 9 November 1978.

63. *Video Games*, Mackintosh Publications, 1978.

64. 'The Personal Computer Strives to Come of Age', *New Scientist*, 19 May 1979; *Personal Computers*, SRI International Business Intelligence Program, Guidelines no. 1034, August 1978.

65. N. Valéry, 'Foot in the Door of the Home Computer', *New Scientist*, 14 April 1977, p. 63-5.

66. J. Martin, *'Future Developments … ' op.cit.* p. 133.

67. See *Television Advisory Committee 1972*, Papers of the Technical Sub-Committee, HMSO, 1973, p. 66.

68. P. Fiddick, 'Towards an electronic democracy?' *The Listener*, 10 May 1979; 'The Cable-TV Industry Gets Moving Again', *Business Week*, 21 November 1977.

69. P. Bonner. 'Talking Back on Television', *The Listener*, 19 April 1979; 'Wired City: Industrial Testbed', *Economist*, 13 January 1979.

70. *Computers and Telecommunications*, Paris, OECD, 1973, p. 122.

71. See, *inter alia*, R. Field, 'Videocassettes: What and Where They Are', *Science Digest*, (83), January 1978, p. 79-83.

72. See *Screen Digest*, November 1978, p. 211-14.

73. *Forbes*, 1 June 1976, p. 24; 'Videodiscs: the Expensive Race to be First', *Business Week*, 15 September 1975.

74. *The Futurist*, October 1977, p. 312.

75. A. Horder, 'Videodiscs—their Potential for Information Storage and Retrieval', *Reprographics Quarterly*, Spring, 1979.

76. J. Chittock, *Financial Times*, 23 November 1978, p. 26.

77. M. Aglietta, *A Theory of Capitalist Regulation*, NLB, 1979, p. 111.

78. *ibid*, p. 117.

79. A. Gramsci, *Selections from the Prison Notebooks*, Lawrence and Wishart, 1971, p. 312.

80. K. Marx, *Grundrisse*, Penguin, 1973, p. 694.

81. For an overview of sectors that will be influenced by micro-electronics see 'Coming to Terms with Micro-chips', *Economist*, 2 June 1979.

82. *Financial Times*, 24 November 1978.

83. Taylor's Testimony Before the Special House Committee, in F.W. Taylor, *Scientific Management*, Harper and Row, 1964, p. 40. (The continuity between Taylorism and post-industrialism is made clear by Peter Drucker, a leading advocate of the 'information society', when he notes that 'the most important step towards the "knowledge economy" was ... Scientific Management (which understood that) the key to productivity was knowledge, not sweat'. P. Drucker. *The Age of Discontinuity*. Heinemann, 1969, p. 254.

RADICAL SCIENCE AND ITS ENEMIES

Hilary Rose and Steven Rose

In the 1972 *Socialist Register* we analysed the development of the radical science movement from its birth in the struggle against the genocidal science rained upon the peoples of Indochina to its often halting and uneven attempts to develop theory[1]. Although we called that paper 'The Radicalization of Science', it actually spoke of the double process by which science which had been seen as socially and technically progressive was increasingly recognized as incorporated within the state, and the radicalization of *scientists* in opposition to this process. As part of that movement, we saw its task as the winning and transformation of the scientific knowledge itself, the making of a science for the people. Whilst it was easy to see the immediate tasks of opposition to the development and uses of particular science and technologies, the theoretical task the movement set itself was more fundamental. Was science a timeless, autonomous intellectual system which stood apart from and above social conflict, or was it part of that conflict, and, if so, how? Whilst the movement had few clear theoretical formulations, it had, in common with the rest of the New Left, certain sharp insights, primarily that the understanding of the social functions of science would be forged out of the contradictions of experience; theory could not be developed from within an ivory tower, even if Marxism was inscribed in gold over the entrance. The May 1968 events, the cultural revolution and the Tet offensive were part of a revolutionary optimism, shared by the radical science movement, of the realizable prospect of human liberation.

Today, in the context of the deepening crisis of capital, economic struggles are central, and the clarity and optimism of the earlier period has retreated. Whilst at the height of the extra-parliamentary movement it was a matter of indifference just what was the flavour of the state machinery managing British capitalism, the mere nuances of Wilson or Heath, Callaghan or Thatcher, today these differences are seen as matters impinging on survival. There has been a corresponding ideological struggle waged over the

317

challenge to bourgeois hegemony made in the wake of '68. Symbolized by the *Berufsverbot* in West Germany, with its refractions in Britain through the pusillanimous Gould Report, the ideological issues are also fundamental to an understanding of the strengths (and weaknesses) of British fascism and the rise to power of the most reactionary conservative administration for many decades.

It is not our purpose here to document the history of specific organizations within the radical science movement. Instead, grasping the old nettle of red and expert, we want to talk about those struggles in which the movement has had a particular part to play, those which have been located primarily within the ideological domain and have at their core the question of the nature of scientific knowledge itself.

The themes which, we argued in 1972, informed the developing movement were these: of the use and abuse of science, the neutrality of science and the self-management of science. As the decade advanced, questions originally posed as those of the use and abuse of science were gradually recognized as a feature of the incorporation of science into the machinery of the capitalist state, making it possible to begin the development of a political economy of science.[2] The radical science movement of the seventies thus only slowly recaptured and moved beyond the level of theoretical analysis achieved much earlier by a previous generation. More than forty years ago, in a book written by an anonymous collective of a dozen communist economists, scientists and technicians, *Britain Without Capitalists*[3] there is a key chapter, (actually written by Desmond Bernal) 'Science and Education', which begins bluntly, 'It is not usual to think of science as an industry', and goes on to show that it is, but 'unlike other industries that are concerned in keeping a certain state of production going, science is concerned with changing that state'. This analysis was lost in the exigencies of war, the inheritance of Stalinism, the cold war and the subsequent dissipation of the 1930s science movement into either techno-economism or an increasingly vacuous internationalism. A Marxist interpretation of the radical science movement of the 1930s which also recognizes its subsequent fate, remains to be made. The only account to date of some of its key activists is by Werskey[4] who interprets history in terms of the psychological and social origins of the individuals themselves. His failure to understand the political forces which led workers and intellectuals to join the Communist Party in the 1930s gives his work an unfortunate cold war flavour, of intellectuals manipulated by Comintern intrigue.

To return to the theoretical developments of the 1970s, the analysis of the neutrality of science led to the exploration of the possibilities of making a new socialist science and to the re-examination of the consequences of Stalinism in science, the Lysenko question in the USSR, now illuminated by the work of Lecourt [5] and of Lewontin and Levins.[6] Self management led to the hard practical realization of the near impossibility of creating socialism in one laboratory[7] and to the theoretical clarification of Levy-Leblond with his distinction between the ideology of and in science.[8].

We cannot consider further the present dimension of these theoretical issues, though, without first referring to the practical struggles in which scientific and technical workers have been engaged. In part, these have inevitably reflected a tightening job situation, resulting in the unionization of scientists and technologists, especially through ASTMS and TASS. Within these unions, scientists have fought on issues which have not only defended their economic position but also fused science and politics. A vital area has been that of health and safety at work, a struggle in which ASTMS in particular has been deeply involved and which was symbolized by the ASTMS-led campaign in the aftermath of the death from smallpox of the Birmingham University technician, Janet Parker, infected from a laboratory on a floor below her own work. The inquiry following her death revealed the gross mismanagement of the laboratory, and the resulting hazards to technicians and scientists working in its vicinity—an issue on which ASTMS had been campaigning since the mid 1960s. A decade of technology-based accidents, from Flixborough and Séveso to Harrisburg has also been one of increasing involvement of left scientists and engineers with shop stewards' movements in the campaigns towards the implementation of the health and safety legislation and the demands of workers to understand and to secure protection from the hazards of their work. It is this area where health groups, scientists, militants, and left groups have been able most effectively to join forces to combat the human destructiveness of the labour process under capital. These actions have ranged from the exposure of the use of toxic chemicals in the leather processing industry in Naples and the carcinogenic nature of vinylchloride used in British factories, and bringing to womens' attention the danger of cancer from hair dyes, to opposition to the use of 2, 4, 5-T, once a defoliant in Vietnam, now a dangerous herbicide rejected by American rural communities resisting the health hazards imposed upon them by agribusiness.

The second symbol within Britain of the fusion of science and politics in a shopfloor campaign is that of the Lucas Aerospace Combine Committee. At Lucas, the workers were faced with structural changes in engineering, electronics and aerospace, generated by cut-backs in defence spending and the transformation of a British company into a multinational switching investments across national boundaries. Going beyond the forms of struggle developed in the late sixties of occupations and factory work-ins and transforming the rhetoric of the popular calls of the mid 1970s for worker participation in management, the Stewards' Combine Committee developed an entire alternative 'corporate plan' for Lucas. The political and industrial strengths of a combine committee which ranged through the big engineering sections to the highly technically qualified draughtsmen of TASS were brought to bear on showing how the skills of the Lucas workforce and fixed capital of the plants could be used in the generation, not of military or aerospace hardware or alienating and de-skilling robotics, but of socially usefully technologies. The strategy of the development of alternative plans as part of the struggle against factory closures in the technology-based industries in the late 1970s has now been generalized far beyond Lucas, although the particular combination of political skills, technological vision and industrial muscle have not always been so abundantly available. How far this strategy will survive the changed political climate of the 1980s, however, cannot be taken for granted. If the re-inflation of the defence budget by the new Conservative administration results in a surge of new orders for British aerospace companies, for instance, the Combine's demands for socially useful work may weaken where the work force is relieved to have any jobs at all. Further, as the Combine is very well aware, there is a continuous danger either of co-option, by being outmanoeuvred by management, or anaesthetized by being taken out of the factories and into the only too eager hands of the universities and polytechnics.

The systematic agitation and education conducted through the collectively produced magazines and pamphlets of the radical science movement contributed to the placing of science and technology on to the agenda of the labour movement, not only as a material force of production but as one indifferent to its human toll. The critique of Taylorism and the work of Braverman drew theoretical attention to the deskilling nature of the new labour processes. *Impascience* in France, *Sapere* in Italy, the long standing *Science for the People* in the United States and *Science for People* in the

U.K. spoke on these issues from the socialist wing of the movement. The anarchist wing, reflected in such publications as *Undercurrents,* while often naive about alternative solutions (so that for the energy crisis they tended to look to windmills and the domestic production of methane) nonetheless were able to respond to ecological issues such as those posed by Concorde, with which the left, trapped by its concern to maintain employment, failed to grapple. Something of the same difficulty has been reflected in the anti-nuclear movement in France: while the *gauchiste* scientists joined the movement, the Communist Party slowly and with difficulty came down on the side of the nuclear power station programme. Not only have such issues been raised by the magazines produced specifically by the radical science movement: they have been taken up and further disseminated by the new abundance of left and alternative publications—for instance, the bringing together of both the technical and economic implications of micro-processor technology by Counter Information Services in its pamphlet *The New Technology.*

By the end of the decade, consciousness of the implications of the new technologies, and actions against them by community groups and the labour movement were widespread, from the local groups opposing the siting of the third London Airport and the rapid growth of the anti-nuclear movement, especially in Europe and the U.S., to the work in the unions on the consequences of the introduction of micro-processors. While there is some danger that these struggles may be presented merely as opposition to an autonomous technological determinism, rather than to the invention, development and application of big technology in the interests of capitalist rationality and the movement of finance capital, these questions are now a significant arena for political struggle.

We can return to our main themes, those within the ideological domain, by way of the reception accorded to the publication in 1977 of a pamphlet by Gould and his fellow committee members entitled 'The Attack on Higher Education: Marxist and Radical Penetration'[9] to a well-orchestrated trumpeting of media publicity. The Left was not slow to see its significance and to counter-attack[10]. The sponsorship of Gould's committee by an organization committed to counter-insurgency propaganda, the Institute for the Study of Conflict, and the stridently Macarthyite tone of its claim that Marxists and radicals constituted a 'clear and present danger' and its 'naming of names' made the purpose of the pamphlet clear.

Gould exhibited the anxiety of the right as the students of '68 took their places within the cultural apparatus. No longer psychologized away as anti-authoritarians raised on demand feeding, or the products of overcrowding in the institutions of higher education, the new Marxists and radicals were seen as constituting a latter-day Comintern plot, a tightly knit group held together by a common theory of the long march through the institutions. The counter-insurgency theorists argued that the radical intellectuals sought to occupy the institutions of higher education so as to subvert the hearts and minds of the young, who in their turn would enter the professions, spreading the deadly poison of creeping socialism. The right-wing belief that when the students entered professional work they would abandon their radical and revolutionary commitment seemed sadly shaken. The Report focused on school-teaching and social work as the professions where the radical mode of scholarship had penetrated furthest, though it promised further instalments on subversion in the media and in publishing.

In Gould and his co-authors' eyes, the threat of the radicals is the attack on the norms of that liberal scholarship which takes as its premise the existence and accessibility of the 'objective standards' of knowledge and of truth. Hence radical philosophy, and above all radical science, which question the bases of these objective standards are seen as the main enemies. Philosophy and science are claimed to have fallen victim to either the critique of ideology or the new sociology of knowledge, Marxists and philosphical relativists jumbled in one paragraph. Any sort of social criticism, inside or outside the dominant ideology—even the writings of Kuhn and Levi-Strauss—is exposed by the Institute's pamphleteers as a threat to the social order. That it singled out in its 'naming of names' only a few of those whose writings have contributed to the movement, and is indeed singularly unscholarly in its discussion of these, does not diminish this point. For despite their uneasy awareness of differences within this heterogenous group, Gould and his co-pamphleteers wanted to insist on a central unity of purpose. Indeed, in their conspiracy theory, it is almost more interesting whom they omit than whom they include; thus the feminist critique is as invisible to them as it is to many of the old left. Like Canute's advisers, Gould and his fellow pamphleteers seek to order back the waves of the new left critique, judiciously hinting at the scope of the traditional administrative mechanisms of restrictions on promotions and appointments, a discreet British version of the *Berufsverbot*.

How could anyone come to jumble so completely the different strands of thought within the ranks of the social critics? The origins must be sought in the continuous process of the renewal of bourgeois culture through the incorporation of ideas arising from the social and intellectual upheavals of the decade. (Take, for example, the way that self management was to appear on the bourgeois agenda as 'participation' blessed by the most advanced sections of capital, or how the critique of deskilling was to be taken on board by car manufacturers such as Volvo in the reorganization of the labour process.)

This incorporation can be seen in the context of the relationship between the left critique of science and the development of the new sociology of knowledge. Academic interest in the interrelations of science and society developed during the 1960s period of techno-economism, when state and industry were persuaded of the validity of the thirties Marxist understanding of science as a material force of production.

By the end of the sixties the gathering economic crisis demonstrated that techno-economism could not guarantee economic growth. Scientists began to be seen as yet another pressure group demanding more funding for their own interests. With this new critical perspective, and in the face of mounting evidence of public concern over pollution and the less desirable consequences of unrestricted technological growth, the glamour of science began to look distinctly tatty, and both the interest and the money began to wane. It only remained for state and industry to make it plain that, apart from some money allocated for basic science, the science budget as a whole would be conditional on delivering the goods to the paymasters.

Pioneering the new language which was to permeate British political life in the seventies, the Rothschild report of 1971[11] enshrined the principle of the scientific contract. The state and industry were to be the customers, research workers the contractors. The old argument in favour of the autonomy of scientific research was abandoned, scientists working on governmental or industrial research were no longer to receive grants; instead the customer offered them a contract. The new language reflected the now incorporated status of science and the age of judicious autonomy was over.

The academic science studies units concerned with the impact of technology, science and society, science of science and science policy could not be immune to this shift, but were required to choose whether to move almost entirely towards the world of contract research or towards basic science. Contract research would investigate links between scientific and technological innovation and economic growth. Basic research took them into the sociology and philosophy of science and explored the relationship of natural science to other forms of knowledge. This new sociology of science returned to the externalist theory of the growth of scientific knowledge. While the socialists returned to Hessen[12], Bernal[13] and their contemporaries, the new sociology armed itself with Kuhn[14] whose work seemed to offer a social interpretation of the growth of science. Almost simultaneously the radical science movement concluded that science was not neutral whilst the new sociology of science discovered that internalist explanations of the growth of science were inadequate and that a structural functionalist account of the social organization of science was a mystification. The consequence was the rapid march toward alternative formulations which were to lead, not merely to the sociological relativism inherent in either a Marxist or sociological theory of knowledge, but beyond, to the adoption of a full philosophical relativism which has characterized the writings of much of the new sociology and philosophy of knowledge and certain influential theoreticians within the radical science movement.

It is this philosophical relativism which has moved from being a critique of other knowledges to an auto-critique of one's own knowledge and on towards an escalating reflexivity. It is a hyper-reflexivity[15][16] spoken of as the 'disembodied dialectic'[17] which, both within the sociology of scientific knowledge and within the radical movement, threatens to consume not only 'ideology' but science itself. The certainties of the Althusserian distinction between scientific knowledge and ideology[18] are to be obliterated, dissolved into their social determinations and a belief in the equality of discourses. The socially constructed nature of 'reality' becomes merely a defence against the 'irreality of chaos and nothingness' which allegedly lies behind all human creations of order[19]. In this irreality there is nothing to distinguish true from false theories; a new equality prevails between knowledges. 'Authenticity', far from offering to humanity the possibility that, through struggle, thought can be de-fetishized and reality known, offers instead 'consciously understanding and admitting the essentially arbitrary nature of the behaviour and identity we choose'[20]. To be cool, to be aware that we are playing in nothing more than a series of more or less elaborate games, constitutes the new authenticity. The politics of subjectivism replace the pursuit of the rational society.

One of the games players par excellence of this new authenticity is Feyerabend.[21] It is perhaps significant that his *Against Method* and

Science in a Free Society have been published in Britain by New Left Books. It seems that it is not merely within bourgeois thought in Britain that the divisions represented by C. P. Snow's *Two Cultures* continue to operate. Both the New Left Review and New Left Books, for example, have slowly acknowledged the existence of science, but when they do enter this territory they choose to publish the writings of philosophers or historians such as Lecourt or Bachelard, literary critics such as Timpanaro. Thus the new Marxism, in dealing at last with Lysenko, or grappling with the inheritance of the Dialectics of Nature, does so purely through philosophical analysis; and the questions thrown up by the actual study of the physical and biological worlds are neglected.

But there is also a contrast between the writings of Feyerabend and the body of work of the Frankfurt School, where Habermas in particular has both laid bare the domination exercised through instrumental rationality, and also set forth the contradiction between this instrumental rationality and the pursuit of the rational society. An uninitiated reading of *Against Method* and *Science in a Free Society* would suggest that Feyerabend is out to destroy not only the claims of expertise and instrumental rationality but reason and rationality themselves. In his envisaged 'free society' science, and indeed any intellectual activity, simply become one tradition amongst many, one ideology against competing ideologies. 'All traditions', he writes, 'have equal rights and equal access to education and other positions of power'[22].

But an initiated reader will recognize that Feyerabend is the self-appointed jester of the court of science. His critique of the formalism of Popperian philosophy is launched from an examination of the practice of science: thus he criticizes the philosopher's conception of scientific method rather than science itself. The practice of science, which Feyerabend usually speaks of as 'research', remains relatively unscathed. Despite his manifest sociological relativism he separates himself very firmly from that 'philosophical relativism' which takes the view that 'ideas are equally true or equally false' or, in an even more radical formulation 'that any distribution of truth values is acceptable'.

But those who do fall into the philosophical relativisit trap which Feyerabend himself avoids springing, go well beyond his ingenious attack on the scientists who have witch-hunted astrology. One influential journal which has at present adopted this line—and indeed brooks no alternative within its pages—is *Radical Science Journal* (RSJ). Thus the mathematician Hodgkin writes, 'I would be happy to accept Althusser's definition of scientific practice (working on knowledges to produce new ones) *without* his implication that there is a line that can be drawn separating scientific practices from ideological ones ... [hence] ... astrology done seriously [is a science]'[23].

Hodgkin travels precisely down the path Feyerabend refuses, with only the moralistic criterion of 'seriously' (which is not spelt out) to ensure the conditions under which astrology is to take its place in the new egalitarianism of knowledges. Yet it is precisely this position which disarms radical scientists, amongst whom Hodgkin must be numbered, when faced with the ideological counter-attack, which Gould symbolized. For instance, when the ideologues of scientific racism, such as Jensen and Eysenck 'work on knowledge', is what they produce new knowledge, and if not, what is it? If it is fetishized consciousness, as RSJ argues, there are no rational grounds for opposing it and the opposition to scientific racism must be seen exclusively in personal and moral terms. If we adopt the position of what is called 'the strong programme' in the sociology of knowledge, then we must presumably regard all these cultural products as new knowledges. Certainly the sociologist of knowledge Barnes[24] as an advocate of the strong programme, is logically consistent when he calls these exponents of the new scientific racism 'new·Galileos', for within his framework of philosophical relativism, anything does indeed go. If the criterion of truth has been relativized away, the possibility of determining what is science and what ideology has been abandoned. The criterion of 'seriousness' Hodgkin would have us adopt seems a very weak substitute.

It is this thesis which is spelt out in greater detail in the article by Young, 'Science is Social Relations'[25]. which has been taken as the major statement of RSJ's theoretical position. Although we have dealt critically with this article elsewhere[26] it is important to look at its main claims and implications here. Young's article constitutes a repeated assertion that science is, or may be reduced to, social relations, that is, despite the claims of science to be concerned with an understanding of the natural world, it can only represent a series of social constructs reflective of the social order. Despite its claims, this position is the antithesis of Marxism and in developing it, Young draws heavily on the writings of Feyerabend and a particular reading of Sohn-Rethel.[27]

Sohn-Rethel's thesis is that the emergence of physical science can be linked to the development of abstract thought, itself a product of the formation of commodity exchange relationships and the separation of mental and manual labour in, above all, ancient Greece. Sohn-Rethel thus points to the social origins of science. But as a materialist he eschews the claim that the existence of social determinants of a phenomenon dissolves the phenomenon itself, and nothing less than this constitutes the enterprise which Young sets himself. The core of Young's case is the claim that 'the economy and the factory are known by socialists to be social relations'. Hence by extension, commodities are social relations, and as scientific facts 'are' commodities, they too are social relations. His approach transforms a mediation into an identity. But a factory is at the same moment part of the reality of social relations and is itself objectively real. Its own material reality does not cease because it is part of social reality. Similarly its products and the skills of the workers embodied in those products are both materially real and objectively part of social relations; they are not reducible to social relations. Young's argument replaces materialism by idealism—only take thought, and the factory will become transformed, the state wither and the millenium arrive. This triumph of the idea is to reverse the achievement of Marx in setting Hegel on his feet—philosophical relativism upends Marx and rediscovers a new Hegelianism. The theoretical criticism is further compounded by Young's understanding of the term 'social relations'. For him, a victim of hyper-reflexitivity, the concept is synonymous with interpersonal relations, and he transforms the slogan of 1968 'the personal is the political' into its converse 'the political is the personal'. But although an apple is a fruit, not all fruits are apples. Lastly he confuses the social determinants of a phenomenon for the phenomenon itself—it is not the social relations of the Hebden Bridge asbestos factory which penetrated the lungs of the workers, but the asbestos fibres. The asbestosis and painful death of the workers are not *merely* social relations either. The failure to make the distinction between the field of study and the organization by which it is used, means that nothing in nature can ever be transformed and any act of understanding is impossible. The authenticity of critical reason, which for Marx affirms humanity's capacity through struggle to de-fetishize thought and 'know the thing itself'[28], has been ceded to the new hip authenticity.

The mistake of bourgeois science is to ignore that objects within nature itself have relationships and histories and are capable of transformation. For reductionist science, nature is locked in a universal present whose multifarious phenomena are nothing but an expression of the unchanging and static properties of individual atoms engaged in a timeless dance.

It is this mechanical, materialistic reductionism which constitutes the dominant ideology of today's reductionist science. By contrast the new idealist ideology pretends that objects do not exist at all but are merely manifestations of 'social' (i.e., interpersonal) relations, a sort of twentieth century ectoplasm. Within this miasma of philosophical reductionism which reduces the phenomenon to its social determinants, how can we say that one brick wall is better built than another, let alone one theory or experiment. What is done is to deny the achievements of human labour, whether these are in bricklaying, cooking or scientific experimentation. It also denies the autonomy of separate knowledges and the problems of discriminating between them and within them. Thus conflicts within fields of knowledge reduce solely to 'social relations', a stance of such monolithic reductionism that paradoxically it enters into complicity with the crudest of economic or biological reductionisms. The political dangers of this philosophical relativism, to say nothing of its theoretical inadequacy are manifest.

Once Marx, invoking the metaphor of a walnut, wrote of revealing the rational kernel within Hegel. For the new philosophical relativism, the metaphor must be that of the onion. First reflexivity usefully peels the skin away, then hyper-reflexivity takes over and strips away the remaining layers until nothing—for an onion has no kernel—remains. In keeping with the present preoccupation with personal feelings, this onion-peeling practice is a painful business. This new subjectivist radicalism, stemming from the agonies of intellectuals trapped within an incorporated science, tests its theories by their moral fervour rather than by their efficacy.

Mao wrote of a revolutionist's theory of knowledge, 'The Marxist philosophy of dialectical materialism has two outstanding characteristics. One is its class nature; it openly avows that dialectical materialism is in the service of the proletariat. The other is its practicality, it emphasizes the dependence of theory on practice, emphasizes that theory is based on practice and serves practice. The truth of any knowledge or theory is not determined by subjective feelings but by objective results in social practice.'[29] In contrast to this, the new relativists of RSJ speak of a theory and practice based 'in the end' on 'personal commitment'.[30]

Such a stance, which goes beyond critique and auto-critique, despite all its radical affirmation, reaches out with unseen hands towards an old enemy. It cannot then come as any surprise to note the speed with which in the last few years the fashionable trend amongst intellectuals has been to turn away from Marx and indeed any revolutionary commitment at all and into the new enchantments presented by the kaleidoscopic gyrations of the latest gurus. Althusserianism was replaced with structuralism, and now an enthusiasm for Foucault, Lacan and the Nouveaux Philosophes. In a search for a theory which would help overturn the world and which the practice of the early 1970s alone was insufficient to achieve, revolutionaries moved out of the streets and into the library. Some remained in its safety, locked into their own private practices of the living out of the personal as the political, ensconced in small groups with their separate gurus. There is a danger that such intellectuals may not even notice that the storm clouds are rising. Indeed for some of them having dropped the term Marxism from the mast-heads of their journals because 'We aren't really sure we know what it means or whether we are Marxists at all now', the storm may seem to signify as little as did the rise of fascism to the thirties logical positivists or surrealists. But the storm is threatening and could blow them, willy nilly, away along with the rest. And it is to the storm itself that we turn.

Earlier in this essay we discussed the Gould pamphlet because its attack on the radical science movement symbolized many of the preoccupations of the ideological counter-attack which has begun to gather momentum in the late 1970s, and it is now necessary to consider the more serious forms that this has taken over the last decade. The essence of an ideological counter-attack is that it must defend the structures and ideas under siege, not merely by isolating their enemies and pursuing them intellectually, politically and administratively, but by asserting the naturalness and inevitability of those ideas themselves, for the importance of ideology is that it is most powerful when invisible, when the natural order of things is not the *subject* for debate but the *premise* upon which that debate is built. The strength of the left during the late sixties and the first half of the seventies, based on the burgeoning economic and social crisis, was to shake the ideological foundations of patriarchal capitalism; as the revolutionary culture flourished, proliferating innumerable small magazines, and boosting the sales of the decidedly non-revolutionary publishers who eagerly sought to print the new critics, the cultural centre of gravity of Britain, like that of the rest of the Western world lurched decidedly to the left. The urgent task of the right was to re-establish the naturalness and inevitability of the *status quo*, and the impossibility of the changes demanded by the revolutionaries. The source of authority for the rejection of revolutionary values was to be just that unchallengeable science which the radical movement was criticizing. Hence the anger shown, for instance by Gould, at the blasphemy of the attacks on science (no one, he remarks with incomprehension and indeed ignorance, would expect to seek for ideology in physics!).[31]

The ideology of a racist and patriarchal capitalism maintains that class, race and sex divisions within the social order are the innate consequences of human biology. The radical science movement has intervened to contest this persistent attempt to reduce the social to the biological.

The ideological counter-attack took shape with the revival, first in the US and almost immediately afterwards in Britain, of the eugenicism surrounding the use of psychometric measures as the IQ test; the IQ testing movement resurrected by Jensen in the US and Eysenck in Britain claimed that intelligence was largely inherited and that differences in school performance and subsequent job expectations between classes, sexes and races were due not to the class nature of the educational system or a racist and sexist society but to the workings out of biological predestination. The appeal of this claim to capital is obvious; its persistent refraction through the media despite the fact that its scientific untenability has been frequently demonstrated at all levels from the experimental to the theoretical testifies to its importance. It has even survived the total destruction of the scientific reputation of one of its key figures, Cyril Burt. His claims for the hereditary bases of differences in intelligence have been shown to be fraudulent. The attack by the left on IQ testing and its ramifications was one of the earliest, and has been one of the most long standing of the campaigns taken up by radical science movement in Britain and the US. At its best the critical intellectual attack was part and parcel of a more general struggle shared with black parents and teachers.[32]

But by the mid 1970s it had become clear that the campaign to re-establish the theory of the heritability of intelligence was but one shot in a much wider battle. The arguments about the naturalness and biological inevitablity of the social order were widened into the grandiloquent claims of a new discipline, sociobiology, argued by its leading exponent, Wilson, to be about to engulf and transform the study of economics, sociology, history and psychology.[33] Sociobiology at its strongest claims that the complex forms of human society are the products of a genetic inheritance; today's Western capitalist societies are the inevitable consequences of genes specified as a result of generations of evolution (or rather that they should be); running through sociobiological thinking is a distinct echo of nineteenth-century social Darwinism; laissez faire is felt to be more biologically sound than monopoly or welfare capitalism; as Dawkins puts it in his popular book *The Selfish Gene*[34] where he criticizes the 'unnatural' welfare state in which

> ... we (sic) have abolished the family as a unit of economic self-sufficiency and substituted the state. But the privilege of guaranteed support for children should not be abused ... Individual humans who have more children than they are capable of raising are probably too ignorant in most cases to be accused of conscious malevolent exploitation. Powerful institutions and leaders who deliberately encourage them to do so seem to me less free from suspicion.

Without wishing to read off the new superstructural forms from the economic base, the correspondence between the economic theory underlying the policy of the Thatcher government and the new individualistic and familial biologism should not pass unnoticed. It leaves behind the biological determination of a Lorenz or a Morris, whose theories, fashionable in the 1950s and early 1960s had argued that co-operative behaviour evolved amongst animals because it was in the interest of the group as a whole that it should do so (group selection). Now, in the hands of Wilson and Trivers in the US, Hamilton, Maynard Smith and Dawkins in Britain, the argument was transformed from group to kin selection in which the individual was the agent of evolution. Animals and, by extrapolation, humans only *appeared* to act co-operatively ('altruistically'); *in fact* they acted selfishly in their own genetic interest to propagate their own genes and those of their close relatives; genetic (kin) not class (or group) loyalties are the key to success. 'Genetic man' in this model comes close to the autonomous figment of bourgeois economics, 'economic man' who calculates the appropriate investment to be made in rearing offspring or rescuing a sibling from a predator's attack*. Evolution centres around the development of adaptive strategies towards stable states. Historians of social thought might be excused

---

* This is not a metaphor: sociobiologists indeed constantly use the term investment and base their mathematical models upon it. Neither the summary of sociobiological thinking here nor the quotation from Dawkins would be regarded as out of context or extreme within sociobiological writing.

for concluding that structural functionalism, having been more-or-less driven from sociology, seeks to reoccupy biology.

By the late 1970s sociobiological reductionism had widened its boundaries indefinitely to claim that aggressiveness, acquisitiveness, territoriality, racism and male supremacy were programmed into the genes along with genes for altruism and spite, homosexuality, male sexual philandering, female sexual constancy, childhood dislike of spinach, political attitudes and the tendency to answer questionnaires inconsistently. The facts of biology, according to Wilson, lie athwart our desires for a transformation of the capitalist order;[35] the 'inevitability of patriarchy' according to Goldberg is an inexorable obstacle to the demands of the feminists.[36]

The critique of sociobiology has been strongly developed by the American radical science movement.[37] To a considerable extent this debate, perhaps as a consequence of the vigour of the response, has been contained within the arena of the campus. In Britain sociobiology has been more quickly taken up by both conservative and the new fascist thought.

It is not for nothing that the monetary economists are now claiming that the 'facts' of sociobiology lend justification to their social theorizing. Biologism, as Billig[38] and Barker[39] have recently documented, is also central to the ramshackle collection of doctrines that provide intellectual sustenance for the National Front. The claims that innate biological differences determine racial characteristics and legitimize white supremacy are fundamental to fascism and the NF was quick to seize on Eysenck and Jensen as 'proving' their point. The NF national organizer, Webster, claims that Jensen's publication was a crucial factor in the collapse of morale amongst multi-racialists and the growth of racism in the 1970s.[40] Scientific racism is a mainstay of NF publications like *Spearhead*, and late in 1977, the NF published a leaflet, distributed in large numbers to school children, together with a longer pamphlet on 'How to Combat Red Teachers'. A central point of both leaflet and pamphlet were the claims that Eysenck and Jensen had 'proved' that there were innate differences in intelligence between blacks and whites, and that 'red' teachers (their cartoon teacher is an unequivocally anti-semitic stereotype) spread multi-racial lies and denigrate 'sound scientists'—the same claim appeared in an election address by the NF in 1979. In the same year, the NF's 'theoretician', Verrall, embraced the entire sociobiological thesis in another *Spearhead* article,[41] now using it to justify arguments not merely for racial inequalities but sexual inequalities as well. The NF stereotype of passive *Kinder-Küchen-Kirche* female and dominant Aryan male is neatly in accord with the sociobiological theses of the inevitability of patriarchy and Verrall was not slow to see the connections.

The widespread struggle against racism and fascism, and the success of the Anti-Nazi League in mobilizing the youth and combating the rise of the NF, was reflected in the derisory electoral performance of fascism in the May 1979 elections, and has held the extreme right in its most virulent form in check. However the sweeping electoral victory of the most reactionary Conservative administration for many years shows the extent to which the ideological counter-attack has successfully penetrated. Biological reductionism has been as integral a part of the Conservative ideological baggage as monetarism. The themes of the conservative election campaign and around which they have ordered their initial policy pronouncements are not *ad hoc* legislative changes but are based upon a concept of the naturalness of a particular competitive capitalist order. Note how often the concept of naturalness appears, for example, in the speeches of Thatcher or her lieutenants. 'One of the most important driving forces in human nature, people passing things on to their children and grandchildren', said Thatcher to the Scottish Conservative Party conference in May 1979. And a few weeks later the thought was echoed in his budget speech by Geoffrey Howe, the Chancellor. 'It is perfectly natural that people should wish to build up capital of their own and pass it on to their children.' The naturalness of capitalism, of the xenophobia of a British 'race' swamped by aliens, of the class order ('we are all unequal. We believe that everyone has the right to be unequal') are all expressions of a particular ideology. This is more than merely a reassertion of the Conservative belief that they are the natural party of government; it is a claim that 'science' is firmly on their side. The terrain won by the left and by critical scholarship in the aftermath of 1968 is now once more to be fought over. Within the framework of a world capitalism wracked by economic, political and energy crises, and the specific situation of a de-industrializing British economy, the battles of the immediate future are likely to be fierce. In this context there is a need not only to respond to specific ideological challenges but to stay on the offensive and produce more and better socialist scholarship which will serve the struggle for human liberation. Radical science will have its part to play within this.

NOTES

1. Rose, H. and Rose, S., 'The Radicalisation of Science', in *Socialist Register 1972,* eds. Miliband R. and Saville J., Merlin, 1972.
2. Rose, H. and Rose, S. (eds.) *The Political Economy of Science,* Macmillan, 1976.
3. Anon., *Britain Without Capitalists,* Lawrence and Wishart, 1936.
4. Werskey, G., *The Visible College,* Allen Lane, 1978.
5. Lecourt, D., *Proletarian Science?* New Left Books, 1977.
6. Levins, R., and Lewontin, R.C., 'The Problem of Lysenkoism', in *The Radicalisation of Science,* eds. Rose, H. and Rose, S. Macmillan, 1976.
7. Lewontin, R., *Work Collectives—Utopian and Otherwise.* Forthcoming.
8. Levy Leblond, J.-M., 'Ideology of/in Contemporary Physics', in *The Radicalisation of Science, op.cit.*
9. (Gould Report) *The Attack on Higher Education: Marxist and Radical Penetration,* Institute for the Study of Conflict, 1977.
10. (CAFD) *The Attack on Higher Education: Where Does It Come From?* Council for Academic Freedom and Democracy, 1977.
11. (Rothschild Report) *A Framework for Government Research and Development* Cmnd 1272 HMSO, 1972.
12. Hessen, B., 'The Social and Economic Roots of Newton's *Principia',* in *Science at the Crossroads,* eds. Bukharin, N. *et al,* Kniga, 1931.
13. Bernal, J.D., *The Social Functions of Science,* Routledge, 1939.
14. Kuhn, T., *The Structure of Scientific Revolutions,* Chicago University Press, 1962.
15. Rose, H., 'Hyper-Reflexivity: A New Danger for the Counter-Movements', in *Countermovements of the Sciences* eds. Nowotny, H. and Rose., H., Reidel, 1979.
16. Heller, A., 'On the New Adventures of the Dialectic', *Telos 33,* 1977.
17. Carveth, D., 'The Disembodied Dialectic: A Psychoanalytic Critique of Sociological Relativism', *Theory and Society 4* (1), 1977.
18. Althusser, L., *For Marx,* Allen Lane, 1965.
19. Carveth, D., *op.cit.*
20. Carveth, D., *op.cit.*
21. Feyerabend, P., *Against Method* and *Science in a Free Society,* New Left Books, 1975 and 1978.
22. Feyerabend, 1978, *op.cit.*
23. Hodgkin, L., 'A Note on Scientism', *Radical Science Journal 5,* 1977.
24. Barnes, B., *Scientific Knowledge and Sociological Theory,* Routledge Kegan Paul, 1974.
25. Young, R., 'Science *Is* Social Relations', *Radical Science Journal 5,* 1977.
26. Rose, H., and Rose, S., 'The Metaphor Goes into Orbit: Science is *not* all Social Relations', *Science Bulletin,* 1979 (in press).
27. Sohn-Rethel, A., *Mental and Manual Labour,* Macmillan, 1978.
28. Heller, *op.cit.*
29. Mao Tse Tung 'On Practice', 1937 *Selected Works,* People's Publishing House, Peking, 1965.

30. Young, M.F.D., 'Taking Sides Against the Probable: Problems of Relativism and Commitment in Teaching and the Sociology of Knowledge', *Educational Review, 25(3)* 1973.

31. Clearly neither Professor Gould nor his fellow committee members had read much in this area. For instance, whilst neither a radical, let alone Marxist account, these issues have been painstakingly documented for the Soviet Union by Dr Graham in Graham, L., *Science and Philosophy in the Soviet Union,* Knopf, 1972.

32. A full footnoting of this conflict would be formidable and is perhaps out of place here, but see:- Kamin, L., *The Science and Politics of IQ,* Penguin, 1976; Rose, S., Hambley J. and Haywood J., 'Science, Racism and Ideology', *Socialist Register 1973;* Rose H. and Rose S., 'The IQ Myth', *Race and Class 20(1)* 1978; Hearnshaw, L.S., *Cyril Burt: Psychologist,* Hodder and Stoughton, 1979.

33. Wilson, E.O., *Sociobiology, The New Synthesis,* Harvard University Press, 1975.

34. Dawkins, R., *The Selfish Gene,* Oxford University Press, 1977.

35. Wilson, E.O., *On Human Nature,* Harvard University Press, 1978.

36. Goldberg, S., *The Inevitability of Patriarchy,* Morrow, 1973.

37. See, for instance, Science for the People Collective, *Biology as a Social Weapon,* Ann Arbor, 1978, *Genes and Gender,* eds. Hubbard, R. and Lowe, M. Gordian, 1979,' "Its Only Human Nature", the Sociobiologist's Fairyland', Rose, S., *Race and Class, 20, (3),* 1979.

38. Billig, M., *Fascists: a Social Psychological View of the National Front,* Academic Press, 1978.

39. Barker, M., 'Racism—The New Inheritors', *Radical Philosophy 21,* 1979.

40. Walker, M., *The National Front,* Fontana, 1977.

41. Verrall, R., 'Sociobiology: The Instincts in our Genes', *Spearhead,* May 1979.

CONTENTS OF PREVIOUS ISSUES

1966

The Labour Government and Beyond—*Ralph Miliband*
The Italian Left—*Lelio Basso*
The Crisis of Belgian Social Democracy—*Marcel Liebman*
The Spanish Left: Illusion and Reality—*L. Torres*
British Trade Unionism in the Sixties—*J. Hughes*
Jugoslavia's Crossroads—*B. McFarlane*
European Capitalism and World Trade—*M. Barratt Brown*
Natural Science and Human Theory:
  A Critique of Herbert Marcuse—*P. Sedgwick*
The Outlook for Africa—*Basil Davidson*
Varieties of African Socialism—*J. Mohan*
The New Class and Rebellion in the Congo—*J. Gerard-Libois*
Problems of Socialism in South East Asia—*Malcolm Caldwell*
India and Pakistan: Twenty Years After—*V. H. Kiernan*

1967*

Vietnam and Western Socialism—*Ralph Miliband*
International Capitalism and 'Supra-Nationality'—*Ernest Mandel*
Labourism and the Labour Government—*John Saville*
The New Left in the United States—*Ronald Aronson and*
  John Cowley
System, Structure and Contradiction in **Capital**—*Maurice Godelier*
Marx and Engels and thhe Concept of the Party—*Monty Johnstone*
Marx and India—*Victor Kiernan*
Nkrumah and Nkrumahism—*Jitendra Mohan*
Insecure Democracy—*Conor Cruise O'Brien*
The Working Class in Latin America: Some Theoretical Problems—
  Ioan Davies and Shakuntala De Miranda

1968

Ideological Trends in the USSR—*Isaac Deutscher*
Lessons of the Soviet Economic Reform—*Michael Ellman*
Two Years of the Cultural Revolution—*K. S. Karol*
Black Power—*Franklin Hugh Adler*
Reform and Revolution—*André Gorz*
Theory and Practice in Gramsci's Marxism—*John Merrington*
Notes on Marxism in 1968—*V. G. Kiernan*
Professor Galbraith and American Capitalism—*Ralph Miliband*
The centenary of the British Trades Union Congress, 1868—1968
  V. L. Allen

1969*

Roots of Bureaucracy—*Isaac Deutscher*
The May Events and Revolution in the West—*Lucio Magri*
Notes on the Intelligentsia—*V. G. Kiernan*
The Strange Death of the Liberal University—*John Cowley*
Moral and Material Incentives—*Peter Clecak*
Nationalism and Revolution in Sub-Saharan Africa—
  Giovanni Arrighi and John S. Saul

1973

An Open Letter to Leszek Kolakowski—*E. P. Thompson*
Industrial Conflict and the Political Economy—*Richard Hyman*
Socialists and the Labour Party—*Ken Coates*
Up Against the Welfare State: The Claimants' Unions—
  Hilary Rose
For a Political Economy of Mass Communications—
  Graham Murdock and Peter Golding
Science, Racism and Ideology—*Steven Rose,*
  John Hambley and Jeff Haywood
The Old Alliance: England and Portugal—*V. G. Kiernan*
A Report on the Further Liberation of Guiné—*Basil Davidson*
Neo-Colonialism vs Liberation Struggle—*John Saul*
Southern Africa: Problems of Armed Struggle—*Joe Slovo*
South Africa: The Search for a Strategy—*Ben Turok*
Stalin and After—*Ralph Miliband*
The Downfall of the Dollar—*H. L. Robinson*
The Coup in Chile—*Ralph Miliband*

1974

My Correct Views on Everything—*Leszek Kolakowski*
Revolutionary Intellectuals and the Soviet Union—
  Rossana Rossanda
Sozhenitsyn: A Political Analysis—*Jean-Marie Chauvier*
Marx on Democratic Forms of Government—*Hal Draper*
Gramsci and Lenin 1917-1922—*Alastair Davidson*
Reconstructing Australian Communism—*Winton Higgins*
Structuralism—Science or Ideology?—*Raoul Makarius*
Class Struggle and the Industrial Revolution—*John Saville*
Workers' Control and Revolutionary Theory—*Richard Hyman*
The Multi-National Corporation—*Walter Goldstein*
American Hegemony Under Revision—*V. G. Kiernan*
The Second Coming of Daniel Bell—*George Ross*
The State in Post-Colonial Societies: Tanzania—*John S. Saul*

1975*

Jean-Paul Sartre: A Critical Tribute—*Istvan Meszaros*
Sartre's Political Practice—*Rossana Rossanda*
Bukharinism, Revolution and Social Development—*Marcel Liebman*
Liebman and Leninism—*Ernest Mandel*
Maoism and the Chinese Revolution—*Roland Lew*
India and the Colonial Mode of Production—*Hamza Alavi*
Notes on the Revolution in Somalia—*Basil Davidson*
What is Violence?—*Anthony Arblaster*
The Struggle Against the Housing Finance Act—*Leslie Sklair*
Workers' Control versus 'Revolutionary' Theory—
  Michael Barratt Brown, Ken Coates & Tony Topham
Political Forms and Historical Materialism—*Ralph Miliband*

* Out of Print